Mission Praise

Compiled by
Peter Horrobin and Greg Leavers

COMBINED MUSIC EDITION

Marshall Pickering
An Imprint of HarperCollins*Publishers*

Marshall Pickering is an imprint of
HarperCollins*Religious*,
Part of HarperCollins*Publishers*,
77–85 Fulham Palace Road
Hammersmith, London W6 8JB

First published in Great Britain in 1990 by
Marshall Pickering

Reprinted: 95 94 93 92 91
Impression number: 10 9 8 7 6 5 4 3 2

ISBN 0 551 01986 7

Words edition   ISBN 0 551 01979 4 (Single copy)
                         ISBN 0 551 01977 8 (Pack of 25)
Easy-to-read edition   ISBN 0 551 02627 8
Large Print edition   ISBN 0 551 01978 6
Musicians' Edition vol. 1 ISBN 0 551 02266 3
Musicians' Edition vol. 2 ISBN 0 551 02267 1
Musicians' Edition vol. 3 ISBN 0 551 02268 X
Musicians' Edition   ISBN 0 551 02313 9 (Pack of three volumes)

Printed and bound in Great Britain by
Richard Clay Ltd of Bungay

A catalogue record for this book
is available from the British Library

Preface

This combined volume of Mission Praise brings together the original volume that was compiled for Mission England with the second and supplementary volumes. The contents of these three books, with the addition of some extra items, and now numbering 798 songs, has been structured so as to be a comprehensive hymn and song book for church and general use.

The success of Mission Praise owes much to its strategy of embracing the best of the old with the best of the new, freely mixing together both traditional hymns and modern songs. As such the volumes have gained wide acceptance with all ages and, indeed, a very wide range of church congregations.

The large and comprehensive subject and music indexes will be an invaluable aid to the selection of items for use throughout the church's year, at all special events in church and family life and for other special services.

The vision for the original Mission Praise volume eventually extended far beyond our initial expectations, and we give thanks to God for the way in which the collection opened up major new dimensions of praise and worship in many churches. Our prayer for this combined edition is that the blessings enjoyed by those who used the first volume of Mission Praise will be shared by all who use this combined volume.

Peter Horrobin and Greg Leavers

1   A new commandment

Words: from John 13
Music: Unknown
arranged Andy Silver

A new com-mand-ment I give un-to you, that you love one an-oth-er as I have loved you, that you love one an-oth-er as I have loved you. By this shall all men know that you are My dis-ci-ples, if

you have love one for an - oth - er._____ By

this shall all men know that you are My dis - ci - ples, if

you have love one for an - oth - er._____

A new commandment I give unto you,
that you love one another as I have loved you,
that you love one another as I have loved you.

By this shall all men know that you are My disciples,
if you have love one for another.
By this shall all men know that you are My disciples,
if you have love one for another.

2 A safe stronghold

EIN' FESTE BURG   87 87 66 667

Words: Martin Luther (1483–1546)
tr. Thomas Carlyle (1795–1881)
Music: melody by Martin Luther (1483–1546)

A safe strong-hold our God is still, a trus - ty_ shield and_ wea - pon; He'll help us_ clear_ from all_ the ill that has us_ now o'er - tak - en. The an-cient prince of hell has_ risen with pur-pose fell; strong mail of craft and power he

wear-eth in＿ this＿ hour; on earth is＿ not his＿ fel - low.

1 A safe stronghold our God is still,
   a trusty shield and weapon;
   He'll help us clear from all the ill
   that has us now o'ertaken.
   The ancient prince of hell
   has risen with purpose fell;
   strong mail of craft and power
   he weareth in this hour;
   on earth is not his fellow.

2 With force of arms we nothing can,
   full soon were we down-ridden;
   but for us fights the proper Man
   whom God Himself has bidden.
   Ask ye: Who is this same?
   Christ Jesus is His name,
   the Lord Sabaoth's Son;
   He, and no other one,
   shall conquer in the battle.

3 And were this world all devils o'er,
   and watching to devour us,
   we lay it not to heart so sore;
   not they can overpower us.
   And let the prince of ill
   look grim as e'er he will,
   he harms us not a whit;
   for why? his doom is writ;
   a word shall quickly slay him.

4 God's word, for all their craft and force,
   one moment will not linger,
   but, spite of hell, shall have its course;
   'tis written by His finger.
   And though they take our life,
   goods, honour, children, wife,
   yet is their profit small;
   these things shall vanish all,
   the city of God remaineth.

3 Abba Father

Words and music: Dave Bilbrough
Music arranged Roland Fudge

Ne - ver let my heart grow cold,

ne - ver let___ me go,_____

Ab - ba Fa - ther, let me be

Yours and Yours___ a - lone._____

4

Abide with me

EVENTIDE 10 10 10 10

Words: H F Lyte (1793–1847)
Music: W H Monk (1823–89)

1 Abide with me; fast falls the eventide;
   the darkness deepens; Lord, with me abide;
   when other helpers fail, and comforts flee,
   help of the helpless, O abide with me.

2 Swift to its close ebbs out life's little day;
   earth's joys grown dim, its glories pass away;
   change and decay in all around I see:
   O Thou who changest not, abide with me!

3 I need Thy presence every passing hour;
   what but Thy grace can foil the tempter's power?
   Who like Thyself my guide and stay can be?
   Through cloud and sunshine, O abide with me.

4 I fear no foe with Thee at hand to bless;
   ills have no weight, and tears no bitterness.
   Where is death's sting? where, grave, thy victory?
   I triumph still, if Thou abide with me.

5 Hold Thou Thy cross before my closing eyes,
   shine through the gloom, and point me to the skies;
   heaven's morning breaks, and earth's vain shadows flee:
   in life, in death, O Lord, abide with me!

5   Above the voices of the world

Words: Timothy Dudley-Smith
Music: Phil Burt

1 A - bove the voi - ces of the world a - round me,_____ my_
2 What can I of - fer Him who calls me to_ Him?_____ On -
3 Lord, I be - lieve; help now my un - be - liev - ing;_____ I_

hopes and dreams, my cares and loves and fears,_____ the_
- ly the wastes of sin and self and shame;_____ a_
come in faith be - cause Your pro - mise stands;_____ Your

long a - wait - ed call of Christ has found me,_____ the_
mind con - fused, a heart that ne - ver knew Him,_____ a_
word of par - don and of peace re - ceiv - ing,_____ all_

voice of Je - sus e - choes in my ears:_____
tongue un - skilled at nam - ing Je - sus' name._____
that I am_ I place with - in Your hands._____

6   Ah Lord God

Words and music: Kay Chance

Words and music: © Kay Chance,
Glaubensentrum, Gruner Plaz 12, 3340 Wolfenbuttel, West Germany

7   All creatures of our God and King

LASST UNS ERFREUEN   88 44 88 with refrain

Words: St Francis of Assisi (1182–1226)
tr. William Henry Draper (1855–1933)
Music: melody from *Geistliche Kirchengessang*
Cologne, 1623
arranged R Vaughan Williams (1872–1958)

All crea-tures of our God and King, lift up your voice and with us sing: Hal - le - lu - jah, hal - le - lu - jah! Thou burn-ing sun with gold-en beam, thou sil-ver moon with soft-er gleam: O__ praise Him, O__ praise Him, Hal - le -

-lu - jah, hal-le - lu - jah, hal-le - lu - - - jah!

1 All creatures of our God and King,
   lift up your voice and with us sing:
   Hallelujah, hallelujah!
   Thou burning sun with golden beam,
   thou silver moon with softer gleam:
       O praise Him, O praise Him,
       Hallelujah, hallelujah, hallelujah!

2 Thou rushing wind that art so strong,
   ye clouds that sail in heaven along,
   O praise Him, hallelujah!
   Thou rising morn, in praise rejoice,
   ye lights of evening, find a voice:
       O praise Him . . .

3 Thou flowing water, pure and clear,
   make music for thy Lord to hear,
   Hallelujah, hallelujah!
   Thou fire so masterful and bright,
   that givest man both warmth and light:
       O praise Him . . .

4 And all ye men of tender heart,
   forgiving others, take your part,
   O sing ye, hallelujah!
   Ye who long pain and sorrow bear,
   praise God and on Him cast your care:
       O praise Him . . .

5 Let all things their Creator bless,
   and worship Him in humbleness,
   O praise Him, hallelujah!
   Praise, praise the Father, praise the Son,
   and praise the Spirit, Three-in-One:
       O praise Him . . .

All earth was dark

Words and music: J Daniels
and P Thompson
Music arranged Christopher Norton

migh - ty___ flame,   till   ev - ery heart,   con -

- sumed by love, shall_ rise   to___ praise Your ho - ly

name.

1   All earth was dark until You spoke,
then all was light and all was peace.
Yet still, oh God, so many wait,
to see the flame of love released.
Lights to the world, oh Light of man,
kindle in us a mighty flame,
till every heart, consumed by love,
shall rise to praise Your holy name.

2 In Christ You gave Your gift of life
to save us from the depth of night.
Oh come and set our spirits free,
and draw us to Your perfect light.
Lights to the world, . . .

3 Where there is fear, may we bring joy,
and healing to a world in pain.
Lord, build Your kingdom through our lives,
till Jesus walks this earth again.
Lights to the world, . . .

4 O burn in us that we may burn
with love that triumphs in despair.
And touch our lives with such a fire,
that souls may search and find You there.
Lights to the world, . . .

9 All glory, laud and honour

ST THEODULPH   76 76 D

Words: Theodulph of Orleans (c750–821)
tr. J M Neale (1818–66)
Melody by Melchior Teschner (c1615)
Harmony from J S Bach (1685–1750)

All glo-ry, laud and hon-our to Thee, Re-deem-er, King, to whom the lips of child-ren made sweet ho-san-nas ring. Thou art the King of Is-rael, Thou Da-vid's roy-al Son, who

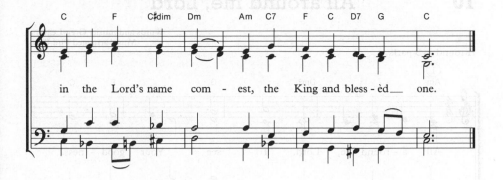

in the Lord's name com - est, the King and bless - èd___ one.

1   All glory, laud and honour
    to Thee, Redeemer, King,
    to whom the lips of children
    made sweet hosannas ring.
    Thou art the King of Israel,
    Thou David's royal Son,
    who in the Lord's name comest,
    the King and blessèd one.

2   The company of angels
    are praising Thee on high,
    and mortal men and all things
    created make reply.
    The people of the Hebrews
    with psalms before Thee went;
    our praise and prayer and anthems
    before Thee we present.

3   To Thee before Thy passion
    they sang their hymns of praise;
    to Thee now high exalted
    our melody we raise.
    Thou didst accept their praises;
    accept the prayers we bring,
    who in all good delightest,
    Thou good and gracious King.

10 All around me, Lord

Words and music: Greg Leavers
Music arranged Phil Burt

A round in 3 parts

All around me, Lord, I see Your goodness,
all creation sings Your praises,
all the world cries, 'God is love!'

All hail King Jesus

Words and music: Unknown
Music arranged Roland Fudge

All hail King Je - sus, all hail Em - man - u - el;_____ King of kings, Lord of lords, bright Morn-ing Star, ev - ery day You give me breath, I'll sing Your prais - es_____ and I'll reign with You through - out e - ter - ni - ty._____

All hail the Lamb

Words and music: Dave Bilbrough

All hail the Lamb en-throned on high, His praise shall be our__ bat - tle cry.

13(i) All hail the power of Jesus' name!

MILES LANE   CM

Words: Edward Perronet (1726–92)
and John Rippon (1751–1836)
Music: W Shrubsole (1760–1806)

1   All hail the power of Jesus' name!
    let angels prostrate fall;
    bring forth the royal diadem,
    and crown Him Lord of all.

2   Crown Him, ye martyrs of our God,
    who from His altar call;
    extol the stem of Jesse's rod,
    and crown Him Lord of all.

3   Ye seed of Israel's chosen race,
    and ransomed from the fall,
    hail Him who saves you by His grace,
    and crown Him Lord of all.

4   Let every kindred, every tribe,
    on this terrestrial ball,
    to Him all majesty ascribe,
    and crown Him Lord of all.

5   O that with yonder sacred throng
    we at His feet may fall,
    join in the everlasting song,
    and crown Him Lord of all!

13(ii) All hail the power of Jesus' name!

DIADEM 86 86 extended

Music: James Ellor (1819–99)

All hail the power of Je - sus' name! let an - gels pros-trate fall;— let an - gels pros - trate fall; bring forth the roy - al di - a - dem,— and crown_____ Him, crown Him,

crown Him,

crown Him, crown Him, crown Him, crown_____

crown Him, crown Him, and crown_ Him Lord of all.

14 All heaven declares

Words: Tricia Richards
Music: Noel Richards

With majesty

Capo 1(A)

1 All heaven de - clares the glo - ry of the
2 I will pro - claim the glo - ry of the

ris - en Lord; who can com - pare
ris - en Lord, who once was slain

with the beau - ty of the Lord? For ev - er He will
to re - con - cile_ man to God. For ev - er You will

be the Lamb up - on_ the throne;
be the Lamb up - on_ the throne;

All heaven waits

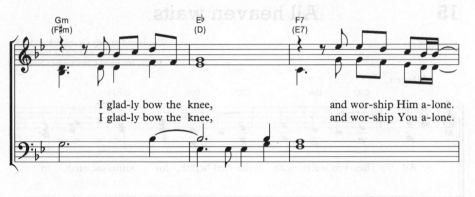

I glad-ly bow the knee,   and wor-ship Him a-lone.
I glad-ly bow the knee,   and wor-ship You a-lone.

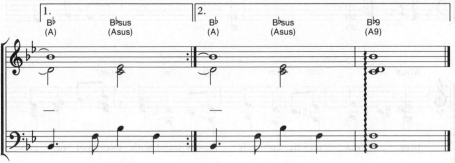

1 All heaven declares
   the glory of the risen Lord;
   who can compare
   with the beauty of the Lord?
   For ever He will be
   the Lamb upon the throne;
   I gladly bow the knee,
   and worship Him alone.

2 I will proclaim
   the glory of the risen Lord,
   who once was slain
   to reconcile man to God.
   For ever You will be
   the Lamb upon the throne;
   I gladly bow the knee,
   and worship You alone.

15

All heaven waits

Words and music: Graham Kendrick
and Chris Rolinson
Music arranged Christopher Norton

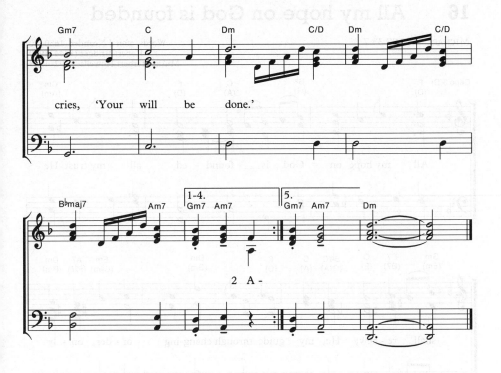

cries, 'Your will be done.'

2 A-

1 All heaven waits with bated breath,
  for saints on earth to pray;
  majestic angels ready stand
  with swords of fiery blade.
  Astounding power awaits a word
  from God's resplendent throne;
  but God awaits our prayer of faith
  that cries, 'Your will be done.'

2 Awake, O Church, arise and pray,
  complaining words discard;
  the Spirit comes to fill your mouth
  with truth, His mighty sword.
  Go place your feet on Satan's ground,
  and there proclaim Christ's name;
  in step with heaven's armies march
  to conquer and to reign!

WOMEN
3 Now in our hearts and on our lips
  the word of faith is near;
  let heaven's will on earth be done,
  let heaven flow from here.
MEN
  Come blend your prayers with Jesus' own,
  before the Father's throne;
  and as the incense clouds ascend,
  God's holy fire rains down.

4 Soon comes the day when, with a shout,
  King Jesus shall appear;
  and with Him all the Church
  from every age shall fill the air.
  The brightness of His coming shall
  consume the lawless one;
  as with a word the breath of God
  tears down his rebel throne.

5 One body here by heaven inspired,
  we seek prophetic power;
  in Christ agreed one heart and voice
  to speak this day, this hour.
  In every place where chaos rules,
  and evil forces brood,
  let Jesus' voice speak like the roar
  of a great multitude.

16   All my hope on God is founded

MICHAEL   87 87 33 7

Words: after J Neander (1650–80)
Robert Bridges (1844–1930)
Music: Herbert Howells (1892–1983)

Music: © Novello & Co Ltd
8–10 Lower James Street, London W1R 3PL

1 All my hope on God is founded,
all my trust He shall renew;
He, my guide through changing order,
only good and only true.
God unknown,
He alone
calls my heart to be His own.

2 Pride of man and earthly glory,
sword and crown betray His trust;
all that human toil can fashion,
tower and temple, fall to dust.
But God's power,
hour by hour,
is my temple and my tower.

3 Day by day our mighty giver
grants to us His gifts of love;
in His will our souls find pleasure,
leading to our home above.
Love shall stand
at His hand,
joy shall wait for His command.

4 Still from man to God eternal
sacrifice of praise be done,
high above all praises praising
for the gift of Christ His Son.
Hear Christ's call
one and all:
we who follow shall not fall.

17 All my life, Lord

Words and music: Andy and Becky Silver

For two groups of singers

18 All over the world

Words and music: Roy Turner
Music arranged Roland Fudge

All o-ver the world the Spi-rit is mov-ing,
All o-ver His church God's Spi-rit is mov-ing,
Right here in this place the Spi-rit is mov-ing,

all o-ver the world as the pro-phet said it would be;
all o-ver His church as the pro-phet said it would be;
right here in this place as the pro-phet said it would be;

all o-ver the world there's a migh-ty re-ve-la-tion of the
all o-ver His church there's a migh-ty re-ve-la-tion of the
right here in this place there's a migh-ty re-ve-la-tion of the

glo-ry of the Lord, as the wa-ters co-ver the sea.
glo-ry of the Lord, as the wa-ters co-ver the sea.
glo-ry of the Lord, as the wa-ters co-ver the sea.

19 All praise to our redeeming Lord

LUCIUS   CM

Words: Charles Wesley (1707–88)
Music: attributed to *Templi Carmina*, 1829

1 All praise to our redeeming Lord,
   who joins us by His grace,
   and bids us each to each restored,
   together seek His face.

2 He bids us build each other up;
   and, gathered into one,
   to our high calling's glorious hope
   we hand in hand go on.

3 The gift which He on one bestows,
   we all delight to prove;
   the grace through every vessel flows,
   in purest streams of love.

4 Ev'n now we think and speak the same,
   and cordially agree;
   concentrated all, through Jesus's name,
   in perfect harmony.

5 We all partake the joy of one,
   the common peace we feel,
   a peace to sensual minds unknown,
   a joy unspeakable.

6 And if our fellowship below
   in Jesus be so sweet,
   what heights of rapture shall we know
   when round His throne we meet!

20 All people that on earth do dwell

OLD HUNDREDTH   LM

Words: William Kethe (1520–94)
Music: Melody from the *Genevan Psalter*, 1551

1 All people that on earth do dwell,
   Sing to the Lord with cheerful voice;
   Him serve with mirth, His praise forth tell;
   come ye before Him and rejoice.

2 The Lord, ye know, is God indeed:
   without our aid He did us make:
   we are His folk, He doth us feed;
   and for His sheep He doth us take.

3 O enter then His gates with praise,
   approach with joy His courts unto;
   praise, laud, and bless His name always,
   for it is seemly so to do.

4 For why? The Lord our God is good;
   His mercy is for ever sure;
   His truth at all times firmly stood,
   and shall from age to age endure.

All the riches of His grace

Words and music: Jan Harrington

With simplicity, flowing

All the rich - es of His grace, all the ful - ness of His bless-ings, all the sweet - ness of His love___ He gives to you,___ He gives to me. All the me.

1 Oh, the blood of___ Je - sus, oh, the blood of___ Je - sus,
2 Oh, the word of___ Je - sus, oh, the word of___ Je - sus,
3 Oh, the love of___ Je - sus, oh, the love of___ Je - sus,

22　All the way

ALL THE WAY　87 87 D

Words: Frances van Alstyne (1820–1915)
(Fanny J Crosby)
Music: Robert Lowry (1826–99)
arranged Phil Burt

All the way my Sav-iour leads me; what have I to ask be - side? Can I doubt His ten-der mer - cy, who through life has been my guide? Heaven-ly peace, di - vin - est com - fort, here by faith in Him to dwell! For I

know   what-e'er be - fall   me,   Je - sus   do - eth all things well.

1   All the way my Saviour leads me;
     what have I to ask beside?
     Can I doubt His tender mercy,
     who through life has been my guide?
     Heavenly peace, divinest comfort,
     here by faith in Him to dwell!
     For I know whate'er befall me,
     Jesus doeth all things well.

2   All the way my Saviour leads me,
     cheers each winding path I tread,
     gives me grace for every trial,
     feeds me with the living bread.
     Though my weary steps may falter,
     and my soul a-thirst may be,
     gushing from the rock before me,
     Lo! a spring of joy I see.

3   All the way my Saviour leads me,
     O the fulness of His love!
     Perfect rest to me is promised
     in my Father's house above.
     When my spirit, clothed, immortal,
     wings its flight to realms of day,
     this, my song through endless ages:
     Jesus led me all the way!

23(i) All things bright and beautiful

ALL THINGS BRIGHT AND BEAUTIFUL   76 76 with refrain   Words: Cecil F Alexander (1818–95)
Music: W H Monk (1823–89)

All things bright and beau - ti-ful, all__ crea-tures great and small,__

all things wise and won - der-ful, the__ Lord God__ made them all.

Each lit - tle flower that o - pens, each lit - tle bird that sings,___ He

made their glow-ing co - lours, He made their ti - ny wings.

All things bright and beautiful,
all creatures great and small,
all things wise and wonderful,
the Lord God made them all.

1 Each little flower that opens,
each little bird that sings,
He made their glowing colours,
He made their tiny wings.
All things bright . . .

2 The purple-headed mountain,
the river running by,
the sunset, and the morning
that brightens up the sky;
All things bright . . .

3 The cold wind in the winter,
the pleasant summer sun,
the ripe fruits in the garden,
He made them every one.
All things bright . . .

4 He gave us eyes to see them,
and lips that we might tell
how great is God almighty,
who has made all things well.
All things bright . . .

23(ii) All things bright and beautiful

ROYAL OAK   76 76 with refrain

Words: Cecil F Alexander (1818–95)
Music: Traditional English melody
arranged Martin Shaw (1875–1958)

All things bright and beau-ti-ful, all crea-tures great and small,

all things wise and won-der-ful, the Lord God made them all.

Each lit-tle flower that o-pens, each lit-tle bird that sings, He_

made their glow-ing_ col-ours, He_ made their ti-ny_ wings.

Music arrangement: © J Curwen & Sons Ltd/William Elkin Music Services,
Station Road Industrial Estate, Salhouse, Norwich, Norfolk NR13 6NY, UK

All things bright and beautiful,
all creatures great and small,
all things wise and wonderful,
the Lord God made them all.

1 Each little flower that opens,
  each little bird that sings,
  He made their glowing colours,
  He made their tiny wings.
    All things bright . . .

2 The purple-headed mountain,
  the river running by,
  the sunset, and the morning
  that brightens up the sky;
    All things bright . . .

3 The cold wind in the winter,
  the pleasant summer sun,
  the ripe fruits in the garden,
  He made them every one.
    All things bright . . .

4 He gave us eyes to see them,
  and lips that we might tell
  how great is God almighty,
  who has made all things well.
    All things bright . . .

24 All things praise Thee

Te Laudant Omnia   77 77 77

Words: G W Conder (1821–74)
Music: J F Swift (1847–1931)

All things praise Thee, Lord most high, heaven and earth and sea and sky,

all were for Thy glo-ry made, that Thy great-ness, thus dis-played,

should all wor-ship bring to Thee; all things praise Thee: Lord, may we.

1   All things praise Thee, Lord most high,
    heaven and earth and sea and sky,
    all were for Thy glory made,
    that Thy greatness, thus displayed,
    should all worship bring to Thee;
    all things praise Thee: Lord, may we.

2   All things praise Thee: night to night
    sings in silent hymns of light;
    all things praise Thee: day to day
    chants Thy power in burning ray;
    time and space are praising Thee;
    all things praise Thee: Lord, may we.

3   All things praise Thee, high and low,
    rain and dew, and seven-hued bow,
    crimson sunset, fleecy cloud,
    rippling stream, and tempest loud,
    summer, winter – all to Thee
    glory render: Lord, may we.

4   All things praise Thee, heaven's high
        shrine
    rings with melody divine;
    lowly bending at Thy feet,
    seraph and archangel meet;
    this their highest bliss, to be
    ever praising: Lord, may we.

5   All things praise Thee, gracious Lord,
    great Creator, powerful Word,
    omnipresent Spirit, now
    at Thy feet we humbly bow,
    lift our hearts in praise to Thee;
    all things praise Thee: Lord, may we.

25 All to Jesus I surrender

Words: J W Van De Venter
Music: W S Weedon
arranged Roland Fudge

1 All to Je - sus I sur-ren-der, all to Him I free - ly give;
2 All to Je - sus I sur-ren-der, hum - bly at His feet I bow;
3 All to Je - sus I sur-ren-der, make me, Sav-iour, whol-ly Thine;
4 All to Je - sus I sur-ren-der, Lord, I give my - self to Thee;
5 All to Je - sus I sur-ren-der, now I feel the sac - red flame;

I will ev - er love and trust Him, in His pres-ence dai - ly live.
world - ly plea-sures all for-sa - ken, take me, Je - sus, take me now.
let me feel the Ho - ly Spi - rit, tru - ly know that Thou art mine.
fill me with Thy love and pow - er, let Thy bless-ing fall on me.
oh, the joy of full sal - va - tion! Glo - ry, glo - ry to His name!

I sur-ren - der all,____ I sur-ren - der all,____

all to Thee, my bless - ed Sav-iour, I sur-ren - der all.

26

All you that pass by

WAREHAM 55 11 D

Words: Charles Wesley (1707–88) altd.
Music: W Knapp (1698–1768)

All you that pass by, to Je-sus draw nigh;

to you is it no-thing that Je-sus should die?

Your ran-som and peace, your sure-ty He is,

come, see if there ev-er was sor-row like His.

1 All you that pass by,
  to Jesus draw nigh;
  to you is it nothing that Jesus should die?
  Your ransom and peace,
  your surety He is,
  come, see if there ever was sorrow like His.

2 He dies to atone
  for sins not His own.
  Your debt He has paid and your work He has done:
  you all may receive
  the peace He did leave,
  who made intercession, 'My Father, forgive.'

3 For you and for me
  He prayed on the tree:
  the prayer is accepted, the sinner is free.
  The sinner am I,
  who on Jesus rely,
  and come for the pardon God cannot deny.

4 His death is my plea;
  my advocate see,
  and hear the blood speak that has answered for me:
  He purchased the grace
  which now I embrace;
  O Father, You know Jesus died in my place!

27 Almighty God

Words and music: Austin Martin
Music arranged Roland Fudge

Al-migh-ty God, we bring You praise for Your Son, the Word of God; by whose power the world was made, by whose blood we are re-deemed.

Morn-ing Star,_____ the Fa - ther's glo - ry,_____

_ we now wor - ship_____ and a - dore You;_____

_ in our hearts_____ Your light has ris - en;_____

_ Je - sus, Lord,_____ we wor - ship You.

28 Almighty God, our heavenly Father

Words: from *The Alternative Service Book 1980*
Music: Chris Rolinson

With feeling

Al-migh-ty God, our hea-ven-ly Fa-ther, we have sinned a-gainst___ You and a-gainst our fel-low men,_____ in thought and word and deed, through neg - li - gence,___ through weak - ness, through our

Music: © 1987 Thankyou Music,
PO Box 75, Eastbourne, East Sussex BN23 6NW, UK

Alleluia

Words and music: Anon
Music arranged Betty Pulkingham

With quiet adoration

1 Alleluia (*8 times*)

2 How I love Him

3 Blessed Jesus

4 My Redeemer

5 Jesus is Lord

6 Alleluia

Music arrangement: © 1971, 1975 Celebration,
administered in Europe by Thankyou Music,
PO Box 75, Eastbourne, East Sussex BN23 6NW

30 Alleluia, alleluia, give thanks

ALLELUIA NO. 1

Words and music: Donald Fishel
Music arranged Betty Pulkingham

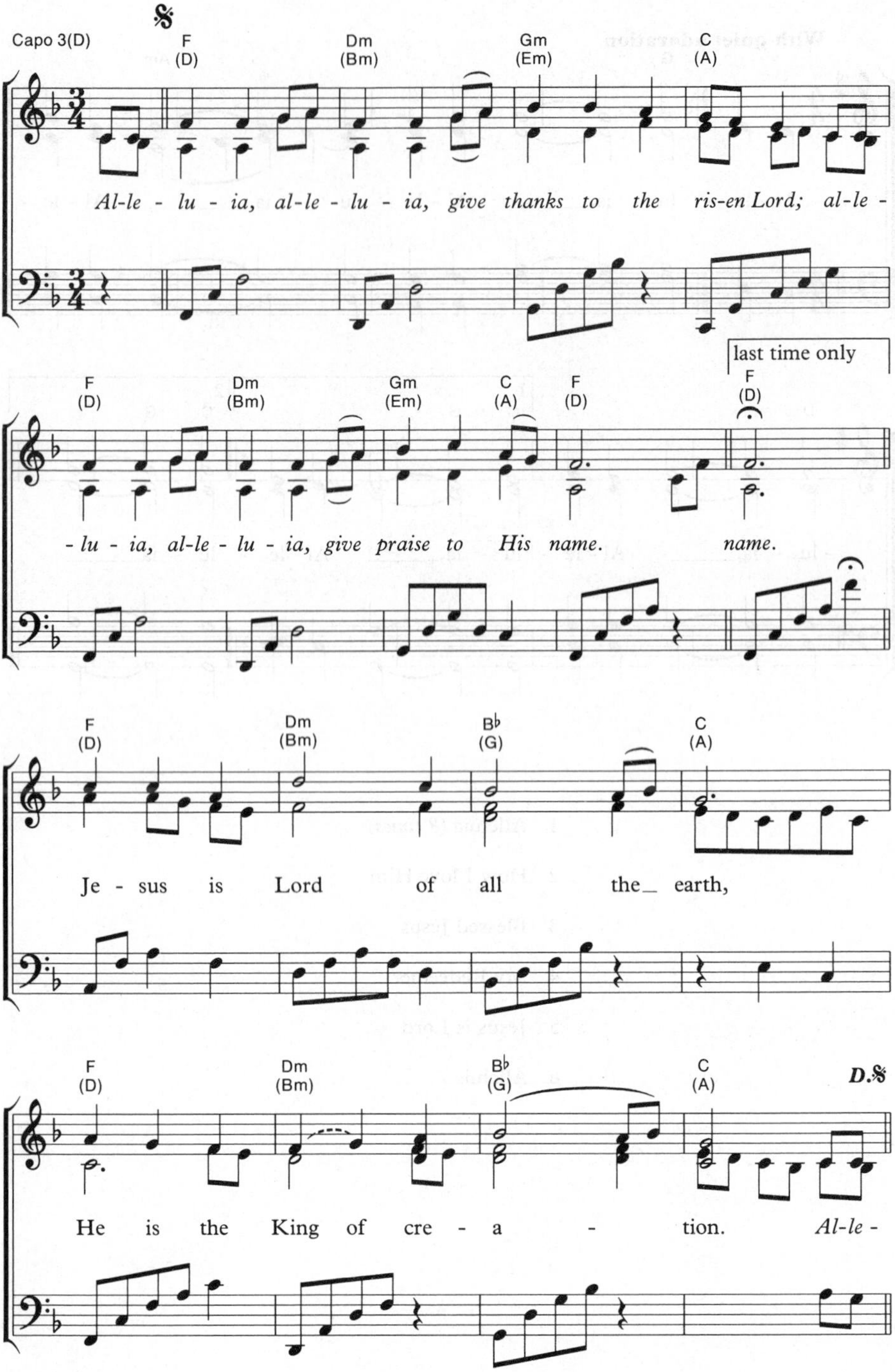
Capo 3(D)
F (D) Dm (Bm) Gm (Em) C (A)
Al-le - lu - ia, al-le - lu - ia, give thanks to the ris-en Lord; al-le -
F (D) Dm (Bm) Gm (Em) C (A) F (D)
last time only
F (D)
- lu - ia, al-le - lu - ia, give praise to His name. name.
F (D) Dm (Bm) B♭ (G) C (A)
Je - sus is Lord of all the_ earth,
F (D) Dm (Bm) B♭ (G) C (A)
D.𝄋
He is the King of cre - a - tion. Al-le -

Alleluia, alleluia,
give thanks to the risen Lord;
alleluia, alleluia,
give praise to His name.

1 Jesus is Lord of all the earth,
   He is the King of creation.
   Alleluia, alleluia . . .

2 Spread the good news o'er all the earth,
   Jesus has died and has risen.
   Alleluia, alleluia . . .

3 We have been crucified with Christ;
   now we shall live for ever.
   Alleluia, alleluia . . .

4 God has proclaimed the just reward,
   life for all men, alleluia.
   Alleluia, alleluia . . .

5 Come let us praise the living God,
   joyfully sing to our Saviour:
   Alleluia, alleluia . . .

31

Amazing grace

AMAZING GRACE   CM

Words: John Newton (1725–1807)
Music: Traditional
arranged Roland Fudge

1   Amazing grace – how sweet the sound –
    that saved a wretch like me!
    I once was lost, but now am found,
    was blind, but now I see.

2   'Twas grace that taught my heart to fear,
    and grace my fears relieved;
    how precious did that grace appear
    the hour I first believed.

3   Through many dangers, toils and snares,
    I have already come;
    'tis grace hath brought me safe thus far,
    and grace will lead me home.

4   When we've been there ten thousand years
    bright shining as the sun,
    we've no less days to sing God's praise
    than when we've first begun.

32   An army of ordinary people

Words and music: Dave Bilbrough
Music arranged Roland Fudge

With feeling

An ar-my of or-di-na-ry peo-ple,_____ a king-dom where love is the key,_____ a ci-ty, a light to the na-tions,___ heirs to the pro-mise are we._____ A peo-ple_ whose life is in Je-sus,_____ a na-tion to-ge-ther we

but the time has now come,   *when the child-ren of*

pro-mise___   *shall flow to-ge-ther as*   *one._____*

1 An army of ordinary people,
   a kingdom where love is the key,
   a city, a light to the nations,
   heirs to the promise are we.
   A people whose life is in Jesus,
   a nation together we stand;
   only through grace are we worthy,
   inheritors of the land.
      A new day is dawning,
      a new age to come,
      when the children of promise
      shall flow together as one:
      a truth long neglected,
      but the time has now come,
      when the children of promise
      shall flow together as one.

2 A people without recognition,
   but with Him a destiny sealed,
   called to a heavenly vision:
   His purpose shall be fulfilled.
   Come let us stand strong together,
   abandon ourselves to the King;
   His love shall be ours for ever,
   this victory song we shall sing.
      A new day . . .

33 And can it be

SAGINA 88 88 88

Words: Charles Wesley (1707–88)
Music: Thomas Campbell (1825–76)

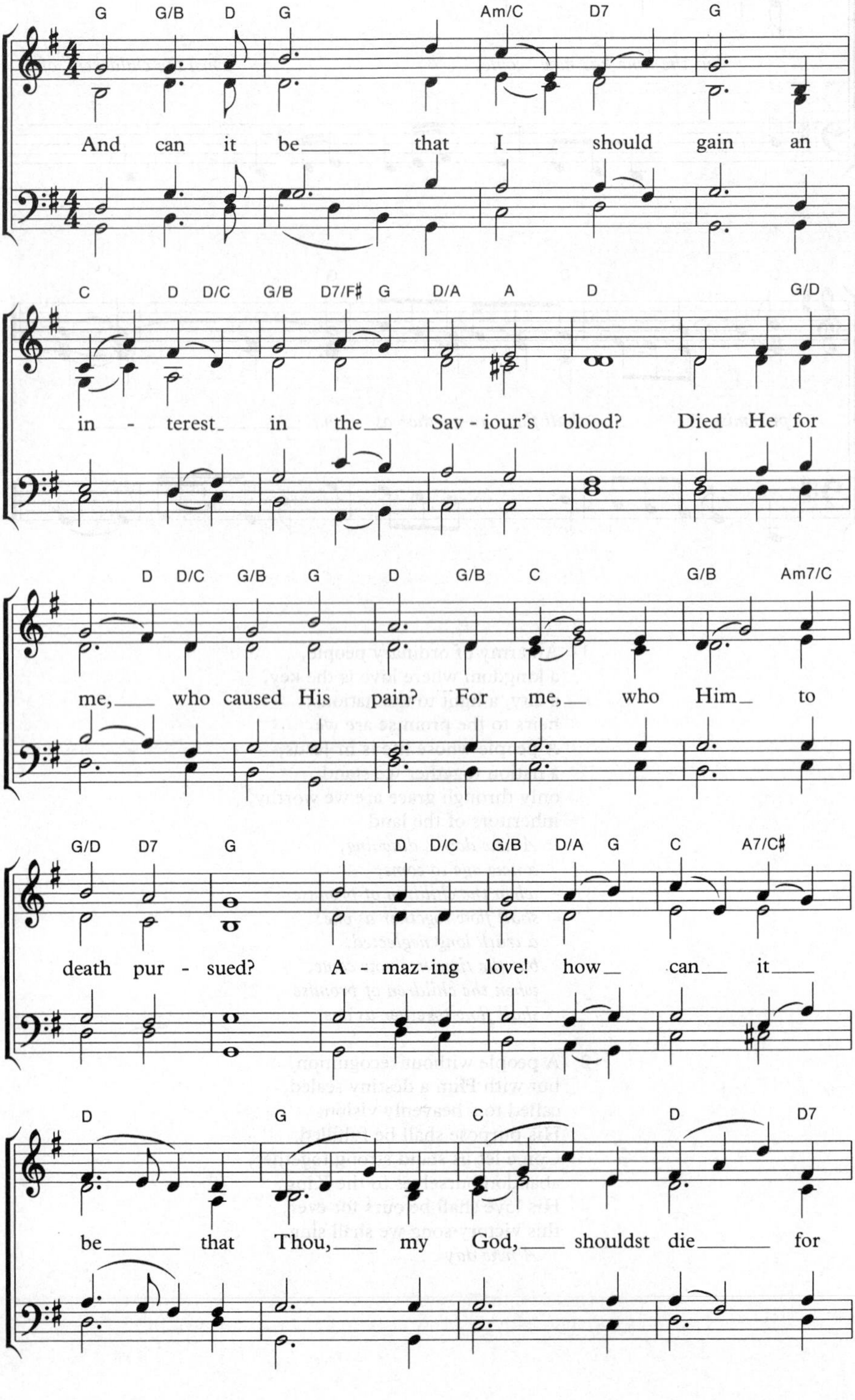

G G/B D G Am/C D7 G
And can it be that I should gain an
C D D/C G/B D7/F♯ G D/A A D G/D
in - terest in the Sav - iour's blood? Died He for
D D/C G/B G D G/B C G/B Am7/C
me, who caused His pain? For me, who Him to
G/D D7 G D D/C G/B D/A G C A7/C♯
death pur - sued? A - maz-ing love! how can it
D G C D D7
be that Thou, my God, shouldst die for

34

me! A - maz - ing love! how can it

be that Thou, my God, shouldst die for me!

1 And can it be that I should gain
   an interest in the Saviour's blood?
   Died He for me, who caused His pain?
   For me, who Him to death pursued?
   Amazing love! how can it be
   that Thou, my God, shouldst die for me!

2 'Tis mystery all! The Immortal dies:
   who can explore His strange design?
   In vain the first-born seraph tries
   to sound the depths of love divine.
   'Tis mercy all! let earth adore,
   let angel minds inquire no more.

3 He left His Father's throne above –
   so free, so infinite His grace –
   emptied Himself of all but love,
   and bled for Adam's helpless race.
   'Tis mercy all, immense and free;
   for, O my God, it found out me!

4 Long my imprisoned spirit lay
   fast bound in sin and nature's night;
   Thine eye diffused a quickening ray –
   I woke, the dungeon flamed with light;
   my chains fell off, my heart was free.
   I rose, went forth, and followed Thee.

5 No condemnation now I dread;
   Jesus, and all in Him, is mine!
   Alive in Him, my living Head,
   and clothed in righteousness divine,
   bold I approach the eternal throne,
   and claim the crown, through Christ, my own.

34   Angel voices ever singing

ANGEL VOICES   85 85 843

Words: Francis Pott (1832–1909)
Music: Edwin George Monk (1819–1900)

1   Angel voices ever singing
    round Thy throne of light,
    angel harps for ever ringing,
    rest not day nor night;
    thousands only live to bless Thee,
    and confess Thee Lord of might.

2   Thou who art beyond the farthest
    mortal eye can scan,
    can it be that Thou regardest
    songs of sinful man?
    Can we know that Thou art near us
    and wilt hear us? Yes, we can.

3   Yes, we know that Thou rejoicest
    o'er each work of Thine;
    Thou didst ears and hands and voices
    for Thy praise design;
    craftsman's art and music's measure
    for Thy pleasure all combine.

4   In Thy house, great God, we offer
    of Thine own to Thee;
    and for Thine acceptance proffer,
    all unworthily,
    hearts and minds and hands and voices
    in our choicest psalmody.

5   Honour, glory, might, and merit
    Thine shall ever be:
    Father, Son, and Holy Spirit,
    Blessèd Trinity:
    of the best that Thou hast given,
    earth and heaven render Thee.

35 Angels from the realms of glory

IRIS   87 87 with refrain

Words: J Montgomery (1771–1854)
in this version Jubilate Hymns
Music: French carol melody

An-gels from the_ realms of glo-ry, wing your flight through all the earth;

her-alds of cre - a-tion's sto-ry now pro-claim Mes - si-ah's birth!

Come_____ and_

wor - ship Christ, the new - born King;_____

wor - ship Christ the new - born King.

1 Angels from the realms of glory,
   wing your flight through all the earth;
   heralds of creation's story
   now proclaim Messiah's birth!
   Come and worship
   Christ, the new-born King;
   come and worship,
   worship Christ the new-born King.

2 Shepherds in the fields abiding,
   watching by your flocks at night,
   God with man is now residing:
   see, there shines the infant light!
   Come and worship . . .

3 Wise men, leave your contemplations!
   brighter visions shine afar;
   seek in Him the hope of nations,
   you have seen His rising star:
   Come and worship . . .

4 Though an infant now we view Him,
   He will share His Father's throne,
   gather all the nations to Him;
   every knee shall then bow down:
   Come and worship . . .

36   Arise, shine

Words and music: Eric Glass
Music arranged Mimi Farra

With strength

1 Be - hold, the_ dark - ness shall cov - er_ the earth,_ and
2 The Gen - tiles shall_ come to thy light,_ and
3 Lift up thine_ eyes round a - bout_ and_ see,_ they
4 Then shalt thou_ see and flow_ to - geth - er, and thy
5 The sun shall no more go_ down,_ nei - ther shall the

gross_ dark - ness_ the peo - ple;_ but the
kings_ to the bright - ness of thy ris - ing:_ and_
gath - er_ them - selves_ to - geth - er;_ and_
heart_ shall_ be_ en - larged;_ the a -
moon_ with - draw_ it - self;_ but the

Lord_ shall a - rise up - on_ thee,_ and His_
they_ shall_ call thee the ci - ty of the Lord, the_
they_ shall_ come, thy_ sons_ from a - far, and thy
- bun-dance of the sea is con - ver - ted un - to thee, and the
Lord_ shall_ be thine_ ev - er - last - ing light, and the

37　As the deer

Words and music: Martin Nystrom

Flowing

As the deer pants for the wa-ter, so my soul longs af - ter
You. You a - lone are my heart's de - sire__ and I
long to wor - ship You. *You a - lone are my*
strength, my shield, to You a - lone may my spi - rit yield.

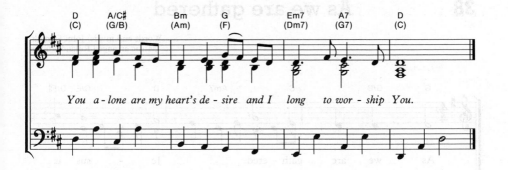

You a-lone are my heart's de-sire and I long to wor-ship You.

1 As the deer pants for the water,
so my soul longs after You.
You alone are my heart's desire
and I long to worship You.
You alone are my strength, my shield,
to You alone may my spirit yield.
You alone are my heart's desire
and I long to worship You.

2 I want You more than gold or silver,
only You can satisfy.
You alone are the real joy-giver
and the apple of my eye.
You alone are . . .

3 You're my Friend and You're my Brother,
even though You are a king.
I love You more than any other,
so much more than anything.
You alone are . . .

38 As we are gathered

Words and music: John Daniels
Music arranged Roland Fudge

As we are gath-ered, Je-sus is here, one with each o-ther, Je-sus is here; joined by the Spi-rit, washed in His Blood,

part of the Bo - dy, the Church of

God. As we are gath - ered,

Je - sus is here, one with each

o - ther, Je - sus is here.

39

As with gladness

Dix   77 77 77

Words: W C Dix (1837–98)
altered Horrobin/Leavers
Music: from a chorale by C Kocher (1786–72)

As with glad-ness men of old did the guid-ing star be-hold;

as with joy they hailed its light, lead-ing on-ward, beam-ing bright,

so, most gra-cious God, may we led by You for ev - er be.

1 As with gladness men of old
did the guiding star behold;
as with joy they hailed its light,
leading onward, beaming bright,
so, most gracious God, may we
led by You for ever be.

2 As with joyful steps they sped,
Saviour, to Your lowly bed,
there to bend the knee before
You whom heaven and earth adore,
so may we with one accord,
seek forgivness from our Lord.

3 As they offered gifts most rare,
gold and frankincense and myrrh,
so may we, cleansed from our sin,
lives of service now begin,
as in love our treasures bring,
Christ, to You our heavenly King.

4 Holy Jesus, every day
keep us in the narrow way;
and when earthly things are past,
bring our ransomed souls at last
where they need no star to guide,
where no clouds Your glory hide.

5 In the heavenly country bright
need they no created light;
You its light, its joy, its crown,
You its sun which goes not down.
There for ever may we sing
Hallelujahs to our King.

40 Ascribe greatness

Words and music: Unknown
Music arranged Roland Fudge

Richly

As - cribe great - ness to our God the rock,____

His work is per - fect and all His ways are just.____

A God of faith - ful - ness____ and

with - out____ in - just - ice;____ good and up - right is

He.____ up - right is He.____

41(i) At the name of Jesus

EVELYNS   65 65 D

Words: Caroline Noel (1817–77)
Music: W H Monk (1823–89)

At the name of Je - sus___ ev - ery knee shall bow,

ev - ery tongue con - fess___ Him___ King of glo - ry___ now.___

'Tis the Fa-ther's plea - sure___ we___ should call Him Lord,___

who from the be - gin - ning___ was the migh - ty Word.

1 At the name of Jesus
   every knee shall bow,
   every tongue confess Him
   King of glory now.
   'Tis the Father's pleasure
   we should call Him Lord,
   who from the beginning
   was the mighty Word.

2 Mighty and mysterious
   in the highest height,
   God from everlasting,
   very Light of light.
   In the Father's bosom,
   with the Spirits blest,
   love, in love eternal,
   rest, in perfect rest.

3 Humbled for a season,
   to receive a name
   from the lips of sinners
   unto whom He came;
   faithfully He bore it
   spotless to the last,
   brought it back victorious,
   when from death He passed.

4 Bore it up triumphant
   with its human light,
   through all ranks of creatures,
   to the central height;
   to the throne of Godhead,
   to the Father's breast,
   filled it with the glory
   of that perfect rest.

5 In your hearts enthrone Him;
   there let Him subdue
   all that is not holy,
   all that is not true;
   crown Him as your captain
   in temptation's hour,
   let His will enfold you
   in its light and power.

6 Brothers, this Lord Jesus
   shall return again,
   with His Father's glory,
   with His angel-train;
   for all wreaths of empire
   meet upon His brow,
   and our hearts confess Him
   King of glory now.

41(ii) At the name of Jesus

CAMBERWELL   65 65 D

Words: C M Noel (1817–77)
Music: Michael Brierley

At the name of Je - sus ev - ery knee shall bow, ev - ery tongue con - fess Him King of glo - ry___ now. 'Tis the Fa - ther's plea - sure we should call Him Lord,

who from the be - gin - ning was the migh - ty Word.

p＿＿＿＿＿＿＿＿＿ now.

1 At the name of Jesus
every knee shall bow,
every tongue confess Him
King of glory now.
'Tis the Father's pleasure
we should call Him Lord,
who from the beginning
was the mighty Word.

2 Mighty and mysterious
in the highest height,
God from everlasting,
very Light of light.
In the Father's bosom,
with the Spirits blest,
love, in love eternal,
rest, in perfect rest.

3 Humbled for a season,
to receive a name
from the lips of sinners
unto whom He came;
faithfully He bore it
spotless to the last,
brought it back victorious,
when from death He passed.

4 Bore it up triumphant
with its human light,
through all ranks of creatures,
to the central height;
to the throne of Godhead,
to the Father's breast,
filled it with the glory
of that perfect rest.

5 In your hearts enthrone Him;
there let Him subdue
all that is not holy,
all that is not true;
crown Him as your captain
in temptation's hour,
let His will enfold you
in its light and power.

6 Brothers, this Lord Jesus
shall return again,
with His Father's glory,
with His angel-train;
for all wreaths of empire
meet upon His brow,
and our hearts confess Him
King of glory now.

42   At this time of giving

Words and music: Graham Kendrick
Music arranged Christopher Norton

Accelerating with each verse

At this time_ of_ giv-ing, glad-ly now_ we_
bring gifts of good - ness and mer - cy
from a heaven-ly_ King. Earth could not con -
-tain the trea - sures hea - ven holds for you,

per - fect joy and last - ing plea-sures, love so strong and__

true.   lai.

At this time of giving,
gladly now we bring
gifts of goodness and mercy
from a heavenly King.

1   Earth could not contain the treasures
    heaven holds for you,
    perfect joy and lasting pleasures,
    love so strong and true.
        At this time of giving . . .

2   May His tender love surround you
    at this Christmastime;
    may you see His smiling face
    that in the darkness shines.
        At this time of giving . . .

3   But the many gifts He gives
    are all poured out from one;
    come receive the greatest gift,
    the gift of God's own Son.
        At this time of giving . . .

    Last two choruses and verses:
    Lai, lai, lai . . . (etc.)

43   At even, ere the sun was set

ANGELUS   LM

Words: Henry Twells (1823–1900)
Music: Melody by Georg Joseph
in Scheffler's *Heilige Seelenlust*, 1657

1 At even, ere the sun was set,
  the sick, O Lord, around Thee lay;
  O in what divers pains they met!
  O with what joy they went away!

2 Once more 'tis eventide, and we,
  oppressed with various ills, draw near;
  what if Thy form we cannot see?
  we know and feel that Thou art here.

3 O Saviour Christ, our woes dispel:
  for some are sick, and some are sad,
  and some have never loved Thee well,
  and some have lost the love they had;

4 And some have found the world is vain,
  yet from the world they break not free;
  and some have friends who give them pain,
  yet have not sought a friend in Thee;

5 And none, O Lord, have perfect rest,
  for none are wholly free from sin;
  and they who fain would serve Thee best
  are conscious most of wrong within.

6 O Saviour Christ, Thou too art man;
  Thou hast been troubled, tempted, tried;
  Thy kind but searching glance can scan
  the very wounds that shame would hide.

7 Thy touch has still its ancient power,
  no word from Thee can fruitless fall;
  hear, in this solemn evening hour,
  and in Thy mercy heal us all.

44   At Your feet, O Lord

Words and music: Janis Miller

Unhurried

At Your feet, O Lord, we wait for You,
yearn-ing Lord, hun-gry Lord, for more of You.
Bowed be-fore You, Lord, we de-sire on-ly You:
fill us Lord, re-vive us Lord, with more of You.

45   At Your feet we fall

Words and music: Dave Fellingham
Music arranged David Peacock

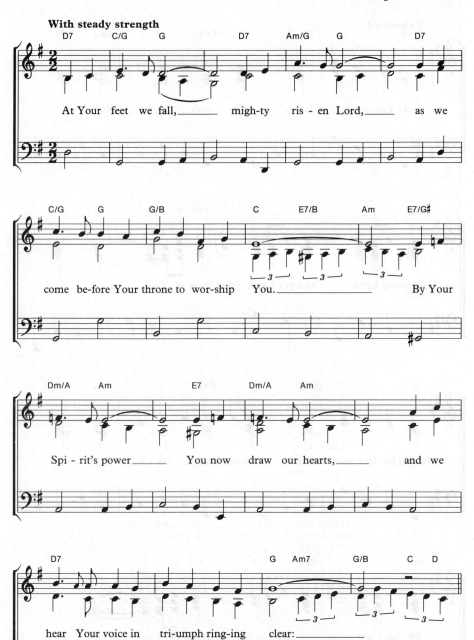

At Your feet we fall,___ migh-ty ris-en Lord,___ as we come be-fore Your throne to wor-ship You.___ By Your Spi-rit's power___ You now draw our hearts,___ and we hear Your voice in tri-umph ring-ing clear:___

Words and music: © 1982 Thankyou Music,
PO Box 75, Eastbourne, East Sussex BN23 6NW, UK

'I am He that liv-eth, that liv-eth and was dead. Be-hold, I am a-live for ev-er-more.

1 At Your feet we fall, mighty risen Lord,
as we come before Your throne to worship You.
By Your Spirit's power You now draw our hearts,
and we hear Your voice in triumph ringing clear:
  'I am He that liveth,
  that liveth and was dead.
  Behold, I am alive
  for evermore.

2 There we see You stand, mighty risen Lord,
clothed in garments pure and holy, shining bright;
eyes of flashing fire, feet like burnished bronze,
and the sound of many waters is Your voice.
  'I am He that liveth . . .

3 Like the shining sun in its noon-day strength,
we now see the glory of Your wondrous face:
once that face was marred, but now You're glorified;
and Your words, like a two-edged sword have mighty power.
  'I am He that liveth . . .

46

Awake, awake, O Zion

Words and music: David J Hadden

A - wake, a - wake, O Zi - on, come clothe your - self with strength._____ A-

Put on your gar - ments of splen - dour, O Je - ru - sa - lem;_____

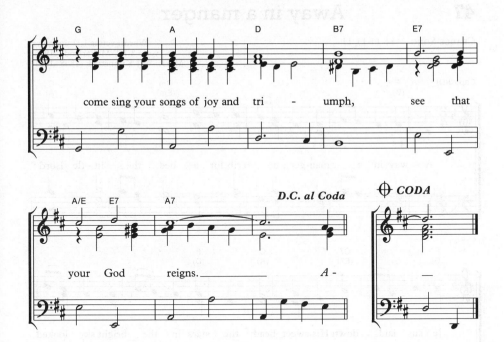

come sing your songs of joy and tri - umph,   see   that

your   God   reigns._____   A -

_____

Awake, awake, O Zion,
come clothe yourself with strength.
Awake, awake, O Zion,
come clothe yourself with strength.

1   Put on your garments of splendour,
    O Jerusalem;
    come sing your songs of joy and triumph,
    see that your God reigns.
        Awake, awake . . .

2   Burst into songs of joy together,
    O Jerusalem;
    the Lord has comforted His people,
    the redeemed Jerusalem.
        Awake, awake . . .

47   Away in a manger

CRADLE SONG   11 11 11 11

Words: verses 1, 2 unknown
verse 3 J T McFarland (c1906)
Music: W J Kirkpatrick (1838–1921)

1   Away in a manger, no crib for a bed,
the little Lord Jesus laid down His sweet head;
the stars in the bright sky looked down where He lay;
the little Lord Jesus asleep in the hay.

2   The cattle are lowing, the Baby awakes,
but little Lord Jesus, no crying He makes:
I love You, Lord Jesus! look down from the sky
and stay by my side until morning is nigh.

3   Be near me, Lord Jesus; I ask You to stay
close by me for ever and love me, I pray;
bless all the dear children in Your tender care,
and fit us for heaven to live with You there.

48   Be still and know

Words and music: Unknown
Music arranged Roland Fudge

1   Be still and know that I am God.
     Be still and know that I am God.
     Be still and know that I am God.

2   I am the Lord that healeth thee.
     I am the Lord that healeth thee.
     I am the Lord that healeth thee.

3   In Thee, O Lord, I put my trust.
     In Thee, O Lord, I put my trust.
     In Thee, O Lord, I put my trust.

49 Be bold, be strong

Words and music: Morris Chapman
Music arranged Andy Silver

I am not dis - mayed, (Not me!) for I'm

walk - ing in faith and vic - to - ry:___ come on and

walk in faith and vic - to - ry,___ for the Lord your

God is with_____ you.

50 Be still, for the presence of the Lord

Words and music: David J Evans

Unhurried

Be still, for the pre-sence of the Lord, the Ho-ly One, is here; come bow be-fore Him now with re-ver-ence and fear: in Him no sin is found — we stand on ho-ly ground. Be still, for the

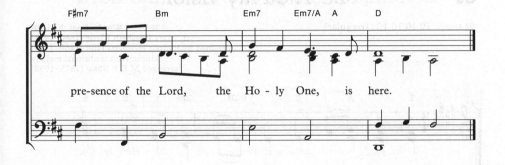

pre-sence of the Lord, the Ho - ly One, is here.

1 Be still,
    for the presence of the Lord,
       the Holy One, is here;
    come bow before Him now
    with reverence and fear:
    in Him no sin is found –
    we stand on holy ground.
    Be still,
    for the presence of the Lord,
       the Holy One, is here.

2 Be still,
    for the glory of the Lord
       is shining all around;
    He burns with holy fire,
    with splendour He is crowned:
    how awesome is the sight –
    our radiant King of light!
    Be still,
    for the glory of the Lord
       is shining all around.

3 Be still,
    for the power of the Lord
       is moving in this place:
    He comes to cleanse and heal,
    to minister His grace –
    no work too hard for Him.
    In faith receive from Him.
    Be still,
    for the power of the Lord
       is moving in this place.

51 Be Thou my vision

SLANE   10 10 10 10 (Irregular)

Words: from the Irish
tr. Mary Elizabeth Byrne (1880–1931)
Versified by Eleanor Henrietta Hull (1860–1935)
Music: Irish traditional melody
arranged M E F Shaw (1875–1958)

Be Thou my vis-ion, O Lord of my heart;
naught be all else to me, save that Thou art –
Thou my best thought, by day or by night,
wak-ing or sleep-ing, Thy presence my light.

1 Be Thou my vision, O Lord of my heart;
   naught be all else to me, save that Thou art –
   Thou my best thought, by day or by night,
   waking or sleeping, Thy presence my light.

2 Be Thou my wisdom, Thou my true Word;
   I ever with Thee, Thou with me, Lord;
   Thou my great Father, I Thy true son;
   Thou in me dwelling, and I with Thee one.

3 Be Thou my battle-shield, sword for the fight,
   be Thou my dignity, Thou my delight.
   Thou my soul's shelter, Thou my high tower:
   raise Thou me heavenward, O Power of my power.

4 Riches I heed not, nor man's empty praise,
   Thou mine inheritance, now and always:
   Thou and Thou only, first in my heart,
   High King of heaven, my treasure Thou art.

5 High King of heaven, after victory won,
   may I reach heaven's joys, O bright heaven's Sun!
   Heart of my own heart, whatever befall,
   still be my vision, O ruler of all.

52

Because He lives

Words: Gloria and William J Gaither
Music: William J Gaither

1 God sent His Son, they called Him Je - sus; He came to love, heal, and for - give; He lived and died to buy my par - don, an emp-ty grave is there to prove my Sav-iour lives.

2 How sweet to hold a new-born ba - by, and feel the pride and joy he gives; but great - er still the calm as - sur - ance, this child can face un-cer-tain days be-cause He lives.

3 And then one day I'll cross the ri - ver; I'll fight life's fi - nal war with pain; and then as death gives way to vic - tory, I'll see the lights of glo - ry and I'll know He lives.

Be - cause He lives_____ I can face to - mor - row;___

_ be - cause He lives_____ all fear is gone;_____

_ be - cause I know_____ He holds the fu - ture,___

_ and life is worth the liv - ing just be-cause He lives.___

53 Because Your love is better than life

Words and music: Phil Potter
Music arranged Andrew Maries

1 Be-cause Your love is bet-ter than life, with my lips I will glo-ri-fy You; I will praise You as long as I live, in Your name I lift my hands.

2 Be-cause Your Son____ has giv-en me life,
3 Be-cause Your Spi - rit____ is fill-ing my life, with my
4 Be-cause Your love____ is bet-ter than life,

lips I will glo - ri - fy__ You, I will praise You__ as long as I

live, in Your name____ I lift my hands.____

OPTIONAL INSTRUMENTAL PART

(Voices)

54 Bind us together, Lord

Words and music: Bob Gillman
Music arranged Norman Warren

Bind us to-geth-er, Lord, bind us to-geth-er with cords that can-not be bro-ken; bind us to-geth-er, Lord, bind us to-geth-er, O bind us to-geth-er with love.

Fine

1 There is on-ly one God, there is on-ly one
2 Made for the glo-ry of God, pur-chased by His pre-cious
3 You are the fam-i-ly of God, You are the pro-mise di -

King,   there is on - ly one Bo - dy
Son.   Born with the right to be clean,   for
- vine,   You are God's cho - sen de - sire,

that   is why we sing:
Je - sus the vic - tory has won.
You are the glo - rious new wine.

D.C. al Fine

Bind us together, Lord,
bind us together
with cords that cannot be broken;
bind us together, Lord,
bind us together,
O bind us together with love.

1 There is only one God,
there is only one King,
there is only one Body –
that is why we sing:
    Bind us together . . .

2 Made for the glory of God,
purchased by His precious Son.
Born with the right to be clean,
for Jesus the victory has won.
    Bind us together . . .

3 You are the family of God,
You are the promise divine,
You are God's chosen desire,
You are the glorious new wine.
    Bind us together . . .

55   Beneath the cross of Jesus

ST CHRISTOPHER   76 86 86 86

Words: Elizabeth Clephane (1830–69)
Music: Frederick C Maker (1844–1927)

1 Be - neath the cross of Je - sus I fain would take my stand –
2 Up - on that cross of Je - sus mine eye at times can see
3 I take, O cross, thy sha - dow, for my a - bid - ing - place!

the sha - dow of a migh - ty rock with - in a wea - ry land;
the ve - ry dy - ing form of One who suf - fered there for me;
I ask no o - ther sun-shine than the sun-shine of His face;

a home with - in a wil - der-ness, a rest up - on the way,
and from my strick-en heart, with tears, two won - ders I con - fess –
con - tent to let the world go by, to know no gain or loss –

from the burn-ing of the noon-tide heat and the bur-den of the day.
the__ won-ders of re - deem-ing love, and__ my own worth-less - ness.
my__ sin - ful self my on - ly shame, my__ glo - ry all – the cross.

56   Bless the Lord, O my soul

BLESS THE LORD

Words and music: Andrea Crouch

57   Bless the Lord, O my soul

Words: from Psalm 103
Music: Unknown
arranged Roland Fudge

With breadth

Bless the Lord, O my soul, bless the Lord, O my soul, and all that is with-in me bless His ho-ly name. Bless the Lord, O my soul, bless the Lord, O my soul, and all that is with-

58 Blessed are the pure in heart

Words and music: Betty Lou Mills
Music arranged Christopher Norton

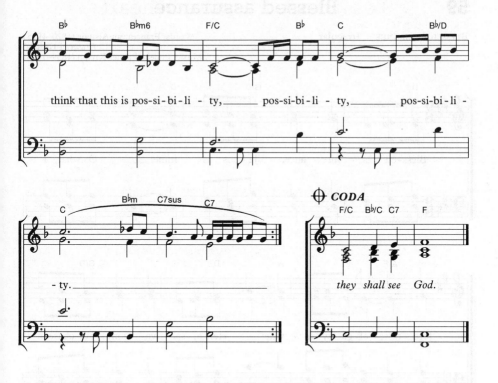

think that this is pos-si-bi-li - ty,_____ pos-si-bi-li - ty,_____ pos-si-bi-li - ty._____

CODA

they shall see God.

Blessed are the pure in heart,
for they shall see God;
blessed are the pure in heart,
for they shall see God.

1 To see God, the alpha and omega,
   to see God, creator, life-sustainer,
   to see God, to think that this is possibility.
   Blessed are . . .

2 To see God, the everlasting Father,
   to see God, whose love endures for ever,
   to see God, how wonderful to think that this could be.
   Blessed are . . .

3 To see God, the God who talked with Moses,
   to see God, whose mercies are so endless,
   to see God, what better incentive for purity.
   Blessed are . . .

4 To see God, the One I've loved and longed for,
   to see God, the Father of my Saviour,
   to see God, a dream come true, at last His face I'll see.
   Blessed are . . .

59 Blessed assurance

BLESSED ASSURANCE   Irregular

Words: Frances van Alstyne (1820–1915)
(Fanny J Crosby)
Music: Phoebe Palmer Knapp (1839–1908)

Bless-ed as - sur - ance, Je - sus is mine:___ O what a
fore - taste of glo-ry di - vine!___ Heir of sal - va - tion, pur-chase of
God;___ born of His Spi - rit, washed in His blood.___
This is my sto - ry, this is my song,___ prais-ing my

Sav - iour all the day long.___ This is my sto - ry, this is my song,___ prais-ing my Sav - iour all the day long.___

1 Blessed assurance, Jesus is mine:
  O what a foretaste of glory divine!
  Heir of salvation, purchase of God;
  born of His Spirit, washed in His blood.
     This is my story, this is my song,
     praising my Saviour all the day long;
     this is my story, this is my song,
     praising my Saviour all the day long.

2 Perfect submission, perfect delight,
  visions of rapture burst on my sight;
  angels descending, bring from above
  echoes of mercy, whispers of love.
     This is my story . . .

3 Perfect submission, all is at rest,
  I in my Saviour am happy and blest;
  watching and waiting, looking above,
  filled with His goodness, lost in His love.
     This is my story . . .

60 Blest be the tie that binds

DENNIS SM

Words: John Fawcett(1740–1817) altd.
Music: J G Nägeli (1768–1836)
arranged Phil Burt

Blest be___ the tie___ that binds our hearts_ in
Christ - ian love; the fel - low - ship___ of
kin - dred minds_ is like___ to that___ a - bove.

1 Blest be the tie that binds
  our hearts in Christian love;
  the fellowship of kindred minds
  is like to that above.

2 Before our Father's throne
  we pour our ardent prayers;
  our fears, our hopes, our aims are one,
  our comforts and our cares.

3 We share our mutual woes,
  our mutual burdens bear,
  and often for each other flows
  the sympathizing tear.

4 When for awhile we part,
  this thought will soothe our pain,
  that we shall still be joined in heart,
  and hope to meet again.

5 This glorious hope revives
  our courage by the way,
  while each in expectation lives,
  and longs to see the day.

6 From sorrow, toil, and pain,
  and sin we shall be free;
  and perfect love and friendship reign
  through all eternity.

61   Born by the Holy Spirit's breath

WHITSUN PSALM   LM

Words: From Romans 8
Timothy Dudley-Smith
Music: Noël Tredinnick

Born by the Ho - ly Spi - rit's breath,
loosed from the law of sin and death, now cleared in Christ from
ev - ery claim, no judge-ment stands a - gainst our name.

1 Born by the Holy Spirit's breath,
   loosed from the law of sin and death,
   now cleared in Christ from every claim,
   no judgement stands against our name.

2 In us the Spirit makes His home
   that we in Him may overcome;
   Christ's risen life, in all its powers,
   its all-prevailing strength, is ours.

3 Sons, then, and heirs of God most high,
   we by His Spirit 'Father' cry;
   that Spirit with our spirit shares
   to frame and breathe our wordless prayers.

4 One is His love, His purpose one:
   to form the likeness of His Son
   in all who, called and justified,
   shall reign in glory at His side.

5 Nor death nor life, nor powers unseen,
   nor height nor depth can come between;
   we know through peril, pain and sword,
   the love of God in Christ our Lord.

62   # Born in the night

MARY'S CHILD   Words and music: Geoffrey Ainger

1 Born in the night,
    Mary's child,
a long way from Your home;
coming in need,
    Mary's child,
born in a borrowed room.

2 Clear shining light,
    Mary's child,
Your face lights up our way:
light of the world,
    Mary's child,
dawn on our darkened day.

3 Truth of our life,
    Mary's child,
You tell us God is good:
prove it is true,
    Mary's child,
go to Your cross of wood.

4 Hope of the world,
    Mary's child,
You're coming soon to reign:
King of the earth,
    Mary's child,
walk in our streets again.

63 Break forth into joy

Words and music: Anon
Music arranged Roland Fudge

Lively

Break forth in-to joy O my soul;_____ break

forth in-to joy O my soul. In the

pre-sence of the Lord there is joy for ev-er-more; break

forth,_____ break forth__ in-to joy.

64   Break Thou the bread of life

LATHBURY   64 64 D

Words: Mary A Lathbury (1841–1913)
and Alexander Groves (1843–1909)
Music: William F Sherwin (1826–88)

Break Thou the bread of life, dear Lord to me,

as Thou didst break the bread be - side the___ sea;

be - yond the sa - cred page I seek Thee, Lord;___

my spi - rit longs for Thee, Thou liv - ing Word!

1 Break Thou the bread of life,
    dear Lord to me,
as Thou didst break the bread
    beside the sea;
beyond the sacred page
    I seek Thee, Lord;
my spirit longs for Thee,
    Thou living Word!

2 Thou art the bread of life,
    O Lord, to me,
Thy holy word the truth
    that saveth me;
give me to eat and live
    with Thee above,
teach me to love Thy truth,
    for Thou art love.

3 O send Thy Spirit, Lord,
    now unto me,
that He may touch my eyes,
    and make me see;
show me the truth concealed
    within Thy word,
and in Thy book revealed
    I see Thee, Lord.

4 Bless Thou the bread of life
    to me, to me,
as Thou didst bless the loaves
    by Galilee;
then shall all bondage cease,
    all fetters fall,
and I shall find my peace,
    my all in all!

65 Brightest and best

EPIPHANY HYMN   11 10 11 10

Words: Reginald Heber (1783–1826)
Music: J F Thrupp (1827–67)

Bright-est and best of the sons of the morn-ing,
dawn on our dark-ness and lend us thine aid;
star of the east_ the ho-ri-zon a-dor-ing,_
guide_ where our in-fant Re-deem-er is laid.

1 Brightest and best of the sons of the morning,
   dawn on our darkness and lend us thine aid;
   star of the east the horizon adoring,
   guide where our infant Redeemer is laid.

2 Cold on His cradle the dew-drops are shining;
   low lies His head with the beasts of the stall:
   angels adore Him, in slumber reclining,
   maker and monarch, and Saviour of all.

3 Say, shall we yield Him, in costly devotion,
   odours of Edom, and offerings divine;
   gems of the mountain, and pearls of the ocean,
   myrrh from the forest, or gold from the mine?

4 Vainly we offer each ample oblation;
   vainly with gifts would His favour secure;
   richer by far is the heart's adoration;
   dearer to God are the prayers of the poor.

5 Brightest and best of the sons of the morning,
   dawn on our darkness and lend us thine aid;
   star of the east the horizon adoring,
   guide where our infant Redeemer is laid.

66   Broken for me

Words and music: Janet Lunt

Words and music: © 1978 Mustard Seed Music,
PO Box 356, Leighton Buzzard LU7 8WP

Je-sus was bro - ken _____ that we might be whole: *Bro-ken for* _____ *bro-ken for you.*

⊕ *CODA*

Broken for me, broken for you,
the body of Jesus broken for you.

1 He offered His body, He poured out His soul,
  Jesus was broken that we might be whole:
      Broken for me . . .

2 Come to My table and with Me dine,
  eat of My bread and drink of My wine:
      Broken for me . . .

3 This is My body given for you,
  eat it remembering I died for you:
      Broken for me . . .

4 This is My blood I shed for you,
  for your forgiveness, making you new:
      Broken for me . . .

67   Breathe on me, breath of God

TRENTHAM   SM

Words: Edwin Hatch (1835–89)
Music: Robert Jackson (1840–1914)

1   Breathe on me, breath of God,
    fill me with life anew,
    that I may love what Thou dost love,
    and do what Thou wouldst do.

2   Breathe on me, breath of God,
    until my heart is pure,
    until with Thee I will one will,
    to do and to endure.

3   Breathe on me, breath of God,
    till I am wholly Thine,
    until this earthly part of me
    glows with Thy fire divine.

4   Breathe on me, breath of God,
    so shall I never die,
    but live with Thee the perfect life
    of Thine eternity.

68 Cause me to come

Words and music: R Edward Miller

Thoughtfully

Cause me to come to Thy ri-ver,___ O Lord,
cause me to come to Thy ri-ver,___ O Lord,
cause me to come to Thy ri-ver,___ O Lord, cause me to
come, cause me to drink, cause me to live.

1 Cause me to come to Thy river, O Lord, (*3 times*)
   cause me to come, cause me to drink, cause me to live.

2 Cause me to drink from Thy river, O Lord, (*3 times*)
   cause me to come, cause me to drink, cause me to live.

3 Cause me to live by Thy river, O Lord, (*3 times*)
   cause me to come, cause me to drink, cause me to live.

69 Change my heart, O God

Words and music: Eddie Espinosa
Music arranged David Peacock

Children of Jerusalem

CHILDREN'S PRAISE   77 77 with refrain

Words: John Henley (1800–42)
Music: from Curwen's *Tune Book*, 1842

Child-ren of Je - ru - sa-lem sang the praise of Je - sus' name;

child - ren, too, of mo - dern days, join to sing the

Sav-iour's praise: *Hark! hark! hark! while child-ren's voi-ces sing,*

Hark! hark! hark! while child-ren's voi-ces sing loud ho-san-nas,

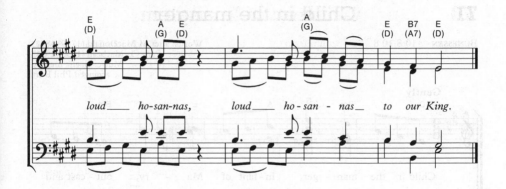

loud____ ho-san-nas, loud____ ho-san - nas__ to our King.

1 Children of Jerusalem
   sang the praise of Jesus' name;
   children, too, of modern days,
   join to sing the Saviour's praise:
     Hark, hark, hark! while children's voices sing,
     hark, hark, hark! while children's voices sing
     loud hosannas, loud hosannas,
     loud hosannas to our King.

2 We are taught to love the Lord,
   we are taught to read His word,
   we are taught the way to heaven;
   praise for all to God be given:
     Hark, hark, hark . . .

3 Parents, teachers, old and young,
   all unite to swell the song;
   higher and yet higher rise,
   till hosannas reach the skies:
     Hark, hark, hark . . .

Child in the manger

BUNESSAN   10 8 10 8

Words: after M MacDonald (1789–1872)
L Macbean (1853–1931)
Music: Gaelic melody
arranged Phil Burt

1 Child in the manger, infant of Mary,
   outcast and stranger, Lord of all!
   Child who inherits all our transgressions,
   all our demerits on Him fall.

2 Once the most holy child of salvation
   gentle and lowly lived below:
   now as our glorious mighty Redeemer,
   see Him victorious over each foe.

3 Prophets foretold Him, infant of wonder;
   angels behold Him on His throne:
   worthy our Saviour of all their praises;
   happy for ever are His own.

72   Christ is the answer

Words and music: Major T W Maltby

Christ is the ans-wer to my ev-ery need; Christ is the ans-wer, He is my friend in-deed. Prob-lems of life my spi-rit may as-sail, with Christ my Sav-iour I need ne-ver fail, for Christ is the ans-wer to my need.

73 Christ is made the sure foundation

WESTMINSTER ABBEY   87 87 87

Words: from the Latin, J M Neale (1818–66)
in this version Jubilate Hymns
Music: H Purcell (1659–95)

Christ is made the sure foun - da - tion, Christ the head and cor - ner - stone cho - sen of the Lord and pre - cious, bind - ing all the Church in one; ho - ly Zi - on's help for

ev - er, and her con - fi - dence___ a - lone.

1 Christ is made the sure foundation,
  Christ the head and corner-stone
  chosen of the Lord and precious,
  binding all the Church in one;
  holy Zion's help for ever,
  and her confidence alone.

2 All within that holy city
  dearly loved of God on high,
  in exultant jubilation
  sing, in perfect harmony;
  God the One-in-Three adoring
  in glad hymns eternally.

3 We as living stones invoke you:
  Come among us, Lord, today!
  with Your gracious loving-kindness
  hear Your children as we pray;
  and the fulness of Your blessing
  in our fellowship display.

4 Here entrust to all Your servants
  what we long from You to gain –
  that on earth and in the heavens
  we one people shall remain,
  till united in Your glory
  evermore with You we reign.

5 Praise and honour to the Father,
  praise and honour to the Son,
  praise and honour to the Spirit,
  ever Three and ever One:
  one in power and one in glory
  while eternal ages run.

74 Christ is risen! hallelujah

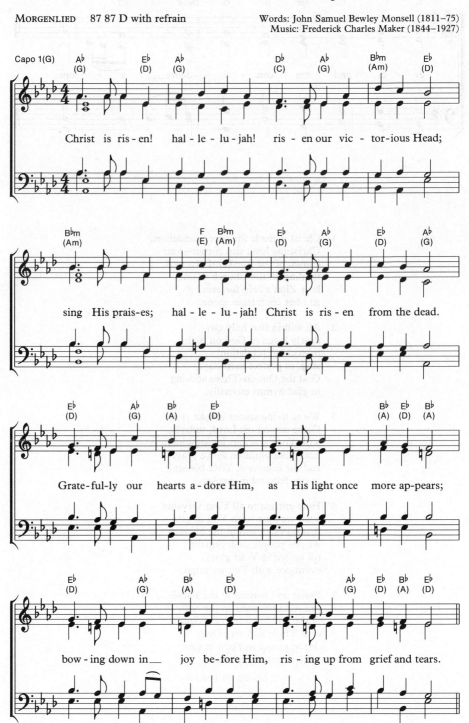

MORGENLIED   87 87 D with refrain

Words: John Samuel Bewley Monsell (1811–75)
Music: Frederick Charles Maker (1844–1927)

Christ is ris-en! hal-le-lu-jah! ris-en our vic-tor-ious Head;

sing His prais-es; hal-le-lu-jah! Christ is ris-en from the dead.

Grate-ful-ly our hearts a-dore Him, as His light once more ap-pears;

bow-ing down in __ joy be-fore Him, ris-ing up from grief and tears.

Christ is ris-en! hal-le-lu-jah! ris-en our vic-tor-ious Head;

sing His prais-es; hal-le-lu-jah! Christ is ris-en from the dead.

1 Christ is risen! hallelujah!
   risen our victorious Head;
   sing His praises; hallelujah!
   Christ is risen from the dead.
   Gratefully our hearts adore Him,
   as His light once more appears;
   bowing down in joy before Him,
   rising up from grief and tears.
   Christ is risen! hallelujah!
   risen our victorious Head;
   sing His praises; hallelujah!
   Christ is risen from the dead.

2 Christ is risen! all the sadness
   of His earthly life is o'er;
   through the open gates of gladness
   He returns to life once more.
   Death and hell before Him bending,
   He doth rise the victor now,
   angels on His steps attending,
   glory round His wounded brow.
   Christ is risen! . . .

3 Christ is risen! henceforth never
   death or hell shall us enthral;
   we are Christ's, in Him for ever
   we have triumphed over all;
   all the doubting and dejection
   of our trembling hearts have ceased.
   'Tis His day of resurrection;
   let us rise and keep the feast.
   Christ is risen! . . .

75 Christ is surely coming

LAND OF HOPE AND GLORY 11 11 11 11 11

Words: from Revelation 22
Christopher Idle
Music: Edward Elgar (1857–1934)
arranged Robin Sheldon

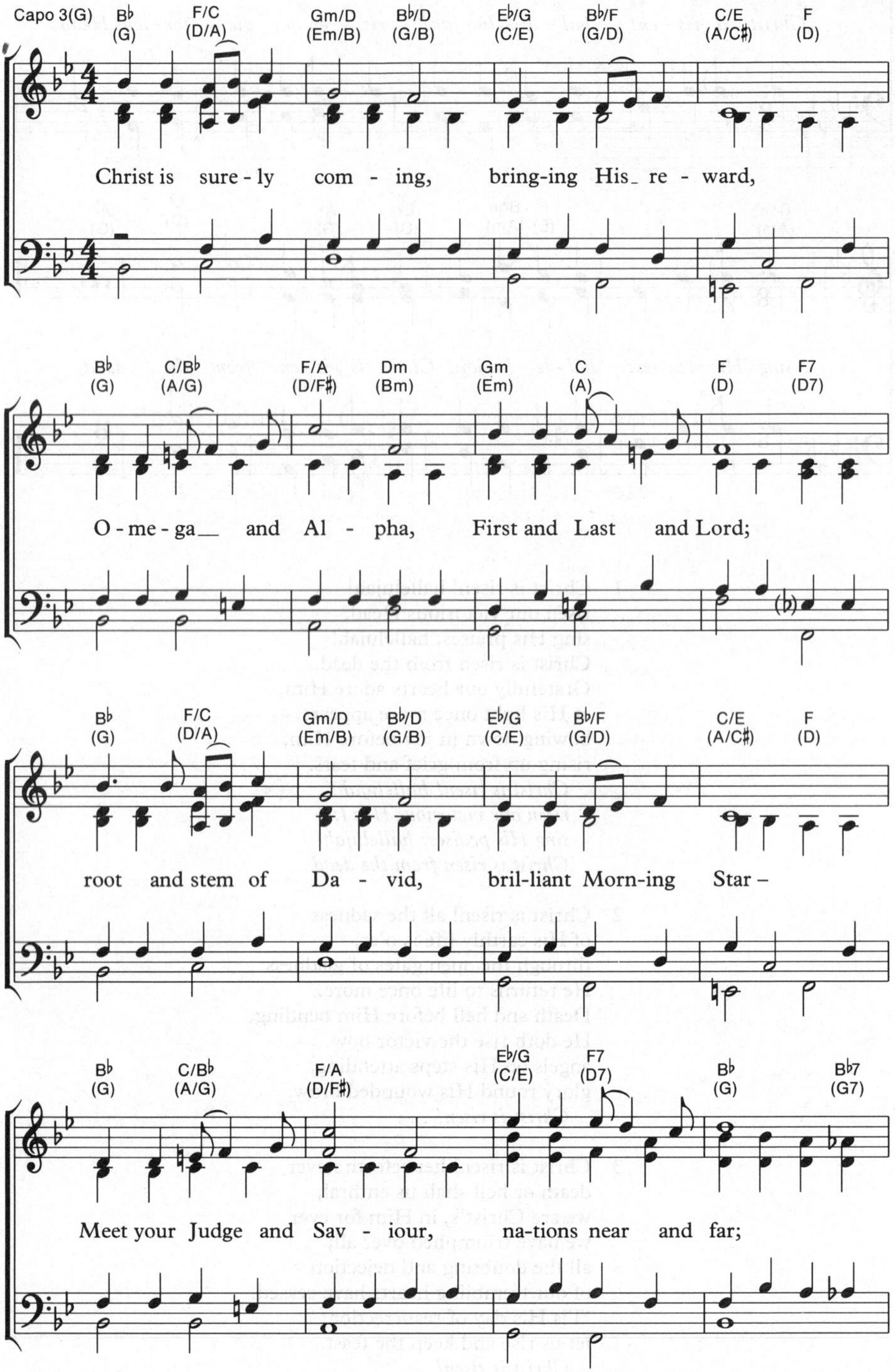

Capo 3(G)
B♭ (G) F/C (D/A) Gm/D (Em/B) B♭/D (G/B) E♭/G (C/E) B♭/F (G/D) C/E (A/C♯) F (D)
Christ is sure - ly com - ing, bring-ing His_ re - ward,
B♭ (G) C/B♭ (A/G) F/A (D/F♯) Dm (Bm) Gm (Em) C (A) F (D) F7 (D7)
O - me - ga__ and Al - pha, First and Last and Lord;
B♭ (G) F/C (D/A) Gm/D (Em/B) B♭/D (G/B) E♭/G (C/E) B♭/F (G/D) C/E (A/C♯) F (D)
root and stem of Da - vid, bril-liant Morn-ing Star –
B♭ (G) C/B♭ (A/G) F/A (D/F♯) E♭/G (C/E) F7 (D7) B♭ (G) B♭7 (G7)
Meet your Judge and Sav - iour, na-tions near and far;

| Eb (C) | F/Eb (D/C) | Bb/D (G/B) | Gm (Em) | Cm7 (Am7) | F7 (D7) | Bb (G) |

meet   your Judge   and   Sav - iour,   na - tions   near   and   far!

1   Christ is surely coming, bringing His reward,
    Omega and Alpha, First and Last and Lord;
    root and stem of David, brilliant Morning Star –
        Meet your Judge and Saviour, nations near and far;
        meet your Judge and Saviour, nations near and far!

2   See the holy city! There they enter in,
    men by Christ made holy, washed from every sin;
    thirsty ones, desiring all He loves to give:
        Come for living water, freely drink, and live;
        come for living water, freely drink, and live!

3   Grace be with God's people! Praise His holy name –
    Father, Son, and Spirit, evermore the same!
    Hear the certain promise from the eternal home:
        'Surely I come quickly!' – Come, Lord Jesus, come;
        'Surely I come quickly!' – Come, Lord Jesus, come!

76 Christ the Lord is risen today

EASTER HYMN   77 77 with Hallelujahs

Words: Charles Wesley (1707–88)
Music: *Lyra Davidica*, 1708
arranged W A Monk (1823–89)

Christ the Lord is risen to-day;_ Hal — — le - lu - jah!

sons of men and an - gels say:_ Hal — — le - lu - jah!

raise your joys and_ tri-umphs high; Hal — — le - lu - jah!

sing, ye heavens; thou earth, re - ply:_ Hal — — le - lu - jah!

1 Christ the Lord is risen today;
   Hallelujah!
   sons of men and angels say:
   raise your joys and triumphs high;
   sing, ye heavens; thou earth, reply:

2 Love's redeeming work is done,
   fought the fight, the battle won;
   Lo! our sun's eclipse is o'er,
   Lo! He sets in blood no more:

3 Vain the stone, the watch, the seal;
   Christ hath burst the gates of hell;
   death in vain forbids Him rise;
   Christ hath opened paradise;

4 Lives again our glorious King;
   where, O death, is now thy sting?
   Once He died our souls to save;
   where thy victory, O grave?

5 Soar we now where Christ hath led,
   following our exalted Head;
   made like Him, like Him we rise;
   ours the cross, the grave, the skies:

6 Hail the Lord of earth and heaven,
   praise to Thee by both be given:
   Thee we greet, in triumph sing
   Hail, our resurrected King:

77 Christ triumphant

CHRIST TRIUMPHANT   85 85 79

Words: Michael Saward
Music: Michael Baughen

With triumphant vigour

Capo 3(D)

Christ tri-um-phant, ev-er reign-ing, Sav-iour, Mas-ter, King,___ Lord of heaven, our lives sus--tain-ing, hear us as we sing:___ *Yours the glo-ry and the crown,___ the high re-*

- nown,_____ the e - ter - nal name._____

1 Christ triumphant, ever reigning,
   Saviour, Master, King,
   Lord of heaven, our lives sustaining,
   hear us as we sing:
      Yours the glory and the crown,
      the high renown, the eternal name.

2 Word incarnate, truth revealing,
   Son of Man on earth!
   power and majesty concealing
   by your humble birth:
      Yours the glory . . .

3 Suffering servant, scorned, ill-treated,
   victim crucified!
   death is through the cross defeated,
   sinners justified:
      Yours the glory . . .

4 Priestly King, enthroned for ever
   high in heaven above!
   sin and death and hell shall never
   stifle hymns of love:
      Yours the glory . . .

5 So, our hearts and voices raising
   through the ages long,
   ceaselessly upon You gazing,
   this shall be our song:
      Yours the glory . . .

78   Christ the Way of life possess me

Words: Timothy Dudley-Smith
Music: Phil Burt

Christ the Way of life pos - sess me, lift my heart to love and praise; guide and keep, sus-tain and bless me, all my days, all my days.

1 Christ the Way of life possess me,
lift my heart to love and praise;
guide and keep, sustain and bless me,
all my days, all my days.

2 Well of life, for ever flowing,
make my barren soul and bare
like a watered garden growing
fresh and fair, fresh and fair.

3 May the Tree of life in splendour
from its leafy boughs impart
grace divine and healing tender,
strength of heart, strength of heart.

4 Path of life before me shining,
let me come when earth is past,
sorrow, self and sin resigning,
home at last, home at last.

79   Christel, whose glory fills the skies

RATISBON   77 77 77

Words: Charles Wesley (1707–88)
Music: melody from J G Werner's *Choralbuch*, Leipzig, 1815
arranged W H Havergal (1793–1870)

1   Christ, whose glory fills the skies,
    Christ, the true, the only light,
    Sun of righteousness, arise,
    triumph o'er the shades of night:
    Day-spring from on high, be near;
    Day-star, in my heart appear.

2   Dark and cheerless is the morn
    unaccompanied by Thee;
    joyless is the day's return,
    till Thy mercy's beams I see;
    till they inward light impart,
    glad my eyes, and warm my heart.

3   Visit then this soul of mine;
    pierce the gloom of sin and grief;
    fill me, radiancy divine;
    scatter all my unbelief;
    more and more Thyself display,
    shining to the perfect day.

80 Christians awake!

YORKSHIRE   10 10 10 10 10 10

Words: John Byrom (1692–1763) altd.
Music: John Wainwright (1723–68)

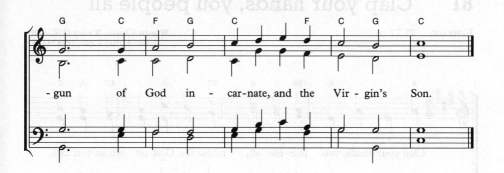

- gun   of   God   in - car-nate, and   the   Vir - gin's   Son.

1   Christians awake! salute the happy morn,
     whereon the Saviour of mankind was born;
     rise to adore the mystery of love
     which hosts of angels chanted from above;
     with them the joyful tidings first begun
     of God incarnate, and the Virgin's Son.

2   Then to the watchful shepherds it was told,
     who heard the angelic herald's voice 'Behold,
     I bring good tidings of a Saviour's birth
     to you and all the nations upon earth:
     this day hath God fulfilled His promised word,
     this day is born a Saviour, Christ the Lord.'

3   He spake; and straightway the celestial choir,
     in hymns of joy unknown before conspire;
     the praises of redeeming love they sang,
     and heaven's whole orb with hallelujahs rang:
     God's highest glory was their anthem still,
     'On earth be peace, and unto men goodwill.'

4   To Bethlehem straight the enlightened shepherds ran,
     to see the wonder God had wrought for man;
     then to their flocks, still praising God, return,
     and their glad hearts with holy rapture burn;
     amazed, the wondrous tidings they proclaim,
     the first apostles of His infant fame.

5   Then may we hope, the angelic hosts among,
     to sing, redeemed, a glad triumphal song:
     He that was born upon this joyful day
     around us all His glory shall display;
     saved by His love, incessant we shall sing
     eternal praise to heaven's almighty King.

81   Clap your hands, you people all

EPHRAIM   77 77

Words: Charles Wesley (1707–88)
Music: Henry Leslie (c1825–76)

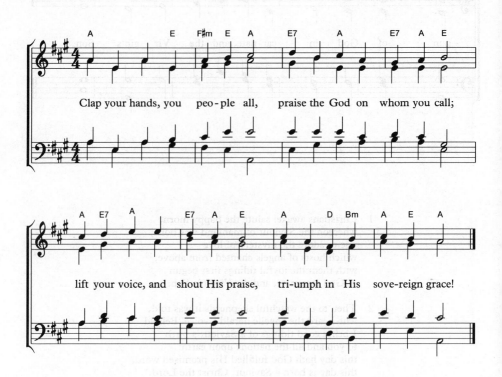

Clap your hands, you peo-ple all, praise the God on whom you call;

lift your voice, and shout His praise, tri-umph in His sove-reign grace!

1 Clap your hands, you people all,
   praise the God on whom you call;
   lift your voice, and shout His praise,
   triumph in His sovereign grace!

2 Glorious is the Lord Most High,
   terrible in majesty;
   He His sovereign sway maintains,
   King o'er all the earth He reigns.

3 Jesus is gone up on high,
   takes His seat above the sky:
   shout the angel-choirs aloud,
   echoing to the trump of God.

4 Sons of earth, the triumph join,
   praise Him with the host divine;
   emulate the heavenly powers,
   their victorious Lord is ours.

5 Shout the God enthroned above,
   trumpet forth His conquering love;
   praises to our Jesus sing,
   praises to our glorious King!

6 Power is all to Jesus given,
   power o'er hell, and earth, and heaven!
   Power He now to us imparts;
   praise Him with believing hearts.

7 Wonderful in saving power,
   Him let all our hearts adore;
   earth and heaven repeat the cry,
   'Glory be to God most high!'

82   Cleanse me from my sin

Words and music: R Hudson Pope (1879–1967)

Cleanse me from my sin, Lord, put Thy power with - in, Lord,

take me as I__ am, Lord, and make me all Thine own.____

Keep me day by day, Lord, un - der-neath Thy sway, Lord,

make my heart Thy pal - ace, and Thy roy - al__ throne.

Words and music: © Scripture Gift Mission
Radstock House, 3 Eccleston Street, London SW1W 9LZ

83 Come and join the celebration

CELEBRATIONS 11 14 with refrain

Words and music: Valerie Collison

Moderato

Come and join the ce-le-bra-tion, it's a ve-ry spe-cial day;

come and share our ju-bi-la-tion, there's a new King born to-day! *Fine*

1 See the shep-herds hur-ry down to Beth-le-hem;

gaze in won-der at the Son of God who lay be-fore them.

2nd time **D.C. al Fine**

84   Come and praise the living God

Words and music: Mike Kerry
Music arranged Roland Fudge

Come and praise the living God,
come and worship, come and worship.
He has made you priest and king,
come and worship the living God.

1 We come not to a mountain of fire and smoke,
   not to gloom and darkness or trumpet sound;
   we come to the new Jerusalem,
   the holy city of God.
       Come and praise . . .

2 By His voice He shakes the earth,
   His judgements known throughout the world.
   But we have a city that for ever stands,
   the holy city of God.
       Come and praise . . .

85 Come and see

Words and music: Graham Kendrick
Music arranged Christopher Norton

Worshipfully

1 Come and see, come and see, come and see the King of love; see the
2 Come and weep, come and mourn for your sin that pierced Him there; so much
3 Man of heaven, born to earth to re - store us to Your heaven. Here we

pur - ple robe and crown of thorns He wears. Sol - diers
deep - er than the wounds of thorn and nail. All our
bow in awe be - neath Your search - ing eyes. From Your

mock, ru - lers sneer as He lifts the cru - el cross; lone and
pride, all our greed, all our fall - en - ness and shame; and the
tears comes our joy, from Your death our life shall spring; by Your

friend - less now, He climbs to - wards the hill. We
Lord has laid the pun - ish - ment on Him.
re - sur - rec - tion pow - er we shall rise.

86 Come and see the shining hope

MARCHING THROUGH GEORGIA 13 13 13 8 10 10 13 8

Words: from Revelation 4 and 5
Christopher Idle
Music: American traditional melody
arranged David Wilson

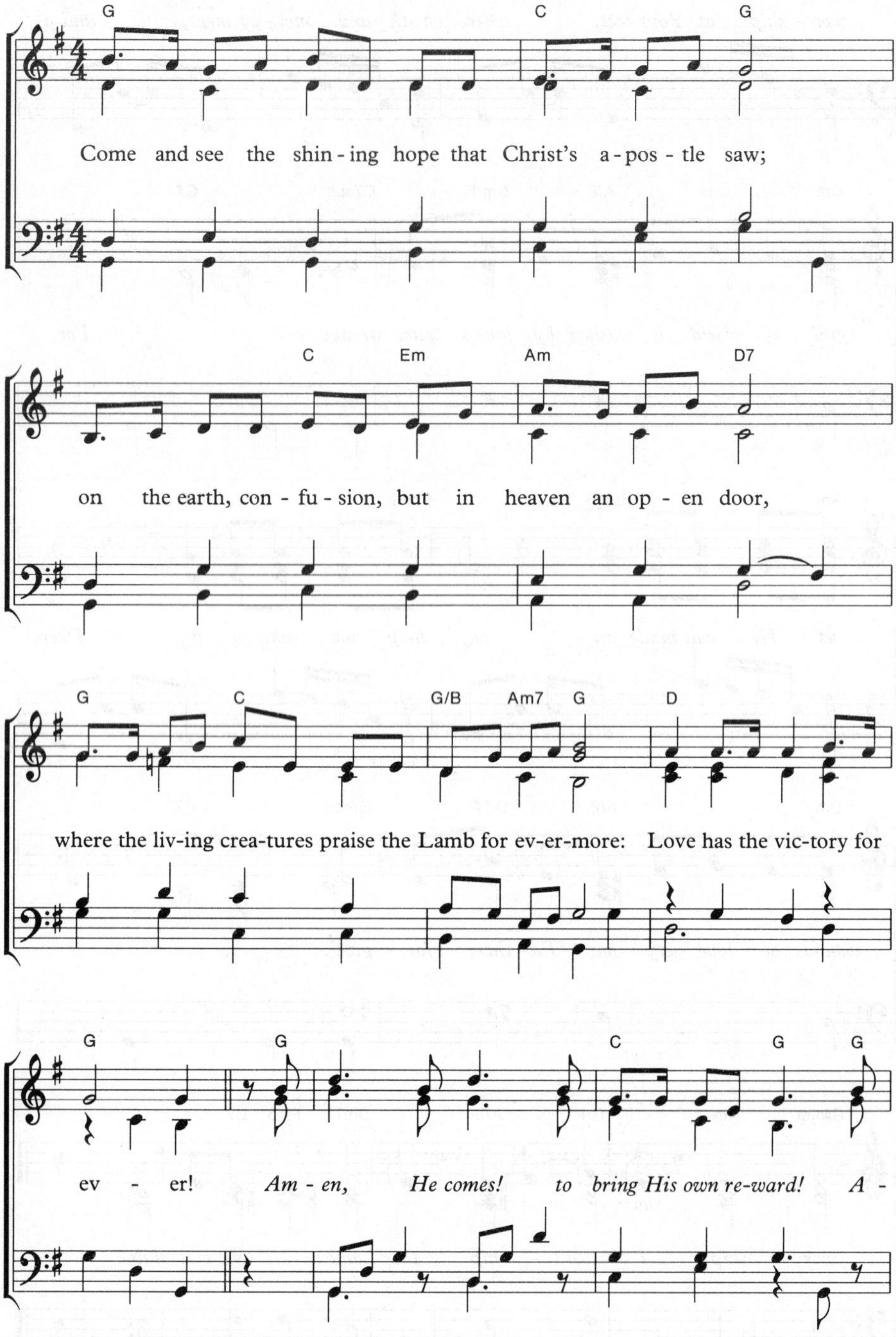

G C G
Come and see the shin-ing hope that Christ's a-pos-tle saw;
C Em Am D7
on the earth, con-fu-sion, but in heaven an op-en door,
G C G/B Am7 G D
where the liv-ing crea-tures praise the Lamb for ev-er-more: Love has the vic-tory for
G G C G G
ev - er! *Am - en, He comes! to bring His own re-ward! A -*

- men, praise God! for jus-tice now re-stored; king-doms of the world be-come the king-doms of the Lord: Love has the vic-tory for ev - er!

1   Come and see the shining hope that Christ's apostle saw;
    on the earth, confusion, but in heaven an open door,
    where the living creatures praise the Lamb for evermore:
    Love has the victory for ever!
      Amen, He comes!
      to bring His own reward!
      Amen, praise God!
      for justice now restored;
      kingdoms of the world
      become the kingdoms of the Lord:
      Love has the victory for ever!

2   All the gifts You send us, Lord, are faithful, good, and true;
    holiness and righteousness are shown in all You do:
    who can see Your greatest Gift and fail to worship You?
    Love has the victory for ever!
      Amen, He comes . . .

3   Power and salvation all belong to God on high!
    So the mighty multitudes of heaven make their cry,
    singing Alleluia! where the echoes never die:
    Love has the victory for ever!
      Amen, He comes . . .

87 Come and praise Him

Words and music: A Carter
Music arranged Roger Mayor

With majesty

Come and praise Him,_____ roy - al priest - hood,_____

_____ come and wor - ship,_____ ho - ly na - tion,_____

_____ wor-ship Je - sus,_____ our Re - deem - er,_____

_____ He is pre - cious,_____ King of glo - ry._____

Come bless the Lord

Words: from Psalm 134
Music: Anon
arranged Roger Mayor

89   Come down, O love divine

DOWN AMPNEY   6 6 11 D

Words: after Bianco da Siena
R F Littledale (1833–90)
Music: R Vaughan Williams (1872–1958)

Come down, O love di - vine, seek Thou this soul of mine and vi - sit it with Thine own ar - dour glow - ing; O Com-for - ter, draw near, with - in my heart ap - pear, and kin - dle it Thy ho - ly flame be - stow - ing.

1 Come down, O love divine,
   seek Thou this soul of mine
   and visit it with Thine own ardour glowing;
   O Comforter, draw near,
   within my heart appear,
   and kindle it, Thy holy flame bestowing.

2 O let it freely burn,
   till earthly passions turn
   to dust and ashes, in its heat consuming;
   and let Thy glorious light
   shine ever on my sight,
   and clothe me round, the while my path illuming.

3 Let holy charity
   mine outward vesture be,
   and lowliness become mine inner clothing;
   true lowliness of heart,
   which takes the humbler part,
   and o'er its own shortcomings weeps with loathing.

4 And so the yearning strong,
   with which the soul will long,
   shall far outpass the power of human telling;
   for none can guess its grace,
   till he become the place
   wherein the Holy Spirit makes His dwelling.

90 Come, Holy Ghost

VENI CREATOR   LM

Words: after R Maurus (c776–856)
J Cosin (1594–1672)
Music: from proper plainsong melody
arranged Roland Fudge

Flowing

Come, Ho - ly Ghost, our souls_ in - spire,

and light-en with_ ce - les - tial fire: Thou the_ a - noint - ing

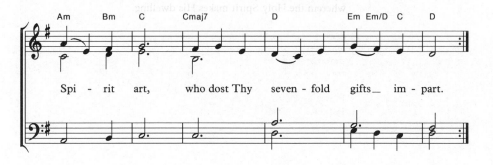

Spi - rit art, who dost Thy seven - fold gifts_ im - part.

After verse 4

Praise_____ to Thy_ e - ter - nal me - rit,

Fa - ther, Son,_ and Ho - ly Spi-rit! A - men.

1 Come, Holy Ghost, our souls inspire,
and lighten with celestial fire:
Thou the anointing Spirit art,
who dost Thy sevenfold gifts impart.

2 Thy blessèd unction from above
is comfort, life, and fire of love:
enable with perpetual light
the dullness of our blinded sight.

3 Anoint and cheer our soilèd face
with the abundance of Thy grace:
keep far our foes, give peace at home –
where Thou art guide no ill can come.

4 Teach us to know the Father, Son,
and Thee, of both to be but One;
that, through the ages all along,
this, this may be our endless song:

Praise to Thy eternal merit,
Father, Son, and Holy Spirit! Amen.

91   Come let us bow down in worship

Words and music: Andy Silver

He is our God, the peo-ple of__ His pas-ture, the

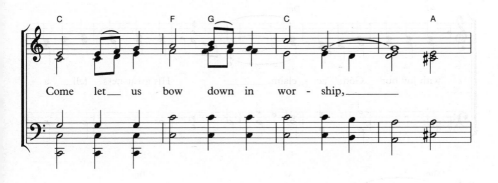

flock un - der His care._____

Come let__ us bow down in wor - ship,_____

let us kneel__ be - fore_____ the Lord.

92   Come, let us praise the Lord

CHILEAN VENITE   66 66 44 44

Words: from Psalm 95
Timothy Dudley-Smith
Music: Chilean folk-song
adapted and arranged Michael Paget

Steadily ♩. = 54

Come, let us praise the Lord, with joy our God ac - claim,____ His great-ness tell_ a - broad____ and bless His sav - ing name.____

If sung in harmony, the words of the bass part are the same as for the tune,
but sung to the bass rhythm one syllable to each note.

Music: © 1988 Oxford University Press
from *New Songs of Praise 4*. Reprinted by permission.

Lift_____ high your songs_____ be -

- fore_ His throne_____ to whom a -

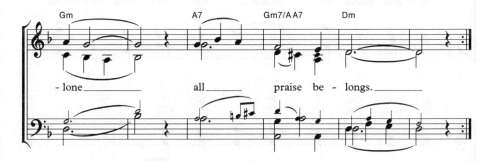

- lone_____ all_____ praise be - longs._____

1 Come, let us praise the Lord,
with joy our God acclaim,
His greatness tell abroad
and bless His saving name.
  Lift high your songs
  before His throne
  to whom alone
  all praise belongs.

2 Our God of matchless worth,
our King beyond compare,
the deepest bounds of earth,
the hills, are in His care.
  He all decrees,
  who by His hand
  prepared the land
  and formed the seas.

3 In worship bow the knee,
our glorious God confess;
the great Creator, He,
the Lord our righteousness.
  He reigns unseen:
  his flock He feeds
  and gently leads
  in pastures green.

4 Come, hear His voice today,
receive what love imparts;
His holy will obey
and harden not your hearts.
  His ways are best;
  and lead at last,
  all troubles past,
  to perfect rest.

93 Come, let us join our cheerful songs

NATIVITY   CM

Words: Isaac Watts (1674–1748)
Music: Henry Lahee (1826–1912)

1 Come, let us join our cheerful songs
   with angels round the throne;
   ten thousand thousand are their tongues,
   but all their joys are one.

2 'Worthy the Lamb that died!' they cry,
   'to be exalted thus';
   'Worthy the Lamb!' our lips reply,
   'for He was slain for us.'

3 Jesus is worthy to receive
   honour and power divine;
   and blessings more than we can give
   be, Lord, for ever Thine.

4 The whole creation join in one,
   to bless the sacred name
   of Him that sits upon the throne,
   and to adore the Lamb.

94 Come let us sing

WONDERFUL LOVE   10 4 10 7 4 10

Words: Robert Walmsley (1831–1905)
Music: F Luke Wiseman (1858–1944)

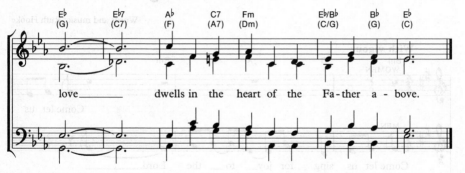

love_____ dwells in the heart of the Fa-ther a - bove.

1 Come let us sing of a wonderful love,
   tender and true;
   out of the heart of the Father above,
   streaming to me and to you:
   Wonderful love
   dwells in the heart of the Father above.

2 Jesus, the Saviour, this gospel to tell,
   joyfully came;
   came with the helpless and hopeless to dwell,
   sharing their sorrow and shame;
   seeking the lost,
   saving, redeeming at measureless cost.

3 Jesus is seeking the wanderers yet;
   Why do they roam?
   Love only waits to forgive and forget;
   Home! weary wanderers, home!
   Wonderful love
   dwells in the heart of the Father above.

4 Come to my heart, O Thou wonderful love,
   come and abide,
   lifting my life till it rises above
   envy and falsehood and pride;
   seeking to be
   lowly and humble, a learner of Thee.

95

Come let us sing

Words and music: Ruth Hooke

Words and music: © 1987 Ruth Hooke,
9 Cypress Grove, Lostock Hall, Preston PR5 5BB

96   Come let us worship

I Am The Bread Of Life

Words: after S Suzanne Toolan
Michael Baughan
Music: Suzanne Toolan
arranged Christian Strover

Come, let us wor-ship Christ to the glo-ry of God the Fa-ther, for He is wor-thy of all our love; He died and rose for us! praise Him as Lord and Sav-iour. *And when the trum - pet shall sound, and Je-sus comes in great power,__ then He will raise us to be with Him for ev - er - more.*

1   Come, let us worship Christ
     to the glory of God the Father,
     for He is worthy of all our love;
     He died and rose for us!
     praise Him as Lord and Saviour.
        And when the trumpet shall sound,
        and Jesus comes in great power,
        then He will raise us to be with Him
        for evermore.

2   'I am the Bread of Life;
     he who comes to Me shall not hunger:
     and all who trust in Me shall not thirst' –
     this is what Jesus said:
     praise Him as Lord and Saviour.
        And when the trumpet . . .

3   'I am the door to life;
     he who enters by Me is saved,
     abundant life he will then receive' –
     this is what Jesus said:
     praise Him as Lord and Saviour.
        And when the trumpet . . .

4   'I am the Light of the world;
     if you follow Me, darkness ceases,
     and in its place comes the light of life' –
     this is what Jesus said:
     praise Him as Lord and Saviour.
        And when the trumpet . . .

5   Lord, we are one with You;
     we rejoice in Your new creation:
     our hearts are fired by Your saving love –
     take up our lives, O Lord,
     and use us for Your glory.
        And when the trumpet . . .

97 Come, let us worship

Words: from Psalm 95
Sarah Turner-Smith
Music: Paul Herrington
arranged Phil Burt

Words and music: © Ears and Eyes Music Ltd/Boosey & Hawkes Music Publishers Ltd,
295 Regent Street, London W1R 8JH

-giv - - ing, make a joy - ful noise;_____
pas - - ture, the sheep of His hand:_____
Fa - - ther, praise to Christ His Son;_____

_ for the Lord_ is a great
_ for Christ the Lord_ is our Shep -
_ praise be to God the Ho - ly Spi -

God: King a - bove all gods._____
- herd, He will lead us home._____
- rit: bless the Three-in - One!_____

name,_____ ho - ly is His name.__

98 Come now with awe

FINLANDIA 11 10 11 10 11 10

Words: Timothy Dudley-Smith
Music: J Sibelius (1865–1957)

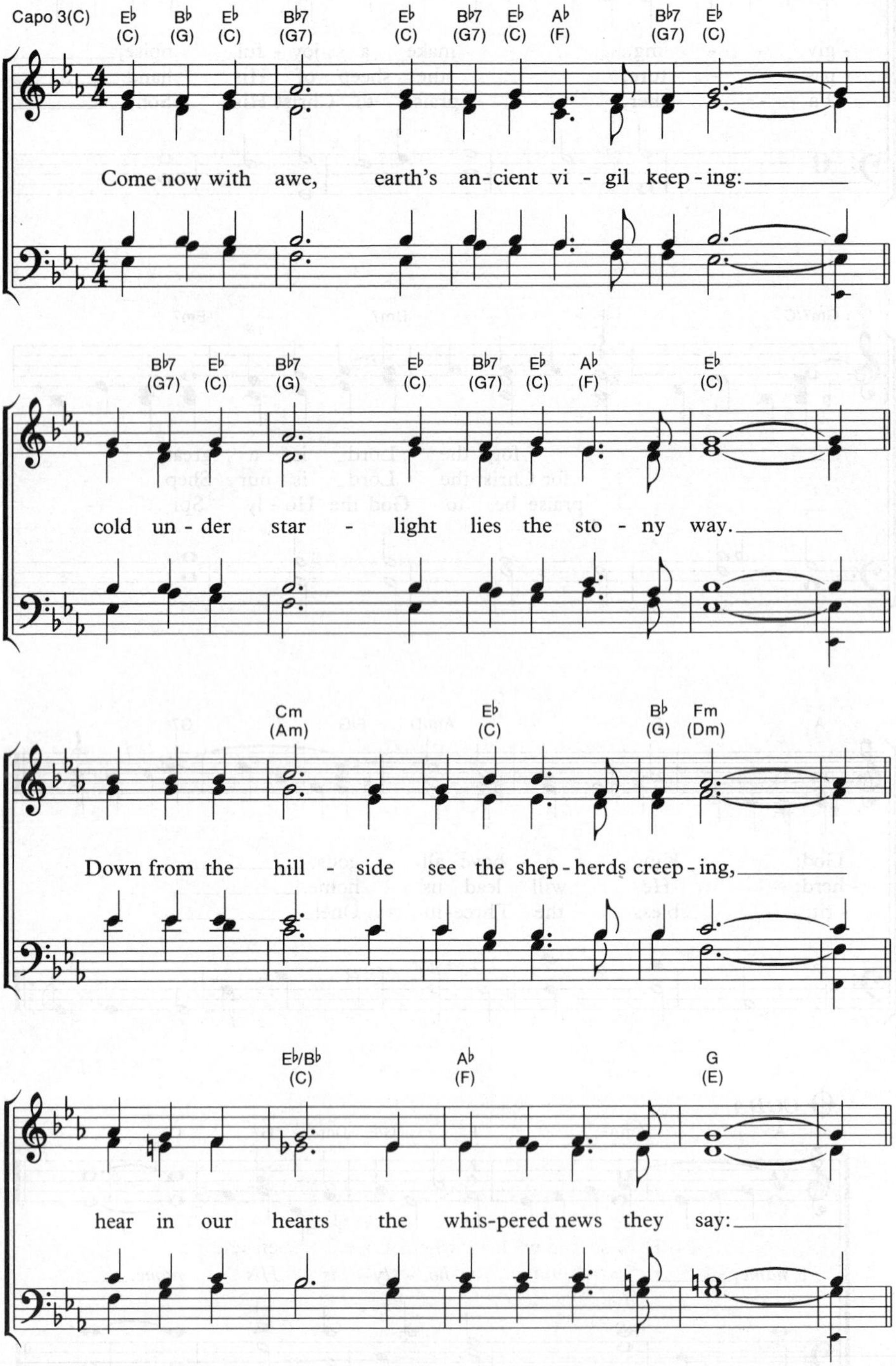

Capo 3(C)
E♭ (C) B♭ (G) E♭ (C) B♭7 (G7) E♭ (C) B♭7 (G7) E♭ (C) A♭ (F) B♭7 (G7) E♭ (C)
Come now with awe, earth's an-cient vi - gil keep - ing:
B♭7 (G7) E♭ (C) B♭7 (G) E♭ (C) B♭7 (G7) E♭ (C) A♭ (F) E♭ (C)
cold un - der star - light lies the sto - ny way.
Cm (Am) E♭ (C) B♭ (G) Fm (Dm)
Down from the hill - side see the shep - herds creep - ing,
E♭/B♭ (C) A♭ (F) G (E)
hear in our hearts the whis-pered news they say:

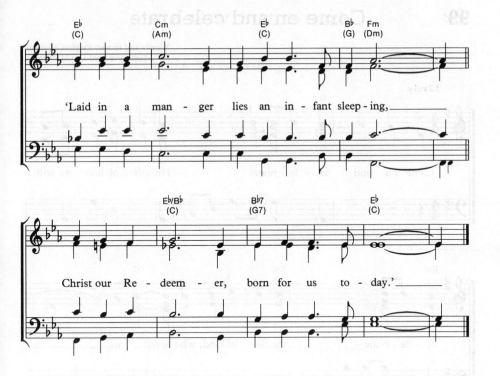

'Laid in a man - ger lies an in - fant sleep - ing,

Christ our Re - deem - er, born for us to - day.'

1 Come now with awe, earth's ancient vigil keeping:
cold under starlight lies the stony way.
Down from the hillside see the shepherds creeping,
hear in our hearts the whispered news they say:
'Laid in a manger lies an infant sleeping,
Christ our Redeemer, born for us today.'

2 Come now with joy to worship and adore Him;
hushed in the stillness, wonder and behold –
Christ in the stable where His mother bore Him,
Christ whom the prophets faithfully foretold:
High King of ages, low we kneel before Him,
starlight for silver, lantern-light for gold.

3 Come now with faith, the age-long secret guessing,
hearts rapt in wonder, soul and spirit stirred –
see in our likeness love beyond expressing,
All God has spoken, all the prophets heard;
born for us sinners, bearer of all blessing,
Flesh of our flesh, behold the eternal Word!

4 Come now with love: beyond our comprehending
Love in its fulness lies in mortal span!
How should we love, whom Love is so befriending?
Love rich in mercy since our race began
now stoops to save us, sighs and sorrows ending,
Jesus our Saviour, Son of God made man.

99

Come on and celebrate

Words and music: Patricia Morgan
Music arranged David Peacock

Lively

Come on and ce - le - brate! His gift of love we will

ce - le - brate – the Son of God, who loved___ us___

___ and gave us life._____ We'll shout Your

praise, O King: You give us joy no-thing else can bring;

Words and music: © 1984 Thankyou Music,
PO Box 75, Eastbourne, East Sussex BN23 6NW, UK

100 Come see the beauty of the Lord

Words and music: Graham Kendrick
Music arranged Christopher Norton

Moderato

Come see the beau-ty of__ the Lord,
But on-ly love pours from His heart,

(Response)

come see the beau-ty of__ His face.
as si-lent-ly He takes__ the blame.

See the Lamb that once was slain,
He has my name up-on His lips,

see on His palms is carved your__ name.
my con-dem-na-tion falls on__ Him.

Words and music: © 1985 Make Way Music,
administered in Europe by Thankyou Music,
PO Box 75, Eastbourne, East Sussex BN23 6NW, UK

101   Come sing the praise of Jesus

Words: J C Winslow (1882–1974)
Music: American traditional melody
arranged D J Langford

praise and glo-ry be to Je - sus, praise and glo-ry be to Je - sus, for Je - sus Christ is King!

1 Come sing the praise of Jesus,
   sing His love with hearts aflame,
   sing His wondrous birth of Mary,
   when to save the world He came;
   tell the life He lived for others,
   and His mighty deeds proclaim,
   for Jesus Christ is King.
      Praise and glory be to Jesus,
      praise and glory be to Jesus,
      praise and glory be to Jesus,
      for Jesus Christ is King!

2 When foes arose and slew Him,
   He was victor in the fight;
   over death and hell He triumphed
   in His resurrection-might;
   He has raised our fallen manhood
   and enthroned it in the height,
   for Jesus Christ is King.
      Praise and glory . . .

3 There's joy for all who serve Him,
   more than human tongue can say;
   there is pardon for the sinner,
   and the night is turned to day;
   there is healing for our sorrows,
   there is music all the way,
   for Jesus Christ is King.
      Praise and glory . . .

4 We witness to His beauty,
   and we spread His love abroad;
   and we cleave the host of darkness,
   with the Spirit's piercing sword;
   we will lead the souls in prison
   to the freedom of the Lord,
   for Jesus Christ is King.
      Praise and glory . . .

5 To Jesus be the glory,
   the dominion, and the praise;
   He is Lord of all creation,
   He is guide of all our ways;
   and the world shall be His empire
   in the fulness of the days,
   for Jesus Christ is King.
      Praise and glory . . .

102   Come, thou long-expected Jesus

STUTTGART   87 87

Words: Charles Wesley (1707–88)
Music: melody by C F Witt (1660–1716)

Come, Thou long-ex-pect-ed Je-sus, born to set Thy peo-ple free;

from our fears and sins re-lease us; let us find our rest in Thee.

1   Come, Thou long-expected Jesus,
     born to set Thy people free;
     from our fears and sins release us;
     let us find our rest in Thee.

2   Israel's strength and consolation,
     hope of all the earth Thou art;
     dear desire of every nation,
     joy of every longing heart.

3   Born Thy people to deliver;
     born a child, and yet a King;
     born to reign in us for ever;
     now Thy gracious kingdom bring.

4   By Thine own eternal Spirit
     rule in all our hearts alone:
     by Thine all-sufficient merit
     raise us to Thy glorious throne.

103 Come, ye faithful

NEANDER   87 87 87

Words: Job Hupton (1762–1849)
and J M Neale (1818–66)
Music: from Chorale *Unser Herrscher*
by J Neander (1650–80)

Come, ye faith-ful, raise the an-them, cleave the_ skies with shouts of praise;

sing to Him who found the ran-som, An - cient of e - ter - nal days,

God e-ter-nal, Word in-car-nate, whom the heaven of heaven o-beys.

1 Come, ye faithful, raise the anthem,
  cleave the skies with shouts of praise;
  sing to Him who found the ransom,
  Ancient of eternal days,
  God eternal, Word incarnate,
  whom the heaven of heaven obeys.

2 Ere He raised the lofty mountains,
  formed the sea, or built the sky,
  love eternal, free, and boundless,
  forced the Lord of life to die,
  lifted up the Prince of princes
  on the throne of Calvary.

3 Now on those eternal mountains
  stands the sapphire throne, all bright,
  with the ceaseless alleluias
  which they raise, the sons of light;
  Sion's people tell His praises,
  victor after hard-won fight.

4 Laud and honour to the Father,
  laud and honour to the Son,
  laud and honour to the Spirit,
  ever Three and ever One,
  One in love, and One in splendour,
  while unending ages run.

104   Come to the waters

Words and music: Jodi Page Clark

1 Je - sus said,_____ 'Come un - to
2 Je - sus said,_____ of the wa - ters
3 Je - sus said,_____ 'He__ who be -
4 So with joy_____ we__ shall draw

Me_____ all ye wea -
that He gave, 'He who drinks_____
- lieves in Me,__ out of him shall
wa - ter__ out of wells_____

- ry, hea - vy la - den.'_____
__ shall ne - ver thirst a - gain.'_____
flow liv - ing wa - ters.'_____
_____ of sal - va - tion._____

D.C.

105   Come, watch with us

Words: Timothy Dudley-Smith
Music: Phil Burt

Em   F#   Bdim   Em/A   A   D

wake   their watch to   keep   and we will   watch____ with them.

1 Come, watch with us this Christmas night;
   our hearts must travel far
   to darkened hills and heavens bright
   with star on shining star;
   to where in shadowy silence sleep
      the fields of Bethlehem,
   as shepherds wake their watch to keep
   and we will watch with them.

2 Who would not join the angel songs
   that tell the Saviour's birth?
   The Lord for whom creation longs
   has come at last to earth;
   the fulness of the Father's love
      is ours at Bethlehem,
   while angels throng the skies above
   and we will sing with them.

3 Who would not journey far to share
   the wisdom of the wise,
   and gaze with them in wonder where
   the world's Redeemer lies?
   The Lord of all the lords that are
      is born at Bethlehem,
   and kings shall kneel beneath His star
   and we will bow with them.

4 Lift every heart the hymn of praise
   that all creation sings;
   the angel host its homage pays,
   the shepherds and the kings.
   For earth and sky with one accord,
      O Child of Bethlehem,
   are come to worship Christ the Lord
   and we will come with them.

106 Come, you thankful people, come

St George's, Windsor   77 77 D

Words: H Alford (1810–71)
in this version Jubilate Hymns
Music: C J Elvey (1816–93)

Come, you thank-ful peo-ple, come, raise the song of har-vest home!

fruit and crops are gath-ered in safe be-fore the storms be-gin:

God our ma-ker will pro-vide for our needs to be sup-plied;

come, with all His peo-ple, come, raise the song of har-vest home!

1 Come, you thankful people, come,
   raise the song of harvest home!
   fruit and crops are gathered in
   safe before the storms begin:
   God our maker will provide
   for our needs to be supplied;
   come, with all His people, come,
   raise the song of harvest home!

2 All the world is God's own field,
   harvests for His praise to yield;
   wheat and weeds together sown
   here for joy or sorrow grown:
   first the blade and then the ear,
   then the full corn shall appear –
   Lord of harvest, grant that we
   wholesome grain and pure may be.

3 For the Lord our God shall come
   and shall bring His harvest home;
   He Himself on that great day,
   worthless things shall take away,
   give His angels charge at last
   in the fire the weeds to cast,
   but the fruitful ears to store
   in His care for evermore.

4 Even so, Lord, quickly come –
   bring Your final harvest home!
   gather all Your people in
   free from sorrow, free from sin,
   there together purified,
   ever thankful at Your side –
   come, with all Your angels, come,
   bring that glorious harvest home!

107(i)   Cradled in a manger

PLEADING SAVIOUR (SALTASH)   87 87 D

Words: George Stringer Rowe (1830–1913)
Music: melody from *Plymouth Collection*, USA, 1855
arranged R Vaughan Williams (1872–1958)

Cradled in a manger, meanly laid the Son of Man His head;
sleeping His first earthly slumber where the oxen had been fed.
Happy were those shepherds listening to the holy angel's word;
happy they within that stable, worshipping their infant Lord.

1 Cradled in a manger, meanly
　　laid the Son of Man His head;
sleeping His first earthly slumber
　　where the oxen had been fed.
Happy were those shepherds listening
　　to the holy angel's word;
happy they within that stable,
　　worshipping their infant Lord.

2 Happy all who hear the message
　　of His coming from above;
happier still who hail His coming,
　　and with praises greet His love.
Blessèd Saviour, Christ most holy,
　　in a manger thou didst rest;
canst Thou stoop again, yet lower
　　and abide within my breast?

3 Evil things are there before Thee;
　　in the heart, where they have fed,
wilt Thou pitifully enter,
　　Son of Man, and lay Thy head?
Enter, then, O Christ most holy;
　　make a Christmas in my heart;
make a heaven on my manger:
　　It is heaven where Thou art.

4 And to those who never listened
　　to the message of Thy birth,
who have winter, but no Christmas
　　bringing them Thy peace on earth,
send to these the joyful tidings;
　　by all people, in each home,
be there heard the Christmas anthem:
　　Praise to God, the Christ has come!

107(ii) Cradled in a manger

St Winifred   87 87 D

Words: George Stringer Rowe (1830–1913)
Music: S J P Dunman (1843–1913)

Crad-led in a man-ger, mean-ly laid the Son of Man His head;

sleep-ing His first earth-ly slum-ber where the ox - en had been fed.

Hap-py were those shep-herds listen-ing to the ho - ly an-gel's word;

hap-py they with-in that sta - ble, wor-ship-ping their in-fant Lord.

1 Cradled in a manger, meanly
   laid the Son of Man His head;
 sleeping His first earthly slumber
   where the oxen had been fed.
 Happy were those shepherds listening
   to the holy angel's word;
 happy they within that stable,
   worshipping their infant Lord.

2 Happy all who hear the message
   of His coming from above;
 happier still who hail His coming,
   and with praises greet His love.
 Blessèd Saviour, Christ most holy,
   in a manger thou didst rest;
 canst Thou stoop again, yet lower
   and abide within my breast?

3 Evil things are there before Thee;
   in the heart, where they have fed,
 wilt Thou pitifully enter,
   Son of Man, and lay Thy head?
 Enter, then, O Christ most holy;
   make a Christmas in my heart;
 make a heaven on my manger:
   It is heaven where Thou art.

4 And to those who never listened
   to the message of Thy birth,
 who have winter, but no Christmas
   bringing them Thy peace on earth,
 send to these the joyful tidings;
   by all people, in each home,
 be there heard the Christmas anthem:
   Praise to God, the Christ has come!

108   Create in me

Words and music: Dave Fellingham
Music arranged Roland Fudge

Warmly

Cre-ate in me a clean heart, O God, and re-

-new a right spi-rit in me.

Cre-ate in me a clean heart, O God, and re-

-new a right spi-rit in me.

109 Crown Him with many crowns

DIADEMATA DSM

Words: Matthew Bridges (1800–94)
and Godfrey Thring (1823–1903)
Music: George Elvey (1816–93)

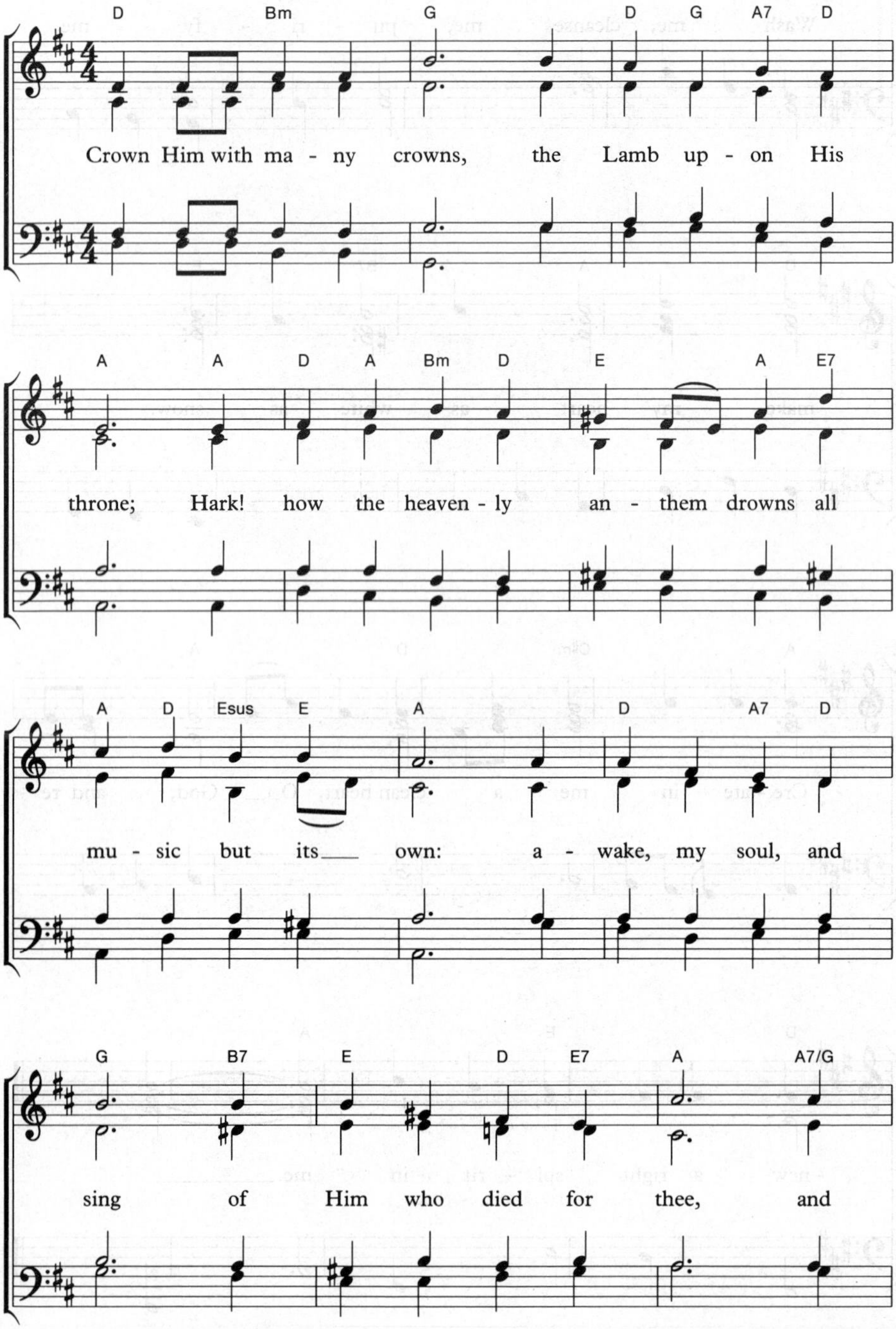

D Bm G D G A7 D
Crown Him with ma - ny crowns, the Lamb up - on His
A A D A Bm D E A E7
throne; Hark! how the heaven - ly an - them drowns all
A D Esus E A D A7 D
mu - sic but its___ own: a - wake, my soul, and
G B7 E D E7 A A7/G
sing of Him who died for thee, and

hail Him as thy cho-sen King through all e-ter-ni-ty.

1 Crown Him with many crowns,
the Lamb upon His throne;
Hark! how the heavenly anthem drowns
all music but its own:
awake, my soul, and sing
of Him who died for thee,
and hail Him as thy chosen King
through all eternity.

2 Crown Him the Son of God
before the worlds began;
and ye who tread where He hath trod,
crown Him the Son of Man,
who every grief hath known
that wrings the human breast,
and takes and bears them for His own,
that all in Him may rest.

3 Crown Him the Lord of life,
who triumphed o'er the grave,
and rose victorious in the strife,
for those He came to save:
His glories now we sing,
who died and rose on high,
who died eternal life to bring,
and lives that death may die.

4 Crown Him the Lord of heaven,
enthroned in worlds above;
crown Him the King to whom is given
the wondrous name of love:
all hail, Redeemer, hail!
for Thou hast died for me;
Thy praise shall never, never fail
throughout eternity.

110 Darkness like a shroud

ARISE, SHINE

Words and music: Graham Kendrick

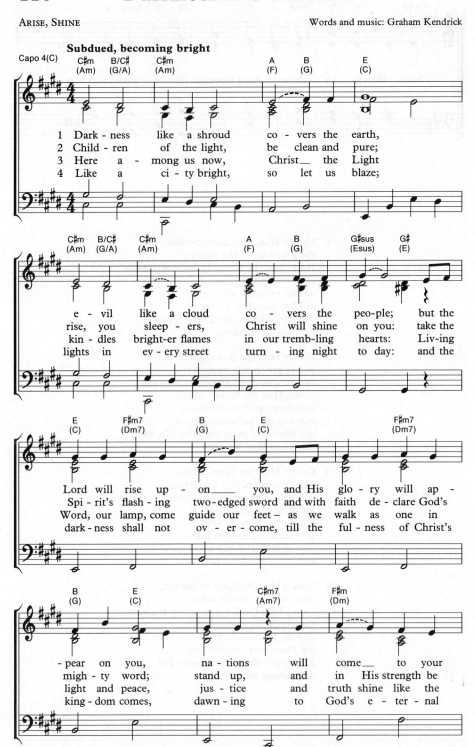

Subdued, becoming bright

Capo 4(C)

1 Dark - ness like a shroud co - vers the earth,
2 Child - ren of the light, be clean and pure;
3 Here a - mong us now, Christ the Light
4 Like a ci - ty bright, so let us blaze;

e - vil like a cloud co - vers the peo - ple; but the
rise, you sleep - ers, Christ will shine on you: take the
kin - dles bright - er flames in our trem - bling hearts: Liv - ing
lights in ev - ery street turn - ing night to day: and the

Lord will rise up - on you, and His glo - ry will ap -
Spi - rit's flash - ing two-edged sword and with faith de - clare God's
Word, our lamp, come guide our feet — as we walk as one in
dark - ness shall not ov - er - come, till the ful - ness of Christ's

- pear on you, na - tions will come to your
migh - ty word; stand up, and in His strength be
light and peace, jus - tice and truth shine like the
king - dom comes, dawn - ing to God's e - ter - nal

Words and music: © 1985 Make Way Music,
administered in Europe by Thankyou Music,
PO Box 75, Eastbourne, East Sussex BN23 6NW, UK

111 Dear Lord and Father of mankind

REPTON   86 88 6 extended

Words: John Greenleaf Whittier (1807–82)
Music: C Hubert H Parry (1848–1918)

Dear Lord and Fa - ther— of man-kind, for - give our fool - ish ways; re - clothe us in our right - ful mind; in pur - er lives Thy ser - vice— find, in— deep-er rev - erence, praise, in deep-er rev - erence praise.

1   Dear Lord and Father of mankind,
    forgive our foolish ways;
    re-clothe us in our rightful mind;
    in purer lives Thy service find,
    in deeper reverence, praise.

2   In simple trust like theirs who heard,
    beside the Syrian sea,
    the gracious calling of the Lord,
    let us, like them, without a word
    rise up and follow Thee.

3   O Sabbath rest by Galilee!
    O calm of hills above,
    where Jesus knelt to share with Thee
    the silence of eternity,
    interpreted by love!

4   Drop Thy still dews of quietness,
    till all our strivings cease;
    take from our souls the strain and stress,
    and let our ordered lives confess
    the beauty of Thy peace.

5   Breathe through the heats of our desire
    Thy coolness and Thy balm;
    let sense be dumb, let flesh retire;
    speak through the earthquake, wind, and fire,
    O still small voice of calm!

112   Delight yourself in the Lord

Words and music: Andy Silver

De - light your - self in the Lord,_____ and He will give you the de - sires_ of your heart. Com - mit your way to the Lord;_____ trust in Him and He will make your right-eous-ness shine,_ shin-ing like the dawn and like the noon-day sun.

215 Delight yourselves in the Lord

The right-eous will dwell in the land for ev - er,_ to share His in - her - it - ance._ De - light your - self in the Lord,_____ and He will give you the de - sires_ of your heart. Com - mit your way to the Lord,_____ com - mit your way_____ to the Lord.

113   Delight yourselves in the Lord

Words and music: David Bolton

De-light your-selves in the Lord,___ de-light your-selves in the Lord;___ for He de-lights in the prais-es of His own peo - - ple;___ for He de-lights in the prais-es of His own peo - - ple.

Let your well spring up with-in and o - ver-flow to
one an - oth - er; let your well spring up with-in and
o - ver-flow to the Lord.

Delight yourselves in the Lord,
delight yourselves in the Lord;
for He delights in the praises
of His own people;
for He delights in the praises
of His own people.

Let your well spring up within
and overflow to one another;
let your well spring up within
and overflow to the Lord.

114   Ding dong! Merrily on high

BRANLE DE L'OFFICIAL

Words: George Ratcliffe Woodward (1848–1934)
Music: 16th-cent. French melody
arranged Charles Wood and B V Burnett

1 Ding dong! Mer-ri-ly on high   in heaven the bells are ring-ing.
2 E'en so, here be-low, be-low,   let steep-le bells be swung-en;
3 Pray you, du-ti-ful-ly prime   your ma-tin chime, ye ring-ers;

Ding dong! Ve-ri-ly the sky   is riven with an-gels sing-ing:
and i-o, i-o, i-o,   by priest and peo-ple sung-en!
may you beau-ti-ful-ly rime   your eve-time song, ye sing-ers:

Glo - - - - - - - - - - - ri-a, ho-san-na in ex-cel-sis!

115 Do not be afraid

Words and music: Gerald Markland
Music arranged Roland Fudge

With warmth

Do not be a - fraid, for I have re - deemed you. I have called you by your name; you are Mine.

1 When you walk through the wa - ters I'll be
2 When the fire is burn-ing all a -
3 When the fear of lone - li - ness is
4 When you dwell in the ex - ile of the
5 You are Mine, O My child; I am your

with you; you will ne - ver sink be - neath the waves.
- round you, you will ne - ver be con - sumed by the flames.
loom - ing, then re - mem-ber I am at your side.
stran - ger, re - mem-ber you are pre-cious in My eyes.
Fa - ther, and I love you with a per - fect love.

116   Down from His glory

O Sole Mio   11 12 11 10 with refrain

Words: William E Booth-Clibborn (1893–1969)
Music: Eduardo di Capun
arranged Norman Johnson

Down from His glo-ry, ev-er-liv-ing sto-ry, my God and
Sav-iour came, and Je-sus was His name; born in a man-ger
to His own a stran-ger, a man of sor-rows, tears and a - go-ny!
O how I love Him! how I a - dore Him! My breath, my

sun-shine, my all-in - all!_ The great Cre - a - tor_____ be-came my

Sav - iour, and all God's ful - ness_____ dwell-eth in Him!

1 Down from His glory, ever-living story,
    my God and Saviour came, and Jesus was His name;
    born in a manger to His own a stranger,
    a man of sorrows, tears and agony!
        O how I love Him! how I adore Him!
        My breath, my sunshine, my all-in-all!
        The great Creator became my Saviour,
        and all God's fulness dwelleth in Him!

2 What condescension, bringing us redemption,
    that in the dead of night, not one faint hope in sight;
    God gracious, tender, laid aside His splendour,
    stooping to woo, to win, to save my soul.
        O how I love Him . . .

3 Without reluctance, flesh and blood, His substance,
    He took the form of man, revealed the hidden plan;
    O glorious mystery, sacrifice of Calvary!
    And now I know He is the great 'I AM'!
        O how I love Him . . .

117 Do not be worried and upset

Words: from John 14: 1–6
Music: G Taylor

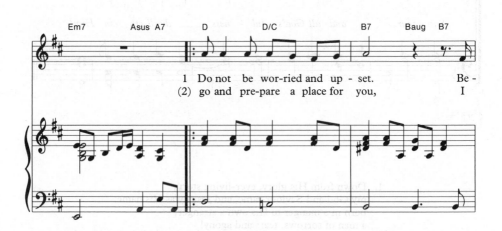

1 Do not be wor-ried and up-set. Be -
(2) go and pre-pare a place for you, I

- lieve in God, be-lieve al - so in Me,
will come back and take you to My - self,

118   Draw near to God

Achor

Draw near to God and He'll draw near to you;

draw near to God and He'll draw near to you.

Lift up ho - ly hands to Him and sing of what He's done;

op - en up your hearts to Him and praise_____ Him for His

Son._____

He'll draw near to you.

to Coda ⊕

⊕ **CODA**

D.C. al Coda

119   El-Shaddai

Words: Michael Card
Music: John Thompson

We will praise___ and lift You high,___ El - Sha - ddai.

1 Through your love ___

El-Shaddai, El-Shaddai
   (God Almighty, God Almighty)
El-Elyon na Adonai
   (God in the highest, Oh Lord)
Age to age You're still the same
by the power of the name.
El-Shaddai, El-Shaddai
   (God Almighty, God Almighty)
Erkamka na Adonai
   (We will love You, Oh Lord)
We will praise and lift You high,
El-Shaddai.

1 Through Your love and through the ram
   You saved the son of Abraham.
   Through the power of Your hand,
   turned the sea into dry land.
   To the outcast on her knees
   You were the God who really sees,
   and by Your might You set Your children free.
     El-Shaddai, El-Shaddai . . .

2 Through the years You made it clear,
   that the time of Christ was near.
   Though the people couldn't see
   what Messiah ought to be.
   Though Your word contained the plan
   they just could not understand.
   Your most awesome work was done
   through the frailty of Your Son.
     El-Shaddai, El-Shaddai . . .

120 Emmanuel

Words: Greg Leavers
Music: Greg Leavers and Phil Burt

Lord of lords ALL is He.
Lord of lords

God Him-self_ will give a sign; a vir-gin shall bear a son who shall be

called Em - ma - nu - el._____

Emmanuel, (Emmanuel,)
God with us, (God with us,)
Wonderful (Wonderful)
Counsellor, (Counsellor,)
Prince of Peace –
a Saviour is born to redeem the world,
and His name is Jesus.
King of kings, (King of kings,)
Lord of lords (Lord of lords)
is He.

1 God Himself will give a sign;
   a virgin shall bear a son
   who shall be called Emmanuel.
      Emmanuel . . .

2 People who now walk in darkness
   soon will see the light of Jesus,
   He is the light of the world.
      Emmanuel . . .

3 Hear a voice cry in the desert,
   clear a way for the Messiah,
   make straight a highway for God.
      Emmanuel . . .

4 Bringing good news, healing heartaches,
   preaching freedom, releasing captives,
   giving a mantle of praise.
      Emmanuel . . .

121 Emmanuel, Emmanuel

Words and music: Bob McGee

122   Eternal Father, strong to save

MELITA   88 88 88

Words: William Whiting (1825–78)
Music: John Bacchus Dykes (1823–76)

1   Eternal Father, strong to save,
    whose arm hath bound the restless wave,
    who bidd'st the mighty ocean deep
    its own appointed limits keep:
    O hear us when we cry to Thee
    for those in peril on the sea.

2   O Christ, whose voice the waters heard,
    and hushed their raging at Thy word,
    who walkedst on the foaming deep,
    and calm amid the storm didst sleep:
    O hear us when we cry to Thee
    for those in peril on the sea.

3   O Holy Spirit, who didst brood
    upon the waters dark and rude,
    and bid their angry tumult cease,
    and give, for wild confusion, peace:
    O hear us when we cry to Thee
    for those in peril on the sea.

4   O Trinity of love and power,
    our brethren shield in danger's hour;
    from rock and tempest, fire and foe,
    protect them wheresoe'er they go:
    thus evermore shall rise to Thee
    glad hymns of praise from land and sea.

123

Eternal God

Words and music: Dave Fellingham
Music arranged Roland Fudge

Lyrics:
E - ter - nal God, we come to You, we come be - fore Your throne; we en - ter by a new and liv - ing way, with con - fi - dence we come.

We de-clare Your faith - ful - ness, Your

pro - mi - ses are true; __ we will now draw near to wor-ship

You. _____ WOMEN O ho - ly ly
MEN O ho - ly God, _____ we come to

God, __ full of jus - tice, wis - dom and right-eous-ness,
You, _____ O ho - ly God, _____ wee see Your

faith-ful-ness and love;__ Your migh - ty
faith-ful-ness and love,__ Your migh-ty power,_____ Your ma - jes -

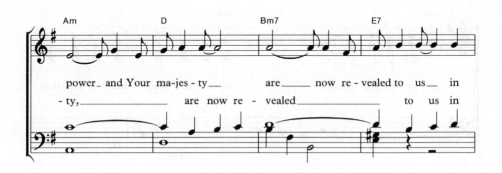

power_ and Your ma-jes - ty__ are_____ now re - vealed to us__ in
- ty,_____ are now re - vealed_____ to us in

Je - sus who has died__ for our sin, Je - sus who was raised from the dead,
Je - sus who has died,__ Je - sus who was raised,

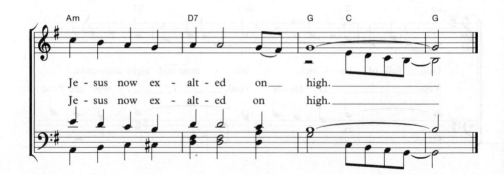

Je - sus now ex - alt - ed on__ high._____
Je - sus now ex - alt - ed on high._____

Eternal God, we come to You,
we come before Your throne;
we enter by a new and living way,
with confidence we come.
We declare Your faithfulness,
Your promises are true;
we will now draw near to worship You.

MEN
O holy God, we come to You,
O holy God, wee see Your faithfulness and love,
Your mighty power, Your majesty,
are now revealed to us in Jesus who has died,
Jesus who was raised,
Jesus now exalted on high.

WOMEN
O holy God, full of justice,
wisdom and righteousness,
faithfulness and love;
Your mighty power and Your majesty
are now revealed to us
in Jesus who has died for our sin,
Jesus who was raised from the dead,
Jesus now exalted on high.

Exalt the Lord our God

Words and music: Rick Ridings
Music arranged Roland Fudge

Steadily

Ex - alt the Lord our God,_____ ex - alt the Lord our God,_____ and wor - ship at His foot - stool, wor - ship at His foot - stool; ho - ly is He, ho - ly is He._____

125   Faithful vigil ended

FAITHFUL VIGIL   65 65

Words: from Luke 2
Timothy Dudley-Smith
Music: David Wilson

Sustained

Faith-ful vi - gil end - ed, watch-ing, wait-ing cease:___

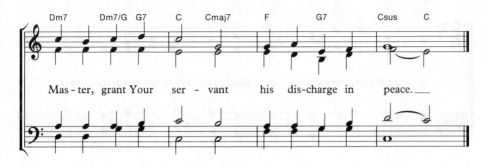

Mas - ter, grant Your ser - vant his dis-charge in peace.___

1 Faithful vigil ended,
   watching, waiting cease:
   Master, grant Your servant
   his discharge in peace.

2 All the Spirit promised,
   all the Father willed,
   now these eyes behold it
   perfectly fulfilled.

3 This Your great deliverance
   sets Your people free;
   Christ their light uplifted
   all the nations see.

4 Christ, Your people's glory!
   Watching, doubting cease:
   grant to us Your servants
   our discharge in peace.

126 Facing a task unfinished

AURELIA 76 76 D

Words: Frank Houghton (1894–1972)
Music: Samuel Sebastian Wesley (1810–76)

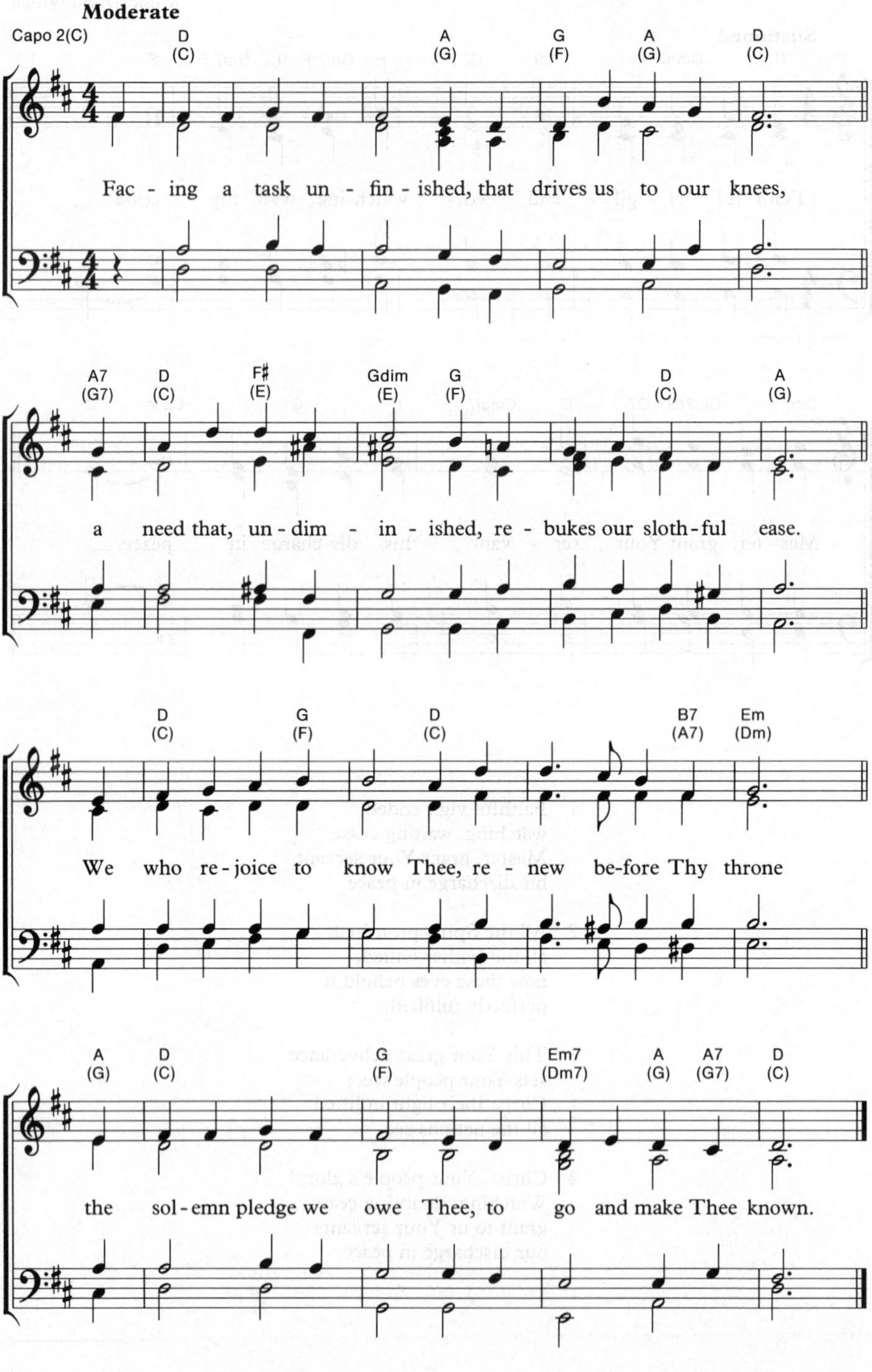

Moderate
Capo 2(C)
D (C) A (G) G (F) A (G) D (C)
Fac - ing a task un - fin - ished, that drives us to our knees,
A7 (G7) D (C) F♯ (E) Gdim (E) G (F) D (C) A (G)
a need that, un - dim - in - ished, re - bukes our sloth - ful ease.
D (C) G (F) D (C) B7 (A7) Em (Dm)
We who re - joice to know Thee, re - new be - fore Thy throne
A (G) D (C) G (F) Em7 (Dm7) A (G) A7 (G7) D (C)
the sol - emn pledge we owe Thee, to go and make Thee known.

1 Facing a task unfinished,
   that drives us to our knees,
   a need that, undiminished,
   rebukes our slothful ease.
   We who rejoice to know Thee,
   renew before Thy throne
   the solemn pledge we owe Thee,
   to go and make Thee known.

2 Where other lords beside Thee
   hold their unhindered sway,
   where forces that defied Thee
   defy Thee still today.
   With none to heed their crying
   for life, and love, and light,
   unnumbered souls are dying,
   and pass into the night.

3 We bear the torch that, flaming,
   fell from the hands of those
   who gave their lives, proclaiming
   that Jesus died and rose.
   Ours is the same commission,
   the same glad message ours,
   fired by the same ambition,
   to Thee we yield our powers.

4 O Father who sustained them,
   O Spirit who inspired,
   Saviour, whose love constrained them
   to toil with zeal untired.
   From cowardice defend us,
   from lethargy awake!
   Forth on Thine errands send us,
   to labour for Thy sake.

127   Father, although I cannot see

MORDEN   86 86 86

Words: John Eddison
Music: Norman Warren

Words: © Scripture Union,
130 City Road, London EC1V 2NJ

1   Father, although I cannot see
    the future You have planned,
    and though the path is sometimes dark
    and hard to understand:
    yet give me faith, through joy and pain,
    to trace Your loving hand.

2   When I recall that in the past
    Your promises have stood
    through each perplexing circumstance
    and every changing mood,
    I rest content that all things work
    together for my good.

3   Whatever, then, the future brings
    of good or seeming ill,
    I ask for strength to follow You
    and grace to trust You still;
    and I would look for no reward,
    except to do Your will.

128 Father God, I wonder

Words and music: Ian Smale
Music arranged David Peacock

Lively Spanish style

Fa - ther God, I won - der how I man-aged to ex - ist with - out the know-ledge of Your par - ent - hood and Your lov - ing care. But now I am Your son, I am a - dopt-ed in Your fam - i - ly, and I can ne - ver

be a-lone_ 'cause, Fa-ther God, You're there be-side me.

I will sing Your prais-es, I will

sing Your prais-es, I will sing Your prais-es

1.
for ev-er-more.

2.
for ev-er-more.

129   Father God, I love You

Words and music: Joan Robinson

Gently

1 Fa - ther God,_____ I love__ You,
2 Je - sus,_____ I love__ You,
3 Spi - rit,_____ I love__ You,
4 Al - le - lu - ia,

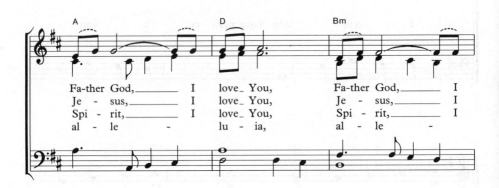

Fa-ther God,_____ I love_ You,   Fa-ther God,_____ I
Je - sus,_____ I love_ You,   Je - sus,_____ I
Spi - rit,_____ I love_ You,   Spi - rit,_____ I
al - le - lu - ia,   al - le -

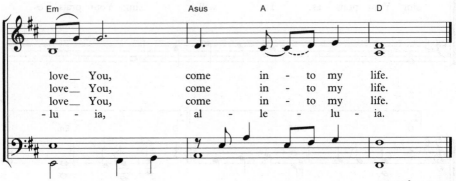

love__ You,   come in - to my life.
love__ You,   come in - to my life.
love__ You,   come in - to my life.
- lu - ia,   al - le - lu - ia.

repeat last verse

130 Father God, the Lord, Creator

WALTHAM 87 87

Words: John Richards
Music: H Albert (1604–51)
harmony by J S Bach (1685–1750)

Fa-ther God, the Lord, Cre-a - tor, by whose hand we all_ are fed,

in Your mer-cy re - cre-ate us at the break-ing of_ the Bread.

1 Father God, the Lord, Creator,
  by whose hand we all are fed,
  in Your mercy recreate us
  at the breaking of the Bread.

2 Christ our Lord, be present with us,
  risen victorious from the dead!
  In Your mercy may we know You,
  in the breaking of the Bread.

3 Holy Spirit, God's empowering,
  by whose life the Church is led;
  in Your mercy, send us strengthened
  from the breaking of the Bread.

4 Father, Son, and Holy Spirit,
  hear our praises – sung and said.
  From our hearts comes our thanksgiving
  for the breaking of the Bread.

131   Father God, we worship You

Words and music: Graham Kendrick
Music arranged Christopher Norton

1 Father God, we worship You,
 make us part of all You do.
 As You move among us now
 we worship You.

2 Jesus King, we worship You,
 help us listen now to You.
 As You move among us now
 we worship You.

3 Spirit pure, we worship You,
 with Your fire our zeal renew.
 As You move among us now
 we worship You.

132   Father, hear the prayer we offer

Sussex   87 87

Words: Love Maria Willis (1824–1908)
Music: English traditional melody
adapted by R Vaughan Williams (1872–1958)

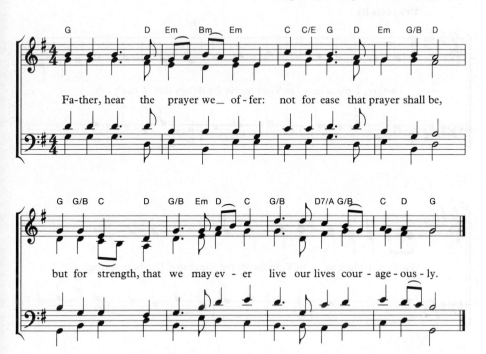

1 Father, hear the prayer we offer:
   not for ease that prayer shall be,
   but for strength, that we may ever
   live our lives courageously.

2 Not for ever in green pastures
   do we ask our way to be:
   but by steep and rugged pathways
   would we strive to climb to Thee.

3 Not for ever by still waters
   would we idly quiet stay;
   but would smite the living fountains
   from the rocks along our way.

4 Be our strength in hours of weakness,
   in our wanderings be our guide;
   through endeavour, failure, danger,
   Father, be Thou at our side.

5 Let our path be bright or dreary,
   storm or sunshine be our share;
   may our souls, in hope unweary,
   make Thy work our ceaseless prayer.

133   Father, I place into Your hands

Words and music: Jenny Hewer

Fa-ther, I place in - to Your hands the things that I can't do.

Fa-ther, I place in - to Your hands the times that I've been through.

Fa-ther, I place in - to Your hands the way that I should go, for I

know I al - ways can trust You.

1   Father, I place into Your hands
    the things that I can't do.
    Father, I place into Your hands
    the times that I've been through.
    Father, I place into Your hands
    the way that I should go,
    for I know I always can trust You.

2   Father, I place into Your hands
    my friends and family.
    Father, I place into Your hands
    the things that trouble me.
    Father, I place into Your hands
    the person I would be,
    for I know I always can trust You.

3   Father, we love to seek Your face,
    we love to hear Your voice.
    Father, we love to sing Your praise,
    and in Your name rejoice.
    Father, we love to walk with You
    and in Your presence rest,
    for we know we always can trust You.

4   Father, I want to be with You
    and do the things You do.
    Father, I want to speak the words
    that You are speaking too.
    Father, I want to love the ones
    that You will draw to You,
    for I know that I am one with You.

134   Father in heaven

Words and music: Dave Bilbrough
Music arranged Christopher Norton

Rhythmic

Fa-ther in hea-ven, our voi-ces we raise: re-ceive our de-vo-tion, re-ceive now our praise as we sing of the glo-ry of all that You've done – the great-est love-sto-ry that's ev-er been sung. *And we will*

1 Father in heaven,
  our voices we raise:
  receive our devotion,
  receive now our praise
  as we sing of the glory
  of all that You've done –
  the greatest love-story
  that's ever been sung.
    And we will crown You Lord of all,
    yes, we will crown You Lord of all,
    for You have won the victory:
    yes, we will crown You Lord of all.

2 Father in heaven,
  our lives are Your own;
  we've been caught by a vision
  of Jesus alone –
  who came as a servant
  to free us from sin:
  Father in heaven,
  our worship we bring.
    And we will crown . . .

3 We will sing Alleluia,
  we will sing to the King,
  to our mighty Deliverer
  our alleluias will ring.
  Yes, our praise is resounding
  to the Lamb on the throne:
  He alone is exalted
  through the love He has shown.
    And we will crown . . .

135 Father in heaven, how we love You

Words and music: Bob Fitts
Music arranged Christopher Norton

Fa-ther in hea-ven, how we love You, __ we lift Your name in all the earth. _ May Your king-dom be es-tab-lished in our prais-es __ as Your peo-ple de-clare Your migh-ty works. Bless-èd be the Lord God Al-migh-ty, __ who was and is and is to come, __ bless-èd be the Lord God Al-migh-ty, __ who reigns for ev - er-more.

136 Father, sending Your anointed Son

St Andrew 87 87

Words: John Richards
Music: E H Thorne (1834–1916)

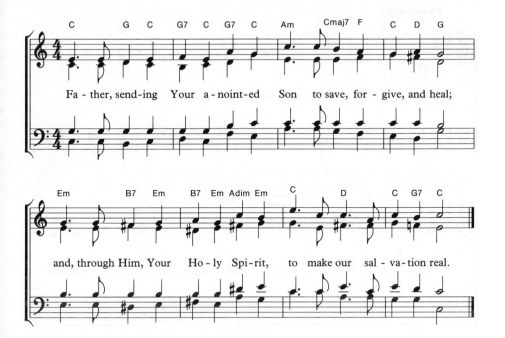

Fa - ther, send-ing Your a - noint-ed Son to save, for - give, and heal;

and, through Him, Your Ho - ly Spi - rit, to make our sal - va-tion real.

1 Father, sending Your anointed
   Son to save, forgive, and heal;
   and, through Him, Your Holy Spirit,
   to make our salvation real.

2 Look upon our ills and trouble,
   and on those who suffer much.
   Send Your church the Spirit's unction
   in Christ's name to heal and touch.

3 Grant forgiveness to the faithful;
   bring to unity their prayer;
   use it for Your work unhindered,
   through both sacrament and care.

OPTIONAL VERSE
FOR WHEN ANOINTING TAKES PLACE
4 May the one/ones to be anointed
   outwardly with oil this hour,
   know Christ's fullest restoration
   through the Holy Spirit's power.

5 Heal Your church! Anoint and send us
   out into the world to tell
   of Your love and blessings to us;
   how, in Christ, 'All will be well.'

137 Father make us one

Words and music: Rick Ridings
Music arranged Christopher Norton

138   Father, never was love so near

Words and music: Graham Kendrick
Music arranged Christopher Norton

1 Fa - ther,_____ ne - ver_ was love so near; ten - der,_____ my deep - est wounds to heal.

2 Je - sus,_____ the heart of God re - vealed, with us,_____ feel - ing_ the pain we feel.

with Him_ gave ev - ery-thing; now He's ev - ery -

- thing to me._____ me._____

And me._____ now

He's ev - ery - thing to me._____

139   Father, we adore You

Words and music: Terrye Coelho

This item may be sung as a 3-part round.

1   Father, we adore You,
    lay our lives before You:
    how we love You!

2   Jesus, we adore You,
    lay our lives before You:
    how we love You!

3   Spirit, we adore You,
    lay our lives before You:
    how we love You!

140 Father, we adore You

Words and music: Carl Tuttle
Music arranged Roland Fudge

1 Fa-ther, we a-dore You, You've drawn us to this place; we bow down be-fore_ You, hum-bly on our face.

2 Je-sus_ we_ love You, be-cause You first loved us; You reached out and healed us with Your migh-ty touch.

3 Spi-rit_ we_ need You, to lift us from this mire; con-sume and em-power us with Your ho-ly fire.

All the earth shall wor-ship at the throne of the

King; of His great and awe - some power,

we shall sing! Ho - ly is

He; Bless - èd is He;

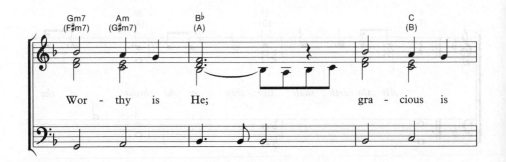

Wor - thy is He; gra - cious is

Words and music © 1982 Maranatha! Music,
administered in Europe by Thankyou Music,
PO Box 75, Eastbourne, East Sussex, BN23 6NW, UK

He;   Faith - ful is He;

awe - some is He;   Sav - iour is

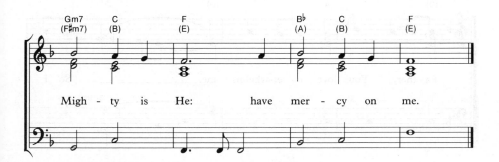

He;   Mas - ter is He;

Migh - ty is He: have mer - cy on me.

141 Father, Your love is precious

Words and music: Everett Perry
Music arranged Roland Fudge

142   Father, we love You

Words and music: Donna Adkins

1 Fa - ther, we love You, we wor - ship and a - dore You:
2 Je - sus, we love You, we wor - ship and a - dore You:
3 Spi - rit, we love You, we wor - ship and a - dore You:

glo - ri - fy Your name in all the earth.

Glo - ri - fy Your name, glo - ri - fy Your name,

glo - ri - fy Your name, in all the earth.

143 Fight the good fight

DUKE STREET   LM

Words: J S B Monsell (1811–75)
Music: John Hatton (d 1793)

Fight the good fight with all thy might; Christ is thy strength, and Christ thy right. Lay hold on life, and it shall be thy joy and crown e - ter - nal - ly.

1 Fight the good fight with all thy might;
   Christ is thy strength, and Christ thy right.
   Lay hold on life, and it shall be
   thy joy and crown eternally.

2 Run the straight race through God's good grace,
   lift up thine eyes, and seek His face;
   life with its path before thee lies;
   Christ is the way, and Christ the prize.

3 Cast care aside, lean on thy guide,
   His boundless mercy will provide;
   lean, and thy trusting soul shall prove
   Christ is thy life, and Christ thy love.

4 Faint not, nor fear, His arm is near,
   He changeth not, and thou art dear;
   only believe, and thou shalt see
   that Christ is all in all to thee.

144   Fear not, rejoice and be glad

Words and music: Priscilla Wright Porter

With breadth

Fear not, re - joice and be glad, the
Lord hath done a great thing; hath poured out His Spi - rit on
all man - kind,__ on those who con - fess His name.____

1 The fig tree is bud - ding, the vine bear - eth fruit, the
2 Ye shall eat in plen - ty and be sa - tis - fied, the
3 My peo - ple shall know__ that I am the Lord, their
4 My child - ren shall dwell in a bo - dy of love, a

Words and music: © 1971, 1975 Celebration,
administered in Europe by Thankyou Music,
PO Box 75, Eastbourne, East Sussex BN23 6NW, UK

wheat fields are gold - en with grain.____ Thrust in the sic - kle, the
moun-tains will drip with sweet wine.____ My child-ren shall drink of the
shame I have tak - en a - way.____ My Spi - rit will lead them to -
light to the world they will be.____ Life shall come forth from the

har - vest is ripe, the Lord_ has giv - en us rain.____
foun-tain of life, My child-ren will know they are Mine.____
- geth - er a - gain, My Spi - rit will show them the way.____
Fa - ther a - bove, My bo - dy will set man-kind free.____

Fear not, rejoice and be glad,
the Lord hath done a great thing;
hath poured out His Spirit on all mankind,
on those who confess His name.

1   The fig tree is budding, the vine beareth fruit,
    the wheat fields are golden with grain.
    Thrust in the sickle, the harvest is ripe,
    the Lord has given us rain.
        Fear not, rejoice . . .

2   Ye shall eat in plenty and be satisfied,
    the mountains will drip with sweet wine.
    My children shall drink of the fountain of life,
    My children will know they are Mine.
        Fear not, rejoice . . .

3   My people shall know that I am the Lord,
    their shame I have taken away.
    My Spirit will lead them together again,
    My Spirit will show them the way.
        Fear not, rejoice . . .

4   My children shall dwell in a body of love,
    a light to the world they will be.
    Life shall come forth from the Father above,
    My body will set mankind free.
        Fear not, rejoice . . .

145 Fill the place Lord with Your glory

Words and music: Chris Bowater

With simplicity

Fill the place, Lord, with Your glo-ry,_____ at this gath-ering of Your own;_____ reign in sove-reign grace and pow-er_____ from Your praise - sur- -round - ed throne._____ Fill the place, Lord, with Your glo-ry,_____ at this gath - ering of Your own;_____

Words and music: © 1983 Lifestyle Music Ltd, PO Box 356,
Leighton Buzzard, Beds LU7 8WP UK

146(i) Fill Thou my life

ST FULBERT   CM

Words: Horatius Bonar (1808–82)
Music: H J Gauntlett (1805–76)

1 Fill Thou my life, O Lord my God,
   in every part with praise,
   that my whole being may proclaim
   Thy being and Thy ways.

2 Not for the lip of praise alone,
   nor e'en the praising heart,
   I ask, but for a life made up
   of praise in every part:

3 Praise in the common things of life,
   its goings out and in;
   praise in each duty and each deed,
   however small and mean.

4 Fill every part of me with praise:
   let all my being speak
   of Thee and of Thy love, O Lord,
   poor though I be and weak.

5 So shalt Thou, Lord, from me, e'en me,
   receive Thy glory due;
   and so shall I begin on earth
   the song for ever new.

6 So shall no part of day or night
   from sacredness be free;
   but all my life, in every step,
   be fellowship with Thee.

146(ii)   Fill Thou my life

RICHMOND   CM

Words: Horatius Bonar (1808–82)
Music: melody by Thomas Haweis (1734–1820)
arranged S Webbe the younger (c1770–1843)

Fill Thou my life, O Lord my God, in ev - ery part with praise, that my whole be - ing may pro - claim Thy be - ing and Thy ways.

1 Fill Thou my life, O Lord my God,
   in every part with praise,
   that my whole being may proclaim
   Thy being and Thy ways.

2 Not for the lip of praise alone,
   nor e'en the praising heart,
   I ask, but for a life made up
   of praise in every part:

3 Praise in the common things of life,
   its goings out and in;
   praise in each duty and each deed,
   however small and mean.

4 Fill every part of me with praise:
   let all my being speak
   of Thee and of Thy love, O Lord,
   poor though I be and weak.

5 So shalt Thou, Lord, from me, e'en me,
   receive Thy glory due;
   and so shall I begin on earth
   the song for ever new.

6 So shall no part of day or night
   from sacredness be free;
   but all my life, in every step,
   be fellowship with Thee.

147   Fill your hearts with joy

REGENT SQUARE   87 87 87

Words: from Psalm 147
Timothy Dudley-Smith
Music: H T Smart (1813–79)

Fill your hearts with joy and glad-ness, sing and praise your
God and mine! Great the Lord in___ love and wis-dom,
might and ma-jes - ty di - vine! He who framed the
star - ry hea-vens knows and names them_ as they shine.

1 Fill your hearts with joy and gladness,
sing and praise your God and mine!
Great the Lord in love and wisdom,
might and majesty divine!
He who framed the starry heavens
knows and names them as they shine.

2 Praise the Lord, His people, praise Him!
wounded souls His comfort know;
those who fear Him find His mercies,
peace for pain and joy for woe;
humble hearts are high exalted,
human pride and power laid low.

3 Praise the Lord for times and seasons,
cloud and sunshine, wind and rain;
spring to melt the snows of winter
till the waters flow again;
grass upon the mountain pastures,
golden valleys thick with grain.

4 Fill your hearts with joy and gladness,
peace and plenty crown your days;
love His laws, declare His judgements,
walk in all His words and ways;
He the Lord and we His children –
praise the Lord, all people, praise!

148   For all the Saints

SINE NOMINE   10 10 10 4

Words: W W How (1823–97)
Music: R Vaughan Williams (1872–1958)

For all the Saints who from their la-bours rest,

who Thee by faith be - fore the world con - fessed,

Thy name, O Je - su, be for ev - er blest.

Al - le - lu - ia, al - le - lu - ia!

1 For all the Saints who from their labours rest,
  who Thee by faith before the world confessed,
  Thy name, O Jesu, be for ever blest.
  Alleluia!

2 Thou wast their Rock, their fortress, and their might;
  Thou, Lord, their Captain in the well fought fight;
  Thou in the darkness drear their one true light.
  Alleluia!

3 O may Thy soldiers, faithful, true and bold,
  fight as the Saints who nobly fought of old,
  and win, with them, the victor's crown of gold!
  Alleluia!

4 O blest communion, fellowship divine!
  We feebly struggle, they in glory shine;
  yet all are one in Thee, for all are Thine.
  Alleluia!

5 And when the strife is fierce, the warfare long,
  steals on the ear the distant triumph song,
  and hearts are brave again, and arms are strong.
  Alleluia!

6 The golden evening brightens in the west;
  soon, soon to faithful warriors cometh rest;
  sweet is the calm of paradise the blest.
  Alleluia!

7 But lo! there breaks a yet more glorious day:
  the Saints triumphant rise in bright array;
  the King of glory passes on His way.
  Alleluia!

8 From earth's wide bounds, from ocean's farthest coast,
  through gates of pearl streams in the countless host,
  singing to Father, Son and Holy Ghost.
  Alleluia!

149 For God so loved the world

Words and music: Graham Kendrick
Music arranged Christopher Norton

WOMEN 1 For God so loved the world that He gave His on‑ly Son; and all who be‑lieve in Him shall not

WOMEN
1 For God so loved the world
   that He gave His only Son;
   and all who believe in Him
   shall not die,
     but have eternal life;
     no, they shall not die,
     but have eternal life.

ALL
2 And God showed His love for you,
   when He gave His only Son;
   and you, if you trust in Him,
   shall not die,
     but have eternal life;
     no you shall not die,
     but have eternal life.

150   For His name is exalted

Words and music: Dale Garratt
Music arranged David Peacock

For His name is ex - alt - ed,_____ His
glo - ry a - bove hea - ven and earth._____
Ho - ly is the Lord God al - migh - ty, who
was and who is and who is to come.

181. For I'm building a people of power

For His name is ex-alt-ed,_____ His glo-ry a-bove hea-ven and earth._____ Ho-ly is the Lord God al-migh-ty, who sit-teth on the throne and who lives for ev-er-more._____

151 For I'm building a people of power

Words and music: Dave Richards
Music arranged Roger Mayor

For I'm build - ing a peo - ple of pow - er___ and I'm

mak - ing a peo - ple of praise, that will move through this land by My

Spi - rit,___ and will glo - ri - fy My pre-cious name. Build Your

Church, Lord, make us strong, Lord, join our hearts, Lord, through Your

Son; make us one, Lord, in Your bo - dy, in the

King - dom of Your Son. Build Your Church, Lord, make us

strong, Lord, join our hearts, Lord, through Your Son; make us

one, Lord, in Your bo - dy, in the King - dom of Your Son.

152 For the beauty of the earth

ENGLAND'S LANE 77 77 77

Words: Folliott Pierpoint (1835–1917)
altered Horrobin/Leavers
Music: from an English melody
adapted by Geoffrey Shaw (1879–1943)

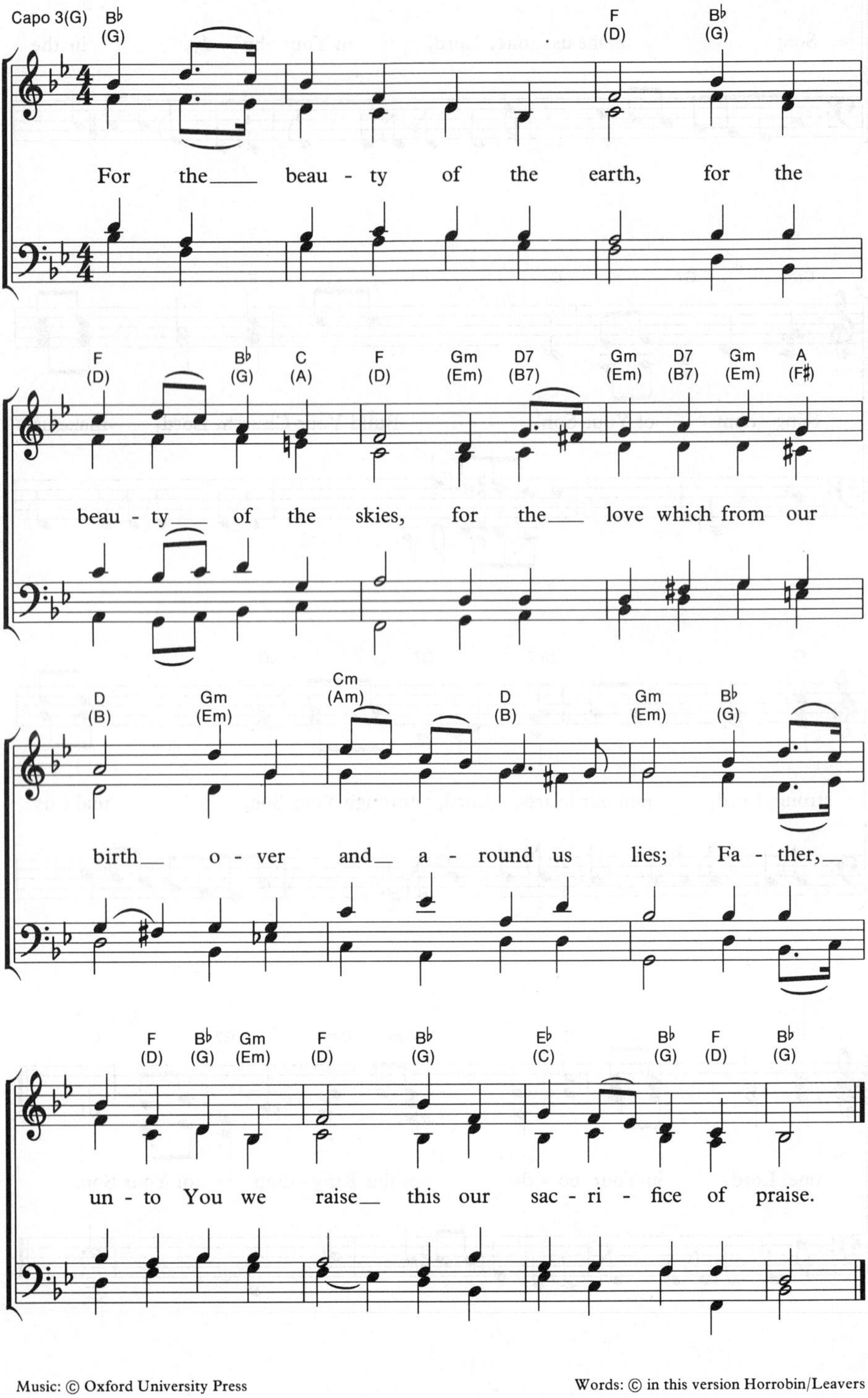

Capo 3(G)
B♭ (G) F (D) B♭ (G)
For the beau - ty of the earth, for the
F (D) B♭ (G) C (A) F (D) Gm (Em) D7 (B7) Gm (Em) D7 (B7) Gm (Em) A (F♯)
beau - ty of the skies, for the love which from our
D (B) Gm (Em) Cm (Am) D (B) Gm (Em) B♭ (G)
birth o - ver and a - round us lies; Fa - ther,
F (D) B♭ (G) Gm (Em) F (D) B♭ (G) E♭ (C) B♭ (G) F (D) B♭ (G)
un - to You we raise this our sac - ri - fice of praise.

1   For the beauty of the earth,
    for the beauty of the skies,
    for the love which from our birth
    over and around us lies;
    Father, unto You we raise
    this our sacrifice of praise.

2   For the beauty of each hour
    of the day and of the night,
    hill and vale, and tree and flower,
    sun and moon, and stars of light;
    Father, unto You we raise
    this our sacrifice of praise.

3   For the joy of love from God,
    that we share on earth below;
    for our friends and family,
    and the love that they can show;
    Father, unto You we raise
    this our sacrifice of praise.

4   For each perfect gift divine
    to our race so freely given,
    thank You Lord that they are mine,
    here on earth as gifts from heaven;
    Father, unto You we raise
    this our sacrifice of praise.

153   For the fruits of His creation

EAST ACKLAM   84 84 88 84

Words: F Pratt Green
Music: Francis Jackson

fu - ture needs in earth's safe keep-ing, thanks be to God!___

1 For the fruits of His creation,
   thanks be to God!
   For His gifts to every nation,
   thanks be to God!
   For the ploughing, sowing, reaping,
   silent growth while we are sleeping;
   future needs in earth's safe keeping,
   thanks be to God!

2 In the just reward of labour,
   God's will is done;
   in the help we give our neighbour,
   God's will is done;
   in our worldwide task of caring
   for the hungry and despairing;
   in the harvests we are sharing,
   God's will is done.

3 For the harvests of the Spirit,
   thanks be to God!
   For the good we all inherit,
   thanks be to God!
   For the wonders that astound us,
   for the truths that still confound us;
   most of all, that love has found us,
   thanks be to God!

154   For the might of Your arm

MOUNTAIN CHRISTIANS   Irregular

Words: Charles Silvester Horne (1865–1914)
Music: attributed to John Mannin (1802–65)
in the *Fellowship Hymn Book*, 1909

For the might of Your arm we bless You, our God, our__ fa-thers'

God; You have kept Your pil-grim peo - ple by the

strength of Your staff and rod; You have called us to the

jour - ney which faith-less feet ne'er trod;_____ *For the*

might of Your arm we— bless You, our   God, our— fa - thers' God.

1 For the might of Your arm we bless You,
   our God, our fathers' God;
   You have kept Your pilgrim people
   by the strength of Your staff and rod;
   You have called us to the journey
   which faithless feet ne'er trod;
       For the might of Your arm we bless You,
       our God, our fathers' God.

2 For the love of Christ constraining,
   that bound their hearts as one;
   for the faith in truth and freedom
   in which their work was done;
   for the peace of God's evangel
   wherewith their feet were shod;
       For the might . . .

3 We are watchers of a beacon
   whose light must never die;
   we are guardians of an altar
   that shows You ever nigh;
   we are children of Your freemen
   who sleep beneath the sod;
       For the might . . .

4 May the shadow of Your presence
   around our camp be spread;
   baptize us with the courage
   You gave unto our dead;
   O keep us in the pathway
   their saintly feet have trod;
       For the might . . .

155   For this purpose

Words and music: Graham Kendrick
Music arranged David Peacock

With conviction

1 For this pur - pose Christ was re -
2 In the name of Je - sus we

- vealed, to des - troy all the works of the
stand; by the power of His blood we now

e - vil one. Christ in
claim this ground: Sa - tan

us has o - ver - come, so with
has no au - tho - ri - ty here, powers of

gladness we sing_____ and welcome His kingdom in._____
darkness must flee,_____ for Christ has the victory._____

MEN   WOMEN
_____ Over sin He has conquered: Halle-

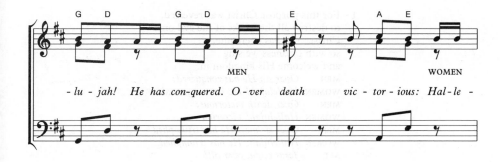

MEN   WOMEN
-lu-jah! He has conquered. Over death victorious: Halle-

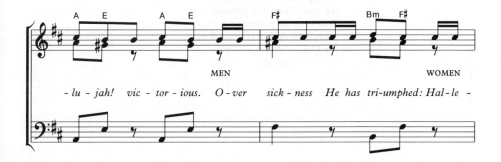

MEN   WOMEN
-lu-jah! victorious. Over sickness He has triumphed: Halle-

- lu-jah! He has tri-umphed. *Je - sus reigns_____ o - ver*

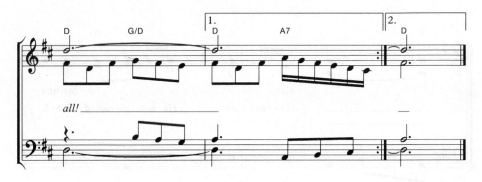

all!_____

1 For this purpose Christ was revealed,
   to destroy all the works of the evil one.
   Christ in us has overcome,
   so with gladness we sing
   and welcome His kingdom in.
   MEN   *Over sin He has conquered:*
   WOMEN *Hallelujah! He has conquered.*
   MEN   *Over death victorious:*
   WOMEN *Hallelujah! victorious.*
   MEN   *Over sickness He has triumphed:*
   WOMEN *Hallelujah! He has triumphed.*
   ALL   *Jesus reigns over all!*

2 In the name of Jesus we stand;
   by the power of His blood
   we now claim this ground:
   Satan has no authority here,
   powers of darkness must flee,
   for Christ has the victory.
            Over sin . . .

156   For unto us a child is born

Words: from Isaiah 9
Music: Unknown
arranged Phil Burt

157   For unto us a child is born

Words and music: David J Hadden

Flowing and expressive

1 For un - to us a child is born, un - to
us a son is given, and the gov - ern - ment shall
be up - on His shoul - der; for un - to
us a child is born, un - to us a son is given,

(2) there shall be no end to the
in - crease of His rule, to the in - crease of His
gov - ern - ment and peace; for He shall
sit on Da - vid's throne up - hold - ing right - eous - ness,

(3) is the Migh - ty God, He
is the Prince of Peace, the King of kings and
Lord of lords: all
hon - our to the King, all glo - ry to His name,

158   For Thou, O Lord

Words and music: Pete Sanchez Jnr

For Thou, O Lord, art high a-bove all the earth; Thou art ex - alt - ed far a-

1. - bove all gods. For Thou, O

2. - bove all gods. I ex -

For Thou, O Lord,
art high above all the earth;
Thou art exalted far above all gods.
For Thou, O Lord,
art high above all the earth;
Thou art exalted far above all gods.
I exalt Thee, I exalt Thee,
I exalt Thee, O Lord;
I exalt Thee, I exalt Thee,
I exalt Thee, O Lord.

159 Forth in Thy name, O Lord, I go

ANGEL'S SONG LM

Words: Charles Wesley (1707–88)
Music: Orlando Gibbons (1583–1625)

Forth in Thy name, O Lord, I go,
my dai - ly la - bour to pur - sue,
Thee, on - ly Thee, re - solved to know
in all I think, or speak, or do.

1 Forth in Thy name, O Lord, I go,
my daily labour to pursue,
Thee, only Thee, resolved to know
in all I think, or speak, or do.

2 The task Thy wisdom hath assigned
O let me cheerfully fulfil;
in all my works Thy presence find,
and prove Thy acceptable will.

3 Thee may I set at my right hand,
whose eyes my inmost substance see;
and labour on at Thy command,
and offer all my works to Thee.

4 Give me to bear Thy easy yoke,
and every moment watch and pray,
and still to things eternal look,
and hasten to Thy glorious day.

5 For Thee delightfully employ
whate'er Thy bounteous grace hath given,
and run my course with even joy,
and closely walk with Thee to heaven.

160   Forty days and forty nights

HEINLEIN   77 77

Words: G H Smyttan (1822–70) altd.
Music: M Herbst (1654–81)

1   Forty days and forty nights
     Thou wast fasting in the wild;
     forty days and forty nights
     tempted and yet undefiled.

2   Sunbeams scorching all the day,
     chilly dew-drops nightly shed,
     prowling beasts about Thy way,
     stones Thy pillow, earth Thy bed.

3   Let us Thy endurance share
     and from earthly greed abstain,
     with Thee watching unto prayer,
     with Thee strong to suffer pain.

4   Then if evil on us press,
     flesh or spirit to assail,
     victor in the wilderness,
     may we never faint or fail!

5   So shall peace divine be ours;
     holier gladness ours shall be;
     come to us angelic powers,
     such as ministered to Thee.

161   Freely, for the love He bears us

Words: Timothy Dudley-Smith
Music: Phil Burt

1 Freely, for the love He bears us,
God has made His purpose plain:
Christ has died and Christ is risen,
Christ will come again.

2 Christ has died, the world's Redeemer,
Lamb of God for sinners slain:
Christ has died . . .

3 Christ is risen, high-ascended,
Lord of all to rule and reign:
Christ has died . . .

4 Christ is coming, King of Glory,
firmly then the faith maintain:
Christ has died . . .

Music: © 1989 Phil Burt

Words: © Timothy Dudley-Smith

162   From heaven You came

THE SERVANT KING

Words and music: Graham Kendrick
Music arranged David Peacock

Worshipfully

Descant *(Ah)*

1 From heaven You came, help-less babe, en-tered our world, Your
2 There in the gar-den of tears my hea-vy load He
3 Come see His hands and His feet, the scars that speak of
4 So let us learn how to serve and in our lives en-

glo - ry veiled,   not to be served but to serve,
chose to bear;   His heart with sor - row was torn,
sac - ri - fice,   hands that flung stars in - to space
- throne Him,   each o - ther's needs to pre - fer,

and give Your life   that we might live.
'Yet not my will   but yours,' He said.
to cru - el nails   sur - rend - ered.
for it is Christ we're serv - ing.

This is our

163   From the rising of the sun

Words and music: Paul Deming

Joyfully

From the ris-ing of the sun   to the go - ing down of the same,_ the Lord's name is to be praised. From the ris - ing of the

Praise ye the Lord,

praise Him O ye ser - vants of the Lord, praise the

name of the Lord; bless - ed be the

name of the Lord from this time forth,

and for ev - er - more.

164   From the sun's rising

Words and music: Graham Kendrick
Music arranged Christopher Norton

1 From the sun's ris-ing un - to the sun's set-ting, Je-sus our Lord shall be great in the earth; and all earth's king-doms shall be His do - mi-nion – all of cre - a - tion shall sing of His worth.

Let ev-ery heart, ev-ery voice,_ ev-ery tongue join with spi - rits a - blaze; one in His love, we will cir - cle the world with the

2 To every tongue, tribe and nation He sends us,
   to make disciples, to teach and baptize;
   for all authority to Him is given;
   now as His witnesses we shall arise.
        Let every heart . . .

3 Come let us join with the Church from all nations,
   cross every border, throw wide every door;
   workers with Him as He gathers His harvest,
   till earth's far corners our Saviour adore.
        Let every heart . . .

        Let all His people rejoice,
        and let all the earth hear His voice!

165 Give me a heart

Words and music: G E Hutchinson

Give me a heart that will love the un-love-ly,
o-pen my eyes to the nee-dy and lost,
help me, O Lord, to show Your love in ac-tion,
give, with-out count-ing the cost,

give,   with-out   count-ing   the   cost.

1   Give me a heart that will love the unlovely,
    open my eyes to the needy and lost,
    help me, O Lord, to show Your love in action,
    give, without counting the cost,
    give, without counting the cost.

2   Help me remember I'm empty without You,
    help me to find my strength only in You.
    I can give nothing unless You first fill me,
    Your love alone must shine through,
    Your love alone must shine through.

3   Make me be willing to go where You send me,
    make me be ready to answer Your call.
    Give me a heart that rejoices to serve You,
    sharing the best love of all,
    sharing the best love of all.

166 Give me a sight, O Saviour

Words and music: Katherine Agnes May Kelly (1869–1942)

Give me a sight, O Sav-iour, of Thy won-drous love to me,___ of the love that brought Thee down to earth, to die on Cal-va-ry.___ O make me un-der-stand it,

Words and music: © National Young Life Campaign
Spring Cottage, Spring Road, Leeds, West Yorks LF6 1AD

help me to take it in;_____ what it meant to Thee, the

Ho - ly One, to bear___ a - way my sin._____

1 Give me a sight, O Saviour,
  of Thy wondrous love to me,
  of the love that brought Thee down to earth,
  to die on Calvary.
      O make me understand it,
      help me to take it in;
      what it meant to Thee,
      the Holy One,
      to bear away my sin.

2 Was it the nails, O Saviour,
  that bound Thee to the tree?
  Nay, 'twas Thine everlasting love,
  Thy love for me, for me.
      O make me understand . . .

3 O wonder of all wonders,
  that through Thy death for me
  my open sins, my secret sins,
  can all forgiven be!
      O make me understand . . .

4 Then melt my heart, O Saviour,
  bend me, yes, break me down,
  until I own Thee – Conqueror,
  and Lord, and Sovereign crown.
      O make me understand . . .

167 Give me oil in my lamp

Words and music: Anon
Music arranged Betty Pulkingham

Brightly

1 Give me oil in my lamp, keep me burn-ing,_____ give me
2 Make me a fish - er of men, keep me seek-ing,_____ make me a
3 Give me joy in my heart, keep me sing-ing,_____ give me
4 Give me love in my heart, keep me serv-ing,_____ give me

oil in my lamp, I pray; give me
fish - er of men, I pray; make me a
joy in my heart, I pray; give me
love in my heart, I pray; give me

oil in my lamp, keep me burn - ing,_____ keep me
fish - er of men, keep me seek - ing,_____ keep me
joy in my heart, keep me sing - ing,_____ keep me
love in my heart, keep me serv - ing,_____ keep me

burn - ing till the break of day.
seek - ing till the break of day.
sing - ing till the break of day.
serv - ing till the break of day.

Words and music: Copyright control
Music arrangement: © 1974, 1975 Celebration,
administered in Europe by Thankyou Music,
PO Box 75, Eastbourne, East Sussex BN23 6NW, UK

Sing ho - san - na, sing ho - san - na,

sing ho - san - na to the King of kings! King. (2) Make

1
Give me oil in my lamp, keep me burning,
give me oil in my lamp, I pray;
give me oil in my lamp, keep me burning,
keep me burning till the break of day.
Sing hosanna, sing hosanna,
sing hosanna to the King of kings!
Sing hosanna, sing hosanna,
sing hosanna to the King.

2
Make me a fisher of men, keep me seeking,
make me a fisher of men, I pray;
make me a fisher of men, keep me seeking,
keep me seeking till the break of day.
Sing hosanna . . .

3
Give me joy in my heart, keep me singing,
give me joy in my heart, I pray;
give me joy in my heart, keep me singing,
keep me singing till the break of day.
Sing hosanna . . .

4
Give me love in my heart, keep me serving,
give me love in my heart, I pray;
give me love in my heart, keep me serving,
keep me serving till the break of day.
Sing hosanna . . .

168 Give me the faith

GIESSEN 88 88 88

Words: Charles Wesley (1707–88)
Music: from Gauntlett's *Comprehensive Tune Book*, 1851

Give me the faith which can re - move and
sink the moun - tain to a plain; give me the
child - like, pray - ing love, which longs to build Thy
house a - gain; Thy love let it my heart o'er -

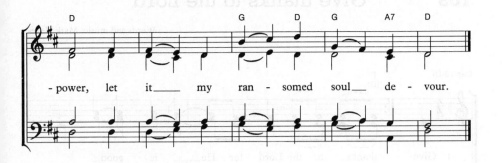

-power, let it___ my ran - somed soul___ de - vour.

1 Give me the faith which can remove
   and sink the mountain to a plain;
   give me the childlike, praying love,
   which longs to build Thy house again;
   Thy love let it my heart o'erpower,
   let it my ransomed soul devour.

2 I would the precious time redeem,
   and longer live for this alone –
   to spend and to be spent for them
   who have not yet my Saviour known;
   fully on these my mission prove,
   and only breathe to breathe Thy love.

3 My talents, gifts, and graces, Lord,
   into Thy blessèd hands receive;
   and let me live to preach Thy word,
   and let me to Thy glory live;
   my every sacred moment spend
   in publishing the sinners' friend.

4 Enlarge, inflame, and fill my heart
   with boundless charity divine;
   so shall I all my strength exert,
   and love them with a zeal like Thine;
   and lead them to Thine open side,
   the sheep for whom their Shepherd died.

169   Give thanks to the Lord

Words and music: Mark Hayes

1 Give thanks to the Lord for He is good,
(2) un-der-stand-ing made the heavens, His
(3) child-ren through the wil-der-ness,
(4) -mem-bered us in our low es-tate,

love en-dures for ev-er. Who / Give thanks to the God
And made the great and shin-
And struck down ma-ny migh-
And freed us from our en-

- of gods,
- ing lights, His love en-dures for ev-er. The
- ty kings, And
- e-mies, To

O give thanks___ to the Lord of lords,
migh-ty sun___ to___ rule the day,___ His love en-dures for___
gave to them an in - he - ri-tance,
ev - ery crea - ture___ He gives food,

To___ Him a-lone___ who does___ great works,
And the moon and the stars to rule___ at___ night. His
A pro-mised land___ for Is - ra - el,___
Give thanks to the God___ of___ heaven,

ev - er.

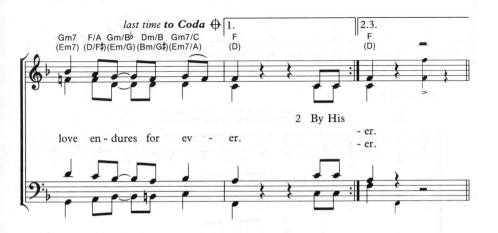

last time **to Coda**

2 By His

love en-dures for ev - er.

- er.
- er.

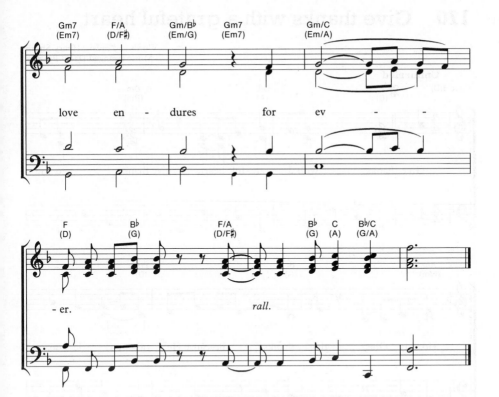

love en - dures for ev - - - er. *rall.*

1   Give thanks to the Lord for He is good,
    His love endures for ever.
    Give thanks to the God of gods,
    His love endures for ever.
    O give thanks to the Lord of lords,
    His love endures for ever.
    To Him alone who does great works,
    His love endures for ever.

2   By His understanding made the heavens,
    His love endures for ever.
    Who made the great and shining lights,
    His love endures for ever.
    The mighty sun to rule the day,
    His love endures for ever.
    And the moon and the stars to rule at night,
    His love endures for ever.
        Hallelujah, Hallelu,
        The Lord Jehovah reigns.
        He is the same from age to age;
        His love will never change.

3   God led His children through the
            wilderness,
    His love endures for ever.
    And struck down many mighty kings,
    His love endures for ever.
    And gave to them an inheritance,
    His love endures for ever.
    A promised land for Israel,
    His love endures for ever.
        Hallelujah . . .

4   He remembered us in our low estate,
    His love endures for ever.
    And freed us from our enemies,
    His love endures for ever.
    To every creature He gives food,
    His love endures for ever.
    Give thanks to the God of heaven,
    His love endures for ever,
    His love endures for ever,
    His love endures for ever.

170   Give thanks with a grateful heart

Words and music: Henry Smith
Music arranged David Peacock

171 Give to our God immortal praise

RIMINGTON LM

Words: Isaac Watts (1674–1748) altd.
Music: F Duckworth (1862–1941)

1 Give to our God immortal praise;
mercy and truth are all His ways:
wonders of grace to God belong,
repeat His mercies in your song.

2 Give to the Lord of lords renown;
the King of kings with glory crown:
His mercies ever shall endure,
when lords and kings are known no more.

3 He built the earth, He spread the sky,
and fixed the starry lights on high:
wonders of grace to God belong,
repeat His mercies in your song.

4 He fills the sun with morning light,
He bids the moon direct the night:
His mercies ever shall endure,
when suns and moons shall shine no more.

5 He sent His Son with power to save
from guilt and darkness and the grave:
wonders of grace to God belong,
repeat His mercies in your song.

172   Glorious Father

Words and music: Danny Reed

Glo-ri-ous Fa-ther we ex-alt You; we wor-ship, hon-our and a-dore You; we de-light to be in Your pres-ence O Lord. We mag-ni-fy Your ho-ly name, and we sing come Lord Je-sus, glo-ri-fy Your name, and we sing come Lord Je-sus, glo-ri-fy Your name.

173 Glorious things of thee are spoken

AUSTRIA   87 87 D

Words: John Newton (1725–1807)
Music: J F Haydn (1732–1809)

Glo-rious things of thee are spo-ken, Zi - on, ci - ty of our God;

He, whose word can - not be bro-ken, formed thee for His own a - bode:

on the Rock of A - ges found-ed, what can＿ shake thy sure re-pose?

With sal-va-tion's walls sur - round-ed, thou may'st smile at＿ all thy foes.

1 Glorious things of thee are spoken,
  Zion, city of our God;
  He, whose word cannot be broken,
  formed thee for His own abode:
  on the Rock of ages founded,
  what can shake thy sure repose?
  With salvation's walls surrounded,
  thou may'st smile at all thy foes.

2 See, the streams of living waters,
  springing from eternal love,
  well supply thy sons and daughters
  and all fear of want remove:
  who can faint, while such a river
  ever flows their thirst to assuage?
  Grace which, like the Lord, the giver,
  never fails from age to age.

3 Saviour, if of Zion's city
  I, through grace, a member am,
  let the world deride or pity,
  I will glory in Thy name:
  fading is the worldling's pleasure,
  all his boasted pomp and show;
  solid joys and lasting treasure
  none but Zion's children know.

174 Glory, glory in the highest

Words and music: Danny Daniels

glo - ry,___ WOMEN glo - ry,___ MEN glo - ry,___ WOMEN glo - ry,___

MEN glo - ry,___ ALL glo - ry to the___ Lamb!___ MEN I give

2nd time **to Coda** ✛   **D.𝄋 al Coda**

ALL I give glo - ry to___ the Lamb!

✛ *CODA*

I give glo - ry to___ the Lamb!

175   Glory be to God in heaven

REGENT SQUARE   87 87 87

Words: John Richards
Music: H Smart (1813–79)

1 Glo-ry be to God in hea-ven, and to all on earth, His peace; Lord and Fa-ther,_ King in glo-ry, gifts of praise in_ us re-lease, so our wor-ship and thanks-giv-ing from our hearts will_ ne-ver cease.

2 Christ in-car-nate, sent by Fa-ther to re-deem, re-new, re-store; ris-en Lamb, in_ glo-ry seat-ed, hear our prayers Lord, we im-plore. Now to Fa-ther, Son, and Spi-rit be all glo-ry_ ev-er-more.

Words: © 1984 John Richards/Renewal Servicing,
PO Box 17 Shepperton, Middlesex TW17 8NU

176   # Glory to You, my God

TALLIS' CANON   LM

Words: T Ken (1637–1710)
in this version Jubilate Hymns
Music: Thomas Tallis (1505–1585)

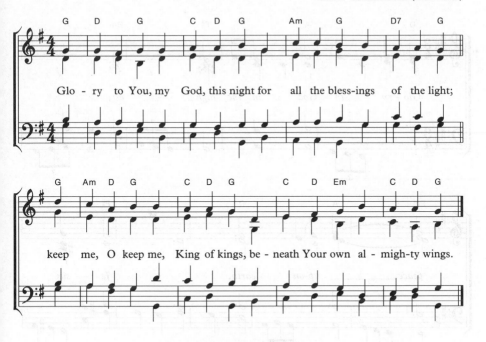

1 Glory to You, my God, this night
for all the blessings of the light;
keep me, O keep me, King of kings,
beneath Your own almighty wings.

2 Forgive me, Lord, through Your dear Son,
the wrong that I this day have done,
that peace with God and man may be,
before I sleep, restored to me.

3 Teach me to live, that I may dread
the grave as little as my bed;
teach me to die, that so I may
rise glorious at the awesome day.

4 O may my soul on you repose
and restful sleep my eyelids close;
sleep that shall me more vigorous make
to serve my God when I awake.

5 If in the night I sleepless lie,
my mind with peaceful thoughts supply;
let no dark dreams disturb my rest,
no powers of evil me molest.

6 Praise God from whom all blessings flow
in heaven above and earth below;
one God, three persons, we adore –
to Him be praise for evermore!

177 Glory to God in the highest

Words and music: Greg Leavers
Music arranged Phil Burt

Glory to God in the highest,
peace upon earth,
Jesus Christ has come to earth;
that's why we sing,
Jesus the King,
Jesus has come for you.

1 The shepherds who were sitting there
were suddenly filled with fear;
the dark night was filled with light,
angels singing everywhere.
    Glory to God . . .

2 The next time we hear a song
of worship from a heavenly throng,
will be when Jesus comes again,
then with triumph we'll all sing:
    Glory to God . . .

178 Go forth and tell

YANWORTH   10 10 10 10

Words: J E Seddon (1915–83)
Music: John Barnard

Go forth and tell! O Church of God, a-wake! God's sav-ing news to all the na-tions take: pro-claim Christ Je-sus, Sav-iour, Lord and king, that all the world His wor-thy praise may sing.

1   Go forth and tell! O Church of God, awake!
    God's saving news to all the nations take:
    proclaim Christ Jesus, Saviour, Lord and King,
    that all the world His worthy praise may sing.

2   Go forth and tell! God's love embraces all;
    He will in grace respond to all who call:
    how shall they call if they have never heard
    the gracious invitation of His word?

3. Go forth and tell! men still in darkness lie;
    in wealth or want, in sin they live and die:
    give us, O Lord, concern of heart and mind,
    a love like Yours which cares for all mankind.

4   Go forth and tell! the doors are open wide:
    share God's good gifts – let no one be denied;
    live out your life as Christ your Lord shall choose,
    Your ransomed powers for His sole glory use.

5   Go forth and tell! O church of God, arise!
    Go in the strength which Christ your Lord supplies;
    go till all nations His great name adore
    and serve Him, Lord and King for evermore.

179 Go, tell it on the mountain

Words and music: Geoffrey Marshall-Taylor
Music arranged: Douglas Coombes

Go, tell it on the moun - tain, o - ver the hills and ev-ery-where; go, tell it on the moun - tain that Je - sus is His name.

He pos-sessed no rich - es, no home to lay His head; He saw the needs of oth - ers and cared for them in - stead._____

Go, tell it on the mountain,
over the hills and everywhere;
go, tell it on the mountain
that Jesus is His name.

1 He possessed no riches, no home to lay His head;
   He saw the needs of others and cared for them instead.
   Go tell it on the mountain . . .

2 He reached out and touched them, the blind, the deaf, the lame;
   He spoke and listened gladly to anyone who came.
   Go tell it on the mountain . . .

3 Some turned away in anger, with hatred in the eye;
   they tried Him and condemned Him, then led Him out to die.
   Go tell it on the mountain . . .

4 'Father, now forgive them' – those were the words He said;
   in three more days He was alive and risen from the dead.
   Go tell it on the mountain . . .

5 He still comes to people, His life moves through the lands;
   He uses us for speaking, He touches with our hands.
   Go tell it on the mountain . . .

180 God came among us

Words and music: Marilyn Baker
Music arranged Phil Burt

God came a - mong us, He be - came a man, be - came a ba - by, though through Him the world be - gan. He came to earth to bring us peace, but where is that peace to - day? It can be found

1 God came among us, He became a man,
   became a baby, though through Him the world began.
   He came to earth to bring us peace,
   but where is that peace today?
   It can be found
   by those who will let Him direct their way.

2 He came to serve, to show us how much He cared;
   our joys and sorrows He so willingly shared.
   He came to earth to bring us joy,
   but where is that joy today?
   It can be found
   by those who let Him wash their guilt away.

3 Death tried to hold Him, but it could not succeed;
   He rose again, and now we can be freed.
   He longs to give eternal life
   to all who will simply receive,
   yes to all who
   will open their hearts and just believe.

181 God forgave my sin

Words and music: Carol Owens

1 God for - gave my sin in Je - sus'
2 All power is given in Je - sus'

name; I've been born a - gain in
name in earth and heaven in

Je - sus' name, and in Je - sus'
Je - sus' name; and in Je - sus'

name I come to you to
name I come to you to

182 God has spoken to His people

Words: Willard Jabusch
Music: Israeli folk melody
arranged Norman Warren

God has spo-ken to His peo-ple, al-le-lu-ia,

and His words are words of wis-dom, al-le-lu-ia!

O - pen your ears, O Christ-ian peo-ple, o - pen your ears and hear good news;

o - pen your hearts, O roy-al priest-hood, God has come to_ you.

God has spoken to His people, alleluia,
and His words are words of wisdom, alleluia!

1 Open your ears, O Christian people,
   open your ears and hear good news;
   open your hearts, O royal priesthood,
   God has come to you.
   God has spoken . . .

2 They who have ears to hear His message,
   they who have ears, then let them hear;
   they who would learn the way of wisdom,
   let them hear God's word!
   God has spoken . . .

3 Israel comes to greet the Saviour,
   Judah is glad to see His day;
   from east and west the peoples travel,
   He will show the way.
   God has spoken . . .

183 God holds the key

Words: Joseph Parker (1830–1902)
Music: George C Stebbins (1846–1945)

1 God holds the key of all unknown,
   and I am glad:
   if other hands should hold the key,
   or if He trusted it to me,
   I might be sad, I might be sad.

2 What if tomorrow's cares were here
   without its rest?
   I'd rather He unlocked the day,
   and, as the hours swing open, say,
   'My will is best, My will is best.'

3 The very dimness of my sight
   makes me secure;
   for, groping in my misty way,
   I feel His hand; I hear Him say,
   'My help is sure, My help is sure.'

4 I cannot read His future plans;
   but this I know:
   I have the smiling of His face,
   and all the refuge of His grace,
   while here below, while here below.

5 Enough: this covers all my wants;
   and so I rest!
   for what I cannot, He can see,
   and in His care I saved shall be,
   for ever blest, for ever blest.

184   God is building a house

Words and music: Anon
Music arranged Phil Burt

1   God is building a house,
    God is building a house,
    God is building a house that will stand.
    He is building by His plan
    with the living stones of man,
    God is building a house that will stand.

2   God is building a house,
    God is building a house,
    God is building a house that will stand.
    With apostles, prophets, pastors,
    with evangelists and teachers,
    God is building a house that will stand.

3   Christ is head of this house,
    Christ is head of this house,
    Christ is head of this house that will stand.
    He abideth in its praise,
    will perfect it in its ways,
    Christ is head of this house that will stand.

4   We are part of this house,
    we are part of this house,
    we are part of this house that will stand.
    We are called from every nation
    to enjoy His full salvation,
    we are part of this house that will stand.

185 God is good

Words and music: Graham Kendrick
Music arranged David Peacock

Lively

God is good — we sing and shout it,__ God is good —
we ce-le-brate; God is good — no more we doubt it,__
God is good — we know it's true!
And when I think of His love for me, my heart fills with praise and I

God is good – we sing and shout it,
God is good – we celebrate;
God is good – no more we doubt it,
God is good – we know it's true!

And when I think of His love for me,
my heart fills with praise
and I feel like dancing;
for in His heart there is room for me,
and I run with arms opened wide.

God is good – we sing and shout it,
God is good – we celebrate;
God is good – no more we doubt it,
God is good – we know it's true! *Hey!*

186 God is in His temple

GRÖNINGEN   668 668 33 66

Words: W T Matson (1833–99)
Music: J Neander (1650–80)

God is in His tem - ple, the Al - migh - ty Fa - ther, round His foot-stool let us ga - ther:

Him with a - dor - a - tion serve, the Lord most ho - ly, who has mer - cy on the low - ly:

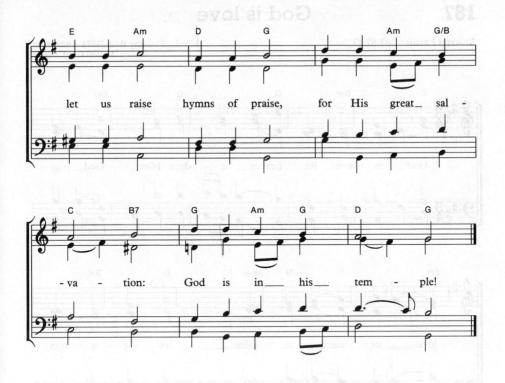

let us raise hymns of praise, for His great salvation: God is in his temple!

1 God is in His temple,
    the Almighty Father,
    round His footstool let us gather:
    Him with adoration
    serve, the Lord most holy,
    who has mercy on the lowly:
      let us raise
      hymns of praise,
    for His great salvation:
      God is in His temple!

2 Christ comes to His temple:
    we, His word receiving,
    are made happy in believing.
    Lo! from sin delivered,
    He has turned our sadness,
    our deep gloom, to light and gladness!
      let us raise
      hymns of praise,
    for our bonds are severed:
      Christ comes to His temple!

3 Come and claim Your temple,
    gracious Holy Spirit!
    In our hearts Your home inherit:
    make in us Your dwelling,
    Your high work fulfilling,
    into ours Your will instilling,
      till we raise
      hymns of praise
    beyond mortal telling,
      in the eternal temple.

187

God is love

ABBOT'S LEIGH   87 87 D

Words: Timothy Rees (1874–1939) altd.
Music: Cyril Taylor

God_ is love: let heaven_ a - dore Him;_ God_ is love:__ let earth_ re - joice;___ let cre - a - tion sing_ be - fore Him, and_ ex - alt_ Him with_ one voice. He_ who laid_ the earth's_ foun - da - tion,_ He_ who

spread the heavens a-bove, He__ who breathes through all__ cre-a-tion,_ He_ is love,_ e-ter-nal love.

1 God is love: let heaven adore Him;
God is love: let earth rejoice;
let creation sing before Him,
and exalt Him with one voice.
He who laid the earth's foundation,
He who spread the heavens above,
He who breathes through all creation,
He is love, eternal love.

2 God is love: and He enfoldeth
all the world in one embrace;
with unfailing grasp He holdeth
every child of every race.
And when human hearts are breaking
under sorrow's iron rod,
all the sorrow, all the aching,
wrings with pain the heart of God.

3 God is love: and though with blindness
sin afflicts the souls of men,
God's eternal loving-kindness
holds and guides them even then.
Sin and death and hell shall never
o'er us final triumph gain;
God is love, so love for ever
o'er the universe must reign.

188 God is our strength and refuge

DAMBUSTERS MARCH   77 75 77 11

Words: from Psalm 46
Richard Bewes
Music: E Coates (1886–1958)
arranged John Barnard

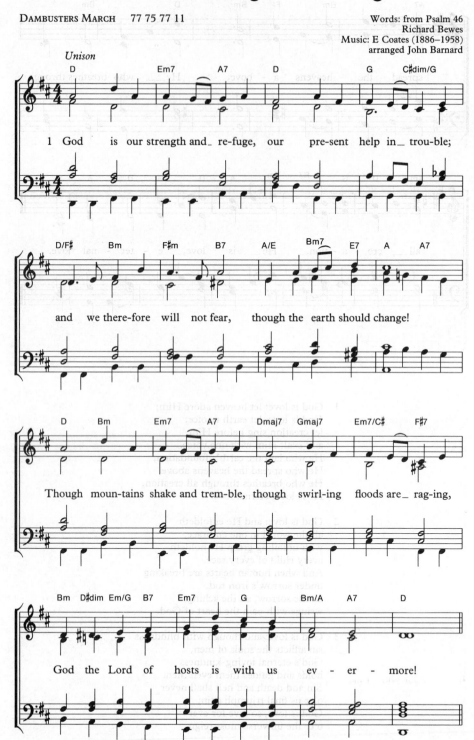

1 God is our strength and refuge, our present help in trouble;
and we therefore will not fear, though the earth should change!
Though mountains shake and tremble, though swirling floods are raging,
God the Lord of hosts is with us evermore!

2 There is a flow-ing_ ri-ver, with-in God's ho-ly_ ci-ty;
3 Come, see the works of our Mak-er, learn of His deeds all-power-ful;

God is in the midst of her — she shall not_ be moved!_
wars will cease a-cross the world when He shat-ters the spear!_

God's help is swift-ly_ giv-en, thrones van-ish at His pres-ence —
Be still and know your Cre-a-tor, up-lift Him in the_ na-tions —

God the Lord of hosts is with us ev-er-more!
God the Lord of hosts is with us ev-er-more!

189 God is working His purpose out

BENSON Irregular

Words: A C Ainger (1841–1919)
in this version Jubilate Hymns
Music: Millicent D Kingham (1866–1927)

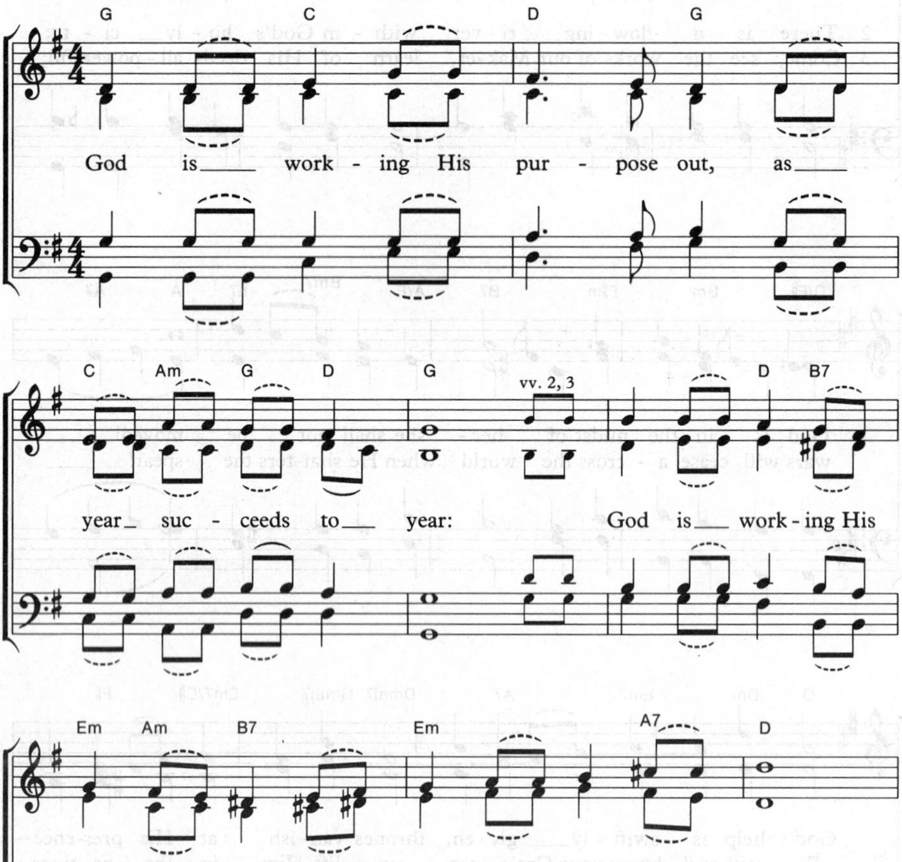

G C D G
God is work - ing His pur - pose out, as
C Am G D G
year suc - ceeds to year:
vv. 2, 3
D B7
God is work - ing His
Em Am B7 Em A7 D
pur - pose out, and the time is draw - ing near:
G
near - er and near - er draws the time, the

time that shall sure - ly be, when the earth shall be filled with the glo - ry of God, as the wa - ters__ co - ver the sea.

1 God is working His purpose out,
  as year succeeds to year:
  God is working His purpose out,
  and the time is drawing near:
  nearer and nearer draws the time,
  the time that shall surely be,
  when the earth shall be filled
  with the glory of God,
  as the waters cover the sea.

2 From utmost east to utmost west
  wherever man has trod,
  by the mouth of many messengers
  rings out the voice of God:
  listen to me you continents,
  you islands look to me,
  that the earth may be filled
  with the glory of God,
  as the waters cover the sea.

3 We shall march in the strength of God,
  with the banner of Christ unfurled,
  that the light of the glorious gospel of truth
  may shine throughout the world;
  we shall fight with sorrow and sin
  to set their captives free,
  that the earth may be filled
  with the glory of God,
  as the waters cover the sea.

4 All we can do is nothing worth
  unless God blesses the deed;
  vainly we hope for the harvest-tide
  till God gives life to the seed:
  nearer and nearer draws the time,
  the time that shall surely be,
  when the earth shall be filled
  with the glory of God,
  as the waters cover the sea.

190   God of all ages

Words: Peter Coutts
Music: Peter Graham

The guitar chords are not compatible with the piano accompaniment

Words and music: © 1988 Oxford University Press
From *New Songs of Praise 4*

1 God of all ages and Lord for all time,
   Creator of all things in perfect design:
   for fields ripe for harvest, for rich golden grain,
   for beauty in nature, we thank You again.

2 God of all nations and Lord of all lands,
   who placed the world's wealth in the palm of our hands,
   we pray for Your guidance to guard against greed.
   though great the resources, still great is the need.

3 God of compassion and Lord of all life,
   we pray for Your people in conflict and strife.
   The earth You created a vast treasure store,
   yet hunger still thrives while men fight to gain more.

4 God of all wisdom, take us by the hand
   and insight bestow when we ruin Your land.
   For rivers polluted, for forests laid bare,
   we pray Your forgiveness for failing to care.

5 God of all greatness and giver of light,
   with each sunlit morning we worship Your might,
   our half-hearted service Your only reward:
   for love beyond measure, we thank You O Lord.

191 God of glory

Words and music: Dave Fellingham
Music arranged David Peacock

1326 God of grace and God of glory

192(i) God of grace and God of glory

WESTMINSTER ABBEY 87 87 87

Words: H E Fosdick (1878–1969)
Music: from *The Psalmist*, 1842
adapted from Henry Purcell (1659–95)

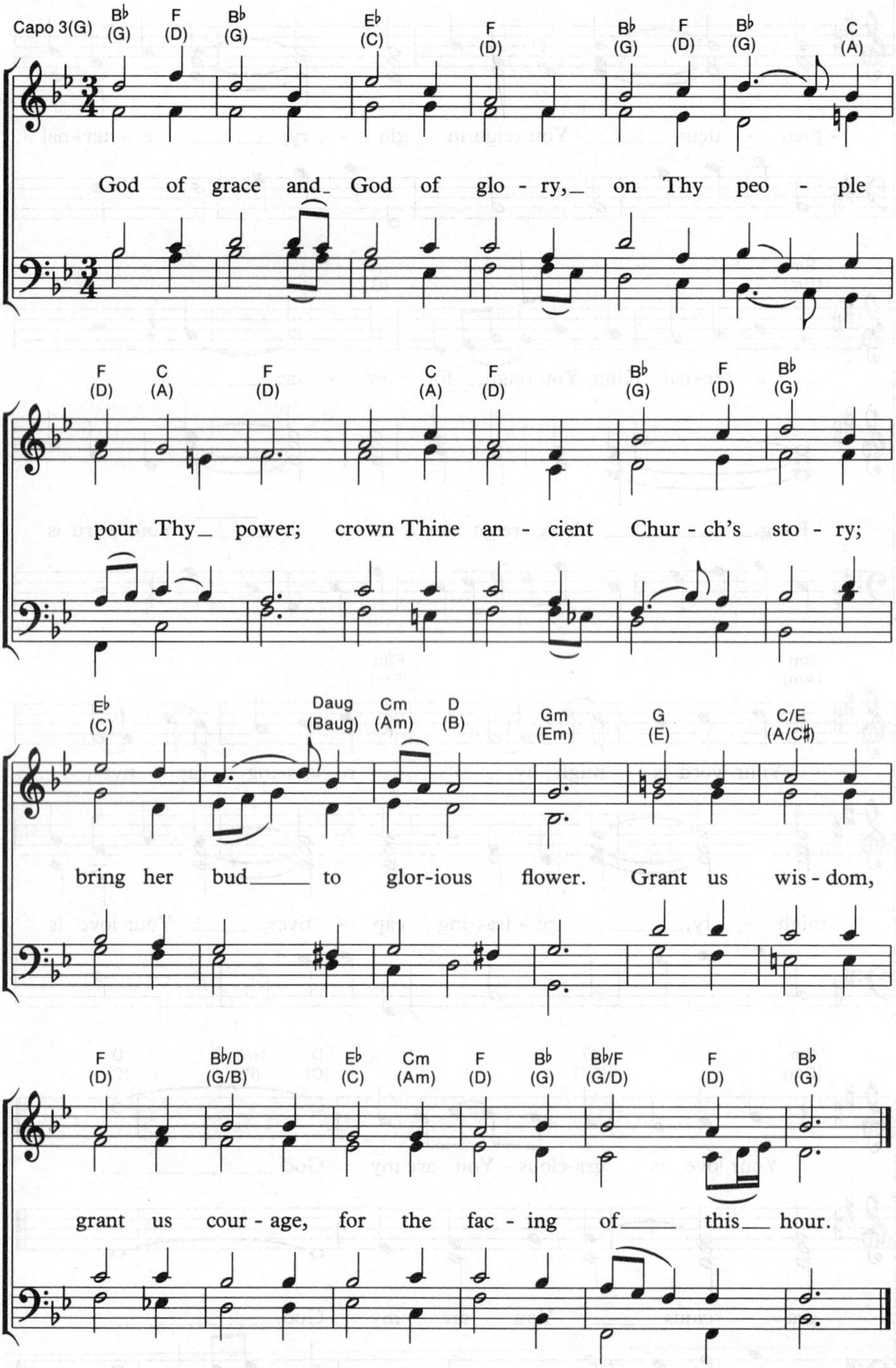

Capo 3(G)
B♭ (G) F (D) B♭ (G) E♭ (C) F (D) B♭ (G) F (D) B♭ (G) C (A)
God of grace and God of glo - ry, on Thy peo - ple
F (D) C (A) F (D) C (A) F (D) B♭ (G) F (D) B♭ (G)
pour Thy power; crown Thine an - cient Chur - ch's sto - ry;
E♭ (C) Daug (Baug) Cm (Am) D (B) Gm (Em) G (E) C/E (A/C♯)
bring her bud to glor-ious flower. Grant us wis - dom,
F (D) B♭/D (G/B) E♭ (C) Cm (Am) F (D) B♭ (G) B♭/F (G/D) F (D) B♭ (G)
grant us cour - age, for the fac - ing of this hour.

1 God of grace and God of glory,
   on Thy people pour Thy power;
   crown Thine ancient Church's story;
   bring her bud to glorious flower.
   Grant us wisdom,
   grant us courage,
   for the facing of this hour.

2 Lo! the hosts of evil round us
   scorn Thy Christ, assail His ways!
   Fears and doubts too long have bound us;
   free our hearts to work and praise.
   Grant us wisdom,
   grant us courage,
   for the living of these days.

3 Heal Thy children's warring madness;
   bend our pride to Thy control;
   shame our wanton, selfish gladness,
   rich in things and poor in soul.
   Grant us wisdom,
   grant us courage,
   lest we miss Thy kingdom's goal.

4 Set our feet on lofty places;
   gird our lives that they may be
   armoured with all Christlike graces
   in the fight to set men free.
   Grant us wisdom,
   grant us courage,
   that we fail not man nor Thee.

5 Save us from weak resignation
   to the evils we deplore;
   let the search for Thy salvation
   be our glory evermore.
   Grant us wisdom,
   grant us courage,
   serving Thee whom we adore.

192(ii) God of grace and God of glory

RHUDDLAN   87 87 87

Words: H E Fosdick (1878–1969)
Music: Welsh traditional melody

God of grace and God of glo-ry, on Thy peo-ple
pour Thy power;_ crown Thine an-cient Chur-ch's sto-ry;
bring her bud to glor-ious flower. Grant us wis-dom,_
grant us cour-age,_ for the fac-ing of this hour.

1 God of grace and God of glory,
   on Thy people pour Thy power;
   crown Thine ancient Church's story;
   bring her bud to glorious flower.
   Grant us wisdom,
   grant us courage,
   for the facing of this hour.

2 Lo! the hosts of evil round us
   scorn Thy Christ, assail His ways!
   Fears and doubts too long have bound us;
   free our hearts to work and praise.
   Grant us wisdom,
   grant us courage,
   for the living of these days.

3 Heal Thy children's warring madness;
   bend our pride to Thy control;
   shame our wanton, selfish gladness,
   rich in things and poor in soul.
   Grant us wisdom,
   grant us courage,
   lest we miss Thy kingdom's goal.

4 Set our feet on lofty places;
   gird our lives that they may be
   armoured with all Christlike graces
   in the fight to set men free.
   Grant us wisdom,
   grant us courage,
   that we fail not man nor Thee.

5 Save us from weak resignation
   to the evils we deplore;
   let the search for Thy salvation
   be our glory evermore.
   Grant us wisdom,
   grant us courage,
   serving Thee whom we adore.

193 God moves in a mysterious way

LONDON NEW   CM

Words: William Cowper (1731–1800)
Music: from *Playford's Psalms*, 1671
adapted from *Scottish Psalter*, 1635

God moves in a mys-ter-ious___ way, His won-ders to___ per-form; He plants His___ foot-steps in the___ sea, and rides up-on the storm.

1 God moves in a mysterious way,
   His wonders to perform;
   He plants His footsteps in the sea,
   and rides upon the storm.

2 Deep in unfathomable mines
   of never-failing skill,
   He treasures up His bright designs,
   and works His sovereign will.

3 Ye fearful saints, fresh courage take;
   the clouds ye so much dread
   are big with mercy, and shall break
   in blessings on your head.

4 Judge not the Lord by feeble sense,
   but trust Him for His grace;
   behind a frowning providence
   He hides a smiling face.

5 His purposes will ripen fast,
   unfolding every hour;
   the bud may have a bitter taste,
   but sweet will be the flower.

6 Blind unbelief is sure to err,
   and scan His work in vain;
   God is His own interpreter,
   and He will make it plain.

194   God save our gracious Queen

NATIONAL ANTHEM   664 6664

Words: Unknown
Music: *Thesaurus Musicus*, 1743

1   God save our gracious Queen,
    long live our noble Queen,
    God save the Queen!
    Send her victorious,
    happy and glorious,
    long to reign over us;
    God save the Queen!

2   Thy choicest gifts in store
    on her be pleased to pour,
    long may she reign;
    may she defend our laws,
    and ever give us cause
    to sing with heart and voice
    God save the Queen!

195   God whose Son was once a man

Words: Peter Horrobin
Music: Greg Leavers

1 God whose Son was once a man on earth gave His life that
2 God whose power fell on the ear - ly Church, sent to earth from
3 Pour Your Spi - rit on the Church to - day, that Your life through

men may live. Ris - en, our as - cend - ed Lord ful -
heaven a - bove; Spi - rit led, by Him or - dained, they
me may flow; Spi - rit filled, I'll serve Your name and

- filled His pro - mised word. *When the Spi - rit came, the*
showed the world God's love.
live the truth I know. (after v. 3) *When the Spi - rit comes, new*

Church was born, God's peo - ple shared in a bright new dawn. *They*
life is born, God's peo - ple share in a bright new dawn. *We'll*

196 Good Christian men, rejoice

IN DULCI JUBILO Irregular

Words: John Mason Neale (1818–66)
Music: German Carol melody, 14th cent.

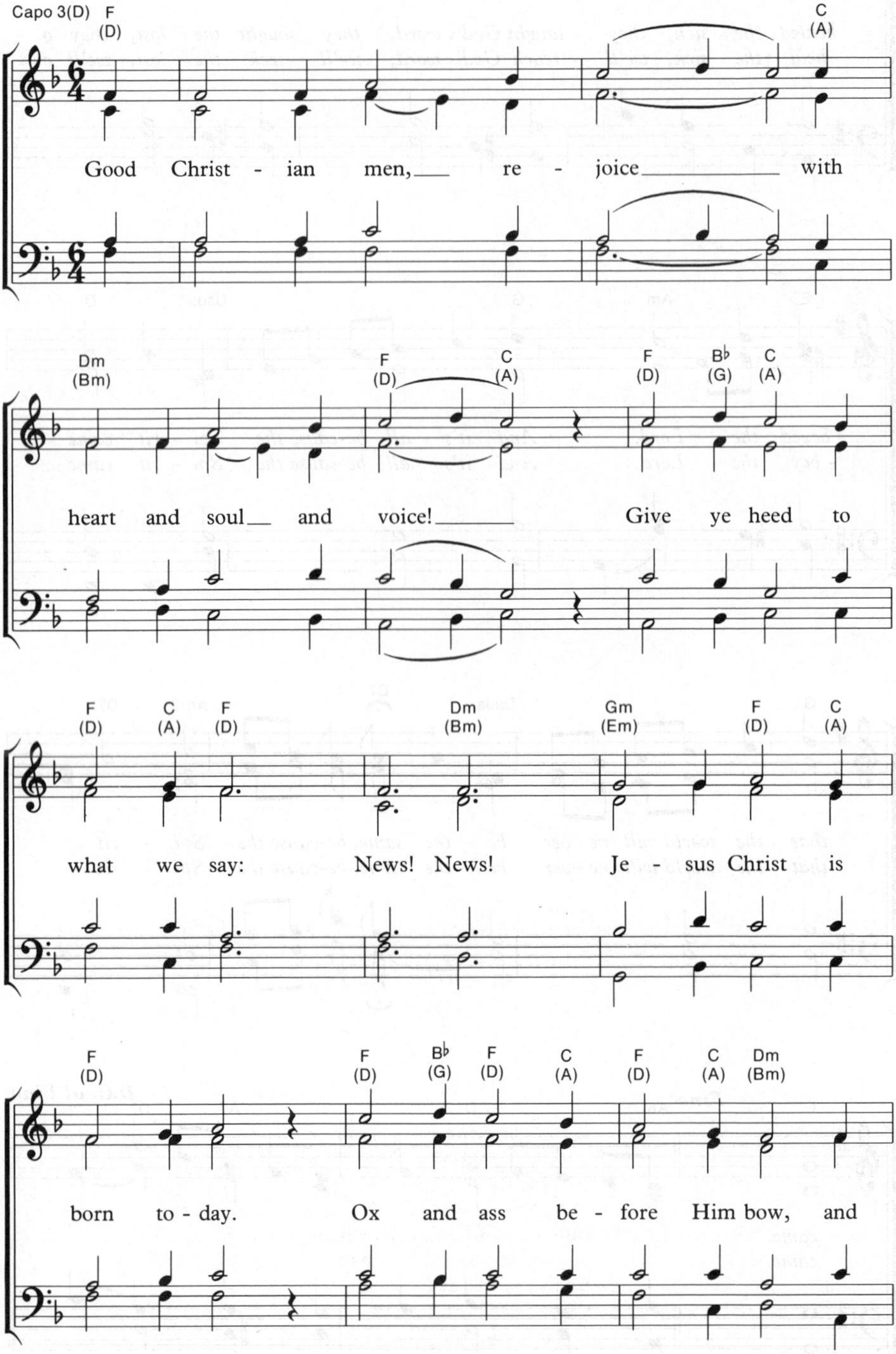

Capo 3(D) F (D) C (A)
Good Christ - ian men, re - joice with
Dm (Bm) F (D) C (A) F (D) B♭ (G) C (A)
heart and soul and voice! Give ye heed to
F (D) C (A) F (D) Dm (Bm) Gm (Em) F (D) C (A)
what we say: News! News! Je - sus Christ is
F (D) F (D) B♭ (G) F (D) C (A) F (D) C (A) Dm (Bm)
born to - day. Ox and ass be - fore Him bow, and

He is in the man-ger now: Christ is born to-day,_____ Christ is born to-day._____

1 Good Christian men, rejoice
with heart and soul and voice!
Give ye heed to what we say:
News! News! Jesus Christ is born today.
Ox and ass before Him bow,
and He is in the manger now:
Christ is born today,
Christ is born today.

2 Good Christian men, rejoice
with heart and soul and voice!
Now ye hear of endless bliss:
Joy! Joy! Jesus Christ was born for this.
He hath ope'd the heavenly door,
and man is blest for evermore:
Christ was born for this,
Christ was born for this.

3 Good Christian men, rejoice
with heart and soul and voice!
Now ye need not fear the grave:
Peace! Peace! Jesus Christ was born to save;
calls you one, and calls you all,
to gain His everlasting hall:
Christ was born to save,
Christ was born to save.

197 Great God of wonders

CAREY (SURREY)   88 88 88

Words: Samuel Davies (1723–61) altd.
Music: H Carey (1692–1743)

Gracious Spirit

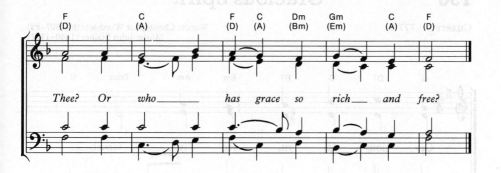

Words: Chrysostom (?) and Worksworth (1807–85)
Music: John Hatton (1400–16)

Thee? Or who_____ has grace so rich___ and free?

CHANT: 77.77

1 Great God of wonders, all Thy ways
   are matchless, godlike and divine;
   but the fair glories of Thy grace
   more godlike and unrivalled shine:
      Who is a pardoning God like Thee?
      Or who has grace so rich and free?

2 Such dire offences to forgive,
   such guilty daring souls to spare;
   this is Thy grand prerogative,
   and none shall in the honour share:
      Who is a pardoning God . . .

3 In wonder lost, with trembling joy,
   we take the pardon of our God,
   pardon for sins of deepest dye,
   a pardon sealed with Jesus' blood:
      Who is a pardoning God . . .

4 O may this glorious matchless love,
   this God-like miracle of grace,
   teach mortal tongues, like those above,
   to raise this song of lofty praise:
      Who is a pardoning God . . .

198 Gracious Spirit

CHARITY   777 5

Words: Christopher Wordsworth (1807–85)
Music: John Stainer (1840–1901)

1 Gracious Spirit, Holy Ghost,
   taught by You, we covet most,
   of Your gifts at Pentecost,
   holy, heavenly love.

2 Faith that mountains could remove,
   tongues of earth or heaven above,
   knowledge, all things, empty prove
   without heavenly love.

3 Though I as a martyr bleed,
   give my goods the poor to feed,
   all is vain if love I need;
   therefore give me love.

4 Love is kind, and suffers long;
   love is meek, and thinks no wrong;
   love, than death itself more strong:
   therefore give us love.

5 Prophecy will fade away,
   melting in the light of day;
   love will ever with us stay:
   therefore give us love.

6 Faith, and hope, and love we see
   joining hand in hand, agree;
   but the greatest of the three,
   and the best, is love.

199 Great is the Lord

Words and music: Steve McEwan

Great_____ is the Lord_ and most wor-thy of

praise, the ci-ty of our God, the ho-ly place, the

joy of the_ whole earth._

Great_____ is the Lord in whom we have the vic - to-ry,_

Lord, we trust in Your un-fail-ing love, for
You a-lone are God e-ter-nal, Through-out earth and hea-ven a-
-bove.

Great is the Lord and most worthy of praise,
the city of our God, the holy place,
the joy of the whole earth.
Great is the Lord in whom we have the victory,
He aids us against the enemy,
we bow down on our knees.

And Lord, we want to lift Your name on high,
and Lord, we want to thank You,
for the works You've done in our lives;
and Lord, we trust in Your unfailing love,
for You alone are God eternal,
throughout earth and heaven above.

200 Great is Thy faithfulness

GREAT IS THY FAITHFULNESS   11 10 11 10 with refrain   Words: T O Chisholm (1866–1960)
Music: W M Runyan (1870–1957)

morn - ing by morn - ing new mer - cies I see;
all I have need - ed Thy hand hath pro - vid - ed, –
great is Thy faith - ful-ness, Lord, un - to me!

1 Great is Thy faithfulness, O God my Father,
  there is no shadow of turning with Thee;
  Thou changest not, Thy compassions they fail not,
  as Thou hast been Thou for ever wilt be.
   Great is Thy faithfulness,
   great is Thy faithfulness;
   morning by morning
   new mercies I see;
   all I have needed
   Thy hand hath provided, –
   great is Thy faithfulness, Lord, unto me!

2 Summer and winter, and spring-time and harvest,
  sun, moon and stars in their courses above,
  join with all nature in manifold witness
  to Thy great faithfulness, mercy and love.
   Great is Thy faithfulness . . .

3 Pardon for sin, and a peace that endureth,
  Thine own dear presence to cheer and to guide;
  strength for today and bright hope for tomorrow,
  blessings all mine, with ten thousand beside!
   Great is Thy faithfulness . . .

201   Guide me, O Thou great Jehovah

CWM RHONDDA   87 87 47 extended

Words: William Williams (1717–91) altd.
Music: John Hughes (1873–1932)

- more,_____ feed me now_ and_ ev - er - more.

1   Guide me, O Thou great Jehovah,
     pilgrim through this barren land;
     I am weak, but Thou art mighty;
     hold me with Thy powerful hand:
         Bread of heaven,
     feed me now and evermore.

2   Open now the crystal fountain,
     whence the healing stream doth flow;
     let the fiery, cloudy pillar
     lead me all my journey through:
         Strong deliverer,
     be Thou still my strength and shield.

3   When I tread the verge of Jordan,
     bid my anxious fears subside:
     death of death, and hell's destruction,
     land me safe on Canaan's side:
         Songs of praises
     I will ever give to Thee.

202 Hail the day

LLANFAIR   77 77 with Alleluias

Words: Charles Wesley (1707–88)
and Thomas Cotterill (1779–1823)
Music: R Williams (1781–1821)

Hail the day that sees Him rise, Al - le - lu - ia,

to His throne be - yond the skies, Al - le - lu - ia,

Christ, the Lamb for sin - ners given, Al - le - lu - ia,___

en - ters now the high - est___ heaven: Al - le - lu - ia.

1 Hail the day that sees Him rise,
  Alleluia,
  to His throne beyond the skies;
  Christ, the Lamb for sinners given,
  enters now the highest heaven.

2 There for Him high triumph waits:
  lift your heads, eternal gates,
  He has conquered death and sin,
  take the King of glory in.

3 See! the heaven its Lord receives,
  yet He loves the earth He leaves;
  though returning to His throne,
  still He calls mankind His own.

4 Still for us He intercedes,
  His prevailing death He pleads,
  near Himself prepares our place,
  He the first-fruits of our race.

5 Lord, though parted from our sight,
  far beyond the starry height,
  lift our hearts that we may rise
  one with You beyond the skies.

6 There with You we shall remain,
  share the glory of Your reign,
  there Your face unclouded view,
  find our heaven of heavens in You.

203 Hail, Thou once despised Jesus

Lux Eoi   87 87 D

Words: John Bakewell (1721–1819)
Music: Arthur S Sullivan (1842–1900)

1 Hail, Thou once despisèd Jesus,
   hail, Thou Galilean King!
   Thou didst suffer to release us,
   Thou didst free salvation bring.
   Hail, Thou agonising Saviour,
   bearer of our sin and shame;
   by Thy merits we find favour;
   life is given through Thy name.

2 Paschal Lamb, by God appointed,
   all our sins on Thee were laid;
   by almighty love anointed,
   Thou hast full atonement made.
   All Thy people are forgiven
   through the virtue of Thy blood;
   opened is the gate of heaven,
   peace is made 'twixt man and God.

3 Jesus, hail! enthroned in glory,
   there for ever to abide;
   all the heavenly hosts adore Thee,
   seated at Thy Father's side:
   there for sinners Thou art pleading,
   there Thou dost our place prepare;
   ever for us interceding,
   till in glory we appear.

4 Worship, honour, power, and blessing,
   Thou art worthy to receive;
   loudest praises, without ceasing,
   meet it is for us to give:
   Help, ye bright angelic spirits!
   bring your sweetest, noblest lays;
   help to sing our Saviour's merits,
   help to chant Immanuel's praise.

204 Hail to the Lord's anointed

CRÜGER 76 76 D

Words: James Montgomery (1771–1854)
Music: adapted by W H Monk (1823–89)
from a chorale by J Crüger (1598–1662)

Hail to the Lord's A - noint - ed, great Da - vid's great - er Son! Hail, in the time ap - point - ed, His reign on earth be - gun! He comes to break op - pres - sion, to set the cap - tive___ free, to

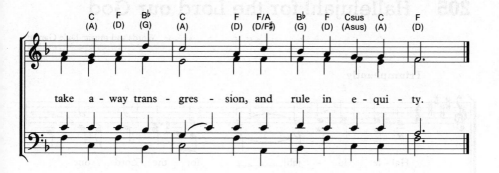

take a-way trans-gres-sion, and rule in e-qui-ty.

1 Hail to the Lord's anointed,
great David's greater Son!
Hail, in the time appointed,
His reign on earth begun!
He comes to break oppression,
to set the captive free,
to take away transgression,
and rule in equity.

2 He comes with succour speedy
to those who suffer wrong;
to help the poor and needy,
and bid the weak be strong;
to give them songs for sighing,
their darkness turn to light,
whose souls, condemned and dying,
were precious in His sight.

3 He shall come down like showers
upon the fruitful earth;
Love, joy, and hope, like flowers,
spring in His path to birth:
before Him, on the mountains,
shall peace the herald go,
and righteousness in fountains
from hill to valley flow.

4 Kings shall fall down before Him,
and gold and incense bring;
all nations shall adore Him,
His praise all people sing;
to Him shall prayer unceasing
and daily vows ascend;
His kingdom still increasing,
a kingdom without end.

5 O'er every foe victorious,
He on His throne shall rest;
from age to age more glorious,
all-blessing and all-blest.
The tide of time shall never
His covenant remove;
His name shall stand for ever,
His changeless name of Love.

205 Hallelujah! for the Lord our God

Words and music: Dale Garratt

Triumphantly

Hal - le - lu - jah!_____ for the Lord our God the Al - migh - ty_____ reigns.

Let us re - joice_____ and be glad_____ and give the glo - ry un - to Him._____ Hal - le - lu - jah! for the Lord our God the Al - migh - ty____ reigns._____

206 Hallelujah, my Father

Words and music: Tim Cullen
Music arranged David Peacock

With quiet devotion

Hal - le - lu - jah, my Father, for giv - ing us Your Son; send - ing Him in to the world to be giv - en up for men, know - ing we would bruise Him and smite Him from the

earth. Hal - le - lu - jah, my _ Fa - ther, in His

death is my birth; _ Hal - le - lu - jah, my _

Fa - ther, in His life _ is my life. _

Hallelujah, my Father,
for giving us Your Son;
sending Him into the world
to be given up for men,
knowing we would bruise Him
and smite Him from the earth.
Hallelujah, my Father,
in His death is my birth;
Hallelujah, my Father,
in His life is my life.

207 Hallelujah! sing to Jesus

HALLELUJAH 87 87 D

Words: W C Dix (1837–98) altd.
Music: S S Wesley (1810–76)

Hal - le - lu - jah! sing to Je - sus, His the scep-tre, His the throne;

Hal - le - lu - jah! His the tri-umph, His the _ vic - to - ry a - lone.

Hark! the songs of peace-ful Si - on thun-der _ like a migh-ty flood;

Je - sus out of ev - ery _ na-tion hath re - deemed us _ by His blood.

1   Hallelujah! sing to Jesus,
     His the sceptre, His the throne;
     Hallelujah! His the triumph,
     His the victory alone.
     Hark! the songs of peaceful Zion
     thunder like a mighty flood;
     Jesus out of every nation
     hath redeemed us by His blood.

2   Hallelujah! not as orphans
     are we left in sorrow now;
     Hallelujah! He is near us,
     Faith believes, nor questions how.
     Though the cloud from sight received Him
     when the forty days were o'er,
     shall our hearts forget His promise,
     'I am with you evermore'?

3   Hallelujah! bread of heaven!
     Thou on earth our food, our stay;
     Hallelujah! here the sinful
     flee to Thee from day to day.
     Intercessor, friend of sinners,
     Earth's Redeemer, plead for me,
     where the songs of all the sinless
     sweep across the crystal sea.

4   Hallelujah! Hallelujah!
     Glory be to God on high;
     to the Father, and the Saviour,
     who has gained the victory;
     glory to the Holy Spirit,
     fount of love and sanctity.
     Hallelujah! Hallelujah!
     to the triune Majesty.

208   'Hallelujah', sing to the Lord

Words and music: Steve and Gina Southworth
Music arranged Christopher Norton

209
Hark, my soul

St Bees   77 77

Words: William Cowper (1731–1800)
Music: John Bacchus Dykes (1823–76)

1 Hark, my soul! it is the Lord;
   'Tis thy Saviour, hear His word;
   Jesus speaks, and speaks to thee,
   'Say, poor sinner, lov'st thou Me?'

2 'I delivered thee when bound,
   and, when bleeding, healed thy wound;
   sought thee wandering, set thee right,
   turned thy darkness into light.'

3 Can a woman's tender care
   cease towards the child she bare?
   Yes, she may forgetful be,
   yet will I remember Thee.

4 'Mine is an unchanging love,
   higher than the heights above,
   deeper than the depths beneath,
   free and faithful, strong as death.'

5 'Thou shalt see My glory soon,
   when the work of grace is done;
   partner of My throne shalt be;
   say, poor sinner, lov'st thou Me?'

6 Lord! it is my chief complaint
   that my love is weak and faint;
   yet I love Thee, and adore:
   O for grace to love Thee more!

210 Hark, the glad sound

St Saviour   CM

Words: Philip Dodderidge (1702–51)
in this version Horrobin/Leavers
Music: F G Baker (1840–1908)

1   Hark, the glad sound! the Saviour comes,
    the Saviour promised long;
    let every heart prepare a throne,
    and every voice a song.

2   He comes, the prisoners to release
    in Satan's bondage held;
    the chains of sin before Him break,
    the iron fetters yield.

3   He comes to free the captive mind
    where evil thoughts control;
    and for the darkness of the blind,
    gives light that makes them whole.

4   He comes the broken heart to bind,
    the wounded soul to cure;
    and with the treasures of His grace
    to enrich the humble poor.

5   Our glad hosannas, Prince of Peace,
    Your welcome shall proclaim;
    and heaven's eternal arches ring
    with Your belovèd name.

211   Hark! the herald-angels sing

MENDELSSOHN   77 77 D with refrain

Words: Charles Wesley (1707–88) and others
Music: F Mendelssohn-Bartholdy (1809–47)
arranged W H Cummings (1831–1915)

Hark! the her - ald - an-gels sing_ 'Glo-ry to the new-born King!

Peace on earth, and mer-cy mild,_ God and sin - ners re - con-ciled.'

Joy-ful, all you na-tions rise,_ join the tri-umph of the skies;_

with th'an-gel - ic host pro - claim,_ 'Christ is_ born in Beth-le-hem!'

Hark! the her-ald - an-gels sing___ 'Glo-ry___ to the new-born King!'

1   Hark! the herald-angels sing
    'Glory to the new-born King!
    Peace on earth, and mercy mild,
    God and sinners reconciled.'
    Joyful, all you nations rise,
    join the triumph of the skies;
    with the angelic host proclaim,
    'Christ is born in Bethlehem!'
        Hark! the herald-angels sing
        'Glory to the new-born King!'

2   Christ by highest heaven adored,
    Christ, the everlasting Lord,
    late in time behold Him come,
    offspring of a virgin's womb!
    Veiled in flesh the Godhead see!
    Hail, the incarnate Deity!
    Pleased as man with man to dwell,
    Jesus, our Immanuel.
        Hark! the herald-angels sing
        'Glory to the new-born King!'

3   Hail, the heaven-born Prince of Peace!
    Hail, the Sun of righteousness!
    Light and life to all He brings,
    risen with healing in His wings.
    Mild He lays His glory by,
    born that man no more may die;
    born to raise the sons of earth,
    born to give them second birth.
        Hark! the herald-angels sing
        'Glory to the new-born King!'

212 Have Thine own way, Lord

THINE OWN WAY, LORD   54 54 D

Words: A A Pollard (1862–1934)
Music: George C Stebbins (1846–1945)

1 Have Thine own way, Lord,
　　have Thine own way;
　Thou art the potter, I am the clay;
　mould me and make me after Thy will,
　while I am waiting, yielded and still.

2 Have Thine own way, Lord,
　　have Thine own way;
　search me and try me, Master, today.
　Whiter than snow, Lord, wash me just now,
　as in Thy presence humbly I bow.

3 Have Thine own way, Lord,
　　have Thine own way;
　wounded and weary, help me, I pray.
　Power, all power, surely is Thine;
　touch me and heal me, Saviour divine.

4 Have Thine own way, Lord,
　　have Thine own way;
　hold o'er my being absolute sway;
　fill with Thy Spirit till all shall see
　Christ only, always, living in me.

213

He gave me beauty

Words and music: Robert Whitney Manzano
Music arranged Christopher Norton

He gave me beau-ty for ash-es,___ the oil of joy for mourn-ing,___ the gar-ment of praise for the spi-rit of hea-vi - ness; that we might be trees of right-eous-ness, the plant-ing of the Lord, that He might be glo - ri - fied.___

214 He gave His life

SELFLESS LOVE 86 86 D

Words: Christopher Porteous
Music: Andrew Maries

He gave His life in self-less love, for sin-ful man He came;

He had no stain of sin Him-self but bore our guilt and shame:

He took the cup of pain and death, His blood was free - ly shed;

we see His bo - dy on the cross, we share the liv - ing bread.

1 He gave His life in selfless love,
  for sinful man He came;
  He had no stain of sin Himself
  but bore our guilt and shame:
  He took the cup of pain and death,
  His blood was freely shed;
  we see His body on the cross,
  we share the living bread.

2 He did not come to call the good
  but sinners to repent;
  it was the lame, the deaf, the blind
  for whom His life was spent:
  to heal the sick, to find the lost –
  it was for such He came,
  and round His table all may come
  to praise His holy name.

3 They heard Him call His Father's name –
  then 'Finished!' was His cry;
  like them we have forsaken Him
  and left Him there to die:
  the sins that crucified Him then
  are sins His blood has cured;
  the love that bound Him to a cross
  our freedom has ensured.

4 His body broken once for us
  is glorious now above;
  the cup of blessing we receive,
  a sharing of His love:
  as in His presence we partake,
  His dying we proclaim
  until the hour of majesty
  when Jesus comes again.

215   He has showed you

Words and music: Graham Kendrick
Music arranged Christopher Norton

God;   but to   act just-ly, and to   love mer-cy, and to

walk   hum - bly___ with   your   God.

to repeat

last time

He has

He has showed you, O man, what is good –
and what does the Lord require of you?
He has showed you, O man, what is good –
and what does the Lord require of you,
but to act justly, and to love mercy,
and to walk humbly with your God;
but to act justly, and to love mercy,
and to walk humbly with your God.
He has showed . . .

216 He is born, our Lord and Saviour

Words and music: Jimmy Owens

born to bring us light and peace;
for our sins to bring for-give-ness,
from our guilt to bring re-lease.

1 He is born, our Lord and Saviour:
   He is born, our heavenly King:
   give Him honour, give Him glory,
   earth rejoice and heaven sing!
   Born to be our sanctuary,
   born to bring us light and peace;
   for our sins to bring forgiveness,
   from our guilt to bring release.

2 He who is from everlasting
   now becomes the incarnate Word;
   He whose name endures for ever
   now is born the Son of God:
   born to bear our griefs and sorrows,
   born to banish hate and strife;
   born to bear the sin of many,
   born to give eternal life!

3 Hail, the Holy One of Israel,
   chosen heir to David's throne;
   hail the brightness of His rising –
   to His light the gentiles come:
   plunderer of Satan's kingdom,
   downfall of his evil power;
   rescuer of all His people,
   conqueror in death's dark hour!

4 He shall rule with righteous judgement,
   and His godly rule extend;
   governor among the nations,
   His great kingdom has no end:
   He shall reign, the King of glory,
   higher than the kings of earth –
   Alleluia, alleluia!
   Praise we now His holy birth!

217

He is exalted

Words and music: Twila Paris

He is ex-alt-ed, the King is ex-alt-ed on high; I will
praise Him. He is ex-alt-ed, for ev-er ex-alt-ed and
I will praise His name!
He is the Lord; for ev-er His truth shall

He is exalted,
the King is exalted on high;
I will praise Him.
He is exalted,
for ever exalted
and I will praise His name!

He is the Lord;
for ever His truth shall reign.
Heaven and earth
rejoice in His holy name.
He is exalted,
the King is exalted on high.

218   He is here, He is here

Words and music: Jimmy Owens
Music arranged Roland Fudge

name._____ praise and a - dore Him yes - ter -
- day and to - day and for ev - er-more the same._____

1   He is here, He is here,
    He is moving among us;
    He is here, He is here,
    as we gather in His name!
    He is here, He is here,
    and He wants to work a wonder;
    He is here as we gather in His name.

2   He is Lord, He is Lord,
    let us worship before Him;
    He is Lord, He is Lord,
    as we gather in His name!
    He is Lord, He is Lord,
    let us praise and adore Him
    yesterday and today and for evermore the same.

219   He that is in us

Words and music: Graham Kendrick
Music arranged Christopher Norton

Lively

He that is in us is great-er than he that is in the world;

He that is in us is great-er than he that is in_____ the world.

There-fore I will sing and I will re-joice, for His

Spi - rit lives in me.   Christ the liv-ing One has
o - ver-come, and we share in His vic - to - ry.

He that is in us is greater
than he that is in the world;
He that is in us is greater
than he that is in the world.

1   Therefore I will sing and I will rejoice,
    for His Spirit lives in me.
    Christ the living One has overcome,
    and we share in His victory.
        He that is in us . . .

2   All the powers of death and hell and sin
    lie crushed beneath His feet.
    Jesus owns the name above all names,
    crowned with honour and majesty.
        He that is in us . . .

    (*Repeat verse 2, slowly and majestically*)

220   He is Lord, He is Lord

Words and music: Marvin Frey
Music arranged Roland Fudge

He is Lord, He is Lord, He is ris-en from the dead and He is Lord! Ev-ery knee shall bow, ev-ery tongue con - fess that Je - sus Christ is Lord.

221   He walked where I walk

Words and music: Graham Kendrick
Music arranged Christopher Norton

LEADER
1 He walked where I___ walk, He walked where I___ walk,
2 One of a ha - ted race, one of a ha - ted race,

LEADER
He stood where I___ stand, He stood where I___ stand,
stung by the pre - ju - dice, stung by the pre - ju - dice,

Allegro moderato

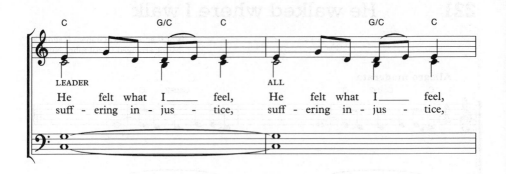

He felt what I____ feel,   He felt what I____ feel,
suff - ering in - jus - tice,   suff - ering in - jus - tice,

He un - der - stands, He un - der - stands.
yet He for - gives, yet He for - gives.

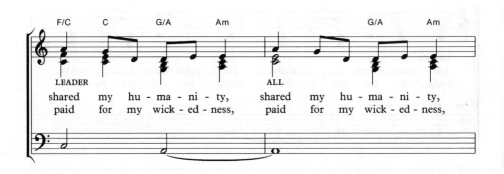

He knows my frail - ty,   He knows my frail - ty,
Wept for my wast - ed years,   wept for my wast - ed years,

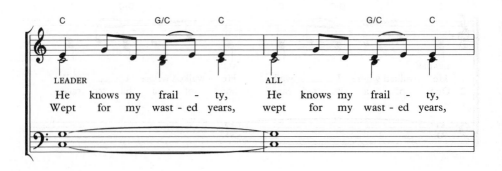

shared my hu - ma - ni - ty,   shared my hu - ma - ni - ty,
paid for my wick - ed - ness,   paid for my wick - ed - ness,

222   He was pierced

Words and music: Maggi Dawn
Music arranged Christopher Norton

1 He was pierced for our trans - gres - sions, ___ and bruised for our in-i - qui - ties; and to bring us peace He was pun - ished, ___ and by His

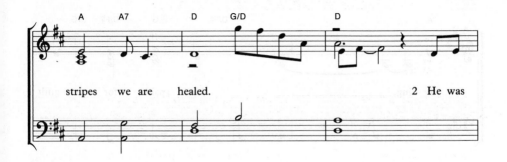

stripes   we are   healed.   2 He was

led   like   a   lamb___   to   the   slaugh-ter,_____

___   al - though He   was   in - no - cent of   crime;

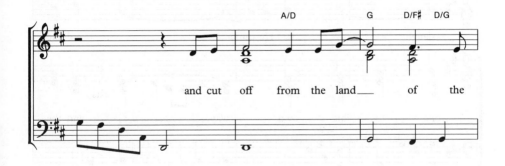

and cut   off   from the land___   of   the

1   He was pierced for our transgressions,
    and bruised for our iniquities;
    and to bring us peace He was punished,
    and by His stripes we are healed.

2   He was led like a lamb to the slaughter,
    although He was innocent of crime;
    and cut off from the land of the living,
    He paid for the guilt that was mine.

    We like sheep have gone astray,
    turned each one to his own way,
    and the Lord has laid on Him
    the iniquity of us all.
    We like sheep . . .

223   He who dwells

Words and music: Chris Bowater

and I'll say of the Lord He is__ my strength._____

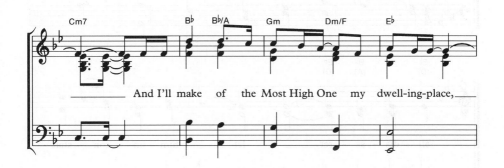

_____ And I'll make of the Most High One my dwell-ing-place,___

_____ and I'll say He is__ my God,___ I'll say He is__ my

God,__ I will say He is my God in whom I trust._____

224 He who would valiant be

MONKS GATE 65 65 66 65

Words: after John Bunyan (1628–88)
Percy Dearmer (1867–1936)
Music: English traditional melody
arranged R Vaughan Williams (1872–1958)

He who would valiant be 'gainst all dis-as-ter, let him in con-stan-cy fol-low the Mas-ter. There's no dis-cour-age-ment shall make him once re-

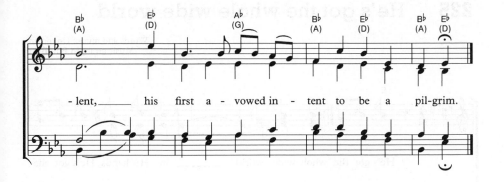

-lent,_____ his first a - vowed in - tent to be a pil-grim.

1 He who would valiant be
  'gainst all disaster,
  let him in constancy
  follow the Master.
  There's no discouragement
  shall make him once relent,
  his first avowed intent
  to be a pilgrim.

2 Who so beset him round
  with dismal stories,
  so but themselves confound –
  his strength the more is.
  No foes shall stay his might,
  though he with giants fight:
  he will make good his right
  to be a pilgrim.

3 Since, Lord, Thou dost defend
  us with Thy Spirit,
  we know we at the end
  shall life inherit.
  Then fancies flee away!
  I'll fear not what men say,
  I'll labour night and day
  to be a pilgrim.

225   He's got the whole wide world

Words and music: Unknown
Music arranged Phil Burt

1 He's got the whole wide world in His hands,
  He's got the whole wide world in His hands,
  He's got the whole wide world in His hands,
  He's got the whole world in His hands.

2 He's got everybody here, in His hands, . . .

3 He's got the tiny little baby, in His hands . . .

4 He's got you and me brother, in His hands . . .

226   Healing God, almighty Father

HYFRYDOL   87 87 D

Words: John Richards
Music: R H Prichard (1811–87)

Heal - ing God,__ al - migh - ty Fa - ther, ac - tive__ through - out__ his - to - ry; ev - er sav - ing, guid - ing, work - ing for__ Your child - ren__ to__ be free. Shep - herd, King,__ in -

-spir - ing pro - phets to____ fore - see____ Your

suf - fering role ___ Lord,_ we raise__ our prayers and

voi - ces;_ make_ us one____ and make us whole.

1 Healing God, almighty Father,
   active throughout history;
   ever saving, guiding, working
   for Your children to be free.
   Shepherd, King, inspiring prophets
   to foresee Your suffering role –
   Lord, we raise our prayers and voices;
   make us one and make us whole.

2 Healing Christ, God's Word incarnate,
   reconciling man to man;
   God's atonement, dying for us
   in His great redemptive plan.
   'Jesus', Saviour, Healer, Victor,
   drawing out for us death's sting;
   Lord, we bow our hearts in worship,
   and united praises bring.

3 Healing Spirit, Christ-anointing,
   raising to new life in Him;
   help the poor; release to captives;
   cure of body; health within.
   Life-renewing and empowering
   Christ-like service to the lost;
   Lord, we pray 'Renew Your wonders
   as of a New Pentecost!'

4 Healing Church, called-out and chosen
   to enlarge God's kingdom here;
   Lord-obeying; Spirit-strengthened
   to bring God's salvation near:
   for creation's reconciling
   gifts of love in us release.
   Father, Son and Holy Spirit
   'Make us instruments of peace.'

227

Hear my cry, O God

Words and music: Andy Silver

Hear my cry, O God, lis - ten to my prayer; from the ends of the earth will I call to You. Hear my cry, O God, when my heart is o - ver - whelmed; lead me to the Rock that is high-er than I.

Teach me to trust in You,_____ to pour out my heart to You;

You're my help, my re-fuge and my strength. Hear my cry, O

God, lis - ten to my prayer; from the

ends of the earth will I call to You; hear my cry, O God.

228 Here from the world we turn

TRYST   64 64 66 64

Words: Frances van Alstyne (1820–1915)
(Fanny J Crosby)
Music: William H Doane (1832–1915)

Here from the world we turn, Je - sus to seek;

here may His lov - ing voice gra - cious - ly speak!

Je - sus, our dear - est friend, while at Thy feet we bend,

oh, let Thy smile de - scend! 'tis Thee we seek.

1 Here from the world we turn, Jesus to seek;
   here may His loving voice graciously speak!
   Jesus, our dearest friend, while at Thy feet we bend,
   oh, let Thy smile descend! 'tis Thee we seek.

2 Come, Holy Comforter, Presence divine,
   now in our longing hearts graciously shine!
   Oh, for Thy mighty power! Oh, for a blessed shower,
   filling this hallowed hour with joy divine.

3 Saviour, Thy work revive! Here may we see
   those who are dead in sin quickened by Thee!
   Come to our hearts' delight, make every burden light,
   cheer Thou our waiting sight; we long for Thee.

229   Here I am

Words and music: Chris Bowater

Here I am, wholly available –
as for me, I will serve the Lord.

1 The fields are white unto harvest
   but oh, the labourers are so few;
   so Lord I give myself to help the reaping,
   to gather precious souls unto You.
     Here I am . . .

2 The time is right in the nation
   for works of power and authority;
   God's looking for a people who are willing
   to be counted in His glorious victory.
     Here I am . . .

3 As salt are we ready to savour,
   in darkness are we ready to be light;
   God's seeking out a very special people
   to manifest His truth and His might.
     Here I am . . .

230 Here, O my Lord

TOULON 10 10 10 10

Words: Horatius Bonar (1808–89)
Music: Louis Bourgeois (1510–61)

Here, O my Lord, I see Thee face to face;

here__ would I touch and han - dle things un - seen,

here grasp with firm - er__ hand th'e - ter - nal grace,

and__ all my wea - ri - ness up - on__ Thee__ lean.

1 Here, O my Lord, I see Thee face to face;
  here would I touch and handle things unseen,
  here grasp with firmer hand th'eternal grace,
  and all my weariness upon Thee lean.

2 Here would I feed upon the bread of God,
  here drink with Thee the royal wine of heaven;
  here would I lay aside each earthly load,
  here taste afresh the calms of sin forgiven.

3 Too soon we rise, the symbols disappear;
  the feast, though not the love, is past and gone;
  the bread and wine remove, but Thou art here,
  nearer than ever, still my shield and sun.

4 I have no help but Thine; nor do I need
  another arm save Thine to lean upon;
  it is enough, my Lord, enough indeed;
  my strength is in Thy might, Thy might alone.

5 Mine is the sin, but Thine the righteousness;
  mine is the guilt, but Thine the cleansing blood;
  here is my robe, my refuge, and my peace –
  Thy blood, Thy righteousness, O Lord my God.

6 Feast after feast thus comes and passes by,
  yet passing, points to the glad feast above,
  giving sweet foretaste of the festal joy,
  the Lamb's great bridal feast of bliss and love.

231 Hévénu shalom

Words: Chorus Israeli traditional song
Verses Michael Baughen
Music: Israeli traditional melody

Hévénu shalom aléchem,
Hévénu shalom aléchem,
Hévénu shalom aléchem,
Hévénu shalom,
shalom, shalom aléchem.

1 Because He died and is risen,
because He died and is risen,
because He died and is risen,
we now have peace with God
    through Jesus Christ our Lord.
    Hévénu shalom . . .

2 His peace destroys walls between us,
His peace destroys walls between us,
His peace destroys walls between us,
for only He can reconcile
    us both to God.
    Hévénu shalom . . .

3 My peace I give you, said Jesus,
My peace I give you, said Jesus,
My peace I give you, said Jesus,
don't let your heart be troubled,
    do not be afraid.
    Hévénu shalom . . .

4 The peace beyond understanding,
the peace beyond understanding,
the peace beyond understanding,
will guard the hearts and minds
    of those who pray to Him.
    Hévénu shalom . . .

232 His hands were pierced

Words and music: D Woods

1 His hands were pierced, the hands that made
   the mountain range and everglade;
   that washed the stains of sin away
   and changed earth's darkness into day.

2 His feet were pierced, the feet that trod
   the furthest shining star of God;
   and left their imprint deep and clear
   on every winding pathway here.

3 His heart was pierced, the heart that burned
   to comfort every heart that yearned;
   and from it came a cleansing flood,
   the river of redeeming blood.

4 His hands and feet and heart, all three
   were pierced for me on Calvary;
   and here and now, to Him I bring
   my hands, feet, heart, an offering.

233

His name is higher

Words and music: Unknown
Music arranged Roger Mayor

234   His name is wonderful

Words and music: Audrey Mieir
Music arranged Norman Warren

His name is won-der-ful, His name is won-der-ful,
He is the migh-ty king, Mas-ter of ev-ery-thing,

His name is won-der-ful, Je-sus my Lord.

Je-sus my Lord. He's the great Shep-herd, the rock of all a-ges,

al-migh-ty God is He;_____ bow down be-fore Him,

love and a-dore Him, His name is won-der-ful, Je-sus my Lord!

235   Hold me Lord

Words and music: Danny Daniels
Music arranged Christopher Norton

236   Holy child

Words: Timothy Dudley-Smith
Music: Michael Baughen
arranged Phil Burt

Tenderly

1 Ho-ly child,_____ how still You lie! safe the man-ger, soft the hay; faint up-on_____ the east-ern sky breaks the dawn of Christ-mas Day.

2 Ho-ly child,_____ whose birth-day brings shep-herds from their field and fold, an-gel

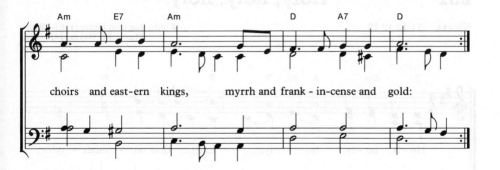

choirs and east-ern kings, myrrh and frank - in-cense and gold:

1 Holy child, how still You lie!
  safe the manger, soft the hay;
  faint upon the eastern sky
  breaks the dawn of Christmas Day.

2 Holy child, whose birthday brings
  shepherds from their field and fold,
  angel choirs and eastern kings,
  myrrh and frankincense and gold:

3 Holy child, what gift of grace
  from the Father freely willed!
  In Your infant form we trace
  all God's promises fulfilled.

4 Holy child, whose human years
  span like ours delight and pain;
  one in human joys and tears,
  one in all but sin and stain:

5 Holy child, so far from home,
  all the lost to seek and save:
  to what dreadful death You come,
  to what dark and silent grave!

6 Holy child, before whose name
  powers of darkness faint and fall;
  conquered death and sin and shame –
  Jesus Christ is Lord of all!

7 Holy child, how still You lie!
  safe the manger, soft the hay;
  clear upon the eastern sky
  breaks the dawn of Christmas Day.

237

Holy, holy, holy

NICAEA 11 12 12 10

Words: Reginald Heber (1783–1826)
Music: J B Dykes (1823–76)

Ho - ly, ho - ly, ho - ly,__ Lord__ God al - migh - ty!

ear - ly in the morn - ing our song shall rise to Thee;__

Ho - ly, ho - ly, ho - ly!__ mer - ci-ful and migh - ty,

God__ in three Per - sons,__ bless - èd Tri - ni - ty!

1 Holy, holy, holy, Lord God almighty!
early in the morning our song shall rise to Thee;
Holy, holy, holy! – merciful and mighty,
God in three Persons, blessèd Trinity!

2 Holy, holy, holy! All the saints adore Thee,
casting down their golden crowns around the glassy sea;
cherubim and seraphim falling down before Thee,
who wast, and art, and evermore shall be.

3 Holy, holy, holy! – though the darkness hide Thee,
though the eye of sinful man Thy glory may not see;
only Thou art holy, there is none beside Thee,
perfect in power, in love, and purity.

4 Holy, holy, holy, Lord God almighty!
all Thy works shall praise Thy name, in earth, and sky, and sea:
Holy, holy, holy! – merciful and mighty,
God in three Persons, blessèd Trinity!

238

Holy, holy

Words and music: Jimmy Owens

Words and music: © 1972 Lexicon Music Inc (USA)/MPI
Ltd/United Nations Music Publishers Ltd/Boosey & Hawkes
Music Publishers Ltd

1   Holy, holy, holy, holy,
    holy, holy, Lord God almighty!
    And we lift our hearts before You
    as a token of our love:
    holy, holy, holy, holy.

2   Gracious Father, gracious Father,
    we're so glad to be Your children, gracious Father;
    as we lift our heads before You
    as a token of our love,
    gracious Father, gracious Father.

3   Precious Jesus, precious Jesus,
    we're so glad that You've redeemed us, precious Jesus;
    and we lift our hands before You
    as a token of our love,
    precious Jesus, precious Jesus.

4   Holy Spirit, Holy Spirit,
    come and fill our hearts anew, Holy Spirit! –
    and we lift our voice before You
    as a token of our love,
    Holy Spirit, Holy Spirit.

5   Hallelujah, hallelujah,
    hallelujah, hallelujah –
    and we lift our hearts before You
    as a token of our love,
    hallelujah, hallelujah.

239   Holy, holy, holy is the Lord

Words and music: Unknown
Music arrangement: Norman Warren

Ho - ly, ho - ly, ho - ly is the Lord;

ho - ly is the Lord God al - migh - ty!

1.

2. - ty! Who was, and is, and is to come!

Ho - ly, ho - ly, ho - ly is the Lord! __

1   Holy, holy, holy is the Lord;
holy is the Lord God almighty!
Holy, holy, holy is the Lord;
holy is the Lord God almighty!
Who was, and is, and is to come!
Holy, holy, holy is the Lord!

2   Jesus, Jesus, Jesus is the Lord;
Jesus is the Lord God almighty!
Jesus, Jesus, Jesus is the Lord;
Jesus is the Lord God almighty!
Who was, and is, and is to come!
Jesus, Jesus, Jesus is the Lord!

3   Worthy, worthy worthy is the Lord;
worthy is the Lord God almighty!
Worthy, worthy worthy is the Lord;
worthy is the Lord God almighty!
Who was, and is, and is to come!
Worthy, worthy, worthy is the Lord!

4   Glory, glory, glory to the Lord;
glory to the Lord God almighty!
Glory, glory, glory to the Lord;
glory to the Lord God almighty!
Who was, and is, and is to come!
Glory, glory, glory to the Lord!

240

Holy is the Lord

Words and music: Kelly Green
Music arranged Christopher Norton

Majestically

MEN AND WOMEN IN CANON

Right-eous-ness_____ and mer - cy,   Judge - ment_____ and

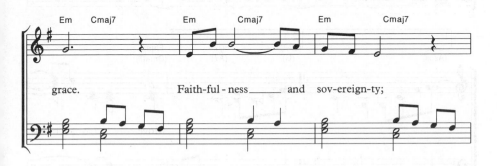

grace.   Faith-ful - ness_____ and sov-ereign-ty;

Ho - ly   is   the Lord,   Ho - ly   is   the

Lord.   Lord._____

241   Holy Spirit, we welcome You

Words and music: Chris Bowater

Ho - ly Spi - rit,— we wel - come You,— Move a - mong us with ho - ly fire— as we lay a - side— all earth - ly de - sire,

2 Holy Spirit, we welcome You,
   Holy Spirit, we welcome You!
   Let the breeze of Your presence blow
   that Your children here might truly know
   how to move in the Spirit's flow.
   Holy Spirit, Holy Spirit,
   Holy Spirit, we welcome You!

3 Holy Spirit, we welcome You,
   Holy Spirit, we welcome You!
   Please accomplish in us today
   some new work of loving grace, we pray –
   unreservedly – have Your way.
   Holy Spirit, Holy Spirit,
   Holy Spirit, we welcome You!

242 Hosanna, hosanna

Words and music: Carl Tuttle

Lively

1 Ho - san - na, ho - san - na, ho-san-na in the high - est; ho - san - na, ho - san - na, ho-san-na in the high - est:
2 Glo - ry, glo - ry, glo-ry to the King of kings; glo - ry, glo - ry, glo-ry to the King of kings:

Lord, we lift up Your name, with hearts full of praise.

1   Hosanna, hosanna, hosanna in the highest;
    hosanna, hosanna, hosanna in the highest:
    Lord, we lift up Your name,
    with hearts full of praise.
    Be exalted, O Lord my God –
    hosanna, in the highest.

2   Glory, glory, glory to the King of kings;
    glory, glory, glory to the King of kings:
    Lord, we lift up Your name
    with hearts full of praise.
    Be exalted, O Lord my God –
    glory to the King of kings.

243 How firm a foundation

MONTGOMERY 11 11 11 11

Words: 'K' in Rippon's *Selection*, 1787 altd.
Music: probably Samuel Jarvis (d 1785)

How firm a foun - da - tion, ye saints of the Lord,

is laid for your faith in His ex - cel - lent word;

what more can He say than to you He hath said, ___

you ___ who un - to Je - sus for re - fuge have fled?

1 How firm a foundation, ye saints of the Lord,
is laid for your faith in His excellent word;
what more can He say than to you He hath said,
you who unto Jesus for refuge have fled?

2 Fear not, He is with thee, O be not dismayed;
for He is thy God, and will still give thee aid:
He'll strengthen thee, help thee, and cause thee to stand,
upheld by His righteous, omnipotent hand.

3 In every condition, in sickness, in health,
in poverty's vale, or abounding in wealth;
at home and abroad, on the land, on the sea,
as thy days may demand shall thy strength ever be.

4 When through the deep waters He calls thee to go,
the rivers of grief shall not thee overflow;
for He will be with thee in trouble to bless,
and sanctify to thee thy deepest distress.

5 When through fiery trials thy pathway shall lie,
His grace all-sufficient shall be thy supply;
the flame shall not hurt thee, His only design
thy dross to consume and thy gold to refine.

6 The soul that on Jesus has leaned for repose
He will not, He will not, desert to its foes;
that soul, though all hell should endeavour to shake,
He'll never, no never, no never forsake.

244 How good is the God we adore

CELESTE LM

Words: Joseph Hart (1712–68)
Music: from *Lancashire Sunday School Songs*, 1857

How good is the God we a-dore! Our faith-ful, un-change-a-ble friend: His love is as great as His power and knows nei-ther mea-sure nor end.

1 How good is the God we adore!
   Our faithful, unchangeable friend:
   His love is as great as His power
   and knows neither measure nor end.

2 For Christ is the first and the last;
   His Spirit will guide us safe home:
   we'll praise Him for all that is past
   and trust Him for all that's to come.

245 How great is our God

Words and music: Unknown
Music arranged Phil Burt

With life

How great is our God,_____ how great is His name,_____

__ how great is His love_____ for - ev - er the same._____

__ He rolled back the wa - ters_____ of the migh-ty Red Sea,_____

__ and He said, 'I'll ne-ver leave you,_____ put your trust in Me.'_____

246 How I love You

Words and music: Keith Green

Brightly

How I love You: You are the One, You are the One;

4th time to Coda

how I love You: You are the One for me!

1 I was so lost, but You showed the way – 'cause You are the Way;
2 I was lied to, but You told the truth – 'cause You are the Truth;
3 I was dy - ing, but You gave me life – 'cause You are the Life;

I was so lost, but You showed the way to me.
I was lied to, but You showed the truth to me.
I was dy - ing, and You gave Your life for me.

⊕ **CODA**

You are the One – God's ri-sen Son, You are the One, for__ me!

4 Hal - le - lu - jah! You are the One,
How I love You: You are the One,_

You are the One;__ Hal - le - lu - jah!
You are the One;__ how I love You:

You are the One for me!
You are the One for me!

247   How lovely is Thy dwelling-place

Words: from Psalm 84
Music: Scottish traditional folk melody
arranged Jonathan Asprey

1 and 4   How_ love - ly   is_____ Thy_____ dwell-ing-place,
2   Ev - en   the spar - row_____ finds a home_
3   And I'd ra - ther be_____ a_____ door-keep-er_

O_ Lord of hosts, to_ me;_____ my_
where_ he can set-tle_ down;_____ and the
and_____ on - ly stay_ a_ day,_____ than_

soul   is   long-ing and   faint - ing   the_ courts of the
swal - low,   she_ can   build a_   nest   where she   may
live   the   life of a   sin -   ner   and_ have to_

Lord   to_   see._   My_ heart   and   flesh, they are
lay_   her_   young,_   with - in   the   courts of the
stay_ a - way._   For the Lord   is   shi - ning

sing - ing   for_ joy   to the   liv - ing_   God;_
Lord_ of_ hosts,   my_ King,   my_ Lord, and my_   God;_
as_ the_ sun,   and the Lord,   He's   like_ a_   shield;_

248 How lovely is Thy dwelling-place

Words: from Psalm 84
Music: Unknown
arranged Phil Burt

How love-ly is Thy dwell-ing-place, O Lord of hosts, my soul longs and yearns for Your courts, _____ and my heart and flesh sing for joy to the liv-ing God. _____ One

249   How lovely on the mountains

Words and music: Leonard E Smith Jnr
Music arranged David Peacock

Lyrics:
How love-ly on the moun-tains are the feet of Him who brings good news, good news, pro-claim-ing peace, an-nounc-ing news of hap-pi-ness, Our God reigns, our God reigns!

Our God reigns,_____ our God reigns,_____

our God reigns,_____ our God reigns!_____

POPULAR VERSION

1 How lovely on the mountains are the feet of Him
   who brings good news, good news,
   proclaiming peace, announcing news of happiness,
   Our God reigns, our God reigns!
       Our God reigns, our God reigns! (*twice*)

2 You watchmen lift your voices joyfully as one,
   shout for your King, your King.
   See eye to eye the Lord restoring Zion:
   your God reigns, your God reigns!

3 Waste places of Jerusalem break forth with joy,
   We are redeemed, redeemed.
   The Lord has saved and comforted His people:
   your God reigns, your God reigns!

4 Ends of the earth, see the salvation of your God,
   Jesus is Lord, is Lord.
   Before the nations He has bared His holy arm:
   your God reigns, your God reigns!

Original version of words overleaf

1 How lovely on the mountains are the feet of Him
  who brings good news, good news,
  proclaiming peace, announcing news of happiness,
  Our God reigns, our God reigns!
      Our God reigns, our God reigns! (*twice*)

2 He had no stately form, He had no majesty,
  that we should be drawn to Him.
  He was despised and we took no account of Him,
  yet now He reigns with the Most High.
      Now He reigns, now He reigns,
      now He reigns with the Most High!

3 It was our sin and guilt that bruised and wounded Him,
  it was our sin that brought Him down.
  When we like sheep had gone astray, our Shepherd came
  and on His shoulders bore our shame.
      On His shoulders, on His shoulders,
      on His shoulders He bore our shame.

4 Meek as a lamb that's led out to the slaughterhouse,
  dumb as a sheep before its shearer,
  His life ran down upon the ground like pouring rain,
  that we might be born again.
      That we might be, that we might be,
      that we might be born again.

5 Out from the tomb He came with grace and majesty,
  He is alive, He is alive.
  God loves us so – see here His hands, His feet, His side,
  Yes, we know He is alive.
      He is alive, He is alive,
      He is alive, He is alive!

6 How lovely on the mountains are the feet of Him
  who brings good news, good news,
  announcing peace, proclaiming news of happiness:
  our God reigns, our God reigns.
      Our God reigns, our God reigns,
      our God reigns, our God reigns!

250 How shall they hear

OMBERSLEY LM

Words: Timothy Dudley-Smith
Music: W H Gladstone (1840–91)

1 How shall they hear, who have not heard
news of a Lord who loved and came?
nor known His reconciling word,
nor learned to trust the Saviour's name?

2 To all the world, to every place,
neighbours and friends and far-off lands,
preach the good news of saving grace;
go while the great commission stands.

3 'Whom shall I send?' who hears the call,
constant in prayer, through toil and pain,
telling of one who died for all,
to bring a lost world home again?

4 'Lord, here am I,' Your fire impart
to this poor cold self-centred soul;
touch but my lips, my hands, my heart,
and make a world for Christ my goal.

5 Spirit of love, within us move:
Spirit of truth, in power come down!
So shall they hear and find and prove
Christ is their life, their joy, their crown.

251 How sweet the name of Jesus

St Peter   CM

Words: John Newton (1725–1807) altd.
Music: A R Reinagle (1799–1877)

1 How sweet the name of Jesus sounds
in a believer's ear!
It soothes his sorrows, heals his wounds,
and drives away his fear.

2 It makes the wounded spirit whole,
and calms the troubled breast;
'tis manna to the hungry soul,
and to the weary rest.

3 Dear name! the rock on which I build,
my shield and hiding-place,
my never-failing treasury, filled
with boundless stores of grace.

4 Jesus! my shepherd, brother, friend,
my prophet, priest and king;
my lord, my life, my way, my end,
accept the praise I bring.

5 Weak is the effort of my heart,
and cold my warmest thought;
but when I see Thee as Thou art,
I'll praise Thee as I ought.

6 Till then I would Thy love proclaim
with every fleeting breath;
and may the music of Thy name
refresh my soul in death!

252 How precious, O Lord

Words and music: Phil Rogers
Music arranged Christopher Norton

Words and music: © 1982 Thankyou Music,
PO Box 75, Eastbourne, East Sussex BN23 6NW, UK

253 Hushed was the evening hymn

SAMUEL 66 66 88

Words: J D Burns (1823–64)
altered Horrobin/Leavers
Music: Arthur S Sullivan (1842–1900)

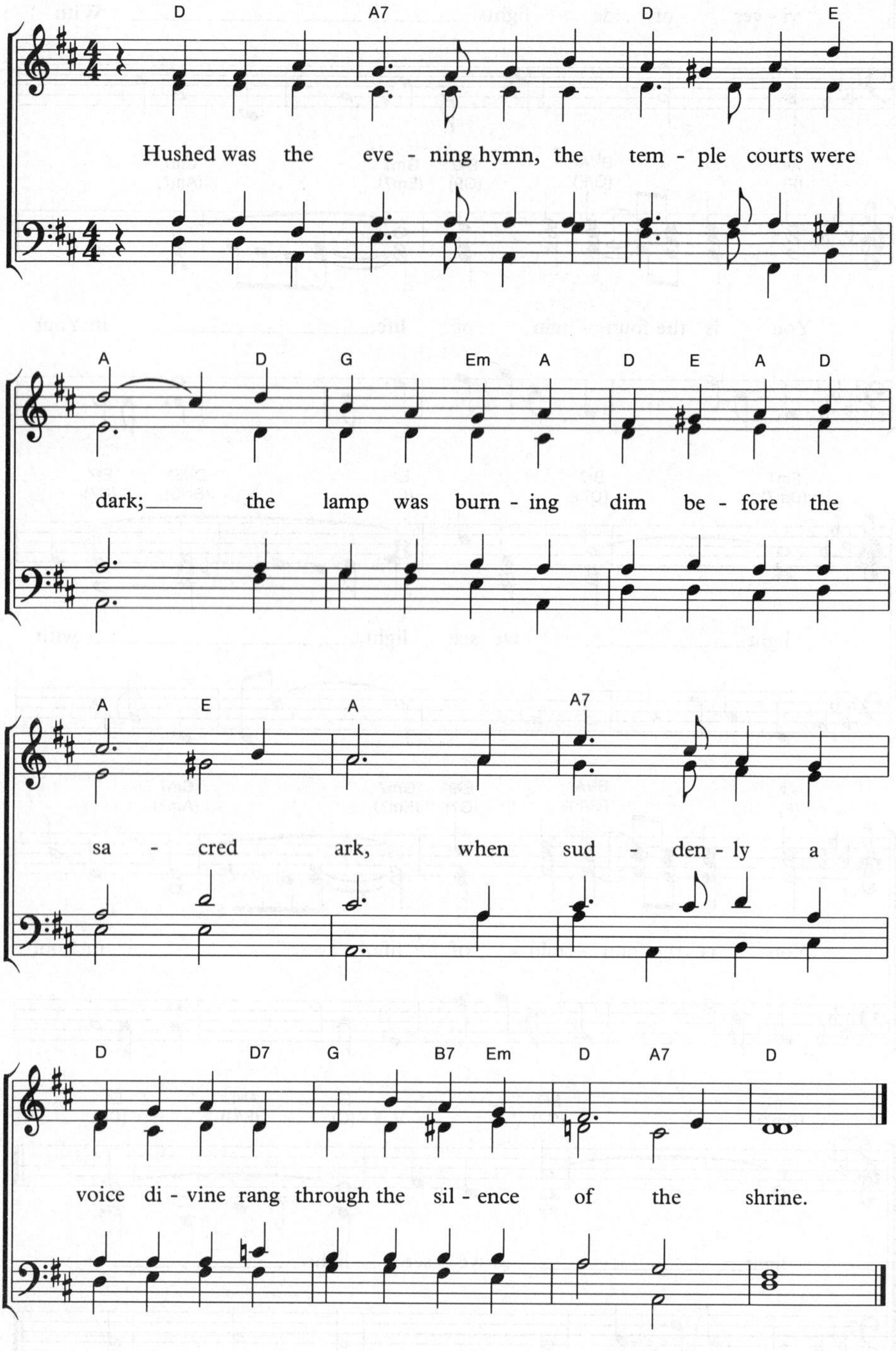

D A7 D E
Hushed was the eve - ning hymn, the tem - ple courts were
A D G Em A D E A D
dark; the lamp was burn - ing dim be - fore the
A E A A7
sa - cred ark, when sud - den - ly a
D D7 G B7 Em D A7 D
voice di - vine rang through the sil - ence of the shrine.

1   Hushed was the evening hymn,
    the temple courts were dark;
    the lamp was burning dim
    before the sacred ark,
    when suddenly a voice divine
    rang through the silence of the shrine.

2   The old man, meek and mild,
    the priest of Israel, slept;
    his watch the temple child,
    the little Samuel, kept:
    and what from Eli's sense was sealed
    the Lord to Hannah's son revealed.

3   O give me Samuel's ear,
    the open ear, O Lord,
    alive and quick to hear
    each whisper of Your word –
    like him to answer at Your call,
    and to obey You first of all.

4   O give me Samuel's heart,
    a lowly heart, that waits
    to serve and play the part
    You show us at Your gates,
    by day and night, a heart that still
    moves at the breathing of Your will.

5   O give me Samuel's mind,
    a sweet, unmurmuring faith,
    obedient and resigned
    to You in life and death,
    that I may read with childlike eyes
    truths that are hidden from the wise.

254   I am a new creation

Words and music: Dave Bilbrough
Music arranged David Peacock

I am a new creation, no more in con-demnation, here in the grace of God I stand. My heart is o-ver-flow-ing, my love just keeps on grow-ing, here in the grace of God I stand. And I will praise

255

I am a wounded soldier

Words and music: Danny Daniels
Music arranged Christopher Norton

Gospel feel

Capo 3(D)

I am a wound-ed sol - dier_ but I will not leave the fight,___ be - cause the Great Phy-si - cian is heal - ing_ me.__ So I'm_ stand-ing in the bat - tle,_ in the

I am a wounded soldier
but I will not leave the fight,
because the Great Physician is healing me.

So I'm standing in the battle,
in the armour of His light,
because His mighty power is real in me.

I am loved, I am accepted
by the Saviour of my soul;
I am loved, I am accepted
and my wounds will be made whole.

256

I am not mine own

Words and music: Chris Bowater

1 I am not mine own,
I've been bought with a price.
Precious blood of Christ,
I am not mine own.

2 I belong to You,
I've been bought with a price.
Precious blood of Christ,
I belong to You.

3 How could I ever say
'I will choose another way',
knowing the price that's paid;
precious blood of Christ.

257

I am not skilled

Ewhurst   88 87

Words: Dora Greenwell (1821–82)
altered Horrobin/Leavers
Music: Cecil John Allen (1886–1973)

1   I am not skilled to understand
    what God has willed, what God has planned;
    I only know at His right hand
    stands One who is my Saviour.

2   I take Him at His word indeed:
    'Christ died for sinners,' this I read;
    and in my heart I find a need
    of Him to be my Saviour.

3   That He should leave His place on high
    and come for sinful man to die,
    you count it strange? so once did I,
    before I knew my Saviour.

4   And O that He fulfilled may see
    the glory of His life in me,
    and with His work contented be,
    as I with my dear Saviour.

5   Yea, living, dying, let me bring
    my life, to Him an offering,
    that He who lives to be my King
    once died to be my Saviour.

258 I am trusting Thee

BULLINGER   85 83

Words: Frances Ridley Havergal (1836–79)
Music: E W Bullinger (1837–1913)

1 I am trusting Thee, Lord Jesus,
   trusting only Thee;
   trusting Thee for full salvation,
   great and free.

2 I am trusting Thee for pardon,
   at Thy feet I bow;
   for Thy grace and tender mercy,
   trusting now.

3 I am trusting Thee for cleansing
   in the crimson flood;
   trusting Thee to make me holy
   by Thy blood.

4 I am trusting Thee to guide me;
   Thou alone shalt lead,
   every day and hour supplying
   all my need.

5 I am trusting Thee for power,
   Thine can never fail;
   words which Thou Thyself shalt give me
   must prevail.

6 I am trusting Thee, Lord Jesus;
   never let me fall;
   I am trusting Thee for ever,
   and for all.

259

I am trusting in You

Words and music: Andy and Becky Silver

260

I am the Bread

Words and music: Brian Hoare

1 I am the Bread, the Bread of Life; who comes to
me will ne - ver hun - ger. I am the Bread, the Bread of
heaven; who feeds on me will ne - ver die. *And as you*
eat, re - mem - ber me — my bo - dy

(2) Vine, the liv - ing Vine; a - part from
me you can do no - thing. I am the Vine, the re - al
Vine: a - bide in me and I in you. *And as you*
drink, re - mem - ber me — my blood was

(3) bread, and drink this wine, and as you
do, re - ceive this life of mine. All that I am I give to
you, that you may live for ev - er - more.

Fine

1 I am the Bread,
   the Bread of Life;
   who comes to me will never hunger.
   I am the Bread,
   the Bread of heaven;
   who feeds on me will never die.
   And as you eat, remember me –
   my body broken on the tree:
   my life was given to set you free,
   and I'm alive for evermore.

2 I am the Vine,
   the living Vine;
   apart from me you can do nothing.
   I am the Vine,
   the real Vine:
   abide in me and I in you.
   And as you drink, remember me –
   my blood was shed upon the tree:
   my life was given to set you free,
   and I'm alive for evermore.

3 So eat this bread,
   and drink this wine,
   and as you do, receive this life of mine.
   All that I am I give to you,
   that you may live for evermore.

261   I am the Bread of Life

Words and music: S Suzanne Toolan
Music arranged Betty Pulkingham

Rich and full

Capo 3(G)

1   I am the Bread of Life;___ he who comes to Me shall not_
(2) bread that_ I will give___ is My flesh for the life of the
(3) -less___ you_ eat___ of the flesh of the Son of_
4   I am the Re - sur - rec - tion, I___ am the_
(5) Lord,___ we be - lieve___ that_ You___ are the_

hun - ger;_ he who believes in Me shall not thirst.   No one can come to
world;___ and he who eats___ of this bread,   he shall_ live for
Man___ and_ drink_ of His blood, and drink___ of His
Life;___ he who be - lieves___ in Me,   ev - en_ if he
Christ,___ the_ Son___ of God, who___ has

Me_ un - less the_ Fa - ther draw him.
ev - er,___ he shall_ live for ev - er.
blood, you shall not have life with - in you.   *And I will*
die,_ he shall_ live for ev - er.
come_ in - to___ the___ world._

Words and music: © 1971 GIA Publications Inc,
7404 S Mason Avenue, Chicago, IL 60638, USA

262   I am waiting for the dawning

THERE'S A LIGHT   87 87 D

Words: S T Francis (1834–1925)
Music: M L Wostenholm (1887–1959)

I am wait-ing for the dawn-ing of the bright and bless-ed day, when the dark-some night of sor-row shall have van-ished far a-way: when for ev-er with the Sav-iour far be-yond this vale of tears, I shall swell the song of

wor-ship through the ev - er - last - ing years.

1   I am waiting for the dawning
    of the bright and blessed day,
    when the darksome night of sorrow
    shall have vanished far away:
    when for ever with the Saviour
    far beyond this vale of tears,
    I shall swell the song of worship
    through the everlasting years.

2   I am looking at the brightness –
    see, it shineth from afar –
    of the clear and joyous beaming
    of the bright and morning Star.
    Through the dark grey mist of morning
    do I see its glorious light;
    then away with every shadow
    of this sad and weary night.

3   I am waiting for the coming
    of the Lord who died for me;
    oh, His words have thrilled my spirit,
    'I will come again for Thee.'
    I can almost hear His footfall,
    on the threshold of the door,
    and my heart, my heart is longing
    to be with Him evermore.

263   I am weak but Thou art strong

Words: Anon
Music: Traditional melody
arranged Roland Fudge

grant it Jesus, this my plea;____ dai - ly walk-ing close with

Thee,____ let it be, dear Lord, let it be. be.

1 I am weak but Thou art strong,
   Jesus keep me from all wrong;
   I'll be satisfied as long
   as I walk, let me walk, close with Thee.
      Just a closer walk with Thee,
      grant it Jesus, this my plea;
      daily walking close with Thee,
      let it be, dear Lord, let it be.

2 Through this world of toils and snares,
   if I falter, Lord, who cares?
   Who with me my burden shares?
   None but Thee, dear Lord, none but Thee.
      Just a closer walk . . .

3 When my feeble life is o'er,
   time for me will be no more,
   guide me gently, safely home,
   to Thy Kingdom's shore, to Thy shore.
      Just a closer walk . . .

264 I believe in Jesus

Words and music: Marc Nelson

Build 2nd and 3rd times

1 I_____ be-lieve in Je - sus,_
2 and 3 I_____ be-lieve in You, Lord,

I be-lieve He is the Son of God.
I be-lieve You are the Son of God;

I be-lieve He died and rose a-gain,
I be-lieve You died and rose a-gain:

1 I believe in Jesus,
  I believe He is the Son of God.
  I believe He died and rose again,
  I believe He paid for us all.
  And I believe He's here now
  standing in our midst,
  here with the power to heal now
  and the grace to forgive.

2 I believe in You, Lord,
  I believe You are the Son of God;
  I believe You died and rose again:
  I believe You paid for us all:
  MEN   And I believe You're here now,
  WOMEN I believe that You're here
  ALL   standing in our midst.
  MEN   Here with the power to heal now,
  WOMEN with the power to heal
  ALL   and the grace to forgive.

3 I believe in You, Lord . . . *(repeat verse 2)*

  And I believe He's here now
  standing in our midst,
  here with the power to heal now
  and the grace to forgive.

265   I cannot count Your blessings

Words and music: Phil Rogers

I can-not count Your bless-ings, Lord, they're won-der-ful;___ I can't be - gin___ to mea - sure Your___ great love;_____ I can-not count the times You have for - giv - en me and changed me by___ Your

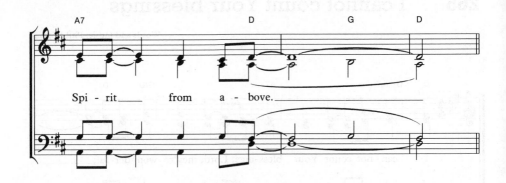

Spi - rit___ from a - bove.___

How I wor - ship You,___ my Fa - ther, You___ are

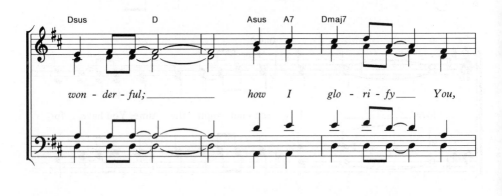

won - der - ful;___ how I glo - ri - fy___ You,

Je - sus, You're my Lord.___ How I praise You, Ho - ly

Spi - rit, You__ have changed my life, and You're

now at work in me to change the world._____

1   I cannot count Your blessings, Lord, they're wonderful;
    I can't begin to measure Your great love;
    I cannot count the times You have forgiven me
    and changed me by Your Spirit from above.
       How I worship You, my Father,
       You are wonderful;
       how I glorify You, Jesus,
       You're my Lord.
       How I praise You, Holy Spirit,
       You have changed my life,
       and You're now at work in me
       to change the world.

2   When I was blind You opened up my eyes to see;
    when I was dead You gave me life anew;
    when I was lost You found me and You rescued me,
    and carried me, rejoicing, home with You.
       How I worship You . . .

3   I cannot count Your mercies, Lord, they're marvellous;
    I can't begin to measure Your great grace;
    I cannot count the times that You have answered me,
    whenever I have prayed and sought Your face.
       How I worship You . . .

4   Whenever I consider what I am to You,
    my heart is filled with wonder, love and awe.
    I want to share with others that You love them too,
    and tell the world of Jesus, more and more.
       How I worship You . . .

266   I cannot tell

LONDONDERRY AIR   Irregular

Words: William Young Fullerton (1857–1932)
Music: Irish traditional melody
arranged Roland Fudge

I can-not tell why He, whom an-gels wor - ship,— should set His love up-on the sons of men,— or why, as Shep - herd, He should seek the wand-erers, to bring them back, they know not how or when.— But this I know, that He was born of Ma - ry,— when Beth - l'em's

man - ger was His on - ly home,____ and that He lived at Na - za - reth and
la - boured, and so the Sav-iour, Sav-iour of the world, is come.__

1   I cannot tell why He, whom angels worship,
    should set His love upon the sons of men,
    or why, as Shepherd, He should seek the wanderers,
    to bring them back, they know not how or when.
    But this I know, that He was born of Mary,
    when Bethlehem's manger was His only home,
    and that He lived at Nazareth and laboured,
    and so the Saviour, Saviour of the world, is come.

2   I cannot tell how silently He suffered,
    as with His peace He graced this place of tears,
    or how His heart upon the cross was broken,
    the crown of pain to three and thirty years.
    But this I know, He heals the broken-hearted,
    and stays our sin, and calms our lurking fear,
    and lifts the burden from the heavy laden,
    for yet the Saviour, Saviour of the world, is here.

3   I cannot tell how He will win the nations,
    how He will claim His earthly heritage,
    how satisfy the needs and aspirations
    of east and west, of sinner and of sage.
    But this I know, all flesh shall see His glory,
    and He shall reap the harvest He has sown,
    and some glad day His sun shall shine in splendour
    when He the Saviour, Saviour of the world, is known.

4   I cannot tell how all the lands shall worship,
    when, at His bidding, every storm is stilled,
    or who can say how great the jubilation
    when all the hearts of men with love are filled.
    But this I know, the skies will thrill with rapture,
    and myriad, myriad human voices sing,
    and earth to heaven, and heaven to earth, will answer:
    At last the Saviour, Saviour of the world, is King!

267   I confess

Words and music: Chris Bowater

I con - fess that Je - sus Christ is Lord,___

I con - fess that Je - sus Christ is Lord.___

He's om - ni - po - tent,_ mag - ni - fi - cent, all glo - rious, vic -

- to - ri - ous;_ I con - fess that Je - sus Christ is Lord.___

268   I delight greatly in the Lord

Words and music: Chris Bowater

269 I do not know what lies ahead

Words and music: Alfred B Smith
and Eugene Clarke

I do not know what lies a-head, the way I can-not see; yet One stands near to be my guide, He'll show the way to me:

I know who holds the fu-ture, and He'll guide me with His hand; with God things don't just hap-pen, ev-ery-thing by Him is planned. So

as I face to-mor-row, with its prob-lems large and small, I'll

trust the God of mir-a-cles, give to Him my all.

1 I do not know what lies ahead,
the way I cannot see;
yet One stands near to be my guide,
He'll show the way to me:
  I know who holds the future,
  and He'll guide me with His hand;
  with God things don't just happen,
  everything by Him is planned.
  So as I face tomorrow,
  with its problems large and small,
  I'll trust the God of miracles,
  give to Him my all.

2 I do not know how many days
of life are mine to spend;
but One who knows and cares for me
will keep me to the end:
  I know who holds . . .

3 I do not know the course ahead,
what joys and griefs are there;
but One is near who fully knows,
I'll trust His loving care:
  I know who holds . . .

270

I get so excited, Lord

Words and music: Mick Ray
Music arranged Christopher Norton

With joy

1 I get so ex-cit - ed, Lord, ev-ery time I re - al - ize

I'm for - giv - en, I'm for - giv - en.

Je - sus Lord, You've done it all, You've paid the price:

I'm for - giv - en, I'm for - giv - en.

Hal - le - lu - jah, Lord, my heart just fills with praise,

1 I get so excited, Lord,
every time I realize
I'm forgiven, I'm forgiven.
Jesus Lord, You've done it all,
You've paid the price:
I'm forgiven, I'm forgiven.
  Hallelujah, Lord,
  my heart just fills with praise,
  my feet start dancing, my hands rise up,
  and my lips they bless Your name.
  I'm forgiven, I'm forgiven, I'm forgiven.
  I'm forgiven, I'm forgiven, I'm forgiven.

2 Living in Your presence, Lord,
is life itself;
I'm forgiven, I'm forgiven.
with the past behind, grace for today,
and a hope to come;
I'm forgiven, I'm forgiven.
  Hallelujah . . .

271   I give You all the honour

Words and music: Carl Tuttle
Music arranged Christopher Norton

Broadly

I give You all the hon-our and praise that's due Your name, for You are the King of glo-ry, the Cre-a-tor of all things._____ *And I wor-ship You,*_____ *I give my life to You,*_____ *I fall*_____ *down on my*

1 I give You all the honour
   and praise that's due Your name,
   for You are the King of glory,
   the Creator of all things.
      And I worship You,
      I give my life to You,
      I fall down on my knees.
      Yes, I worship You,
      I give my life to You,
      I fall down on my knees.

2 As Your Spirit moves upon me now,
   You meet my deepest need,
   and I lift my hands up to Your throne,
   Your mercy, I've received.
      And I worship . . .

3 You have broken chains that bound me,
   You've set this captive free,
   I will lift my voice to praise Your name
   for all eternity.
      And I worship . . .

272   I have decided to follow Jesus

Words and music: Unknown
Music arranged Cliff Barrows
and Don Hustad

1 I have de - cid - ed___ to fo-llow Je - sus,___ I have de -
3 Though none go with me,___ I still will fol - low,___ though none go

-cid - ed___ to fo-llow Je - sus,___ I have de - cid - ed___ to fo-llow
with me,___ I still will fol - low, though none go with me,___ I still will

Je - sus,___ no turn-ing back,___ no turn-ing back.___
fol - low,___ no turn-ing back,___ no turn-ing back.___

2 The world be-hind me,___ the cross be-fore me,___ The world be -
4 Will you de-cide now___ to fol-low Je - sus?___ Will you de -

2 The world be-hind me,___ the cross be-fore me,___
4 Will you de-cide now___ to fol-low Je - sus?___

1   I have decided to follow Jesus, (*3 times*)
    no turning back, no turning back.

2   The world behind me, the cross before me, (*3 times*)
    no turning back, no turning back.

3   Though none go with me, I still will follow, (*3 times*)
    no turning back, no turning back.

4   Will you decide now to follow Jesus? (*3 times*)
    no turning back, no turning back.

273   I hear the sound

Words and music: Dave Moody
Music arranged Roland Fudge

I hear the sound of the ar-my of the Lord;

I hear the sound of the ar-my of the Lord; it's the sound of

praise, it's the sound of war; the ar-my of the Lord, the

ar-my of the Lord, the ar-my of the Lord

is march-ing on.

274   I hear the sound of rustling

Words and music: Ronnie Wilson
Music arranged Roger Mayor

I hear the sound of rust-ling in the leaves of the trees, the
Spi - rit of the Lord has come down on the earth. The
Church that seemed in slum-ber has now ris-en from its knees and
dry bones are res-pond-ing with the fruits of new birth. Oh

what the Fa-ther gives to me I'll sing, I on-ly want to be His breath,____ I on-ly want to glo-ri-fy the King.____

8va

1 I hear the sound of rustling in the leaves of the trees,
the Spirit of the Lord has come down on the earth.
The Church that seemed in slumber has now risen from its knees
and dry bones are responding with the fruits of new birth.
Oh this is now a time for declaration,
the Word will go to all men everywhere,
the Church is here for healing of the nations,
behold the day of Jesus drawing near.
My tongue will be the pen of a ready writer,
and what the Father gives to me I'll sing,
I only want to be His breath,
I only want to glorify the King.

2 And all around the world the body waits expectantly,
the promise of the Father is now ready to fall.
The watchmen on the tower all exhort us to prepare,
and the Church responds – a people who will answer the call.
And this is not a phase which is passing,
it's the start of an age that is to come;
and where is the wise man and the scoffer?
Before the face of Jesus they are dumb.
My tongue will be . . .

3 A body now prepared by God and ready for war,
the prompting of the Spirit is our word of command.
We rise, a mighty army, at the bidding of the Lord,
the devils see and fear, for their time is at hand.
And children of the Lord hear our commission,
that we should love and serve our God as one.
The Spirit won't be hindered by division,
in the perfect work that Jesus has begun.
My tongue will be . . .

275(i) I heard the voice of Jesus say

VOX DILECTI DCM

Words: Horatius Bonar (1808–89)
Music: J B Dykes (1823–76)

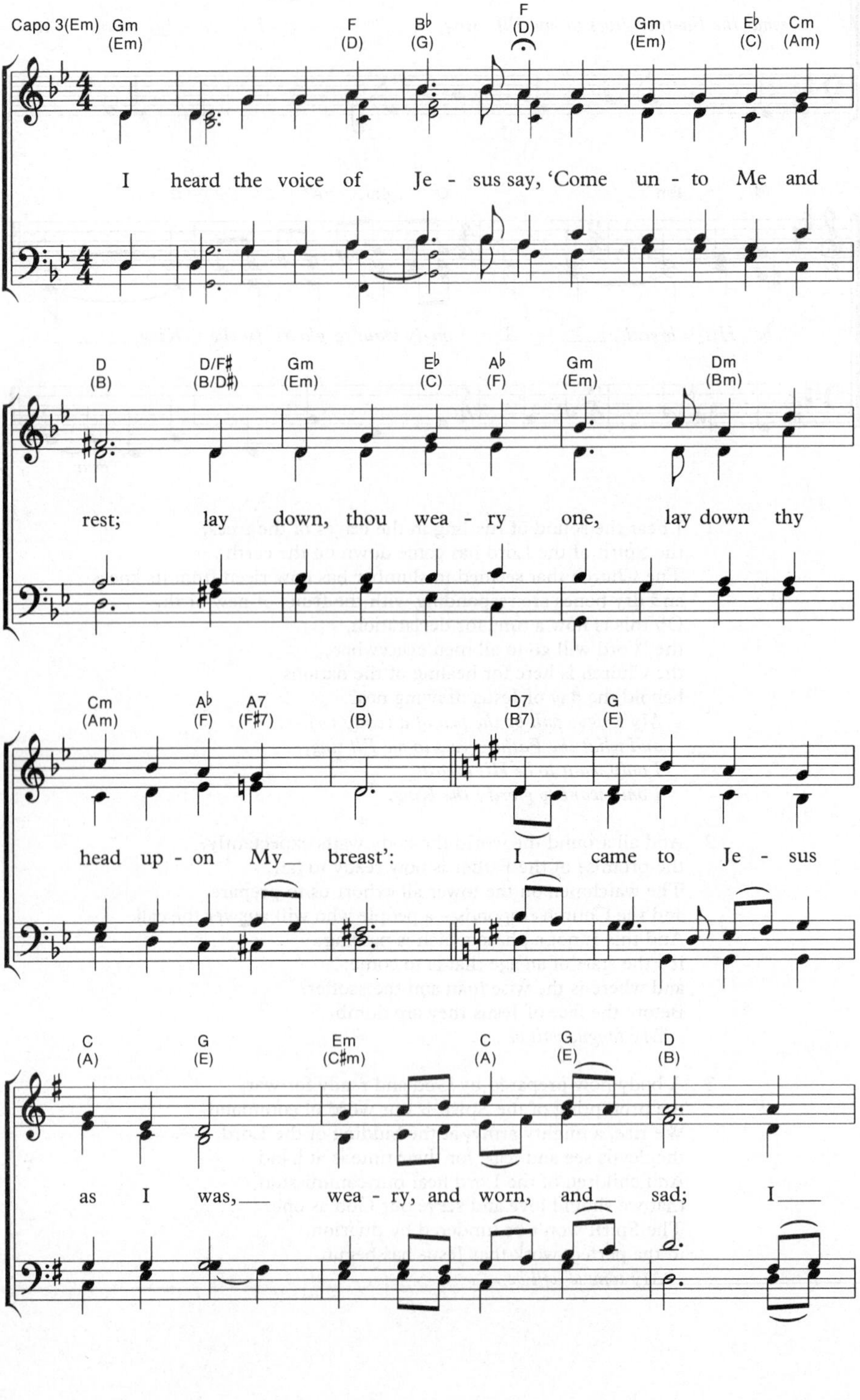

Capo 3(Em)
Gm (Em) F (D) B♭ (G) F (D) Gm (Em) E♭ (C) Cm (Am)
I heard the voice of Je - sus say, 'Come un - to Me and
D (B) D/F♯ (B/D♯) Gm (Em) E♭ (C) A♭ (F) Gm (Em) Dm (Bm)
rest; lay down, thou wea - ry one, lay down thy
Cm (Am) A♭ (F) A7 (F♯7) D (B) D7 (B7) G (E)
head up - on My breast': I came to Je - sus
C (A) G (E) Em (C♯m) C (A) G (E) D (B)
as I was, wea - ry, and worn, and sad; I

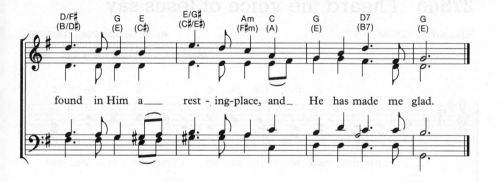

found in Him a___ rest - ing-place, and_ He has made me glad.

1 I heard the voice of Jesus say,
   'Come unto Me and rest;
   lay down, thou weary one, lay down
   thy head upon My breast':
   I came to Jesus as I was,
   weary, and worn, and sad;
   I found in Him a resting-place,
   and He has made me glad.

2 I heard the voice of Jesus say,
   'Behold, I freely give
   the living water; thirsty one,
   stoop down and drink, and live':
   I came to Jesus, and I drank
   of that life-giving stream;
   my thirst was quenched, my soul revived,
   and now I live in Him.

3 I heard the voice of Jesus say,
   'I am this dark world's light;
   look unto Me, thy morn shall rise,
   and all thy day be bright':
   I looked to Jesus and I found
   in Him my star, my sun;
   and in that light of life I'll walk
   till travelling days are done.

275(ii) I heard the voice of Jesus say

KINGSFOLD DCM

Words: Horatius Bonar (1808–89)
Music: English traditional melody
arranged R Vaughan Williams (1872–1958)

I__ heard the__ voice of Je-sus say, 'Come un-to Me__ and rest;____ lay__ down, thou__ wea-ry one, lay down thy__ head up-on__ My__ breast': I__ came to Je-sus as__ I was, wea-ry, and__ worn, and__ sad;____ I__

found in_ Him a_ rest - ing - place, and_ He has made me_ glad.

1 I heard the voice of Jesus say,
   'Come unto Me and rest;
   lay down, thou weary one, lay down
   thy head upon My breast':
   I came to Jesus as I was,
   weary, and worn, and sad;
   I found in Him a resting-place,
   and He has made me glad.

2 I heard the voice of Jesus say,
   'Behold, I freely give
   the living water; thirsty one,
   stoop down and drink, and live':
   I came to Jesus, and I drank
   of that life-giving stream;
   my thirst was quenched, my soul revived,
   and now I live in Him.

3 I heard the voice of Jesus say,
   'I am this dark world's light;
   look unto Me, thy morn shall rise,
   and all thy day be bright':
   I looked to Jesus and I found
   in Him my star, my sun;
   and in that light of life I'll walk
   till travelling days are done.

276   # I just want to praise You

Words and music: Arthur Tannous
Music arranged Christopher Norton

I just want to praise You;
lift my hands and say: 'I love You.'
You are everything to me,
and I exalt Your holy name on high.

I just want to praise You;
lift my hands and say: 'I love You.'
You are everything to me,
and I exalt Your holy name;
I exalt Your holy name,
I exalt Your holy name on high.

277   I know I'll see Jesus some day

I'LL SEE JESUS   10 8 11 8 with refrain

Words: Avis M Christiansen
Music: Scott Lawrence

joy it will be when His face I shall see, I know I'll see Je-sus some day!

1 Sweet is the hope that is thrilling my soul:
   I know I'll see Jesus some day!
   Then what if the dark clouds of sin o'er me roll,
   I know I'll see Jesus some day!
      I know I'll see Jesus some day!
      I know I'll see Jesus some day!
      What a joy it will be
      when His face I shall see,
      I know I'll see Jesus some day!

2 Though I must travel by faith not by sight,
   I know I'll see Jesus some day!
   No evil can harm me, no foe can affright
   I know I'll see Jesus some day!
      I know I'll see Jesus . . .

3 Darkness is gathering, but hope shines within,
   I know I'll see Jesus some day!
   What joy when He comes to wipe out every sin;
   I know I'll see Jesus some day!
      I know I'll see Jesus . . .

278(i) I know that my Redeemer lives

CHURCH TRIUMPHANT   LM

Words: Samuel Medley (1738–99)
Music: J W Elliot (1883–1915)

1 I know that my Redeemer lives!
   What joy the blest assurance gives!
   He lives, He lives, who once was dead;
   He lives, my everlasting Head!

2 He lives, to bless me with His love;
   He lives, to plead for me above;
   He lives, my hungry soul to feed;
   He lives, to help in time of need.

3 He lives, and grants me daily breath;
   He lives, and I shall conquer death;
   He lives, my mansion to prepare;
   He lives, to lead me safely there.

4 He lives, all glory to His name;
   He lives, my Saviour, still the same;
   What joy the blest assurance gives!
   I know that my Redeemer lives!

278(ii) I know that my Redeemer lives

PHILIPPINE LM

Words: Samuel Medley (1738–99)
Music: R E Roberts (1878–1940)

1 I know that my Redeemer lives!
  What joy the blest assurance gives!
  He lives, He lives, who once was dead;
  He lives, my everlasting Head!

2 He lives, to bless me with His love;
  He lives, to plead for me above;
  He lives, my hungry soul to feed;
  He lives, to help in time of need.

3 He lives, and grants me daily breath;
  He lives, and I shall conquer death;
  He lives, my mansion to prepare;
  He lives, to lead me safely there.

4 He lives, all glory to His name;
  He lives, my Saviour, still the same;
  What joy the blest assurance gives!
  I know that my Redeemer lives!

279   I know not why

I KNOW WHOM I HAVE BELIEVED   CM with refrain

Words: D W Whittle (1840–1901)
Music: James McGranahan (1840–1907)

I know not why God's wond-rous grace to me has been made

known; nor why—un-wor-thy— as I am— He

claimed me for— His— own. *But 'I know whom— I have be-*

-liev - ed;—— and am per - suad - ed—— that He is ab - le to

keep that__ which I've com - mit - ted   un - to Him   a-gainst that day.'

1 I know not why God's wondrous grace
   to me has been made known;
   nor why – unworthy as I am –
   He claimed me for His own.
        But 'I know whom I have believed;
        and am persuaded that He is able
        to keep that which I've committed
        unto Him against that day.'

2 I know not how this saving faith
   to me He did impart;
   or how believing in His word
   wrought peace upon my heart.
        But 'I know . . .

3 I know not how the Spirit moves,
   convincing men of sin;
   revealing Jesus through the word,
   creating faith in Him.
        But 'I know . . .

4 I know not what of good or ill
   may be reserved for me –
   of weary ways or golden days
   before His face I see.
        But 'I know . . .

280   I lift my hands

Words and music: Eddie Espinosa
Music arranged Christopher Norton

I lift my__ hands,_____ I raise my__ voice,__ I give my heart to You my Lord,__ and I re-joice. There are ma - ny, ma-ny rea-sons why I do the things I do, O but most of all I praise You, most of all I

Words and music: © 1982 Mercy Publishing,
administered in Europe by Thankyou Music,
PO Box 75, Eastbourne, East Sussex BN23 6NW, UK

praise You, Je - sus,   most   of   all   I   praise You be-cause You're

1.2. You.   2 I   lift   my___   3. You.___

1   I lift my hands,
    I raise my voice,
    I give my heart to You my Lord,
    and I rejoice.
    There are many, many reasons
    why I do the things I do,
    O but most of all I praise You,
    most of all I praise You,
    Jesus, most of all I praise You
    because You're You.

2   I lift my hands,
    I raise my voice,
    I give my life to You my Lord,
    and I rejoice.
    There are many, many reasons
    why I do the things I do,
    O but most of all I love You,
    most of all I love You,
    Jesus, most of all I love You
    because You're You.

3   I lift my hands,
    I raise my voice,
    I give my love to You my Lord,
    and I rejoice.
    There are many, many reasons
    why I love You like I do,
    O but most of all I love You,
    most of all I love You,
    Jesus, most of all I love You
    because You're You.

281

I lift my eyes

Words: Timothy Dudley-Smith
Music: Michael Baughen and Elisabeth Crocker

1 I lift my eyes
   to the quiet hills,
   in the press of a busy day;
   as green hills stand
   in a dusty land,
   so God is my strength and stay.

2 I lift my eyes
   to the quiet hills,
   to a calm that is mine to share;
   secure and still
   in the Father's will,
   and kept by the Father's care.

3 I lift up my eyes
   to the quiet hills,
   with a prayer as I turn to sleep;
   by day, by night,
   through the dark and light,
   my Shepherd will guard His sheep.

4 I lift up my eyes
   to the quiet hills,
   and my heart to the Father's throne;
   in all my ways,
   to the end of days,
   the Lord will preserve His own.

282 I live, I live

Words and music: Rich Cook

283   I look to the hills

Words and music: Greg Leavers
Music arranged Phil Burt

I look to the hills from where shall my help come; my help comes from the Lord, ma-ker of heaven and earth. He will not al-low your foot to ev-er slip;

He who keeps you___ will not sleep. I

I look to the hills
from where shall my help come;
my help comes from the Lord,
maker of heaven and earth.

1 He will not allow
   your foot to ever slip;
   He who keeps you will not sleep.
   I look to the hills . . .

2 He watches over you
   as your shade from moon and sun;
   He will keep you from all harm.
   I look to the hills . . .

3 He will guard your ways
   as you come and as you go;
   from this time and for evermore.
   I look to the hills . . .

284 I love my Lord

Words: J M Barnes
Music: David G Wilson

I love my Lord be - cause He heard my voice. My God, He lis - tens to my prayer. Be-cause He hears me when I call on Him, through all my days I shall pray.

1 I love my Lord because He heard my voice.
My God, He listens to my prayer.
Because He hears me when I call on Him,
through all my days I shall pray.

2 My soul was saved from death; my eyes from tears;
my feet now walk before the Lord;
yet in despair I thought my end was near,
my faith in life disappeared.

3 What can I do to thank God for His love –
for all His benefits to me?
I will lift up salvation's cup on high
and call on Him by His Name.

4 My vows to Him I promise to fulfil,
to Him I sacrifice my life.
He freed me from the servitude of sin
and now I serve as His slave.

5 Unite in praise, great family of God,
His children, bring to Him your thanks.
City of peace, where God has made His home
with one accord, praise His name!

285 I love the name of Jesus

Words and music: Kathleen Thomerson

I love the name of Je-sus, King of my heart, He is
ev-ery-thing to me. I bless the name of Je-sus,
reign in my life, show the Fa-ther's love so free.
Spi-rit of love, Spi-rit of power, shine through e-ter-ni-

1 I love the name of Jesus,
   King of my heart,
   He is everything to me.
   I bless the name of Jesus,
   reign in my life,
   show the Father's love so free.
   Spirit of love,
   Spirit of power,
   shine through eternity.
   I love the name of Jesus,
   Light of the world,
   let me walk each day with Thee.

2 I love the name of Jesus,
   risen above,
   and He loves and prays for me.
   I bless the name of Jesus,
   ruling on high
   with a glorious majesty.
   Spirit of love,
   Spirit of power,
   shine through eternity.
   I praise the name of Jesus,
   Lord of my life,
   for He died to set me free.

3 I love the name of Jesus,
   splendour of God,
   and His face I long to see.
   I bless the name of Jesus,
   Shepherd of men;
   by His side I now can be.
   Spirit of love,
   Spirit of power,
   shine through eternity.
   I praise the name of Jesus,
   for He is love,
   and that love He gives to me.

286 I love You, O Lord, You alone

JANE 88 88 D

Words: Christopher Idle
Music: David Peacock

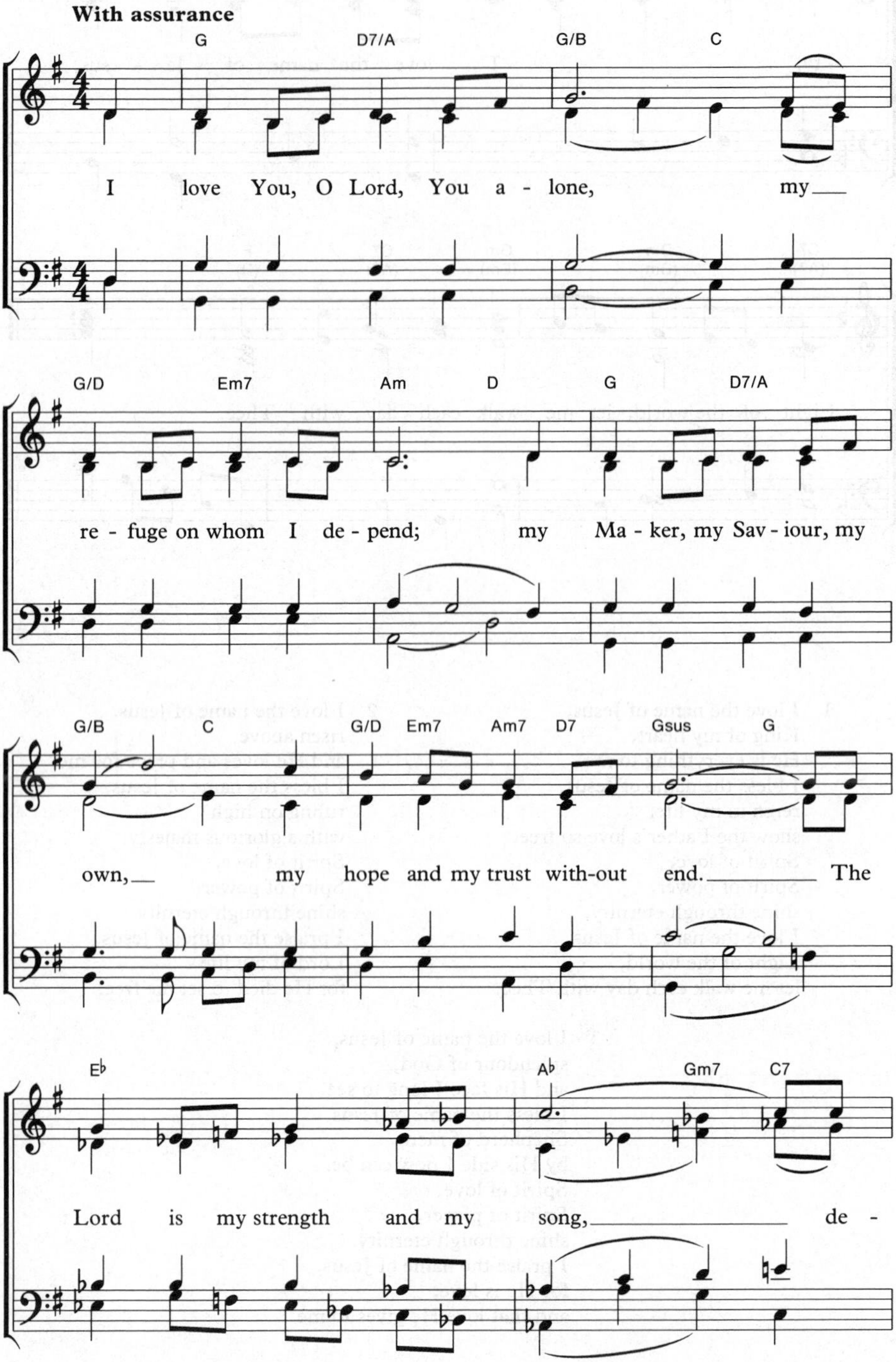
With assurance
G D7/A G/B C
I love You, O Lord, You a - lone, my
G/D Em7 Am D G D7/A
re - fuge on whom I de - pend; my Ma - ker, my Sav - iour, my
G/B C G/D Em7 Am7 D7 Gsus G
own, my hope and my trust with-out end. The
E♭ A♭ Gm7 C7
Lord is my strength and my song, de -

-fen-der and guide of my ways; my Mas-ter to whom I be-long, my God who shall have all my praise.

1 I love You, O Lord, You alone,
   my refuge on whom I depend;
   my Maker, my Saviour, my own,
   my hope and my trust without end.
   The Lord is my strength and my song,
   defender and guide of my ways;
   my Master to whom I belong,
   my God who shall have all my praise.

2 The dangers of death gathered round,
   the waves of destruction came near;
   but in my despairing I found
   the Lord who released me from fear.
   I called for His help in my pain,
   to God my salvation I cried;
   He brought me His comfort again,
   I live by the strength He supplied.

3 The earth and the elements shake
   with thunder and lightning and hail;
   the cliffs and the mountaintops break
   and mortals are feeble and pale.
   His justice is full and complete,
   His mercy to us has no end;
   the clouds are a path for His feet,
   He comes on the wings of the wind.

4 My hope is the promise He gives,
   my life is secure in His hand;
   I shall not be lost, for He lives!
   He comes to my side – I shall stand!
   Lord God, You are powerful to save,
   Your Spirit will spur me to pray;
   Your Son has defeated the grave:
   I trust and I praise You today!

287 I love You, Lord

Words and music: Laurie Klein

288   I need Thee every hour

I NEED THEE   10 10 with refrain

Words: Annie Sherwood Hawks (1835–1918)
Music: R Lowry (1826–99)

I need Thee ev-ery hour, most gra - cious Lord:

no ten - der voice like Thine can peace___ af - ford.

I need Thee, O I need Thee! ev - ery hour I need Thee;

O bless me now, my Sav-iour! I come___ to Thee.

2   I need Thee every hour,
stay Thou near by;
temptations lose their power
when Thou art nigh.
    I need Thee . . .

3   I need Thee every hour,
in joy or pain;
come quickly and abide,
or life is vain.
    I need Thee . . .

4   I need Thee every hour,
teach me Thy will;
and Thy rich promises
in me fulfil.
    I need Thee . . .

5   I need Thee every hour,
most Holy One;
O make me Thine indeed,
Thou blessed Son!
    I need Thee . . .

289

I receive You

Words and music: John Lai
Music arranged Christopher Norton

1 I re-ceive You, O_ Spi-rit of love; how I need Your
(2) feel You, touch-ing me right now; come re-veal Your

heal-ing from a-bove. I re-ceive You, I re-ceive You, I re-
pow-er on me now. I can feel You, I can feel You, I can

- ceive Your heal-ing from a - bove. 2 I can

feel Your pow-er on me

now, I can feel Your pow-er on me now.

290   I receive Your love

Words and music: Paul Armstrong

Gently

1 I re - ceive Your love, I re - ceive Your
2 I con - fess Your love, I con - fess Your

love, in my heart I re - ceive Your love, O
love, in my heart I con - fess Your love, O

Lord, I re - ceive Your love; by Your Spi - rit with -
Lord, I con - fess Your love; by Your Spi - rit with -

- in me I re - ceive, I re - ceive Your love.
- in me I con - fess, I con - fess Your love.

291   I rest in God alone

Words and music: John Daniels
Music arranged Christopher Norton

Lyrics: I rest in God a - lone,___ from_ Him comes my sal - va - tion;___ my soul finds rest in Him,___ my_ for - tress —

292   I see perfection

CHILDREN OF THE KING

Words and music: Chris Eaton
Music arranged Christopher Hayward

1 I   see per - fec - tion as I
2 Your   Ho - ly Spi - rit will for

look   in Your eyes, Lord; there's   no re -
ev - er con - trol me!   I   give my

-jec - tion as I look_____ in Your eyes, Lord.
pre - sent, fu - ture, past, to You com - plete - ly.

Animated

You are_ a ri - ver that is ne - ver dry,

Je-sus, we_ can ne-ver de-ny_ Your love for us_

on the cross now You've made us child-ren of the King.

now You've made us child-ren of the King.

1 I see perfection as I look in Your eyes, Lord;
there's no rejection as I look in Your eyes, Lord.
You are a river that is never dry,
You are the star that lights the evening sky,
You are my God and I will follow You,
and now I know just where I'm going to.
We are children, children of the King;
we will praise Your name,
glorify You, magnify You.
Jesus, we can never deny
Your love for us on the cross
now You've made us children of the King.

2 Your Holy Spirit will for ever control me!
I give my present, future, past, to You completely.
You are a river . . .
now You've made us children of the King!

293   I sing the almighty power of God

JACKSON   CM

Words: Isaac Watts (1674–1748)
Music: Thomas Jackson (1715–81)

1   I sing the almighty power of God,
     that made the mountains rise,
     that spread the flowing seas abroad,
     and built the lofty skies.

2   I sing the wisdom that ordained
     the sun to rule the day;
     the moon shines full at His command,
     and all the stars obey.

3   I sing the goodness of the Lord,
     that filled the earth with food;
     He formed the creatures with His word,
     and then pronounced them good.

4   Creatures, as numerous as they be,
     are subject to His care;
     there's not a place where we can flee
     but God is present there.

5   Lord, how Thy wonders are displayed
     where'er I turn mine eye,
     if I survey the ground I tread,
     or gaze upon the sky.

6   God's hand is my perpetual guard,
     He guides me with His eye;
     why should I then forget the Lord,
     whose love is ever nigh?

294 I sing a new song

Words and music: Carl Tuttle
and John Wimber

I serve a risen Saviour

You, I wor - ship You, _____ I

wor - ship You. _____ 2 I

Fine

bow down _____ my face at the foot - stool of the

Lamb, I lay down _____ my

life at the al - tar of _ God; and I

D.%̸ al Fine

295

I serve a risen Saviour

Words and music: A H Ackley

1 I serve a ris-en Sav-iour, He's in the world to-day; I know that He is liv-ing, what-ev-er men may say. I see His hand of mer-cy, I hear His voice of cheer; and

2 In all the world a-round me I see His lov-ing care, and though my heart grows wea-ry I nev-er will des-pair; I know that He is lead-ing, through all the storm-y blast, the

3 Re-joice, re-joice, O Christ-ian, lift up your voice and sing e-ter-nal hal-le-lu-jahs to Je-sus Christ the King! The hope of all who seek Him, The help of all who find, none

just the time I need Him,___ He's al - ways near.___
day of His ap - pear-ing___ will come at last.___
o - ther is so lov-ing,___ so good and kind.___

He lives,___ He lives,___ Christ Je - sus lives_ to - day!___ He
He lives, He lives,

walks with me and talks with me a - long life's nar - row way.___ He

lives,___ He lives,___ Sal - va - tion to im - part!___ You
He lives, He lives,

ask me how I know He lives? He lives with-in my heart.___

296   I stand amazed in the presence

Words and music: Charles H Gabriel (1858–1932)

I stand a-mazed in the pre-sence of Je-sus the Na-za-rene, and won-der how He could love me, a sin-ner, con-demned, un-clean.

How mar-vel-lous! how won-der-ful!
O, how mar-vel-lous! O, how won-der-ful! *and my song shall ev-er be:*

How mar-vel-lous! how won-der-ful!
O, how mar-vel-lous! O, how won-der-ful! *is my Sav-iour's love for me!*

1   I stand amazed in the presence
     of Jesus the Nazarene,
     and wonder how He could love me,
     a sinner, condemned, unclean.
         How marvellous! how wonderful!
         and my song shall ever be:
         How marvellous! how wonderful!
         is my Saviour's love for me!

2   For me it was in the garden
     He prayed – 'Not My will, but Thine';
     He had no tears for His own griefs,
     but sweat drops of blood for mine.
         How marvellous! . . .

3   In pity angels beheld Him,
     and came from the world of light,
     to comfort Him in the sorrows
     He bore for my soul that night.
         How marvellous! . . .

4   He took my sins and my sorrows,
     He made them His very own;
     He bore the burden to Calvary,
     and suffered, and died alone.
         How marvellous! . . .

5   When with the ransomed in glory
     His face I at last shall see,
     'twill be my joy through the ages
     to sing of His love for me.
         How marvellous! . . .

297   I stand before the presence

Words and music: Mavis Ford

I stand be-fore the pre-sence of the Lord God of hosts, a

child of my Fa-ther and an heir of His grace. For

Je - sus paid the debt for me, the veil was torn in two, and the

Ho - ly of Ho - lies has be - come my dwell-ing - place.

298 I want to learn to appreciate You

Words and music: John Kennett
Music arranged Christopher Norton

Words and music: © 1980 Thankyou Music,
PO Box 75, Eastbourne, East Sussex BN23 6NW, UK

299 # I trust in Thee, O Lord

Words and music: M Warrington
Music arranged Jeanne Harper

2 Bless - ed be__ the Lord,__

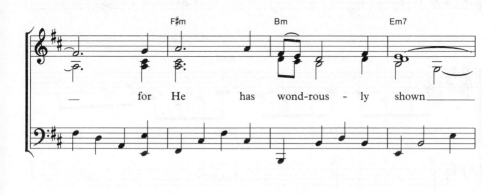

__ for He has wond-rous - ly shown__

__ His stead - fast love__ to me,__

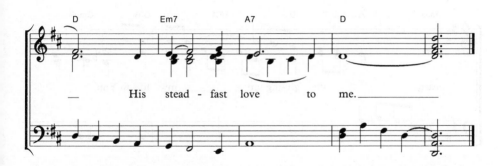

__ His stead - fast love to me.__

300   I want to see Your face

Words and music: Ruth Hooke

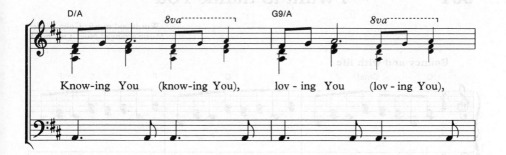

Know-ing You   (know-ing You),   lov-ing You   (lov-ing You),

Lord.   Lord.

I want to see Your face,
I want to see Your face,
give You the worship of my heart, of my heart,
giving up my life to You.
Knowing You (knowing You),
loving You (loving You), Lord.

301 I want to thank You

Words and music: Colin Waller
Music arranged Noël Tredinnick

thank You, I want to praise with Your pow - er,

I want to praise You, Yours is the pow - er,

Yours is the power, the truth, the way.

Yours is the power, the truth, the way.

I want to thank You, I want to praise You,
I want to love You more each day.
I want to thank You, I want to praise You,
Yours is the power, the truth, the way.

1   Father, Your love I feel;
    help me to show it to be real.
    Then I can openly say,
    Yours is the power, the truth, the way.
    I want to thank You . . .

2   Jesus, Your word I hear;
    help me to see its truth so clear.
    So I can openly say,
    Yours is the power, the truth, the way.
    I want to thank You . . .

3   Spirit, Your power I know;
    help me to feel it, and to grow
    stronger in every way, – 'cause
    Yours is the power, the truth, the way.
    I want to thank You . . . (twice)

302   # I want to walk with Jesus

Words: C Simmonds
Music: Swiss folk melody
arranged Phil Burt

I want to walk with Je - sus Christ, all the days I live of this life on earth; to give to Him com - plete con - trol of bo - dy and of soul. *Fol - low Him, fol - low Him, yield your life to*

1 I want to walk with Jesus Christ,
   all the days I live of this life on earth;
   to give to Him complete control
   of body and of soul.
     Follow Him, follow Him,
     yield your life to Him –
     He has conquered death,
     He is King of kings;
     accept the joy which He gives to those
     who yield their lives to Him.

2 I want to learn to speak to Him,
   to pray to Him, confess my sin,
   to open my life and let Him in,
   for joy will then be mine.
     Follow Him, follow Him . . .

3 I want to learn to speak of Him –
   my life must show that He lives in me;
   my deeds, my thoughts, my words must speak
   all of His love for me.
     Follow Him, follow Him . . .

4 I want to learn to read His word,
   for this is how I know the way
   to live my life as pleases Him,
   in holiness and joy.
     Follow Him, follow Him . . .

5 O Holy Spirit of the Lord,
   enter now into this heart of mine;
   take full control of my selfish will
   and make me wholly Thine!
     Follow Him, follow Him . . .

303   I want to serve You, Lord

Words and music: Chris Rolinson

1   I want to serve You, Lord,
      in total abandonment,
   I want to yield my heart to You;
   I want to give my life in all surrender,
   I want to live for You alone.

2   I want to give my all
      in total abandonment,
   releasing all within my grasp;
   I want to live my life in all its fulness,
   I want to worship Christ alone.

3   I want to come to You
      in total abandonment –
   Lord, will You set my heart ablaze?
   I want to love You with all my soul and strength,
   I want to give You all my days.

304 # I want to worship the Lord

Words and music: Robert Cameron
Music arranged Roland Fudge

With quiet adoration

I want to wor-ship the Lord with all of my
heart, give Him my all_____ and not just a
part. Lift up my hands to the King of
kings, praise Him in ev-ery-thing._____

305   I will build my church

Words and music: Graham Kendrick
Music arranged Christopher Norton

Brightly

MEN 'I will build my church, and the
WOMEN I will build my church,

gates of hell, shall not pre - vail, a -
and the gates of hell, shall not pre - vail, a -

1. ALL
- gainst____ it.' I will

2. MEN ALL
- gainst_____ it.' So you

powers in the hea-vens a-bove, bow down! And you powers on the earth be-low,

bow down! And ac-know - ledge that Je - sus,

Je - sus, Je - sus is Lord,_____

— is Lord!   MEN I will

MEN   'I will build my church,
WOMEN   I will build my church,
MEN   and the gates of hell,
WOMEN   and the gates of hell,
MEN   shall not prevail,
WOMEN   shall not prevail,
ALL   against it.'
MEN   I will build . . .

ALL
So you powers in the heavens above,
bow down!
And you powers on the earth below,
bow down!
And acknowledge that Jesus,
Jesus, Jesus is Lord,
is Lord!

306   I will call upon the Lord

Words and music: Rich Cook

307   I will enter His gates

Words and music: Leona van Brethorst

With pace and swing

I will en-ter His gates with thanks-giv-ing in my heart, I will en-ter His courts with praise; I will say this is the day that the Lord has made, I will rejoice for He has made me glad. He has made me glad, He has made me glad; I will re-joice for He has made me glad. He has made me glad, He has made me glad; I will re-joice for He has made me glad.

308   I will give thanks

Words and music: Brent Chambers
Music arranged Roland Fudge

Rich and unhurried

I will give thanks to Thee, O__ Lord, a-mong the

peo - ples, I will sing prais-es to Thee a-mong the

na - tions._____ For Thy stead-fast love is great, is__

great to the hea - vens, and Thy faith-ful-ness, Thy__

I will give You praise

309   I will give You praise

Words and music: Tommy Walker

I will give You praise, I will sing Your song,_ I will

bless Your ho - ly name;_ For there is no o-ther God who is

like un - to You, You're the on - ly way.__ On-ly You

____ are the au - thor of life,_ on-ly You,_____ can bring the

blind their sight,__ on - ly You,_____ are called

Prince of Peace, on - ly You_____ pro-mised You'd ne-ver leave,

on - ly You are God._____

I will give You praise,
I will sing Your song,
I will bless Your holy name;
For there is no other God
who is like unto You,
You're the only way.
Only You are the author of life,
only You, can bring the blind their sight,
only You, are called Prince of Peace,
only You promised You'd never leave,
only You are God.

310   I will magnify Thy name

Words and music: Scott Palazzo

I will mag-ni-fy Thy name a-bove all the earth; I will mag-ni-fy Thy name a-bove all the earth.

I will sing un-to Thee earth.

I will magnify Thy name above all the earth;
I will magnify Thy name above all the earth.
I will sing unto Thee the praises in my heart;
I will sing unto Thee the praises in my heart.

311   I will rejoice, I will rejoice

Words and music: Dave Fellingham
Music arranged Christopher Norton

312 I will rejoice in You

Words and music: Anon
Music arranged Phil Burt

I will re - joice___ in You and be glad,

I will ex - tol__ Your love more than wine;

draw me af - ter You and let us run to - geth - er,

I will re - joice___ in You and be glad._

313 I will sing, I will sing

Words and music: Max Dyer

Liltingly

I will sing, I will sing a song___ un-to the Lord, I will
Al - le - lu, al - le - lu - ia, glo - ry to the Lord, al - le -

sing, I will sing a song___ un-to the Lord, I will sing, I will sing a song
- lu, al - le - lu - ia, glo - ry to the Lord, al - le - lu, al - le - lu - ia, glo -

Repeat for Chorus

___ un-to the Lord, al - le - lu - ia, glo - ry to the Lord.
- ry to the Lord, al - le - lu - ia, glo - ry to the Lord.

2 We will come, we will come as one before the Lord, (*3 times*)
   alleluia, glory to the Lord.
   Allelu, alleluia . . .

3 If the Son, if the Son shall make you free, (*3 times*)
   you shall be free indeed.
   Allelu, alleluia . . .

4 They that sow in tears shall reap in joy, (*3 times*)
   alleluia, glory to the Lord!
   Allelu, alleluia . . .

5 Every knee shall bow and every tongue confess, (*3 times*)
   that Jesus Christ is Lord.
   Allelu, alleluia . . .

6 In His name, in His name we have the victory. (*3 times*)
   Alleluia, glory to the Lord.
   Allelu, alleluia . . .

314   I will sing about Your love

Words and music: Phil Potter
Music arranged David Peacock

Steadily

I will sing a-bout Your love,

I will mag-ni-fy___ Your___ name,

I will be glad___ and re-joice___ in You,

I will praise You a-gain.___

Praise___ the Lord,___ lift your voi - ces high,___

___ praise___ the Lord,___ tell them He's a - live,___

___ praise___ the Lord,___ praise the Lord.

315   I will sing the wondrous story

HYFRYDOL   87 87 D

Words: F H Rawley (1854–1952)
Music: R H Prichard (1811–87)

I＿ will sing＿ the won - drous sto - ry

of＿ the＿ Christ who＿ died＿ for me, – how＿ He

left＿＿ the realms＿ of glo - ry for＿＿ the＿

cross on＿ Cal - va - ry. Yes, I'll sing＿ the

won - drous sto - ry of___ the Christ___ who
died___ for me, –___ sing___ it with___ His saints___ in
glo - ry,___ gath - ered by___ the crys - tal sea.

1 I will sing the wondrous story
   of the Christ who died for me, –
   how He left the realms of glory
   for the cross on Calvary.
   Yes, I'll sing the wondrous story
   of the Christ who died for me, –
   sing it with His saints in glory,
   gathered by the crystal sea.

2 I was lost: but Jesus found me,
   found the sheep that went astray,
   raised me up and gently led me
   back into the narrow way.
   Days of darkness still may meet me,
   sorrow's path I oft may tread;
   but His presence still is with me,
   by His guiding hand I'm led.

3 He will keep me till the river
   rolls its waters at my feet:
   then He'll bear me safely over,
   made by grace for glory meet.
   Yes, I'll sing the wondrous story
   of the Christ who died for me, –
   sing it with His saints in glory,
   gathered by the crystal sea.

316

I will sing unto the Lord

Words and music: Donya Brockway
Music arranged Margaret Evans

317   I will wait upon the Lord

Words and music: Andy Silver

He on-ly is my rock and strength, my re-fuge is in God; I will wait up - on the Lord, my hope is all in Him; He on-ly is my rock and strength, my re-fuge is in God.

318   If my people

Words and music: Graham Kendrick
Music arranged Christopher Norton

then I will hear from hea - ven, I'll hear from

hea - ven and will for - give. I will for-give their

sins and will heal their land— yes___ I will

heal their land.

319   I'd rather have Jesus

Words: Rhea F Miller
Music: Beverly Shea

I'd ra-ther have Je-sus than sil-ver or gold, I'd ra-ther be His than have rich-es un - told;_ I'd ra-ther have Je-sus than hous - es or lands, I'd ra-ther be led by His nail - pierced hand. *Than to be the king of a vast do -*

- main and be held in sin's dread sway;_____ I'd ra - ther have

Je - sus than a - ny - thing this_ world af - fords_ to - day._____

1 I'd rather have Jesus than silver or gold,
  I'd rather be His than have riches untold;
  I'd rather have Jesus than houses or lands,
  I'd rather be led by His nail-pierced hand.
    Than to be the king of a vast domain
    and be held in sin's dread sway;
    I'd rather have Jesus than anything
    this world affords today.

2 I'd rather have Jesus than men's applause,
  I'd rather be faithful to His dear cause;
  I'd rather have Jesus than world-wide fame,
  I'd rather be true to His holy Name.
    Than to be the king . . .

3 He's fairer than lilies of rarest bloom,
  He's sweeter than honey from out the comb;
  He's all that my hungering spirit needs,
  I'd rather have Jesus and let Him lead.
    Than to be the king . . .

320   I'll praise my Maker

Monmouth   888 D

Words: Isaac Watts (1674–1748)
Music: Gabriel Davis (c1768–1824)

life____ and thought___ and be - ing last,____ or im - mor - ta - - - li - ty en - dures.

1 I'll praise my Maker while I've breath,
   and when my voice is lost in death,
   praise shall employ my nobler powers:
   my days of praise shall ne'er be past,
   while life and thought and being last,
   or immortality endures.

2 Happy the man whose hopes rely
   on Israel's God! He made the sky
   and earth and sea, with all their train:
   His truth for ever stands secure;
   He saves the oppressed, He feeds the poor,
   and none shall find His promise vain.

3 The Lord gives eyesight to the blind;
   the Lord supports the fainting mind;
   He sends the labouring conscience peace:
   He helps the stranger in distress,
   the widow and the fatherless,
   and grants the prisoner sweet release.

4 I'll praise Him while He lends me breath;
   and when my voice is lost in death,
   praise shall employ my nobler powers.
   My days of praise shall ne'er be past,
   while life and thought and being last,
   or immortality endures.

321   I'm accepted

Words and music: Rob Hayward
Music arranged Christopher Norton

Worshipfully

I'm ac-cept-ed, I'm for-giv-en, I am fa-thered by the true_ and liv-ing God._ I'm ac-cept-ed, no con-dem-na-tion, I am loved by the true and liv-ing God. There's no

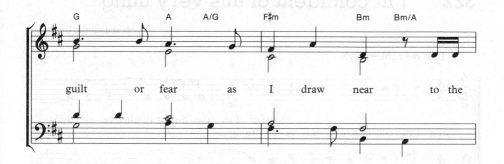

guilt   or   fear   as   I   draw   near   to the

Sav-iour and Cre-a-tor   of the world.   There is   joy   and peace   as

I   re - lease   my   wor - ship to You,   O   Lord.

I'm accepted, I'm forgiven,
I am fathered by the true and living God.
I'm accepted, no condemnation,
I am loved by the true and living God.
There's no guilt or fear as I draw near
to the Saviour and Creator of the world.
There is joy and peace as I release
my worship to You, O Lord.

322   I'm confident of this very thing

Words and music: Unknown

323 I'm not ashamed to own my Lord

JACKSON CM

Words: Isaac Watts (1674–1748)
Music: Thomas Jackson (1715–81)

1 I'm not ashamed to own my Lord,
or to defend His cause;
maintain the honour of His word,
the glory of His cross.

2 Jesus, my God, I know His name;
His name is all my trust;
nor will He put my soul to shame,
nor let my hope be lost.

3 Firm as His throne His promise stands;
and He can well secure
what I've committed to His hands,
till the decisive hour.

4 Then will He own my worthless name
before His Father's face;
and in the new Jerusalem
appoint my soul a place.

I'm redeemed

Words and music: Tony Humphries
Music arranged Christopher Norton

Lively

I'm re-deemed, yes I am, by the blood of the Lamb,

Je - sus Christ has done it__ all for me. I am

His, He is mine, I'm part of the roy-al vine, all my

sins were washed a - way at Cal - va - ry.

I'm special

Once I was lost, I had no-where to go, my

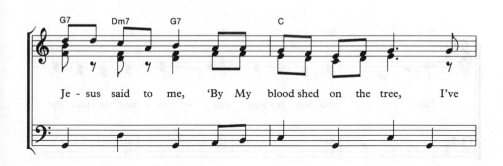

life was just a lone-ly round of sin; till

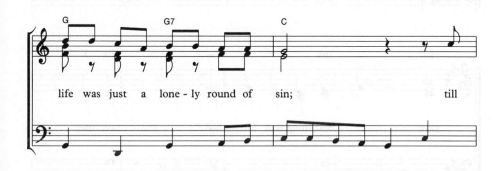

Je-sus said to me, 'By My blood shed on the tree, I've

D.C. al Fine

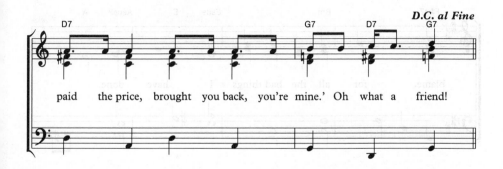

paid the price, brought you back, you're mine.' Oh what a friend!

325

I'm special

Words and music: Graham Kendrick
Music arranged Christopher Norton

With intensity

I'm spe-cial be-cause God has loved me, for He gave the best thing that He had to save me: His own Son Je-sus, cru - ci - fied to take the blame, for all the bad things I have done.

Thank You Je-sus, thank You Lord, for lov-ing me so

much; I know I don't de - serve a-ny - thing,

help me feel Your love right now, to know deep in my

heart that I'm Your spe - cial friend._____

326   Immanuel, O Immanuel

Words and music: Graham Kendrick
Music arranged Christopher Norton

Worshipfully

Im -

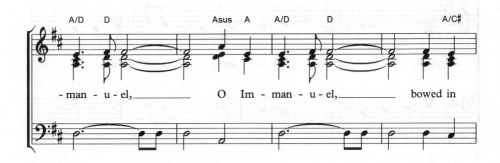

- man - u - el, _____ O Im - man - u - el, _____ bowed in

awe I wor-ship at ___ Your feet, and sing Im -

- man - u - el, _____ God is with ___ us, _____ shar-ing my

words can-not__ ex - plain, all that my heart can-not__ con -

- tain, how great are the glo-ries of__ Your name,_____ Im -

- man - - - u - el._____ Im - __

Immanuel, O Immanuel,
bowed in awe I worship at Your feet,
and sing Immanuel, God is with us,
sharing my humanness, my shame,
feeling my weaknesses, my pain,
taking the punishment, the blame,
Immanuel.
And now my words cannot explain,
all that my heart cannot contain,
how great are the glories of Your name,
Immanuel.

327 # Immortal, invisible

St Denio   11 11 11 11

Words: Walter Chalmers Smith (1824–1908)
Music: Welsh hymn melody

Im - mor - tal, in - vi - si - ble, God on - ly wise,
in light in - ac - ces - si - ble hid from our eyes,
most bless - ed, most glo - rious, the An - cient of __ Days,
al - migh - ty, vic - to - rious, Thy great name we praise.

1 Immortal, invisible, God only wise,
in light inaccessible hid from our eyes,
most blessed, most glorious, the Ancient of Days,
almighty, victorious, Thy great name we praise.

2 Unresting, unhasting, and silent as light,
nor wanting, nor wasting, Thou rulest in might;
Thy justice like mountains high soaring above
Thy clouds, which are fountains of goodness and love.

3 To all, life Thou givest, to both great and small;
in all life Thou livest, the true life of all;
we blossom and flourish as leaves on the tree,
and wither and perish, but nought changeth Thee.

4 Great Father of glory, pure Father of Light,
Thine angels adore Thee, all veiling their sight;
All laud we would render; O help us to see
'tis only the splendour of light hideth Thee.

5 Immortal, invisible, God only wise,
in light inaccessible hid from our eyes,
most blessed, most glorious, the Ancient of Days,
almighty, victorious, Thy great name we praise.

328

Immortal Love

STRACATHRO   CM

Words: John Greenleaf Whittier (1807–92)
Music: C Hutcheson (1792–1860)

Im - mor - tal Love, for ev - er full, for
ev - er flow - ing free, for ev - er shared, for
ev - er whole, a ne - ver - ebb - ing sea:

1   Immortal Love, for ever full,
     for ever flowing free,
    for ever shared, for ever whole,
     a never-ebbing sea:

2   Our outward lips confess the Name
     all other names above;
    love only knoweth whence it came
     and comprehendeth love.

3   We may not climb the heavenly steeps
     to bring the Lord Christ down:
    in vain we search the lowest deeps,
     for Him no depths can drown.

4   In joy of inward peace, or sense
     of sorrow over sin,
    He is His own best evidence,
     His witness is within.

5   For warm, sweet, tender, even yet
     a present help is He;
    and faith still has its Olivet,
     and love its Galilee.

6   The healing of His seamless dress
     is by our beds of pain;
    we touch Him in life's throng and press,
     and we are whole again.

7   Through Him the first fond prayers are said
     our lips of childhood frame,
    the last low whispers of our dead
     are burdened with His name.

8   O Lord and Master of us all,
     whate'er our name or sign,
    we own Thy sway, we hear Thy call,
     we test our lives by Thine.

329 In Christ there is no East or West

ST STEPHEN CM

Words: John Oxenham (1852–1941)
Music: William Jones (1726–1800)

1 In Christ there is no East or West,
   in Him no South or North,
   but one great fellowship of love
   throughout the whole wide earth.

2 In Him shall true hearts everywhere
   their high communion find:
   His service is the golden cord
   Close-binding all mankind.

3 Join hands then, brothers of the faith,
   whate'er your race may be!
   Who serves my Father as a son
   is surely kin to me.

4 In Christ now meet both East and West,
   in Him meet South and North,
   all Christly souls are one in Him,
   throughout the whole wide earth.

330   In full and glad surrender

St Alphege   76 76   Words: Frances Ridley Havergal (1836–79)
Music: H J Gauntlett (1805–76)

1   In full and glad surrender,
    I give myself to Thee,
    Thine utterly and only
    and evermore to be.

2   O Son of God, who lov'st me,
    I will be Thine alone;
    and all I have and am, Lord,
    shall henceforth be Thine own!

3   Reign over me, Lord Jesus,
    O make my heart Thy throne;
    it shall be Thine, dear Saviour,
    it shall be Thine alone.

4   O come and reign, Lord Jesus,
    rule over everything!
    and keep me always loyal
    and true to Thee, my King.

331 In heavenly love abiding

PENLAN 76 76 D

Words: Anna Laetitia Waring (1823–1910)
Music: D Jenkins (1849–1915)

In heaven-ly love a-bid-ing,_____ no
change my heart shall fear;_____ and safe is such con-
-fid-ing,_____ for no-thing chan-ges here._____
The storm may roar with-out me,_____ my heart may

low   be   laid,_____   but   God   is   round_   a -

- bout   me,_____   and   can_   I   be   dis - mayed?_____

1   In heavenly love abiding,
no change my heart shall fear;
and safe is such confiding,
for nothing changes here.
The storm may roar without me,
my heart may low be laid,
but God is round about me,
and can I be dismayed?

2   Wherever He may guide me,
no want shall turn me back;
my Shepherd is beside me,
and nothing can I lack.
His wisdom ever waketh,
His sight is never dim,
He knows the way He taketh,
and I will walk with Him.

3   Green pastures are before me,
which yet I have not seen;
bright skies will soon be o'er me,
where the dark clouds have been.
My hope I cannot measure,
my path to life is free,
my Saviour has my treasure,
and He will walk with me.

332

In Him we live and move

Words and music: Randy Speir
Music arranged Phil Burt

In Him we live and move and have our being;____ in Him we live and move and have our being.____

Make a joy - ful noise, sing un-to____ the Lord,

tell Him of___ your love,   dance be - fore Him;

make a joy - ful noise,   sing un-to___ the Lord,

tell Him of___ your love,   hal - le - lu - -

- jah!   In Him we

CODA

being._____

333 In loving-kindness Jesus came

He Lifted Me   88 86 with refrain   Words and music: C H Gabriel (1856–1932)

In loving-kindness Jesus came, my soul in mercy to reclaim,

and from the depths of sin and shame through grace He lifted me.
(He lifted me.)

From sinking sand He lifted me; with tender hand He lifted me;

from shades of night to plains of light, O praise His name, He lifted me!

1 In loving-kindness Jesus came,
   my soul in mercy to reclaim,
   and from the depths of sin and shame
   through grace He lifted me.
     From sinking sand He lifted me;
     with tender hand He lifted me;
     from shades of night to plains of light,
     O praise His name, He lifted me!

2 He called me long before I heard,
   before my sinful heart was stirred;
   but when I took Him at His word,
   forgiven He lifted me.
     From sinking sand . . .

3 His brow was pierced with many a thorn,
   His hands by cruel nails were torn,
   when from my guilt and grief, forlorn,
   in love He lifted me.
     From sinking sand . . .

4 Now on a higher plane I dwell,
   and with my soul I know 'tis well;
   yet how or why, I cannot tell,
   He should have lifted me.
     From sinking sand . . .

334   In moments like these

Words and music: David Graham
Music arranged G Baker

Lord, sing-ing, I love You Lord,— I love You. Sing-ing You.—

In moments like these I sing out a song,
I sing out a love song to Jesus;
in moments like these I lift up my hands,
I lift up my hands to the Lord:
singing, I love You Lord,
singing, I love You Lord,
singing, I love You Lord,
I love You.

335   In my life Lord, be glorified

Words and music: Bob Kilpatrick
Music arranged Roland Fudge

1 In my life Lord, be glorified, be glorified;
   in my life Lord, be glorified today.

2 In your Church, Lord, be glorified, be glorified;
   in your Church, Lord, be glorified today.

336 In my need Jesus found me

Words and music: Gordon Brattle

337   In the bleak mid-winter

CRANHAM   65 65 D

Words: Christina Georgina Rossetti (1830–94)
Music: Gustav Holst (1874–1934)

1 In the bleak mid - win - ter   fros - ty wind made moan,
2 Our God, heaven can - not hold Him,   nor__ earth sus - tain,
3 An - gels and arch - an - gels   may have gath - ered there,
4 What__ can I give Him,   poor__ as I am?

earth stood hard as   ir - on,   wa - ter like a stone;
heaven and earth shall flee a - way   when He comes to reign;
cher - u - bim and se - ra-phim   thronged__ the air;
If I were a shep - herd,   I would bring a lamb;

snow had fall - en, snow on snow,   snow__ on__ snow,
in the bleak mid - win - ter a sta - ble-place suf - ficed
but His mo - ther on - ly,   in her maid - en bliss,
if I were a wise__ man,   I would do my part; yet

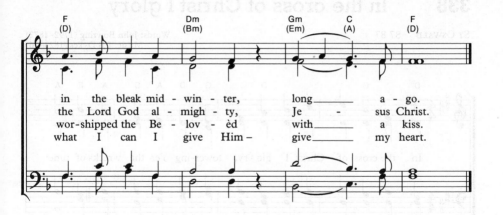

in the bleak mid - win - ter, long_____ a - go.
the Lord God al - migh - ty, Je - sus Christ.
wor-shipped the Be - lov - èd with_____ a kiss.
what I can I give Him – give_____ my heart.

1 In the bleak mid-winter,
    frosty wind made moan,
    earth stood hard as iron,
    water like a stone;
    snow had fallen, snow on snow,
    snow on snow,
    in the bleak mid-winter,
    long ago.

2 Our God, heaven cannot hold Him,
    nor earth sustain,
    heaven and earth shall flee away
    when He comes to reign;
    in the bleak mid-winter
    a stable-place sufficed
    the Lord God almighty,
    Jesus Christ.

3 Angels and archangels
    may have gathered there,
    cherubim and seraphim
    thronged the air;
    but His mother only,
    in her maiden bliss,
    worshipped the Belovèd
    with a kiss.

4 What can I give Him,
    poor as I am?
    If I were a shepherd,
    I would bring a lamb;
    if I were a wise man,
    I would do my part;
    yet what I can I give Him –
    give my heart.

338   In the cross of Christ I glory

St Oswald   87 87

Words: John Bowring (1792–1872)
Music: J B Dykes (1823–76)

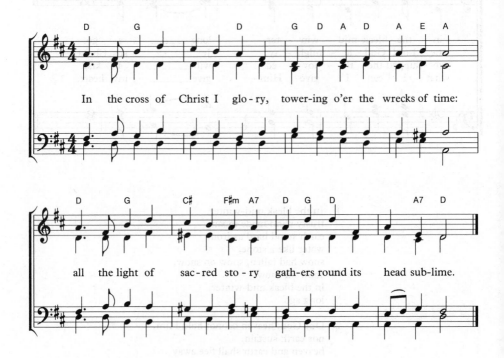

In the cross of Christ I glory, towering o'er the wrecks of time:
all the light of sacred story gathers round its head sublime.

1   In the cross of Christ I glory,
     towering o'er the wrecks of time:
     all the light of sacred story
     gathers round its head sublime.

2   When the woes of life o'ertake me,
     hopes deceive, and fears annoy,
     never shall the cross forsake me;
     Lo! it glows with peace and joy.

3   When the sun of bliss is beaming
     light and love upon my way,
     from the cross the radiance streaming
     adds more lustre to the day.

4   Bane and blessing, pain and pleasure,
     by the cross are sanctified;
     peace is there that knows no measure,
     joys that through all time abide.

5   In the cross of Christ I glory,
     towering o'er the wrecks of time:
     all the light of sacred story
     gathers round its head sublime.

339   In the name of Jesus

Words and music: Unknown
Music arranged Roland Fudge

Joyfully

In the name of Je-sus, in the name of Je-sus, we have the vic-to-

-ry. In the name of Je-sus, in the name of Je-sus,

de-mons will have to flee. Who can tell what

God can do? Who can tell of His love for you?

In the name of Je-sus, Je-sus, we have the vic-to-ry.

340

In the tomb so cold

Words and music: Graham Kendrick
Music arranged Christopher Norton

In the tomb so cold they laid Him, death its vic-tim claimed; powers of hell, they could not hold Him — back to life He came! Christ is ris-en, (Christ is ris-en), death has been con-quered, (death has been con-quered),

Christ is ris - en, (Christ is ris - en): He shall reign for

ev - - er!

last time

1 In the tomb so cold they laid Him,
   death its victim claimed;
   powers of hell, they could not hold Him –
   back to life He came!
       Christ is risen,
       (Christ is risen),
       death has been conquered,
       (death has been conquered),
       Christ is risen,
       (Christ is risen):
       He shall reign for ever!

2 Hell had spent its fury on Him,
   left Him crucified;
   yet by blood He boldly conquered,
   sin and death defied.
       Christ is risen . . .

3 Now the fear of death is broken,
   Love has won the crown.
   Prisoners of the darkness – listen,
   walls are tumbling down!
       Christ is risen . . .

4 Raised from death, to heaven ascending,
   Love's exalted King:
   let His song of joy unending
   through the nations ring!
       Christ is risen . . .

341 In the presence of Your people

Words and music: Brent Chambers

In the pre-sence of Your peo-ple I will praise Your name,

for a-lone you are ho-ly, en-throned on the prais-es of Is-ra-el.

Let us ce-le-brate Your good-ness and your stead-fast love;

may Your name be ex-alt-ed here on_ earth and in heaven a-bove!

342   Infant holy

INFANT HOLY   447 447 44447

From a Polish Carol
Words: tr. E M G Reed (1885–1933)
Music arranged A E Rusbridge (1917–69)

1 In-fant ho-ly, in-fant low-ly, for His bed a cat-tle stall;—
2 Flocks were sleep-ing, shep-herds keep-ing vi-gil till the morn-ing new,—

ox-en low-ing, lit-tle know-ing Christ the babe is Lord of all.
saw the glo-ry, heard the sto-ry— tid-ings of a gos-pel true.

Swift are wing-ing— an-gels sing-ing, no-wells ring-ing, tid-ings bring-ing:
Thus re-joic-ing, free from sor-row, prais-es voic-ing, greet the mor-row:

Christ the babe is— Lord of all;— Christ the babe is Lord of all!
Christ the babe was— born for you;— Christ the babe was born for you!

343   Is this the church of our God?

Words and music: Anne Horrobin
and Stephen Poxon
Music arranged Phil Burt

1 Is this the church of our God?
2 If we're de-pen-dant on Him,

Is this the church of the Word?
if we be-lieve God's own Word,

Is this the church of His Son Je-sus Christ?
if we're re-deemed by the blood of His Son,

Is this the church of His Spi-rit?
if we are filled with His Spi-rit:

3 Then

344   Isn't He beautiful

Words and music: John Wimber
Music arranged Christopher Norton

2 Yes You are beautiful,
   beautiful, yes you are!
   Prince of Peace,
   Son of God,
   yes You are!
   Yes You are wonderful,

wonderful, yes You are!
Counsellor,
Almighty God,
yes You are, yes You are,
yes You are, yes You are,
yes You are!

345 It came upon the midnight clear

NOEL 86 86 D

Words: E H Sears (1810–76)
in this version Jubilate Hymns
Music: English traditional melody
arranged A S Sullivan (1842–1900)

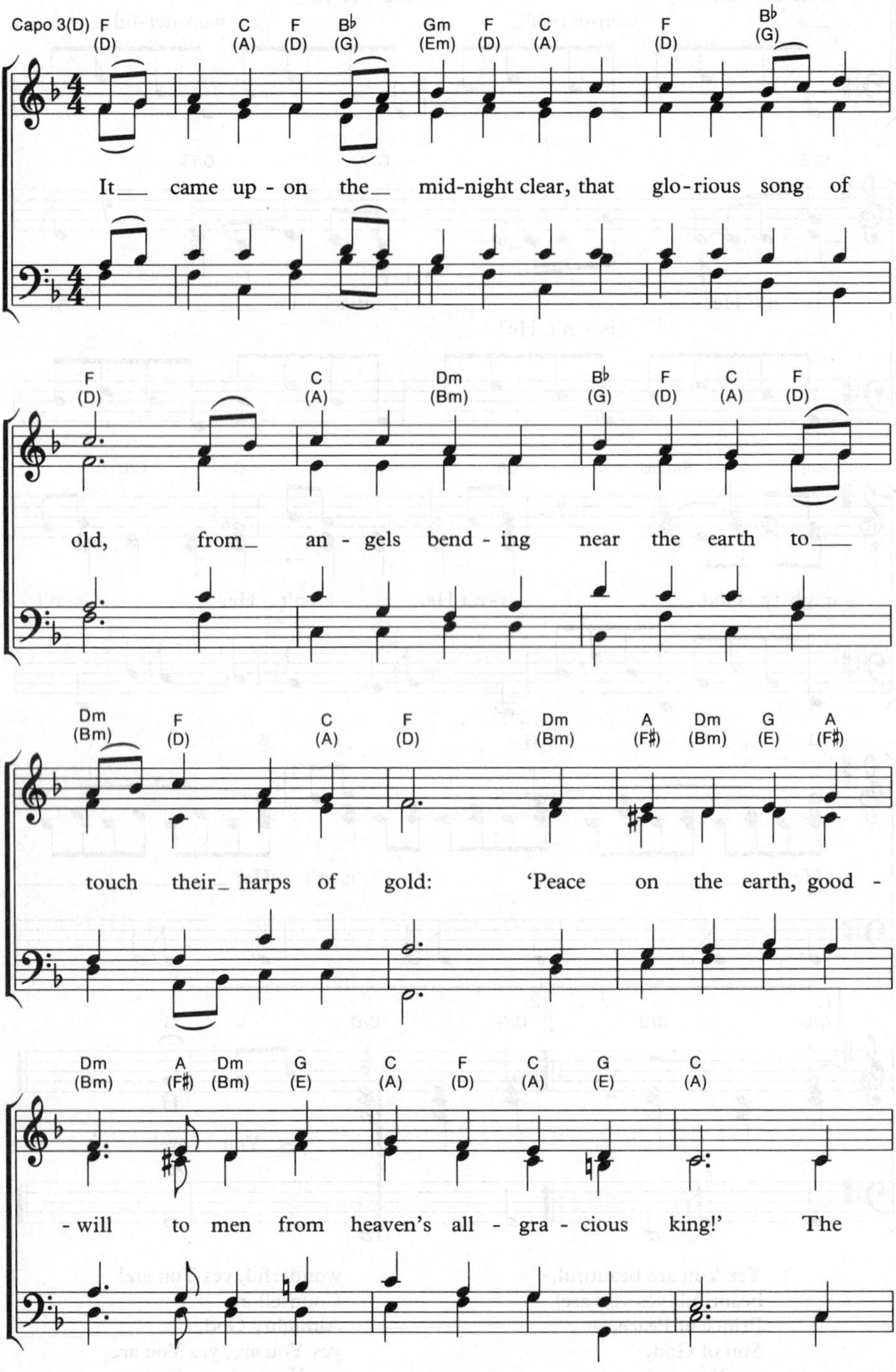

Capo 3(D)
F (D) C (A) F (D) B♭ (G) Gm (Em) F (D) C (A) F (D) B♭ (G)
It came up - on the mid-night clear, that glo-rious song of
F (D) C (A) Dm (Bm) B♭ (G) F (D) C (A) F (D)
old, from angels bend - ing near the earth to
Dm (Bm) F (D) C (A) F (D) Dm (Bm) A (F♯) Dm (Bm) G (E) A (F♯)
touch their harps of gold: 'Peace on the earth, good -
Dm (Bm) A (F♯) Dm (Bm) G (E) C (A) F (D) C (A) G (E) C (A)
- will to men from heaven's all - gra - cious king!' The

world in__ sol - emn still - ness lay to__ hear the__ an - gels sing.

1   It came upon the midnight clear,
     that glorious song of old,
     from angels bending near the earth
     to touch their harps of gold:
     'Peace on the earth, goodwill to men
     from heaven's all-gracious king!'
     The world in solemn stillness lay
     to hear the angels sing.

2   With sorrow brought by sin and strife
     the world has suffered long,
     and, since the angels sang, have passed
     two thousand years of wrong;
     for man at war with man hears not
     the love-song which they bring:
     O hush the noise, you men of strife,
     and hear the angels sing!

3   And those whose journey now is hard,
     whose hope is burning low,
     who tread the rocky path of life
     with painful steps and slow:
     O listen to the news of love
     which makes the heavens ring!
     O rest beside the weary road
     and hear the angels sing!

4   And still the days are hastening on –
     by prophets seen of old –
     towards the fulness of the time
     when comes the age foretold:
     then earth and heaven renewed shall see
     the Prince of Peace, their king;
     and all the world repeat the song
     which now the angels sing.

346   It is a thing most wonderful

BROOKFIELD   LM

Words: William Walsham How (1823–97)
Music: T B Southgate (1814–68)

It is a thing_ most won - der - ful, al - most too

won - der - ful to be, that God's own Son should

come from heaven and die_ to save_ a child_ like me.

1 It is a thing most wonderful,
  almost too wonderful to be,
  that God's own Son should come from heaven
  and die to save a child like me.

2 And yet I know that it is true;
  He chose a poor and humble lot,
  and wept, and toiled, and mourned, and died,
  for love of those who loved Him not.

3 I sometimes think about the cross,
  and shut my eyes and try to see
  the cruel nails and crown of thorns,
  and Jesus crucified for me.

4 But even could I see Him die,
  I could but see a little part
  of that great love, which, like a fire,
  is always burning in His heart.

5 I cannot tell how He could love
  a child so weak and full of sin;
  His love must be most wonderful,
  if He could die my love to win.

6 It is most wonderful to know
  His love for me so free and sure;
  but 'tis more wonderful to see
  my love for Him so faint and poor.

7 And yet I want to love Thee, Lord;
  O light the flame within my heart,
  and I will love Thee more and more,
  until I see Thee as Thou art.

347

It may be at morn

O LORD JESUS HOW LONG   12 12 12 7 with refrain

Words: H L Turner
Music: James McGranahan (1840–1907)

It may be at morn, when the day is a-wak-ing, when
sun-light through dark-ness and sha-dow is break-ing, that
Je-sus will come in the ful-ness of glo-ry, to re-ceive from the
world_ 'His own'. O Lord Je-sus, how long? How

long ere we shout the glad song? Christ re - turn - eth, hal - le -

- lu - jah, hal - le - lu - jah, a - men, hal - le - lu - jah, a - men!

1 It may be at morn, when the day is awaking,
when sunlight through darkness and shadow is breaking,
that Jesus will come in the fulness of glory,
to receive from the world 'His own'.
O Lord Jesus, how long?
How long ere we shout the glad song?
Christ returneth,
hallelujah, hallelujah, amen,
hallelujah, amen!

2 It may be at mid-day, it may be at twilight,
it may be, perchance, that the blackness of midnight
will burst into light in the blaze of His glory,
when Jesus receives 'His own'.
O Lord Jesus . . .

3 While hosts cry hosanna, from heaven descending,
with glorified saints and the angels attending,
with grace on His brow, like a halo of glory,
will Jesus receive 'His own'.
O Lord Jesus . . .

4 Oh, joy! Oh, delight! should we go without dying;
no sickness, no sadness, no dread and no crying;
caught up through the clouds with our Lord into glory,
when Jesus receives 'His own'.
O Lord Jesus . . .

348   It only takes a spark

Words and music: Kurt Kaiser

1 It__ on - ly takes a spark to get a fire__
2 What a won - drous time is spring when all the trees are
3 I__ wish for you, my friend, this hap - pi - ness that

go - ing,____ and soon all those a - round can
bud - ding,____ the birds be - gin to sing; the
I've__ found;____ you can de - pend on Him, it

warm up in its glow - ing;____ that's how it is with
flow - ers start their bloom - ing;____ that's how it is with
mat - ters not where you're bound;____ I'll shout it from the

God's__ love, once you've ex - pe - ri-enced it:__ you
God's__ love, once you've ex - pe - ri-enced it__ you
moun - tain top, I want my world to know; The

spread His love to ev-ery-one; you want to pass it on.___
want to sing, it's fresh like spring; you want to pass it on.___
Lord of love has come to me, I want to pass it on.___

1   It only takes a spark to get a fire going,
    and soon all those around can warm up in its glowing;
    that's how it is with God's love, once you've experienced it:
    you spread His love to everyone;
    you want to pass it on.

2   What a wondrous time is spring when all the trees are budding,
    the birds begin to sing; the flowers start their blooming;
    that's how it is with God's love,
    once you've experienced it you want to sing,
    it's fresh like spring; you want to pass it on.

3   I wish for you, my friend, this happiness that I've found;
    you can depend on Him, it matters not where you're bound;
    I'll shout it from the mountain top,
    I want my world to know;
    The Lord of love has come to me, I want to pass it on.

349   It passeth knowledge

IT PASSETH KNOWLEDGE   10 10 10 10 4

Words: Mary Shekleton (1827–83)
Music: I D Sankey (1840–1908)

It pass - eth know - ledge, that dear love of Thine, my

Sav - iour, Je - sus! yet this soul of mine would

of Thy love, in all its breadth and length, its height and depth, and

ev - er - last - ing strength, knows more and____ more.

1   It passeth knowledge, that dear love of Thine,
my Saviour, Jesus! yet this soul of mine
would of Thy love, in all its breadth and length,
its height and depth, and everlasting strength,
    know more and more.

2   It passeth telling, that dear love of Thine,
my Saviour, Jesus! yet these lips of mine
would fain proclaim, to sinners, far and near,
a love which can remove all guilty fear,
    and love beget.

3   It passeth praises, that dear love of Thine,
my Saviour, Jesus! yet this heart of mine
would sing that love, so full, so rich, so free,
which brings a rebel sinner, such as me,
    nigh unto God.

4   O fill me, Saviour, Jesus, with Thy love;
lead, lead me to the living fount above;
thither may I, in simple faith, draw nigh,
and never to another fountain fly,
    but unto Thee.

5   And then, when Jesus face to face I see,
when at His lofty throne I bow the knee,
then of His love, in all its breadth and length,
its height and depth, its everlasting strength,
    my soul shall sing.

350   It is no longer I that liveth

Words and music: Sally Ellis
Music arranged Christopher Norton

Words and music: © 1980 Thankyou Music,
PO Box 75, Eastbourne, East Sussex BN23 6NW, UK

351 It's Your blood

Words and music: Michael Christ
Music arranged Christopher Norton

Moderato

It's Your blood that clean - ses_ me, it's Your blood that gives me_ life, it's Your blood that took my place in re - deem - ing sac - ri - fice,_____ and wash-es me_____ whit-er than the snow,_____ than the snow. My Je-sus, God's pre-cious sac - ri - fice.

352   I've found a friend

CONSTANCE   87 87 D

Words: J G Small (1817–88)
Music: A S Sullivan (1842–1900)

I've found a friend; O such a friend! He loved me ere I knew Him; He drew me with the— cords of love, and thus He bound me to Him: and round my— heart still— close - ly— twine those ties which nought can se - ver, for

I am His, and He is mine, for ev - er and for ev - er.

1 I've found a friend; O such a friend!
   He loved me ere I knew Him;
   He drew me with the cords of love,
   and thus He bound me to Him:
   and round my heart still closely twine
   those ties which nought can sever,
   for I am His, and He is mine,
   for ever and for ever.

2 I've found a friend; O such a friend!
   He bled, He died to save me;
   and not alone the gift of life,
   but His own self He gave me:
   nought that I have mine own I call,
   I hold it for the giver;
   my heart, my strength, my life, my all,
   are His, and His for ever.

3 I've found a friend; O such a friend!
   all power to Him is given;
   to guard me on my onward course,
   and bring me safe to heaven.
   Eternal glories gleam afar,
   to nerve my faint endeavour;
   so now to watch, to work, to war,
   and then to rest for ever.

4 I've found a friend; O such a friend!
   so kind, and true, and tender!
   So wise a counsellor and guide,
   so mighty a defender!
   From Him who loves me now so well
   what power my soul shall sever?
   Shall life or death? Shall earth or hell?
   No! I am His for ever.

353   I've got peace like a river

Words and music: Traditional
Music arranged Roland Fudge

Quietly

I've got peace like a river, peace like a
river, I've got peace like a river, in my soul;
I've got peace like a river, peace like a
river, I've got peace like a river, in my soul.

Alternative version

Lively

I've got peace like a ri-ver, I've got peace like a
river, I've got peace like a ri-ver in my *(etc.)*

354 Jehovah Jireh

Words and music: Merla Watson
Music arranged Christopher Norton

Je-ho - vah Jir - eh, my pro-vi - der, His grace is suf-fi-cient for me, for me, — for me. me. My God shall sup-ply — all my needs _____ ac - cord-ing to His rich - es in glo - ry; He will give His an - gels_ charge o - ver me. Je-ho - vah Ji-reh cares for me, for me, for me. Je - ho-vah Jir-eh cares for me. __

Words and music: © 1974 Catacombs Productions,
PO Box 4124 Station A, Victoria, BC, Canada

355   Jesus at Your name

Words and music: Chris Bowater

Words and music: © 1982 Lifestyle Music Ltd, PO Box 356,
Leighton Buzzard, Beds LU7 8WP UK

356   Jesus Christ our great Redeemer

Words and music: Peter and Diane Fung

Words and music: © 1983 Thankyou Music,
PO Box 75, Eastbourne, East Sussex BN23 6NW, UK

357 Jesus Christ is risen today

LLANFAIR   77 77 with Hallelujahs

Words: from *Lyra Davidica*, 1708
Music: Melody by Robert Williams (1781–1821)

Unison

suf - fer__ to re - deem our loss. *Hal - le - lu - jah!*

1 Jesus Christ is risen today,
   Hallelujah!
   Our triumphant holy day,
   who did once, upon the cross,
   suffer to redeem our loss.

2 Hymns of praise then let us sing,
   unto Christ, our heavenly King,
   who endured the cross and grave,
   sinners to redeem and save.

3 But the pains which He endured,
   our salvation have procured,
   now in heaven above He's King,
   where the angels ever sing:

358   # Jesus Christ is alive today

Words and music: Unknown
Music arranged Roland Fudge

Joyfully

Je - sus Christ is a - live to-day, I know, I know it's

true.   Sove - reign of the_ U - ni-verse, I

give Him hom-age due.   Seat - ed there at

God's right hand,   I am with Him in the pro - mised land.

Je - sus lives and reigns in me, that's how I know it's true.

Jesus calls us

St Andrew   87 87

Words: Cecil Frances Alexander (1818–95)
Music: E H Thorne (1834–1916)

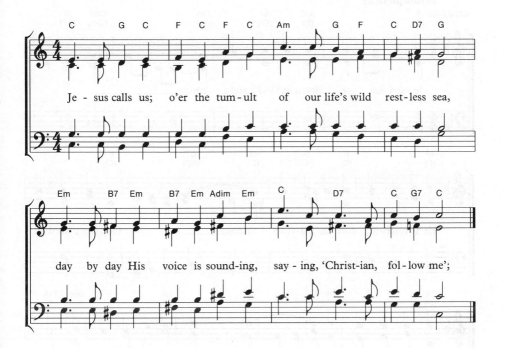

1 Jesus calls us; o'er the tumult
   of our life's wild restless sea,
   day by day His voice is sounding,
   saying, 'Christian, follow me';

2 As of old, apostles heard it
   by the Galilean lake,
   turned from home, and toil, and kindred,
   leaving all for His dear sake.

3 Jesus calls us from the worship
   of the vain world's golden store,
   from each idol that would keep us,
   saying, 'Christian, love Me more.'

4 In our joys and in our sorrows,
   days of toil and hours of ease,
   still He calls, in cares and pleasures,
   'Christian, love Me more than these.'

5 Jesus calls us! By Thy mercies,
   Saviour, may we hear Thy call,
   give our hearts to Thine obedience,
   serve and love Thee best of all.

360

Jesus has sat down

Words and music: Jonathan Wallis
Music arranged David Peacock

Je-sus has sat down at God's right hand,_____

He is reign-ing now on Da-vid's throne;_____ God has placed all

things be-neath His feet,_____ His e-ne-mies will be His

foot-stool._____ *For the gov-ern-ment is now up-on His shoul-der,*_____

_____ *for the gov-ern-ment is now up-on His shoul-der;*_____ *and of the*

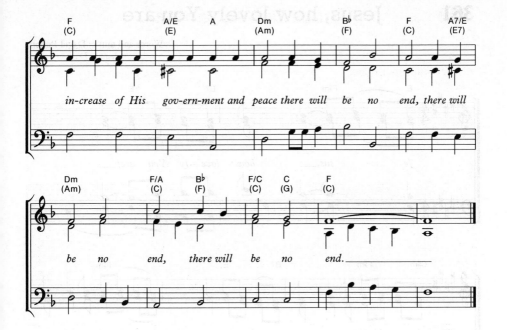

in-crease of His gov-ern-ment and peace there will be no end, there will

be no end, there will be no end._____

1 Jesus has sat down at God's right hand,
  He is reigning now on David's throne;
  God has placed all things beneath His feet,
  His enemies will be His footstool.
  For the government
  is now upon His shoulder,
  for the government
  is now upon His shoulder;
  and of the increase
  of His government and peace
  there will be no end,
  there will be no end,
  there will be no end.

2 God has now exalted Him on high,
  given Him a name above all names;
  every knee will bow, and tongue confess
  that Jesus Christ is Lord.
  For the government . . .

3 Jesus is now living in His church:
  men who have been purchased by His blood –
  they will serve their God, a royal priesthood,
  and they will reign on earth.
  For the government . . .

4 Sound the trumpet – good news to the poor!
  Captives will go free, the blind will see,
  the kingdom of this world will soon become
  the kingdom of our God.
  For the government . . .

361

Jesus, how lovely You are

Words and music: David Bolton

Je - sus,— how love-ly You are!—
You are so gen - tle, so pure and kind, You— shine like the
morn - ing star: Je - sus,— how love-ly You are.—
Al - le - lu - ia, Je - sus is

Jesus, how lovely You are!
You are so gentle, so pure and kind,
You shine like the morning star:
Jesus, how lovely You are.

1 Alleluia, Jesus is my Lord and King;
   Alleluia, Jesus is my everything.
   Jesus, how lovely . . .

2 Alleluia, Jesus died and rose again;
   Alleluia, Jesus forgave all my sin.
   Jesus, how lovely . . .

3 Alleluia, Jesus is meek and lowly;
   Alleluia, Jesus is pure and holy.
   Jesus, how lovely . . .

4 Alleluia, Jesus is the bridegroom;
   Alleluia, Jesus will take His bride soon.
   Jesus, how lovely . . .

362

Jesus, I am resting

TRANQUILITY   87 85 D with refrain

Words: Jean Sophia Pigott (1845–82)
Music: James Mountain (1843–1933)

Je - sus, I am rest-ing, rest-ing, in the joy of what Thou art;

I am find - ing out the great-ness of Thy lov - ing heart.

Thou hast bid me gaze up - on Thee, and Thy beau-ty fills my soul,—

for, by Thy trans - form-ing pow - er, Thou hast made me whole.

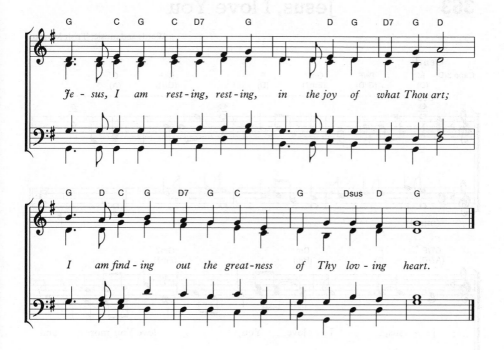

1 Jesus, I am resting, resting,
   in the joy of what Thou art;
   I am finding out the greatness
   of Thy loving heart.
   Thou hast bid me gaze upon Thee,
   and Thy beauty fills my soul,
   for, by Thy transforming power,
   Thou hast made me whole.
     Jesus, I am resting, resting,
     in the joy of what Thou art;
     I am finding out the greatness
     of Thy loving heart.

2 Oh, how great Thy loving kindness,
   vaster, broader than the sea!
   Oh, how marvellous Thy goodness,
   lavished all on me!
   Yes, I rest in Thee, Beloved,
   know what wealth of grace is Thine,
   know Thy certainty of promise,
   and have made it mine.
     Jesus, I am resting . . .

3 Simply trusting Thee, Lord Jesus,
   I behold Thee as Thou art;
   and Thy love so pure, so changeless,
   satisfies my heart.
   Satisfies its deepest longings,
   meets, supplies its every need,
   compasseth me round with blessings;
   Thine is love indeed.
     Jesus, I am resting . . .

4 Ever lift Thy face upon me,
   as I work and wait for Thee;
   resting 'neath Thy smile, Lord Jesus,
   earth's dark shadows flee.
   Brightness of my Father's glory,
   sunshine of my Father's face,
   keep me ever trusting, resting,
   fill me with Thy grace.
     Jesus, I am resting . . .

363   Jesus, I love You

Words and music: Trish Morgan

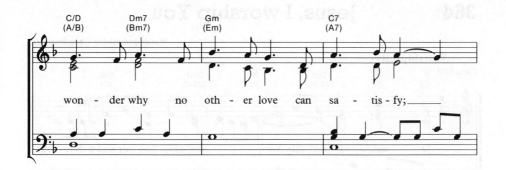

won - der why   no oth - er love   can   sa - tis - fy;_____

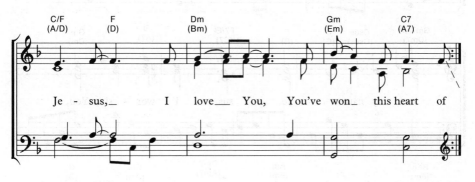

Je - sus,____   I   love____ You,   You've won____ this heart   of

mine!

Jesus, I love You,
love You more and more each day;
Jesus, I love You,
Your gentle touch renews my heart.
It's really no wonder why
no other love can satisfy;
Jesus, I love You,
You've won this heart of mine!

364   Jesus, I worship You

Words and music: Chris Bowater

Words and music: © 1982 Lifestyle Music Ltd, PO Box 356,
Leighton Buzzard, Beds LU7 8WP UK

365 Jesus is Lord of all

Words and music: Marilyn Baker

1 Je - sus is Lord of all,__ Sa - tan is under His feet,__ Je - sus is reign-ing on high,__ and all power is giv - en to Him in heaven and earth.
2 We are__ joined to Him,_ Sa - tan is under our feet,__ we are__ seat - ed on high,__ and all au - tho - ri - ty is given to us through Him.
3 One day we'll be__ like Him,_ per - fect in e - ve - ry way,__ cho - sen to be__ His bride, rul - ing and reign-ing with Him for ev - er - more.

Words and music: © 1983 Word Music (UK), (a division of Word (UK) Ltd)
9 Holdom Avenue, Bletchley, Milton Keynes MK1 1QR, UK

366   Jesus is King

Words and music: Wendy Churchill

1   Jesus is King
        and I will extol Him,
    give Him the glory,
        and honour His name;
    He reigns on high,
        enthroned in the heavens –
    Word of the Father,
        exalted for us.

2   We have a hope
        that is steadfast and certain,
    gone through the curtain
        and touching the throne;
    we have a Priest
        who is there interceding,
    pouring His grace
        on our lives day by day.

3   We come to Him,
        our Priest and Apostle,
    clothed in His glory
        and bearing His name,
    laying our lives
        with gladness before Him –
    filled with His Spirit
        we worship the King:

4   'O Holy One,
        our hearts do adore You;
    thrilled with Your goodness
        we give You our praise!'
    Angels in light
        with worship surround Him,
    Jesus, our Saviour,
        for ever the same.

367   Jesus is Lord

Words and music: David J Mansell

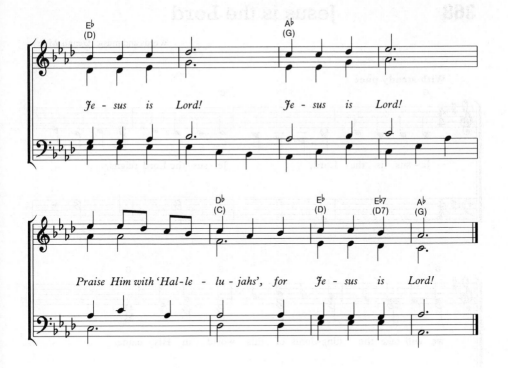

Je - sus   is   Lord!   Je - sus   is   Lord!

Praise Him with 'Hal - le - lu - jahs', for   Je - sus   is   Lord!

1   Jesus is Lord! Creation's voice proclaims it,
     for by His power each tree and flower was planned and made.
     Jesus is Lord! The universe declares it;
     sun, moon and stars in heaven cry: Jesus is Lord!
       Jesus is Lord! Jesus is Lord!
       Praise Him with 'Hallelujahs', for Jesus is Lord!

2   Jesus is Lord! Yet from His throne eternal
     in flesh He came to die in pain on Calvary's tree.
     Jesus is Lord! From Him all life proceeding,
     yet gave His life a ransom thus setting us free.
       Jesus is Lord . . .

3   Jesus is Lord! O'er sin the mighty conqueror,
     from death He rose and all His foes shall own His name.
     Jesus is Lord! God sends His Holy Spirit
     to show by works of power that Jesus is Lord.
       Jesus is Lord . . .

368

Jesus is the Lord

Words and music: Dennis Merry

Je-sus is the Lord, Je-sus the Lord reigns,

we will take the king-doms of this world in His name.

Ev-ery tribe and na-tion, ev-ery si-tu-a-tion,

must de-clare that Je-sus is the Lord._____ For the

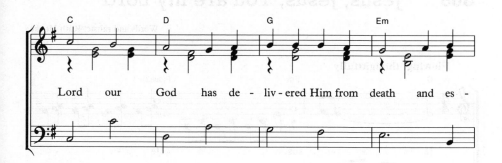

Lord our God has de-liv-ered Him from death and es-

-tab-lished Je-sus as Lord;_____ He has

giv-en Him the power o-ver all that He has made, for our

God has_ made Him Christ the Lord._____

369 Jesus, Jesus, You are my Lord

Words and music: Ruth Hooke

C/G		F/G	G7	Csus		C

keep   us   in _____ Your love. _____

1 Jesus, Jesus,
   You are my Lord and my heart's desire;
   Jesus, Jesus,
   keep us in Your love.

2 Jesus, Jesus,
   You are my King and my Sovereign Master;
   Jesus, Jesus,
   I will serve You Lord.

370   Jesus, Jesus, Jesus

Words and music: Chris Bowater

371

Jesus, Lamb of God

Words and music: Betty Pulkingham

372   Jesus, lover of my soul

ABERYSTWYTH   77 77 D

Words: Charles Wesley (1707–88) altd.
Music: Joseph Parry (1841–1903)

Je - sus,__ lov - er__ of my__ soul,

let me to Thy bo - som fly, while the__ near - er__

wa - ters__ roll, while the__ tem - pest still is__ high:

hide me, O__ my Sav - iour,__ hide,

till the storm of__ life is__ past; safe in - to the

ha - ven guide; O__ re - ceive my__ soul at____ last!

1 Jesus, lover of my soul,
  let me to Thy bosom fly,
  while the nearer waters roll,
  while the tempest still is high:
  hide me, O my Saviour, hide,
  till the storm of life is past;
  safe into the haven guide;
  O receive my soul at last!

2 Other refuge have I none,
  hangs my helpless soul on Thee;
  leave, ah! leave me not alone,
  still support and comfort me:
  all my trust on Thee is stayed;
  all my help from Thee I bring;
  cover my defenceless head
  with the shadow of Thy wing.

3 Thou, O Christ, art all I want;
  more than all in Thee I find;
  raise the fallen, cheer ther faint,
  heal the sick, and lead the blind.
  Just and holy is Thy name,
  I am all unrighteousness;
  false, and full of sin I am,
  Thou art full of truth and grace.

4 Plenteous grace with Thee is found,
  grace to cover all my sin;
  let the healing streams abound,
  make and keep me pure within.
  Thou of life the fountain art,
  freely let me take of Thee;
  spring Thou up within my heart,
  rise to all eternity.

373

Jesus lives

St Albinus 78 78 with Hallelujah

Words: Christian F Gellert (1715–69)
tr. Frances Elizabeth Cox (1812–97)
Music: Henry John Gauntlett (1805–76)

Je - sus lives! thy ter - rors now can, O death, no
more ap - pal us; Je - sus lives! by this we_ know,
thou, O grave, canst not en - thral us. Hal - le - lu - jah!

1 Jesus lives! thy terrors now
   can, O death, no more appal us;
   Jesus lives! by this we know,
   thou, O grave, canst not enthral us.
      Hallelujah!

2 Jesus lives! henceforth is death
   but the gate of life immortal;
   this shall calm our trembling breath,
   when we pass its gloomy portal.
      Hallelujah!

3 Jesus lives! for us He died;
   then, alone to Jesus living,
   pure in heart may we abide,
   glory to our Saviour giving.
      Hallelujah!

4 Jesus lives! our hearts know well,
   naught from us His love shall sever;
   life, nor death, nor powers of hell,
   tear us from His keeping ever.
      Hallelujah!

5 Jesus lives! to Him the throne
   over all the world is given:
   may we go where He is gone,
   rest and reign with Him in heaven.
      Hallelujah!

374   Jesus my Lord

Words and music: Norman J Clayton

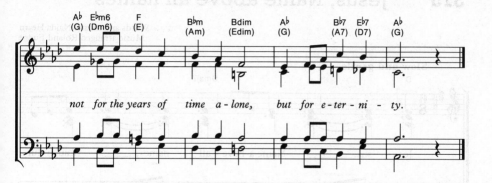

not for the years of time a-lone, but for e-ter-ni - ty.

1 Jesus my Lord will love me for ever,
from Him no power of evil can sever,
He gave His life to ransom my soul,
now I belong to Him:
   Now I belong to Jesus,
   Jesus belongs to me,
   not for the years of time alone,
   but for eternity.

2 Once I was lost in sin's degradation,
Jesus came down to bring me salvation,
lifted me up from sorrow and shame,
now I belong to Him:
   Now I belong . . .

3 Joy floods my soul, for Jesus has saved me,
freed me from sin that long had enslaved me,
His precious blood He gave to redeem,
now I belong to Him:
   Now I belong . . .

375 Jesus, Name above all names

Words and music: Naida Hearn
Music arranged Roland Fudge

Slow and gentle

Je - sus,_____ Name a-bove all names,_____ beau-ti-ful
Sav - iour,_____ glo-ri-ous Lord;_____ Em -
- man - u - el,_____ God is with us,_____ bless-ed Re -
- deem - er,_____ liv - ing Word._____

376 Jesus put this song into our hearts

Words and music: Graham Kendrick
Music arranged David Peacock

Hebrew style, getting faster

1 Je - sus put this song in - to our hearts, _____
2 Je - sus taught us how to live in har - mo - ny,
3 Je - sus taught us how to be a fa - mi - ly,
4 Je - sus turned our sor - row in - to danc - ing,

Je-sus put this song in-to our hearts; ___ it's a song of joy no-one can
Je-sus taught us how to live in har-mo-ny; diff-erent fac-es, diff-erent rac-es,
Je-sus taught us how to be a fa-mi-ly; lov-ing one an-oth-er with the
Je-sus turned our sor-row in-to danc-ing, changed our tears of sad-ness in-to

take__ a-way.___ Je-sus put this song_____ in-to our
He made us one =__ Je-sus taught us how to live_____ in har-mo-
love that He gives – Je-sus taught us how to be_____ a fa-mi-
ri-vers of joy =__ Je-sus turned our sor - row_____ in-to a

hearts._____
- ny._____
- ly._____
dance._____ (Hey!)

377   Jesus, Prince and Saviour

St Gertrude   65 65 D with refrain

Words: Timothy Dudley-Smith
Music: Arthur S Sullivan (1842–1900)

Je - sus, Prince and Sav - iour, Lord of life who died;

Christ, the friend of sin - ners, sin - ners cru - ci - fied.

For a lost world's ran - som, all Him - self He gave,

lay at last death's vic - tim,___ life - less in the grave.

Lord of life tri - um - phant, ris - en now to_ reign!_

King of end - less a - ges, Je - sus lives a - gain!

1 Jesus, Prince and Saviour,
Lord of life who died;
Christ, the friend of sinners,
sinners crucified.
For a lost world's ransom,
all Himself He gave,
lay at last death's victim,
lifeless in the grave.
Lord of life triumphant,
risen now to reign!
King of endless ages,
Jesus lives again!

2 In His power and Godhead
every victory won;
pain and passion ended,
all His purpose done.
Christ the Lord is risen!
sighs and sorrows past,
death's dark night is over,
morning comes at last!
Lord of life . . .

3 Resurrection morning!
sinners' bondage freed;
Christ the Lord is risen –
He is risen indeed!
Jesus, Prince and Saviour,
Lord of life who died,
Christ the King of glory
now is glorified!
Lord of life . . .

378 Jesus shall take the highest honour

Words and music: Chris Bowater

379 Jesus shall reign

TRURO   LM

Words: Isaac Watts (1674–1748)
Music: from *Psalmodia Evangelica*, 1789

Je - sus shall reign wher - e'er the sun does His suc - ces - sive__ jour - neys run; His king - dom stretch from shore to __ shore, till moons shall rise and set no more.

1 Jesus shall reign where'er the sun
   does His successive journeys run;
   His kingdom stretch from shore to shore,
   till moons shall rise and set no more.

2 To Him shall endless prayer be made,
   and princes throng to crown His head;
   His name, like sweet perfume, shall rise
   with every morning sacrifice.

3 People and realms of every tongue
   dwell on His love with sweetest song;
   and infant voices shall proclaim
   their early blessings on His name.

4 Blessings abound where'er He reigns;
   the prisoner leaps to lose his chains,
   the weary find eternal rest,
   and all the sons of want are blest.

5 Let every creature rise and bring
   the highest honours to our King;
   angels descend with songs again,
   and earth repeats the loud 'Amen'.

Jesus, stand among us

CASWELL   65 65

Words: William Pennefather (1816–73)
Music: F Filitz (1804–76)

Je - sus, stand a - mong_ us in Thy ris - en power;

let this time of wor - ship be a hal - lowed hour.

1   Jesus, stand among us
    in Thy risen power;
    let this time of worship
    be a hallowed hour.

2   Breathe the Holy Spirit
    into every heart;
    bid the fears and sorrows
    from each soul depart.

3   Thus with quickened footsteps
    we'll pursue our way,
    watching for the dawning
    of eternal day.

381 Jesus, stand among us

Words and music: Graham Kendrick
Music arranged Roger Mayor

Je - sus, stand a - mong us___ at the meet - ing of___ our lives, be our sweet a - gree - ment at the meet - ing of___ our eyes; O Je - sus, we love You, so we gath - er here, love You,

1   Jesus, stand among us at the meeting of our lives,
      be our sweet agreement at the meeting of our eyes;
      O Jesus, we love You, so we gather here,
      join our hearts in unity and take away our fear.

2   So to You we're gathering out of each and every land,
      Christ the love between us at the joining of our hands;
      O Jesus, we love You, so we gather here,
      join our hearts in unity and take away our fear.

      OPTIONAL VERSE FOR COMMUNION
3   Jesus stand among us at the breaking of the bread;
      join us as one body as we worship You, our Head.
      O Jesus, we love You, so we gather here;
      join our hearts in unity and take away our fear.

382   Jesus take me as I am

Words and music: Dave Bryant
Music arranged Roger Mayor

Words and music: © 1978 Thankyou Music,
PO Box 75, Eastbourne, East Sussex BN23 6NW, UK

Make me like a pre-cious stone,

crys-tal clear__ and fine-ly honed.__

Life of Je-sus shin-ing through,__

giv-ing glo - ry back to You.__

383   Jesus, the joy of loving hearts

MARYTON   LM

Words: from the Latin (12th century)
R Palmer (1808–87)
Music: H P Smith (1825–98)

Je - sus, the joy of lov - ing hearts,
true source of life, and light___ of men:
from the best bliss that earth___ im - parts___ we
turn un - filled to You___ a - gain.

1 Jesus, the joy of loving hearts,
true source of life, and light of men:
from the best bliss that earth imparts
we turn unfilled to You again.

2 Your truth unchanged has ever stood,
You rescue those who on You call:
to those yet seeking, You are good –
to those who find You, all-in-all.

3 We taste of You, the living bread,
and long to feast upon You still;
we drink from You, the fountain-head,
our thirsty souls from You we fill.

4 Our restless spirits long for You,
whichever way our lot is cast,
glad when Your gracious smile we view,
blessed when our faith can hold You fast.

5 Jesus, for ever with us stay,
make all our moments calm and bright;
chase the dark night of sin away,
spread through the world Your holy light.

384 Jesus the Lord

Yisu Ne Kaha

Words: translated from Urdu
Dermott Monahan (1906–57)
Music: Urdu melody
arranged Francis B Westbrook (1903–75)

Je - sus the Lord said: 'I am the Bread, the Bread of___ Life_ for man -

- kind am I, the Bread of___ Life_ for man - kind am I, the

Bread of___ Life_ for man - kind am I.' Je - sus the Lord said:

'I am the Bread, the Bread of___ Life_ for man - kind am I.'

Words: © The Methodist Church,
Division of Education and Youth

1 Jesus the Lord said: 'I am the Bread,
the Bread of Life for mankind am I,
the Bread of Life for mankind am I,
the Bread of Life for mankind am I.'
Jesus the Lord said: 'I am the Bread,
the Bread of Life for mankind am I.'

2 Jesus the Lord said: 'I am the Way,
the true and living Way am I,
the true and living Way am I,
the true and living Way am I.'
Jesus the Lord said: 'I am the Way,
the true and living Way am I.'

3 Jesus the Lord said: 'I am the Light,
the one true Light of the world am I,
the one true Light of the world am I,
the one true Light of the world am I.'
Jesus the Lord said: 'I am the Light,
the one true Light of the world am I.'

4 Jesus the Lord said: 'I am the Shepherd,
the one Good Shepherd of the sheep am I,
the one Good Shepherd of the sheep am I,
the one Good Shepherd of the sheep am I.'
Jesus the Lord said: 'I am the Shepherd,
the one Good Shepherd of the sheep am I.'

5 Jesus the Lord said: 'I am the Life,
the Resurrection and the Life am I,
the Resurrection and the Life am I,
the Resurrection and the Life am I.'
Jesus the Lord said: 'I am the Life,
the Resurrection and the Life am I.'

385   Jesus, the name high over all

LYDIA   CM extended

Words: Charles Wesley (1707–88)
Music: Thomas Phillips (1735–1807)

Je - sus, the name high o - ver all, in hell, or earth, or sky: an - gels and men be - fore it fall, and de - vils fear and fly, and de - vils fear and fly.

1   Jesus, the name high over all,
in hell, or earth, or sky:
angels and men before it fall,
and devils fear and fly.

2   Jesus, the name to sinners dear,
the name to sinners given;
it scatters all their guilty fear,
it turns their hell to heaven.

3   Jesus, the prisoner's fetters breaks,
and bruises Satan's head;
power into strengthless souls He speaks,
and life into the dead.

4   Oh, that the world might taste and see
the riches of His grace!
The arms of love that compass me,
would all mankind embrace.

5   His only righteousness I show,
His saving truth proclaim:
'tis all my business here below
to cry: 'Behold the Lamb!'

6   Happy, if with my latest breath
I may but gasp His name:
preach Him to all, and cry in death:
'Behold, behold the Lamb!'

386   Jesus, the very thought of Thee

St Agnes (Dykes)   CM

Words: Bernard of Clairvaux (1091–1153)
tr. Edward Caswall (1814–78)
Music: J B Dykes (1823–76)

Je - sus, the ve - ry thought_ of Thee
with sweet - ness fills the breast;
but sweet - er far Thy face to see,____
and in Thy pre - sence rest.

1 Jesus, the very thought of Thee
   with sweetness fills the breast;
   but sweeter far Thy face to see,
   and in Thy presence rest.

2 Nor voice can sing, nor heart can frame,
   nor can the memory find
   a sweeter sound than Thy blest name,
   O Saviour of mankind!

3 O hope of every contrite heart,
   O joy of all the meek,
   to those who ask, how kind Thou art!
   how good to those who seek!

4 But what to those who find? Ah, this
   nor tongue nor pen can show:
   the love of Jesus, what it is
   none but His loved ones know.

5 Jesus, our only joy be Thou,
   as Thou our prize wilt be;
   in Thee be all our glory now,
   and through eternity.

387 Jesus, we celebrate Your victory

Words and music: John Gibson

1 It was for free - dom that Christ has set us free,__ no lon -
2 His Spi - rit in__ us__ re - leas - es us from fear,__ the way

- ger to be sub - ject to a yoke of sla - ve - ry.__
__ to Him is o - pen, with bold-ness we draw near;__

So we're re - joic - ing__ in God's vic - to - ry, __ our
and in His pre - sence our prob-lems dis - ap-pear,__ our

hearts re - spond - ing to His love.__
hearts re - spond - ing to His love.__

388   Jesus, we enthrone You

Words and music: Paul Kyle
Music arranged Roland Fudge

389   Jesus, You are changing me

Words and music: Marilyn Baker

Words and music: © 1981 Word Music (UK), (a division of Word (UK) Ltd)
9 Holdom Avenue, Bletchley, Milton Keynes MK1 1QR, UK

390   Jesus, You are the power

Words and music: Dave Fellingham

Je-sus, You are the power, You are the wis - dom ___ that comes from the Lord God, ___ who has re-vealed His love. ___

Our faith now rests ___ on ___ Your power ___ Lord, which Your Spi-rit has poured out on us. ___ We ___ de-clare ___ the mys-tery

391 Jesus, You are the radiance

Words and music: Dave Fellingham
Music arranged David Peacock

Je - sus, You are the rad - iance of the
Fa - ther's glo - - ry, You are the Son, the ap -
- point - ed heir, through whom all things are made;
You are the one who sus - tains all

392   Join all the glorious names

ST GODRIC   66 66 88

Words: Isaac Watts (1674–1748)
Music: J B Dykes (1823–76)

Join all the glo - rious names of wis - dom, love, and power, that ev - er mor - tals knew, that an - gels ev - er bore: all are too mean to speak His worth, too mean to set my Sav - iour forth.

1 Join all the glorious names
of wisdom, love, and power,
that ever mortals knew,
that angels ever bore:
all are too mean to speak His worth,
too mean to set my Saviour forth.

2 Great Prophet of my God,
my tongue would bless Thy name:
by Thee the joyful news
of our salvation came:
the joyful news of sins forgiven,
of hell subdued and peace with heaven.

3 Jesus, my great High Priest,
offered His blood, and died;
my guilty conscience seeks
no sacrifice beside:
His powerful blood did once atone,
and now it pleads before the throne.

4 My Saviour and my Lord,
my conqueror and my King,
Thy sceptre and Thy sword,
Thy reigning grace I sing:
Thine is the power; behold, I sit
in willing bonds beneath Thy feet.

5 Now let my soul arise,
and tread the tempter down:
my captain leads me forth
to conquest and a crown:
march on, nor fear to win the day,
though death and hell obstruct the way.

6 Should all the hosts of death,
and powers of hell unknown,
put their most dreadful forms
of rage and malice on,
I shall be safe; for Christ displays
superior power and guardian grace.

393   Joy to the world

ANTIOCH   CM

Words: Isaac Watts (1674–1748)
Music: G F Handel (1685–1759)
arranged L Mason (1792–1872)

1 Joy to the world, the Lord has come! let
2 Joy to the earth, the Sav - iour reigns! your
3 He rules the world with truth and grace, and

earth re-ceive her King; let ev - ery heart___ pre -
sweet - est songs em - ploy while fields and___ streams___ and
makes the na - tions prove the glo - ries___ of___ His

- pare___ Him___ room_____ and heaven and na - ture sing, and___
hills___ and___ plains___ re - peat the sound-ing joy, re -
right - eous - ness,___ the won - ders of His love, the___

and heaven and na - ture
re - peat the sound-ing
the won - ders of His

heaven and na - ture___ sing,   and___
- peat the sound - ing___ joy,   re -
won - ders of His___ love,   the___

sing,   and heaven and na - ture
joy,   re - peat the sound - ing
love,   the won - ders of His

heaven, and heaven___ and na - ture sing!
- peat,___ re - peat___ the sound - ing joy.
won - ders, won - ders of His love.

sing, and heaven and na - ture sing!
joy, re - peat the sound - ing joy.
love, the won - ders of His love.

1   Joy to the world, the Lord has come!
     let earth receive her King;
     let every heart prepare Him room
          and heaven and nature sing,
          and heaven and nature sing,
          and heaven, and heaven and nature sing!

2   Joy to the earth, the Saviour reigns!
     your sweetest songs employ
     while fields and streams and hills and plains
          repeat the sounding joy,
          repeat the sounding joy,
          repeat, repeat the sounding joy.

3   He rules the world with truth and grace,
     and makes the nations prove
     the glories of His righteousness,
          the wonders of His love,
          the wonders of His love,
          the wonders, wonders of His love.

394   Jubilate, everybody

Words and music: Fred Dunn

395   Judge eternal

RHUDDLAN   87 87 87

Words: Henry Scott Holland (1847–1918) altd.
Music: Welsh traditional melody

1   Judge eternal, throned in splendour,
    Lord of lords and King of kings,
    with Your living fire of judgement
    purge this realm of bitter things;
    solace all its wide dominion
    with the healing of Your wings.

2   Still the weary folk are pining
    for the hour that brings release;
    and the city's crowded clangour
    cries aloud for sin to cease;
    and the homesteads and the woodlands
    plead in silence for their peace.

3   Crown, O God, Your own endeavour;
    cleave our darkness with Your sword;
    feed the faithless and the hungry
    with the richness of Your word;
    cleanse the body of this nation
    through the glory of the Lord.

396(i) Just as I am

WOODWORTH 888 6 extended

Words: Charlotte Elliott (1789–1871)
Music: W B Bradbury (1816–68)

Just as I am, without one plea, but that Thy blood was shed for me, and that Thou bidd'st me come to Thee, O Lamb of God, I come! I come!

1 Just as I am, without one plea,
   but that Thy blood was shed for me,
   and that Thou bidd'st me come to Thee,
   O Lamb of God, I come! I come!

2 Just as I am, and waiting not
   to rid my soul of one dark blot,
   to Thee, whose blood can cleanse each spot
   O Lamb of God, I come! I come!

3 Just as I am, though tossed about
   with many a conflict, many a doubt,
   fightings within, and fears without,
   O Lamb of God, I come! I come!

4 Just as I am, poor, wretched, blind;
   sight, riches, healing of the mind,
   yea, all I need, in Thee to find,
   O Lamb of God, I come! I come!

5 Just as I am, Thou wilt receive,
   wilt welcome, pardon, cleanse, relieve:
   because Thy promise I believe,
   O Lamb of God, I come! I come!

6 Just as I am, Thy love unknown
   hath broken every barrier down;
   now, to be Thine, yea, Thine alone,
   O Lamb of God, I come! I come!

Just as I am

MISERICORDIA   888 6

Words: Charlotte Elliott (1789–1871)
Music: Henry Smart (1813–79)

1 Just as I am, without one plea,
   but that Thy blood was shed for me,
   and that Thou bidd'st me come to Thee,
   O Lamb of God, I come!

2 Just as I am, and waiting not
   to rid my soul of one dark blot,
   to Thee, whose blood can cleanse each spot
   O Lamb of God, I come!

3 Just as I am, though tossed about
   with many a conflict, many a doubt,
   fightings within, and fears without,
   O Lamb of God, I come!

4 Just as I am, poor, wretched, blind;
   sight, riches, healing of the mind,
   yea, all I need, in Thee to find,
   O Lamb of God, I come!

5 Just as I am, Thou wilt receive,
   wilt welcome, pardon, cleanse, relieve:
   because Thy promise I believe,
   O Lamb of God, I come!

6 Just as I am, Thy love unknown
   hath broken every barrier down;
   now, to be Thine, yea, Thine alone,
   O Lamb of God, I come!

397 King of glory, King of peace

GWALCHMAI   74 74 D

Words: George Herbert (1593–1633)
Music: J D Jones (1827–70)

King of glo-ry,__ King of peace, I will love__ Thee;

and, that love_ may_ ne-ver cease, I will move_ Thee.

Thou hast grant-ed my re-quest, Thou hast heard_ me;

Thou didst note my_ work-ing breast, Thou hast spared__ me.

1 King of glory, King of peace,
   I will love Thee;
  and, that love may never cease,
   I will move Thee.
  Thou hast granted my request,
   Thou hast heard me;
  Thou didst note my working breast,
   Thou hast spared me.

2 Wherefore with my utmost art
   I will sing Thee,
  and the cream of all my heart
   I will bring Thee.
  Though my sins against me cried,
   Thou didst clear me;
  and alone, when they replied,
   Thou didst hear me.

3 Seven whole days, not one in seven,
   I will praise Thee;
  in my heart, though not in heaven,
   I can raise Thee.
  Small it is, in this poor sort
   to enrol Thee:
  E'en eternity's too short
   to extol Thee.

398   King of kings and Lord of lords

Words: Sophie Conty and Naomi Batya
Music: Hebrew folk melody

Brightly with increasing pace

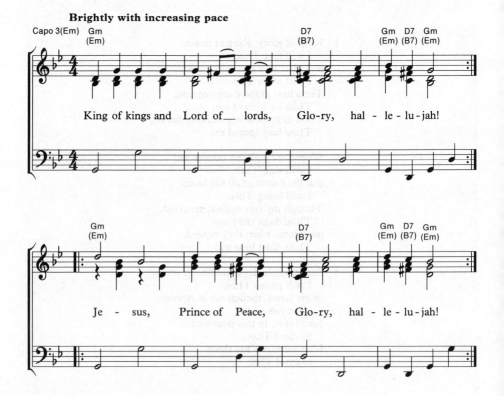

King of kings and Lord of lords,
Glory, hallelujah!
King of kings and Lord of lords,
Glory, hallelujah!
Jesus, Prince of Peace,
Glory, hallelujah!
Jesus, Prince of Peace,
Glory, hallelujah!

(may be sung as a round)

Words and music: © 1980 Maranatha! Music (USA)/Word Music (UK), (a division of Word (UK) Ltd)
9 Holdom Avenue, Bletchley, Milton Keynes MK1 1QR, UK
For British Isles, Republic of Ireland, Continent of Europe (Exc Benelux)

399   # Lead kindly Light

SANDON   10 4 10 4 10 10

Words: J H Newman (1801–90)
Music: C H Purday (1799–1885)

1   Lead kindly Light, amid the encircling gloom,
      lead Thou me on;
   the night is dark, and I am far from home;
      lead Thou me on.
   Keep Thou my feet; I do not ask to see
   the distant scene; one step enough for me.

2   I was not ever thus, nor prayed that Thou
      shouldst lead me on;
   I loved to choose and see my path; but now
      lead Thou me on.
   I loved the garish day, and, spite of fears,
   pride ruled my will: remember not past years.

3   So long Thy power has blest me, sure it still
      will lead me on
   o'er moor and fen, o'er crag and torrent, till
      the night is gone;
   and with the morn those angel faces smile
   which I have loved long since, and lost awhile.

Lead us, heavenly Father

MANNHEIM   87 87 87

Words: James Edmeston (1791–1867)
Music: F Filitz (1804–76)

1 Lead us, heavenly Father, lead us
   o'er the world's tempestuous sea;
   guard us, guide us, keep us, feed us –
   for we have no help but Thee,
   yet possessing every blessing
   if our God our Father be.

2 Saviour, breathe forgiveness o'er us:
   all our weakness Thou dost know:
   Thou didst tread this earth before us,
   Thou didst feel its keenest woe;
   lone and dreary, faint and weary,
   through the desert Thou didst go.

3 Spirit of our God, descending,
   fill our hearts with heavenly joy,
   love with every passion blending,
   pleasure that can never cloy:
   thus provided, pardoned, guided,
   nothing can our peace destroy.

401

Let all that is within me

Words: Melvin Harrell
Music: Anon
arranged Betty Pulkingham

1 Let all that is within me cry, 'Holy';
let all that is within me cry, 'Holy';
holy, holy, holy is the Lamb that was slain.

2 Let all that is within me cry, 'Worthy';
let all that is within me cry, 'Worthy';
worthy, worthy, worthy is the Lamb that was slain.

3 Let all that is within me cry, 'Jesus';
let all that is within me cry, 'Jesus';
Jesus, Jesus, Jesus is the Lamb that was slain.

4 Let all that is within me cry, 'Glory';
let all that is within me cry, 'Glory';
glory, glory, glory to the Lamb that was slain.

402 Led like a lamb

Words and music: Graham Kendrick

1 Led like a lamb to the slaugh - ter, in
2 At break of dawn, poor Ma - ry, still
3 At the right hand of the Fa - ther, now

si - lence and shame, there on Your back You car - ried a world of
weep-ing she came, when through her grief she heard Your voice, now
seat - ed on high, You have be - gun Your e-ter - nal_ reign of

vio-lence and pain. Bleed-ing,_ dy-ing,_
speak-ing her name. Ma - ry!_ Mas-ter!_
jus - tice and joy. Glo-ry,_ glo-ry,_

bleed - ing,___   dy - ing.___
Ma - ry!___   Mas - ter!___   You're a -
glo - ry,___   glo - ry.___

- live, You're a-live, You have ris-en!   *(al-le-lu-ia! al-le-lu-ia!)*
Al-le-lu-ia! _   And the

power and the glo-ry is gi-ven,   *(al-le-lu-ia! al-le-lu-ia!)*
Al-le-lu-ia! _   Je-sus to

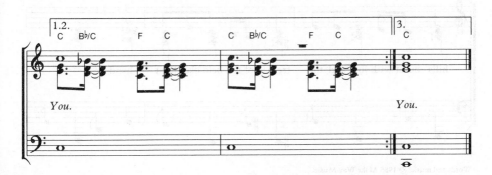

You.   You.

403   Let all the earth

Words and music: Graham Kendrick

Let all the earth hear His voice, let the peo-ple re-joice at the sound of His name; let all the val-leys and hills burst with joy, and the trees of the field clap their hands.

Justice and love He will bring to the world, His kingdom will never fail; held like a two-edged sword in our hand, His word and truth shall prevail, shall prevail!

1 Let all the earth hear His voice,
   let the people rejoice
   at the sound of His name;
   let all the valleys and hills burst with joy,
   and the trees of the field
   clap their hands.
   Justice and love He will bring to the world,
   His kingdom will never fail;
   held like a two-edged sword in our hand,
   His word and truth shall prevail, shall prevail!

2 Let all the earth hear His voice,
   let the prisoners rejoice –
   He is coming to save.
   Satan's dark strongholds crash down
   as with prayer we surround,
   as the cross we proclaim.
   Justice and love . . .

3 Let all the earth hear His song;
   sing it loud, sing it strong –
   it's the song of His praise.
   Silent no more, we cry out –
   let the world hear the shout:
   in the earth the Lord reigns.
   Justice and love . . .

404 Let all the world

LUCKINGTON 10 4 66 66 10 4

Words: George Herbert (1593–1632)
Music: Basil Harwood (1859–1949)

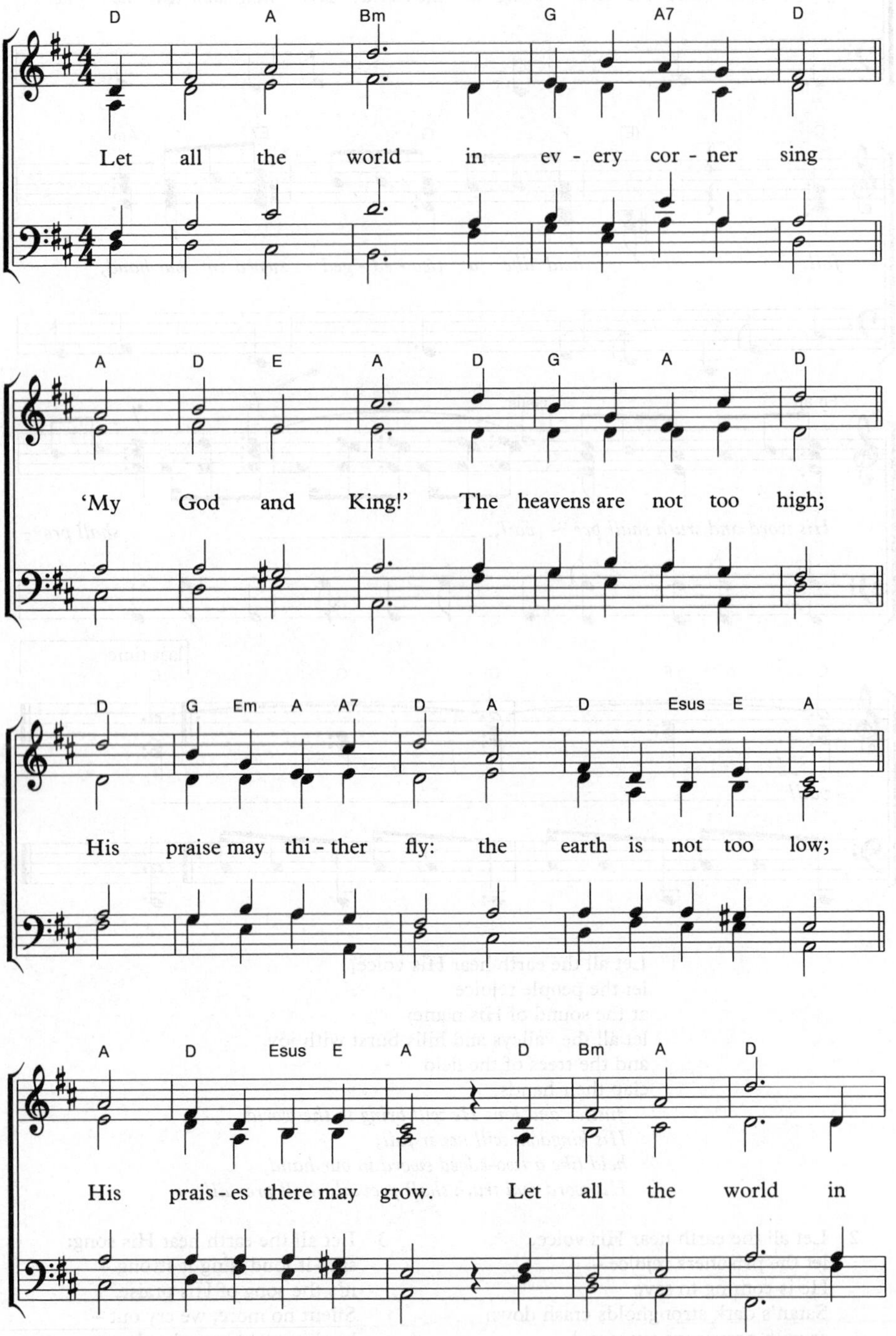

D A Bm G A7 D
Let all the world in ev - ery cor - ner sing
A D E A D G A D
'My God and King!' The heavens are not too high;
D G Em A A7 D A D Esus E A
His praise may thi - ther fly: the earth is not too low;
A D Esus E A D Bm A D
His prais - es there may grow. Let all the world in

ev - ery cor - ner sing 'My God and___ King!'

1 Let all the world in every corner sing
  'My God and King!'
  The heavens are not too high;
  His praise may thither fly:
  the earth is not too low;
  His praises there may grow.
  Let all the world in every corner sing
  'My God and King!'

2 Let all the world in every corner sing
  'My God and King!'
  The Church with psalms must shout,
  no door can keep them out:
  but, above all, the heart
  must bear the longest part.
  Let all the world in every corner sing
  'My God and King!'

405

Let God arise

Words and music: Graham Kendrick
Music arranged David Peacock

Triumphantly

Let God a - rise, and let His e - ne-mies be scat - tered, and

let those who hate Him flee be - fore_ Him;_

let God a - rise, and let His e - ne-mies be scat - tered, and

Fine

let those who hate Him flee a - way._____

Let it be to me

Words and music: Graham Kendrick
Music arranged Christopher Norton

Let it be to me ac - cord - ing to Your

word; let it be to me ac - cord - ing to Your

word. I am Your ser - vant, no rights shall I de -

- mand. Let it be to me, let it be to

me,   let it be to   me   ac -

- cord - ing   to   Your   word._____

Let it be to me according to Your word;
let it be to me according to Your word.
I am Your servant, no rights shall I demand.
Let it be to me, let it be to me,
let it be to me according to Your word.

407 Let Me have My way among you

Words and music: Graham Kendrick
Music arranged David Peacock

Let Me have My way among you, do not strive, do not strive; strive; for

Mine is the pow-er and the glo - ry for ev-er and ev-er the same. Let Me have My way a -

Em   A7   D   D/F#   Em/G   A7   D

- mong___ you,   do not strive,   do not strive.

1 Let Me have My way among you,
   do not strive, do not strive;
   let Me have My way among you,
   do not strive, do not strive;
   for Mine is the power and the glory
   for ever and ever the same.
   Let Me have My way among you,
   do not strive, do not strive.

2 We'll let You have Your way among us,
   we'll not strive, we'll not strive;
   we'll let You have Your way among us,
   we'll not strive, we'll not strive;
   for Yours is the power and the glory
   for ever and ever the same.
   We'll let You have Your way among us,
   we'll not strive, we'll not strive.

3 Let My peace rule within your hearts,
   do not strive, do not strive;
   let My peace rule within your hearts,
   do not strive, do not strive;
   for Mine is the power and the glory
   for ever and ever the same.
   Let My peace rule within your hearts,
   do not strive, do not strive.

4 We'll let Your peace rule within our hearts,
   we'll not strive, we'll not strive;
   we'll let Your peace rule within our hearts,
   we'll not strive, we'll not strive;
   for Yours is the power and the glory
   for ever and ever the same.
   We'll let You have Your way among us,
   we'll not strive, we'll not strive.

Words and music © 1976 Scripture in Song,
administered by Integrity's Hosanna! Music,
PO Box 12, Eastbourne, East Sussex BN23 6NW, UK

408 Let our praise to You be as incense

Words and music: Brent Chambers

Worshipfully

Let our praise to You be as in - cense, let our praise to You be as pil - lars of Your throne; let our praise to You be as in - cense, as we come be - fore You and wor - ship You a - lone.

409 Let saints on earth

DUNDEE CM

Words: Charles Wesley (1707–88)
in this version Jubilate Hymns
Music: from *Scottish Psalter*, 1615

1 Let saints on earth together sing
with those whose work is done;
for all the servants of our King
in earth and heaven, are one.

2 One family, we live in Him,
one church above, beneath,
though now divided by the stream,
the narrow stream of death.

3 One army of the living God,
to His command we bow;
part of His host have crossed the flood
and part are crossing now.

4 But all unite in Christ their head,
and love to sing His praise:
Lord of the living and the dead,
direct our earthly ways!

5 So shall we join our friends above
who have obtained the prize;
and on the eagle wings of love
to joys celestial rise.

410   Let the beauty of Jesus

Words: Albert Orsborn
Music: Rev. Tom Jones

Let the beau-ty of Je-sus be seen in me,_____

all His won-drous com - pas-sion and pu - ri - ty:_____

oh, Thou Spi-rit di - vine, all my na-ture re -

- fine, till the beau-ty of Je-sus be seen in me.

411   Let there be love

Words and music: Dave Bilbrough
Music arranged David Peacock

Let there be love shared a - mong us, let there be love in our
eyes; may now Your love sweep this na-tion, cause us, O Lord,— to a-
-rise: give us a fresh un - der-stand-ing of bro-ther-ly love that is
real; let there be love shared a - mong us, let there be love.———

412   Let's just praise the Lord

Words: Gloria and William J Gaither
Music: William J Gaither

*Alternate lyrics, 'voices', 'hands'.

413   Let us acknowledge the Lord

HOSEA

Words and music: Andy Silver

Let us ac - know - ledge the Lord,

let us press on to ac - know - ledge Him, let us ac -

- know - ledge the Lord.____ Let us ac -

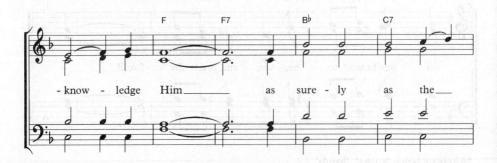

- know - ledge Him____ as sure - ly as the____

sun ris - es; He_____ will ap - pear,_____

_ He will__ come to us like the win - ter

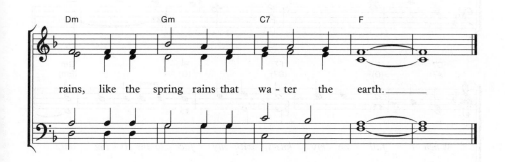

rains, like the spring rains that wa - ter the earth._____

Let us acknowledge the Lord,
let us press on to acknowledge Him,
let us acknowledge the Lord.
Let us acknowledge Him
as surely as the sun rises;
He will appear, He will come to us
like the winter rains,
like the spring rains
that water the earth.

414 Let us break bread together

CALHOUN MELODY

Words: J E Seddon (1915–83)
Music: traditional melody
arranged Norman Warren

Let us break bread to-geth-er on our knees,

let us break bread to-geth-er on our knees:

When I fall on my knees, with my face to the ris-ing sun,

O____ Lord, have____ mer-cy on me!____

TRADITIONAL VERSION

1 Let us break bread together on our knees,
let us break bread together on our knees:
When I fall on my knees,
with my face to the rising sun,
O Lord, have mercy on me!

2 Let us drink wine together on our knees,
let us drink wine together on our knees:
When I fall . . .

3 Let us praise God together on our knees,
let us praise God together on our knees:
When I fall . . .

ALTERNATIVE VERSION

1 Let us praise God together, let us praise;
let us praise God together all our days:
He is faithful in all His ways,
He is worthy of all our praise,
His name be exalted on high!

2 Let us seek God together, let us pray;
let us seek His forgiveness as we pray:
He will cleanse us from all sin,
He will help us the fight to win,
His name be exalted on high!

3 Let us serve God together, Him obey;
let our lives show His goodness through each day:
Christ the Lord is the world's true light –
let us serve Him with all our might,
His name be exalted on high!

415 Let us with a gladsome mind

MONKLAND   77 77

Words: John Milton (1608–74)
Music: John Antes (1740–1811)
arranged John Wilkes (1785–1869)

1   Let us with a gladsome mind
    praise the Lord for He is kind;
    For His mercies shall endure,
    ever faithful, ever sure.

2   He, with all-commanding might,
    filled the new-made world with light:
    For His mercies . . .

3   All things living He doth feed,
    His full hand supplies their need:
    For His mercies . . .

4   He His chosen race did bless
    in the wasteland wilderness:
    For His mercies . . .

5   He hath, with a piteous eye,
    looked upon our misery:
    For His mercies . . .

6   Let us then with gladsome mind,
    praise the Lord for He is kind!
    For His mercies . . .

416 Lift Jesus higher

Words and music: Unknown
Music arranged Phil Burt

Lift Jesus higher, lift Jesus higher,
lift Him up for the world to see.
He said if I be lifted up from the earth
I will draw all men unto me.

417 Lift high the cross

CRUCIFER 10 10 with refrain

Words: G W Kitchen (1827–1912)
and M R Newbolt (1874–1956)
and in this version Jubilate Hymns
Music: S H Nicholson (1875–1947)

Lift high the cross, the love of Christ pro - claim

till all the world_____ a - dores_____ His sac - red name!

Come, Christ - ians, fol - low_____ where the cap - tain trod,

the_____ King vic - to - rious, Christ, the Son of God:

Lift high the cross,
the love of Christ proclaim
till all the world
adores His sacred name!

1   Come, Christians, follow where the captain trod,
     the King victorious, Christ, the Son of God:
       Lift high the cross . . .

2   Each new-born soldier of the crucified
     bears on his brow the seal of Him who died:
       Lift high the cross . . .

3   This is the sign that Satan's armies fear
     and angels veil their faces to revere:
       Lift high the cross . . .

4   Saved by the cross on which their Lord was slain,
     see Adam's children their lost home regain:
       Lift high the cross . . .

5   From north and south, from east and west they raise
     in growing unison their songs of praise:
       Lift high the cross . . .

6   Let every race and every language tell
     of Him who saves our souls from death and hell!
       Lift high the cross . . .

7   O Lord, once lifted on the tree of pain,
     draw all the world to seek You once again:
       Lift high the cross . . .

8   Set up Your throne, that earth's despair may cease
     beneath the shadow of its healing peace:
       Lift high the cross . . .

418 Lift up your heads

Words and music: Steven L Fry

419   Like a mighty river flowing

OLD YEAVERING   88 87

Words: Michael Perry
Music: Noël Tredinnick

1   Like a mighty river flowing,
    like a flower in beauty growing,
    far beyond all human knowing
    is the perfect peace of God.

2   Like the hills serene and even,
    like the coursing clouds of heaven,
    like the heart that's been forgiven,
    is the perfect peace of God.

3   Like the summer breezes playing,
    like the tall trees softly swaying,
    like the lips of silent praying
    is the perfect peace of God.

4   Like the morning sun ascended,
    like the scents of evening blended,
    like a friendship never ended
    is the perfect peace of God.

5   Like the azure ocean swelling,
    like the jewel all-excelling,
    far beyond our human telling
    is the perfect peace of God.

420 Like a candle flame

Words and music: Graham Kendrick
Music arranged Christopher Norton

Gently

Like a can-dle flame, flick-'ring small in our dark-ness.

Un-cre-a-ted light shines through in-fant eyes.

WOMEN *God is with us, al - le -*

MEN *God is with us, al - le - lu - ia,*

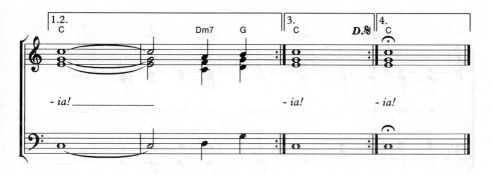

1   Like a candle flame,
    flick'ring small in our darkness.
    Uncreated light
    shines through infant eyes.
    MEN   *God is with us, alleluia,*
    WOMEN   *God is with us, alleluia,*
    MEN   *come to save us, alleluia,*
    WOMEN   *come to save us,*
    ALL   *alleluia!*

2   Stars and angels sing,
    yet the earth sleeps in the shadows;
    can this tiny spark
    set a world on fire?
              God is with us . . .

3   Yet His light shall shine
    from our lives, Spirit blazing,
    as we touch the flame
    of His holy fire.
              God is with us . . .

421 Like a river glorious

WYE VALLEY 65 65 Triple

Words: Frances Ridley Havergal (1836–79)
Music: J Mountain (1844–1933)

Like a ri-ver glo-rious is God's per-fect peace,

o-ver all vic-to-rious, in its bright in-crease:

per-fect, yet it flow-eth ful-ler ev-ery day;

per-fect, yet it grow-eth___ deep-er all the way.

Stayed up - on Je - ho - vah, hearts are ful - ly blest; find - ing, as He pro - mised, _ per - fect peace and rest.

1 Like a river glorious
  is God's perfect peace,
  over all victorious,
  in its bright increase:
  perfect, yet it floweth
  fuller every day;
  perfect, yet it groweth
  deeper all the way.
    Stayed upon Jehovah,
    hearts are fully blest;
    finding, as He promised,
    perfect peace and rest.

2 Hidden in the hollow
  of His blessed hand,
  never foe can follow
  never traitor stand;
  not a surge of worry,
  not a shade of care,
  not a blast of hurry
  touch the Spirit there.
    Stayed upon Jehovah . . .

3 Every joy or trial
  falleth from above,
  traced upon our dial
  by the sun of love.
  We may trust Him fully
  all for us to do;
  They who trust Him wholly
  find Him wholly true.
    Stayed upon Jehovah . . .

422 Light has dawned

Words and music: Graham Kendrick
Music arranged Christopher Norton

ALL 1 Light has dawned that ev - er shall blaze,
WOMEN 2 Sav - iour of the world is___ He,
MEN 3 Life has sprung from hearts of___ stone,
ALL 4 Blood has flowed that clean - ses from sin,

dark - ness flees a - way; Christ the light has
Hea - ven's King come down; judge - ment, love and
by the Spi - rit's breath; hell shall let her
God His love has proved; man may mock and

shone in our hearts, turn - ing night to day.
mer - cy___ meet at His thor - ny crown.
cap - tives_ go, life has con - quered death.
dem - ons may rage – we shall not be moved!

ALL We pro-claim Him King of___ kings, we lift high His___ name;___ Heaven and earth shall bow at His feet,

when He___ comes to reign.

reign. reign.

423   Living under the shadow of His wing

Words and music: David J Hadden
and Bob Silvester

With strength

Liv-ing un - der the sha-dow of His wing we find se - cu - ri - ty. Stand-ing in His pre - sence we will bring our wor - - ship, wor - - ship,

... wor - ship to the King.

1 Living under the shadow of His wing
  we find security.
  Standing in His presence we will bring
  our worship, worship, worship to the King.

2 Bowed in adoration at His feet
  we dwell in harmony.
  Voices joined together that repeat,
  worthy, worthy, worthy is the Lamb.

3 Heart to heart embracing in His love
  reveals His purity.
  Soaring in my spirit like a dove;
  holy, holy, holy is the Lord.

424 Lo! He comes, with clouds descending

HELMSLEY   87 87 47

Words: Charles Wesley (1707–88)
Music: 18th-century English melody

Lo! He comes, with clouds descending,
once for favoured sinners slain:
thousand thousand saints attending,
swell the triumph of His train;
Hallelujah!

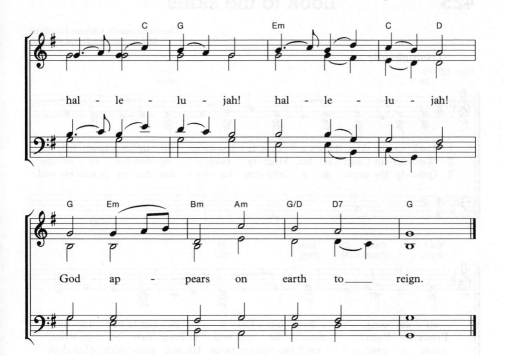

hal - le - lu - jah! hal - le - lu - jah!

God ap - pears on earth to___ reign.

1 Lo! He comes, with clouds descending,
once for favoured sinners slain:
thousand thousand saints attending,
swell the triumph of His train;
   Hallelujah!, hallelujah, hallelujah!
God appears on earth to reign.

2 Every eye shall now behold Him
robed in dreadful majesty;
those who set at nought and sold Him,
pierced, and nailed Him to the tree,
   deeply wailing . . .
shall the true Messiah see.

3 Now redemption, long expected,
see in solemn pomp appear!
All His saints, by man rejected,
now shall meet Him in the air.
   Hallelujah . . .
see the day of God appear.

4 Yea, Amen! let all adore Thee
high on Thy eternal throne;
Saviour, take the power and glory,
claim the kingdom of Thine own;
   Hallelujah . . .
everlasting God, come down!

425
Look to the skies

Words and music: Graham Kendrick
Music arranged David Peacock

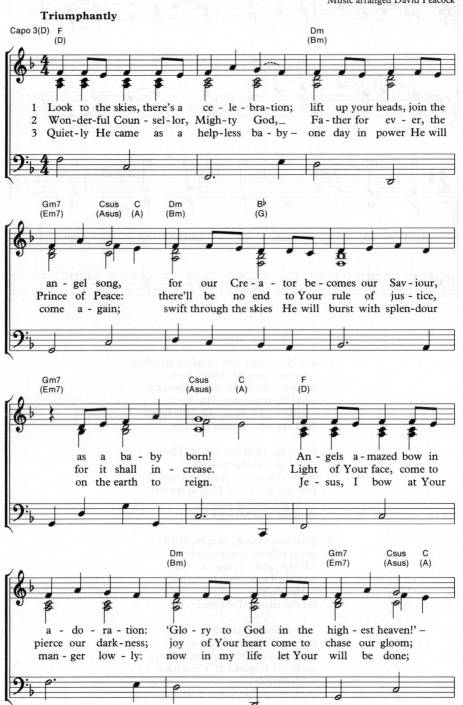

Send the good news out to ev-ery na-tion, for our hope has come.
Star of the morn-ing, a new day dawn-ing, make our hearts Your home.
live in my flesh by Your Spi-rit ho - ly till Your King-dom comes.

Wor - ship the King - come, see His bright-ness; wor - ship the King, His

won - ders tell: Je - sus our King is born to - day — we

wel-come You, Em - man - u - el!

426
Look, ye saints

TRIUMPH   87 87 87

Words: Thomas Kelly (1769–1854)
Music: H J Gauntlett (1805–76)

Look, ye saints, the sight is glo-rious, see the Man of

sor-rows now from the fight re-turned vic-to-rious!

Ev-ery knee to Him shall bow: Crown Him! Crown Him!

Crown Him! Crown Him! Crowns be-come the vic-tor's brow.

1 Look, ye saints, the sight is glorious,
see the Man of sorrows now
from the fight returned victorious!
Every knee to Him shall bow:
  Crown Him! Crown Him!
  Crown Him! Crown Him!
Crowns become the victor's brow.

2 Crown the Saviour, angels, crown Him!
Rich the trophies Jesus brings;
in the seat of power enthrone Him,
while the vault of heaven rings:
  Crown Him! Crown Him!
  Crown Him! Crown Him!
Crown the Saviour King of kings!

3 Sinners in derision crowned Him,
mocking thus the Saviour's claim;
saints and angels crowd around Him,
own His title, praise His name:
  Crown Him! Crown Him!
  Crown Him! Crown Him!
Spread abroad the victor's fame.

4 Hark, those bursts of acclamation!
Hark, those loud triumphant chords!
Jesus takes the highest station:
O what joy the sight affords!
  Crown Him! Crown Him!
  Crown Him! Crown Him!
King of kings, and Lord of lords!

427 Lord, come and heal Your church

Words and music: Chris Rolinson
Music arranged Christopher Norton

1 Lord, come and heal Your church, take our lives and
2 Spi - rit of God, come in and re - lease our
3 Show us Your power, we pray, that___ we may

cleanse with Your fire;___ let Your de - liv - erance
hearts to praise You;___ make us___ whole, for
share in Your glo - ry: we shall a - rise, and

flow as we lift Your name up___ high - er.
ho - ly___ we'll be - come and___ serve You.
go to pro-claim Your works most_ ho - ly.

We will draw near and sur - ren - der our___

fear: *lift* *our* *hands* *to* *pro-claim,* *'Ho - ly*

Fa - ther, *You* *are* *here!'*

1 Lord, come and heal Your church,
  take our lives and cleanse with Your fire;
  let Your deliverance flow
  as we lift Your name up higher.
    We will draw near
    and surrender our fear:
    lift our hands to proclaim,
    'Holy Father, You are here!'

2 Spirit of God, come in
  and release our hearts to praise You;
  make us whole, for
  holy we'll become and serve You.
    We will draw near . . .

3 Show us Your power, we pray,
  that we may share in Your glory:
  we shall arise, and go
  to proclaim Your works most holy.
    We will draw near . . .

428 Lord, for the years

LORD OF THE YEARS   11 10 11 10

Words: Timothy Dudley-Smith
Music: Michael Baughen
arranged David Iliff

Lord, for the years Your love has kept and guid - ed,
urged and in - spired us, cheered us on our way,
sought us and saved us, par - doned and pro - vid - ed:
Lord of the years, we bring our thanks to - day.

1 Lord, for the years Your love has kept and guided,
   urged and inspired us, cheered us on our way,
   sought us and saved us, pardoned and provided:
   Lord of the years, we bring our thanks today.

2 Lord, for that word, the word of life which fires us,
   speaks to our hearts and sets our souls ablaze,
   teaches and trains, rebukes us and inspires us:
   Lord of the word, receive Your people's praise.

3 Lord, for our land in this our generation,
   spirits oppressed by pleasure, wealth and care:
   for young and old, for commonwealth and nation,
   Lord of our land, be pleased to hear our prayer.

4 Lord, for our world where men disown and doubt You,
   loveless in strength, and comfortless in pain,
   hungry and helpless, lost indeed without You:
   Lord of the world, we pray that Christ may reign.

5 Lord for ourselves; in living power remake us –
   self on the cross and Christ upon the throne,
   past put behind us, for the future take us:
   Lord of our lives, to live for Christ alone.

429 Lord have mercy

Words and music: Gerald Markland
Music arranged Roland Fudge

Words and music: © 1978 Kevin Mayhew Ltd,
The Paddock, Rattlesbury, Bury St Edmonds, Suffolk IP30 0SZ

- in you,_
- heart-ed,_

and I'll give
those crushed in

you a heart of flesh.
spi-rit I will save.

Clean wa-ter
So turn to

I will use to cleanse all your wounds,
Me_ for My par-don is great,

My Spi-rit
My word will

I give to you._
heal all your wounds._

D.C.

CODA

peo-ple._

430 Lord have mercy on us

Words and music: Graham Kendrick
Music arranged Phil Burt

Lord have mer-cy on us, come and heal our land; cleanse with Your fire, heal with Your touch: hum-bly we bow and call up-on You now, O

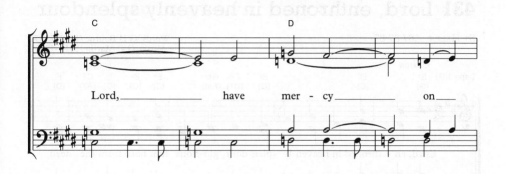

Lord,_____ have mer - cy_____ on_

us,_____ O Lord,_____ have mer - cy_____

_ on_ us._____ _ O Lord,_____

_ have mer - cy_____ on_ us.

431 Lord, enthroned in heavenly splendour

St Helen   87 87 87

Words: G H Bourne (1840–1925)
Music: G C Martin (1844–1916)

Lord, en-throned in heaven-ly splen-dour, glo-rious first born from the dead,

You a-lone our strong de-fend-er, lift-ing up Your peo-ple's head.

Al-le-lu-ia, al-le-lu-ia, Je-sus, true and liv-ing Bread!

1 Lord, enthroned in heavenly splendour,
   glorious first born from the dead,
   You alone our strong defender,
   lifting up Your people's head.
      Alleluia, alleluia,
   Jesus, true and living Bread!

2 Prince of life, for us now living,
   by Your body souls are healed;
   Prince of Peace, Your pardon giving,
   by Your blood our peace is sealed.
      Alleluia, alleluia,
   Word of God in flesh revealed.

3 Paschal Lamb! Your offering, finished
   once for all when You were slain,
   in its fulness undiminished
   shall for evermore remain,
      Alleluia, alleluia,
   cleansing souls from every stain.

4 Great High Priest of our profession,
   through the veil You entered in,
   by Your mighty intercession
   grace and mercy there to win,
      Alleluia, alleluia,
   only sacrifice for sin.

5 Life-imparting heavenly Manna,
   stricken Rock with streaming side,
   heaven and earth with loud hosanna
   worship You, the Lamb who died,
      Alleluia, alleluia,
   risen, ascended, glorified!

432 Lord, I love You

Words and music: Eddie Espinosa
Music arranged Christopher Norton

Lord, I love You, You a-lone did hear my cry;

on - ly You can mend this bro-ken heart of mine.

Yes, I love You, and there is no doubt, Lord, You've

touched me from the in - side out. Lord, I out. Lord, I out.

433(i)   Lord, I was blind

Saxby   LM

Words: W T Matson (1833–99)
in this version Jubilate Hymns
Music: T R Matthews (1826–1910)

Lord, I was blind; I could not see in Your marred vis-age a-ny grace: but now the beau-ty of Your face in ra-diant vis-ion dawns on me.

1 Lord, I was blind; I could not see
   in Your marred visage any grace:
   but now the beauty of Your face
   in radiant vision dawns on me.

2 Lord, I was deaf; I could not hear
   the thrilling music of Your voice:
   but now I hear You and rejoice,
   and all Your spoken words are dear.

3 Lord, I was dumb; I could not speak
   the grace and glory of Your name:
   but now as touched with living flame
   my lips will speak for Jesus' sake.

4 Lord, I was dead; I could not move
   my lifeless soul from sin's dark grave:
   but now the power of life You gave
   has raised me up to know Your love.

5 Lord, You have made the blind to see,
   the deaf to hear, the dumb to speak,
   the dead to live – and now I break
   the chains of my captivity!

433(ii) Lord, I was blind

BODMIN   LM

Words: W T Matson (1833–99)
in this version Jubilate Hymns
Music: A Scott-Gatty (1847–1918)

1 Lord, I was blind; I could not see
   in Your marred visage any grace:
   but now the beauty of Your face
   in radiant vision dawns on me.

2 Lord, I was deaf; I could not hear
   the thrilling music of Your voice:
   but now I hear You and rejoice,
   and all Your spoken words are dear.

3 Lord, I was dumb; I could not speak
   the grace and glory of Your name:
   but now as touched with living flame
   my lips will speak for Jesus' sake.

4 Lord, I was dead; I could not move
   my lifeless soul from sin's dark grave:
   but now the power of life You gave
   has raised me up to know Your love.

5 Lord, You have made the blind to see,
   the deaf to hear, the dumb to speak,
   the dead to live – and now I break
   the chains of my captivity!

434   Lord, it is eventide

CHRIST'S OWN PEACE   Irregular   Words and music: H Ernest Nichol (1862–1926)

Lord, it is e-ven-tide: the light of day is wan-ing;

far o'er the gold-en land earth's voi-ces faint and fall;

low-ly we pray to You for strength and love sus-tain-ing, low-ly we

ask of You Your peace up-on us all. O grant un-to our souls –

Light that grows not pale with day's de - crease,

love that ne-ver can fail till life shall cease;___

joy no tri-al can mar, hope that shines a-far,

faith se - rene as a star, and Christ's own peace.___

2 Lord, it is eventide: we turn to You for healing,
   like those of Galilee who came at close of day;
   speak to our waiting souls, their hidden needs revealing;
   touch us with hands divine that take our sin away.
   O grant unto our souls –
   Light that grows . . .

3 Saviour, You know of every trial and temptation,
   know of the wilfulness and waywardness of youth,
   help us to hold to You, our strength and our salvation,
   help us to find in You the one eternal Truth.
   O grant unto our souls –
   Light that grows . . .

4 Lord, it is eventide: our hearts await Your giving,
   wait for that peace divine that none can take away,
   peace that shall lift our souls to loftier heights of living,
   till we abide with You in everlasting day.
   O grant unto our souls –
   Light that grows . . .

435 Lord Jesus Christ

LIVING LORD 98 88 83

Words and music: Patrick Appleford

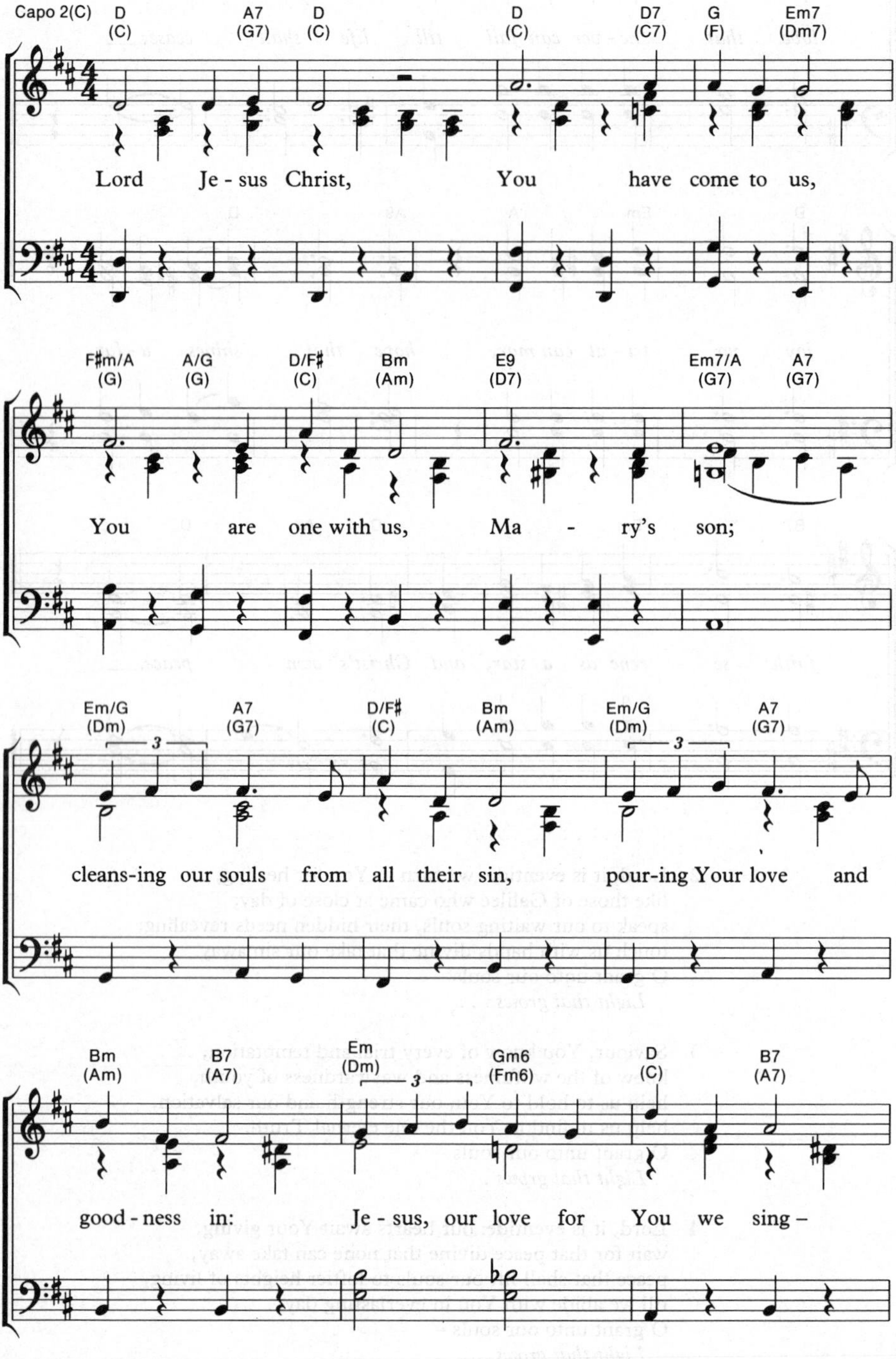

Capo 2(C)
D (C) A7 (G7) D (C) D (C) D7 (C7) G (F) Em7 (Dm7)
Lord Je - sus Christ, You have come to us,
F♯m/A (G) A/G (G) D/F♯ (C) Bm (Am) E9 (D7) Em7/A (G7) A7 (G7)
You are one with us, Ma - ry's son;
Em/G (Dm) A7 (G7) D/F♯ (C) Bm (Am) Em/G (Dm) A7 (G7)
3
cleans-ing our souls from all their sin, pour-ing Your love and
Bm (Am) B7 (A7) Em (Dm) Gm6 (Fm6) D (C) B7 (A7)
good - ness in: Je - sus, our love for You we sing –

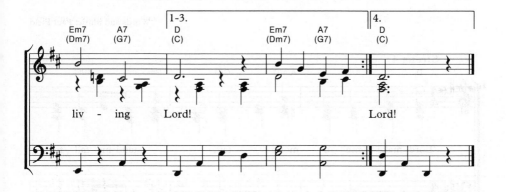

liv - ing Lord! Lord!

1 Lord Jesus Christ, You have come to us,
  You are one with us, Mary's son;
  cleansing our souls from all their sin,
  pouring Your love and goodness in:
  Jesus, our love for You we sing –
      living Lord!

2 Lord Jesus Christ, now and every day
  teach us how to pray, Son of God;
  You have commanded us to do
  this in remembrance, Lord, of You:
  into our lives Your power breaks through –
      living Lord!

3 Lord Jesus Christ, You have come to us,
  born as one of us, Mary's son;
  led out to die on Calvary,
  risen from death to set us free:
  living Lord Jesus, help us see
      You are Lord!

4 Lord Jesus Christ, I would come to You,
  live my life for You, Son of God;
  all Your commands I know are true,
  Your many gifts will make me new:
  into my life Your power breaks through –
      living Lord!

436   Lord, make me a mountain

Words and music: Paul Field

ser - vant   of ev-ery-one   I   meet.   meet.

1   Lord, make me a mountain standing tall for You,
    strong and free and holy, in everything I do.
    Lord, make me a river of water pure and sweet,
    Lord, make me the servant of everyone I meet.

2   Lord, make me a candle shining with Your light,
    steadfastly unflickering, standing for the right.
    Lord, make me a fire burning strong for You,
    Lord, make me be humble in everything I do.

3   Lord, make me a mountain, strong and tall for You,
    Lord, make me a fountain of water clear and new,
    Lord, make me a shepherd that I may feed Your sheep,
    Lord, make me the servant of everyone I meet.

437   Lord, make me an instrument

Words and music: T Hatton
Music arranged Roland Fudge

lift   up   my   hands   in   Thy   name._____

1 Lord, make me an instrument,
   an instrument of worship;
   I lift up my hands in Thy name.
   Lord, make me an instrument,
   an instrument of worship;
   I lift up my hands in Thy name.

2 I'll sing You a love song,
   a love song of worship;
   I lift up my hands in Thy name.
   I'll sing You a love song,
   a love song to Jesus;
   I lift up my hands in Thy name.

3 Lord, make us a symphony,
   a symphony of worship;
   we lift up our hands in Thy name.
   Lord, make us a symphony,
   a symphony of worship;
   we lift up our hands in Thy name.

438
Lord, may we see

Jerusalem DCM

Words: Christopher Porteous
Music: C H H Parry (1848–1918)
arranged Roland Fudge

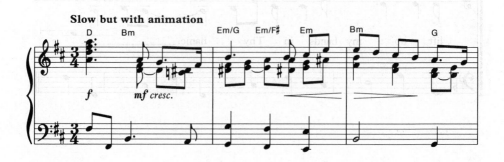

Slow but with animation

1 Lord, may we see Your hands and side, touch You and feel Your pre - sence near; Lord, could our

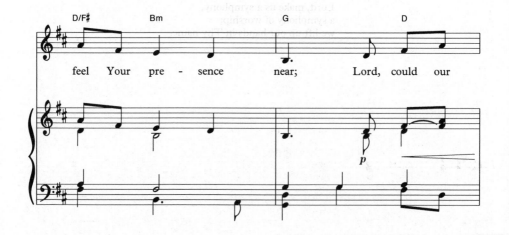

439(i) Lord of all being

MARYTON LM

Words: Oliver Wendell Holmes (1809–94)
Music: H P Smith (1825–98)

1 Lord of all being, throned afar,
  Thy glory flames from sun and star;
  centre and soul of every sphere,
  yet to each loving heart how near.

2 Sun of our life, Thy quickening ray
  sheds on our path the glow of day;
  Star of our hope, Thy softened light
  cheers the long watches of the night.

3 Our midnight is Thy smile withdrawn,
  our noontide is Thy gracious dawn,
  our rainbow arch Thy mercy's sign;
  all, save the clouds of sin, are Thine.

4 Lord of all life, below, above,
  whose light is truth, whose warmth is love,
  before Thy ever-blazing throne
  we ask no lustre of our own.

5 Grant us Thy truth to make us free,
  and kindling hearts that burn for Thee,
  till all Thy living altars claim
  one holy light, one heavenly flame.

439(ii) Lord of all being

OMBERSLEY   LM

Words: Oliver Wendell Holmes (1809–94)
Music: W H Gladstone (1840–91)

1 Lord of all being, throned afar,
   Thy glory flames from sun and star;
   centre and soul of every sphere,
   yet to each loving heart how near.

2 Sun of our life, Thy quickening ray
   sheds on our path the glow of day;
   Star of our hope, Thy softened light
   cheers the long watches of the night.

3 Our midnight is Thy smile withdrawn,
   our noontide is Thy gracious dawn,
   our rainbow arch Thy mercy's sign;
   all, save the clouds of sin, are Thine.

4 Lord of all life, below, above,
   whose light is truth, whose warmth is love,
   before Thy ever-blazing throne
   we ask no lustre of our own.

5 Grant us Thy truth to make us free,
   and kindling hearts that burn for Thee,
   till all Thy living altars claim
   one holy light, one heavenly flame.

440 Lord of creation

CHEDWORTH   10 11 11 11

Words: Jack Winslow (1882–1974)
Music: John Barnard

Lord of cre-a-tion, to You be all praise! Most migh-ty Your work-ing, most won-drous Your ways! Your glo-ry and might are be-yond us to tell, and yet in the heart of the hum-ble You dwell.

1 Lord of creation, to You be all praise!
Most mighty Your working, most wondrous Your ways!
Your glory and might are beyond us to tell,
and yet in the heart of the humble You dwell.

2 Lord of all power, I give You my will,
in joyful obedience Your tasks to fulfil;
Your bondage is freedom, Your service is song,
and, held in Your keeping, my weakness is strong.

3 Lord of all wisdom, I give You my mind,
rich truth that surpasses man's knowledge to find;
what eye has not seen and what ear has not heard
is taught by Your Spirit and shines from Your word.

4 Lord of all bounty, I give You my heart;
I praise and adore You for all You impart,
Your love to inspire me, Your counsel to guide,
Your presence to cheer me, whatever betide.

5 Lord of all being, I give You my all;
for if I disown You I stumble and fall;
but, sworn in glad service Your word to obey,
I walk in Your freedom to the end of the way.

441

Lord of our life

CLOISTERS   11 11 11 5

Words: Philip Pusey (1799–1855)
based on M A von Löwenstern (1594–1648)
Music: Joseph Barnby (1838–96)

Lord of our life, and God of our sal - va - tion,

star of our night, and hope of ev - ery

na - tion, hear and re - ceive___ Thy Chur - ch's sup-pli -

- ca - tion, Lord God Al - migh - ty.

1 Lord of our life, and God of our salvation,
   star of our night, and hope of every nation,
   hear and receive Thy Church's supplication,
     Lord God Almighty.

2 Lord, Thou canst help when earthly armour faileth,
   Lord, Thou canst save when sin itself assaileth;
   Lord, o'er Thy Church nor death nor hell prevaileth;
     grant us Thy peace, Lord.

3 Peace in our hearts, our evil thoughts assuaging;
   peace in Thy Church when disputes are engaging;
   peace, when the world its busy war is waging:
     calm Thy foes' raging.

4 Grant us Thy help till backward they are driven,
   grant them Thy truth, that they may be forgiven;
   grant peace on earth, and after we have striven,
     peace in Thy heaven.

442 Lord of the Church

LONDONDERRY AIR   Irregular

Words: Timothy Dudley-Smith
Music: Irish traditional melody
arranged Roland Fudge

Lord of the church, we pray for our re - new - ing:___ Christ o - ver all, our un - di-vid-ed aim;___ Fire of the Spi - rit, burn for our en - du - ing,__ wind of the Spi - rit, fan the liv-ing flame!___ We turn to Christ a - mid our fear and fail - ing,___ the will that

lacks the cour-age to be free,_____ the wea-ry la - bours, all but un - a - vail - ing,____ to bring us near-er what a church__ should be.____

1 Lord of the church, we pray for our renewing:
   Christ over all, our undivided aim;
   Fire of the Spirit, burn for our enduing,
   wind of the Spirit, fan the living flame!
   We turn to Christ amid our fear and failing,
   the will that lacks the courage to be free,
   the weary labours, all but unavailing,
   to bring us nearer what a church should be.

2 Lord of the church, we seek a Father's blessing,
   a true repentance and a faith restored,
   a swift obedience and a new possessing,
   filled with the Holy Spirit of the Lord!
   We turn to Christ from all our restless striving,
   unnumbered voices with a single prayer –
   the living water for our souls' reviving,
   in Christ to live, and love and serve and care.

3 Lord of the church, we long for our uniting,
   true to one calling, by one vision stirred;
   one cross proclaiming and one creed reciting,
   one in the truth of Jesus and His word!
   So lead us on; till toil and trouble ended,
   one church triumphant one new song shall sing,
   to praise His glory, risen and ascended,
   Christ over all, the everlasting King!

443   Lord of the cross of shame

CROSS OF SHAME   66 11 D

Words: Michael Saward
Music: Michael Baughen

Lord of the cross of shame, set my cold heart a-flame
with love for You, my Sav-iour and my Mas-ter;
who on that lone-ly day bore all my sins a-way,
and saved me from the judge-ment and dis-as-ter.

1 Lord of the cross of shame,
   set my cold heart aflame
   with love for You, my Saviour and my Master;
      who on that lonely day
      bore all my sins away,
   and saved me from the judgement and disaster.

2 Lord of the empty tomb,
   born of a virgin's womb,
   triumphant over death, its power defeated;
      how gladly now I sing
      Your praise, my risen King,
   and worship You, in heaven's splendour seated.

3 Lord of my life today,
   teach me to live and pray
   as one who knows the joy of sins forgiven;
      so may I ever be,
      now and eternally,
   one with my fellow-citizens in heaven.

444 Lord, speak to me

WHITBURN   LM

Words: Frances Ridley Havergal (1836–79)
Music: H Baker (1835–1910)

1 Lord, speak to me, that I may speak
  in living echoes of Thy tone;
  as Thou hast sought, so let me seek
  Thy erring children, lost and lone.

2 O lead me, Lord, that I may lead
  the wandering and the wavering feet;
  O feed me, Lord, that I may feed
  Thy hungering ones with manna sweet.

3 O strengthen me, that, while I stand
  firm on the rock, and strong in Thee,
  I may stretch out a loving hand
  to wrestlers with the troubled sea.

4 O teach me, Lord, that I may teach
  the precious things Thou dost impart;
  and wing my words, that they may reach
  the hidden depths of many a heart.

5 O give Thine own sweet rest to me,
  that I may speak with soothing power
  a word in season, as from Thee,
  to weary ones in needful hour.

6 O fill me with Thy fulness, Lord,
  until my very heart o'erflow
  in kindling thought and glowing word,
  Thy love to tell, Thy praise to show.

7 O use me, Lord, use even me,
  just as Thou wilt, and when, and where,
  until Thy blessed face I see,
  Thy rest, Thy joy, Thy glory share.

445   Lord, the light of Your love

Words and music: Graham Kendrick
Music arranged Christopher Norton

1 Lord, the light of Your love is shin - ing,
2 Lord, I come to Your awe - some pres - ence,
3 As we gaze on Your king - ly bright-ness

in the midst of the dark - ness, shin-ing: Je - sus, Light of the
from the sha - dows in - to Your ra - diance; by Your blood I may
so our fa - ces dis-play Your like-ness, ev - er chang-ing from

world, shine up - on us; set us free by the truth You now bring us -
en - ter Your bright-ness: search me, try me, con-sume all my dark-ness -
glo - ry to glo - ry: mir-rored here, may our lives tell Your sto - ry -

shine on__ me,   shine on__ me.

Shine,   Je - sus, shine,__   fill   this   land   with   the

Fa - ther's glo - ry; blaze,   Spi - rit, blaze,__   set   our

hearts   on   fire.   Flow,   ri - ver, flow,

flood the na - tions with grace and mer - cy;

send forth Your word,___ Lord, and

let there be light!

last time

446   Lord, Thy Word abideth

RAVENSHAW   66 66

Words: Henry Williams Baker (1821–77)
Music: from medieval German melody
arranged W H Monk (1823–89)

1 Lord, Thy Word abideth,
  and our footsteps guideth;
  who its truth believeth
  light and joy receiveth.

2 Who can tell the pleasure,
  who recount the treasure,
  by Thy word imparted
  to the simple-hearted?

3 When the storms are o'er us,
  and dark clouds before us,
  then its light directeth,
  and our way protecteth.

4 When our foes are near us,
  then Thy word doth cheer us,
  word of consolation,
  message of salvation.

5 Word of mercy, giving
  succour to the living;
  word of life, supplying
  comfort to the dying.

6 O that we discerning
  its most holy learning,
  Lord, may love and fear Thee,
  evermore be near Thee!

447   Lord, You are more precious

Words and music: Lynn DeShazo
Music arranged David Peacock

Prayerfully

Lord, You are more pre-cious than sil - ver,

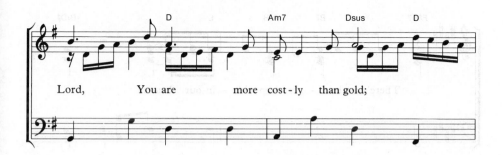

Lord, You are more cost - ly than gold;

Lord, You are more beau - ti - ful __ than dia - monds, and

no-thing I de-sire com-pares with You.

448

Lord we long for You

Words and music: Trish Morgan, Ray Goudie
Ian Townend, Dave Bankhead
Music arranged Christopher Norton

Lord we long for You to move in pow - er.

There's a hun - ger deep with - in our hearts,

to see heal-ing in our na-tion. Send Your Spi-rit to re -

- vive_____ us: *Heal our na - tion!*

Heal our na - tion! Heal our

na - tion! Pour out Your Spi - rit on this land!

1 Lord we long for You to move in power.
   There's a hunger deep within our hearts,
   to see healing in our nation.
   Send Your Spirit to revive us:
       Heal our nation!
       Heal our nation!
       Heal our nation!
       Pour out Your Spirit on this land!

2 Lord we hear Your Spirit coming closer,
   a mighty wave to break upon our land,
   bringing justice, and forgiveness,
   God we cry to You 'Revive us':
       Heal our nation . . .

449

Love divine

BLAENWERN 87 87 D

Words: Charles Wesley (1707–88)
Music: W P Rowlands (1860–1937)

Love di - vine, all loves_ ex - cel - ling, joy_ of heaven, to earth_ come down: fix in us Thy hum - ble dwell - ing, all Thy faith - ful mer - cies_ crown. Je - sus, Thou_ art all_ com - pas - sion, pure, un -

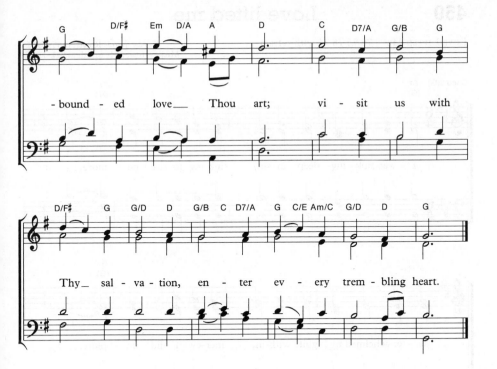

-bound - ed love___ Thou art; vi - sit us with

Thy___ sal - va - tion, en - ter ev - ery trem - bling heart.

1 Love divine, all loves excelling,
  joy of heaven, to earth come down:
  fix in us Thy humble dwelling,
  all Thy faithful mercies crown.
  Jesus, Thou art all compassion,
  pure, unbounded love Thou art;
  visit us with Thy salvation,
  enter every trembling heart.

2 Breathe, O breathe Thy loving Spirit
  into every troubled breast;
  let us all in Thee inherit,
  let us find Thy promised rest.
  Take away the love of sinning,
  Alpha and Omega be;
  end of faith, as its beginning,
  set our hearts at liberty.

3 Come, almighty to deliver,
  let us all Thy grace receive;
  suddenly return, and never,
  never more Thy temples leave.
  Thee we would be always blessing,
  serve Thee as Thy hosts above,
  pray, and praise Thee without ceasing,
  glory in Thy perfect love.

4 Finish then Thy new creation:
  pure and spotless let us be;
  let us see Thy great salvation,
  perfectly restored in Thee:
  Changed from glory into glory,
  till in heaven we take our place,
  till we cast our crowns before Thee,
  lost in wonder, love, and praise.

450 Love lifted me

LOVE LIFTED ME   76 76 76 74 with refrain

Words: James Rowe (1865–1933)
Music: Howard E Smith (1863–1918)

I was sink-ing deep in sin, sink-ing to rise no more, ov-er-whelmed by guilt with-in, mer-cy I did im-plore. Then the Mas-ter of the sea heard my des-pair-ing cry, Christ my Sav-iour lift-ed me, now safe am I.

2   Souls in danger, look above,
    Jesus completely saves;
    He will lift you by His love
    out of the angry waves.
    He's the Master of the sea,
    billows His will obey;
    He your Saviour wants to be,
    be saved today!
        Love lifted me . . .

3   When the waves of sorrow roll,
    when I am in distress,
    Jesus takes my hand in His,
    ever He loves to bless.
    He will every fear dispel,
    satisfy every need;
    all who heed His loving call,
    find rest indeed.
        Love lifted me . . .

451   Love came down at Christmas

HERMITAGE   67 67

Words: Christina Georgina Rossetti (1830–94)
Music: Reginald Owen Morris (1886–1948)

Love came down at Christ - mas,

Love all love - ly, Love di - vine; Love was born at

Christ - mas, star and an - gels gave the sign.

1   Love came down at Christmas,
Love all lovely, Love divine;
Love was born at Christmas,
star and angels gave the sign.

2   Worship we the Godhead,
Love incarnate, Love divine;
worship we our Jesus:
but wherewith for sacred sign?

3   Love shall be our token,
love be yours and love be mine,
love to God and all men,
love for plea and gift and sign.

452   Loved with everlasting love

EVERLASTING LOVE   77 77 D

Words: George Wade Robinson (1838–77)
Music: James Mountain (1843–1933)

2 Heaven above is softer blue,
   earth around is sweeter green;
   something lives in every hue,
   Christless eyes have never seen:
   birds with gladder songs o'erflow,
   flowers with deeper beauties shine,
   since I know, as now I know,
   I am His, and He is mine.

3 His for ever, only His:
   who the Lord and me shall part?
   Ah, with what a rest of bliss
   Christ can fill the loving heart!
   Heaven and earth may fade and flee,
   first-born light in gloom decline;
   but while God and I shall be,
   I am His, and He is mine.

453   Low in the grave He lay

CHRIST AROSE   65 64 with refrain   Words and music: Robert Lowry (1826–99)

Low in the grave He lay, Jesus, my Saviour; waiting the coming day, Jesus, my Lord.

Up from the grave He a-rose, with a mighty triumph o'er His foes; He arose a Victor from the dark domain, and He

lives for ev - er with His saints to reign: He a - rose!_____ He a-

- rose!_____ Hal - le - lu - jah! Christ a - rose!

1 Low in the grave He lay,
   Jesus, my Saviour;
   waiting the coming day,
   Jesus, my Lord.
       Up from the grave He arose,
       with a mighty triumph o'er His foes;
       He arose a victor from the dark domain,
       and He lives for ever with His saints to reign:
       He arose! He arose! Hallelujah! Christ arose!

2 Vainly they watch His bed,
   Jesus, my Saviour;
   vainly they seal the dead,
   Jesus, my Lord.
       Up from the grave . . .

3 Death cannot keep his prey,
   Jesus, my Saviour,
   He tore the bars away,
   Jesus, my Lord.
       Up from the grave . . .

454 Majesty

Words and music: Jack Hayford

Majestically

Ma-jes-ty,_____ wor-ship His Ma-jes-ty;_____ un-to

Je-sus be glo-ry, hon-our and praise._____

Ma-jes-ty,_____ king-dom, au-tho-ri-ty,_____ flows from His

throne un-to His own, His an-them raise._____ So ex-

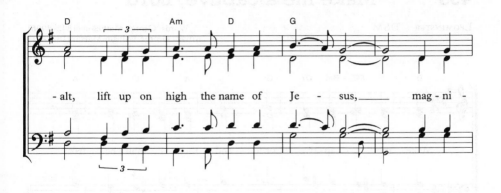

-alt, lift up on high the name of Je - sus,_____ mag - ni -

-fy, come glo - ri - fy, Christ Je-sus the King._____

Ma - jes-ty,_____ wor-ship His Ma - jes-ty,_____ Je-sus who

died, now glo - ri - fied, King of all kings._____

455 Make me a captive, Lord

LEOMINSTER DSM

Words: George Matheson (1842–1906)
Music: George William Martin (1828–81)

Make me a cap-tive, Lord, and then I shall be free;

force me to ren-der up my sword, and I shall con-queror be.

I sink in life's a-larms when by my-self I stand;

im-pri-son me with-in Thine arms, and strong shall be my hand.

1 Make me a captive, Lord,
   and then I shall be free;
   force me to render up my sword,
   and I shall conqueror be.
   I sink in life's alarms
   when by myself I stand;
   imprison me within Thine arms,
   and strong shall be my hand.

2 My heart is weak and poor
   until its master find;
   it has no spring of action sure –
   it varies with the wind.
   It cannot freely move,
   till Thou has wrought its chain;
   enslave it with Thy matchless love,
   and deathless it shall reign.

3 My power is faint and low
   till I have learned to serve;
   it wants the needed fire to glow,
   it wants the breeze to nerve;
   it cannot drive the world,
   until itself be driven;
   its flag can only be unfurled
   when Thou shalt breathe from heaven.

4 My will is not my own
   till Thou hast made it Thine;
   if it would reach a monarch's throne
   it must its crown resign;
   it only stands unbent,
   amid the clashing strife,
   when on Thy bosom it has leant
   and found in Thee its life.

456 Make me a channel of Your peace

St Francis

Words and music: Sebastian Temple
Music arranged Betty Pulkingham

Flowing

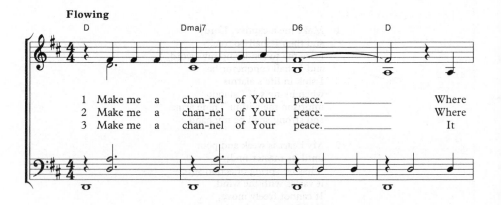

1 Make me a chan-nel of Your peace. _____ Where
2 Make me a chan-nel of Your peace. _____ Where
3 Make me a chan-nel of Your peace. _____ It

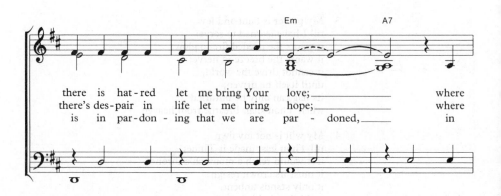

there is hat-red let me bring Your love; _____ where
there's des-pair in life let me bring hope; _____ where
is in par-don - ing that we are par - doned, _____ in

there is in-ju - ry, Your par-don, Lord; _____ and__
there is dark-ness, _____ on - ly light; _____ and__
giv-ing to all men that we re - ceive; _____ and in

457   Make way, make way

Words and music: Graham Kendrick
Music arranged David Peacock

way, *(make way,)* and__ let His king - dom in!

1   Make way, make way,
    for Christ the King in splendour arrives;
    fling wide the gates
    and welcome Him into your lives.
       Make way, make way,
       for the King of kings;
       make way, make way,
       and let His kingdom in!

2   He comes the broken hearts to heal,
    the prisoners to free;
    the deaf shall hear, the lame shall dance,
    the blind shall see.
       Make way . . .

3   And those who mourn with heavy hearts,
    who weep and sigh,
    with laughter, joy and royal crown
    He'll beautify.
       Make way . . .

4   We call You now to worship Him
    as Lord of all,
    to have no gods before Him,
    their thrones must fall!
       Make way . . .

458   Man of Sorrows

GETHSEMANE   777 8   Words and music: Philipp Bliss (1838–76)

1   Man of Sorrows! what a name
for the Son of God, who came
ruined sinners to reclaim!
Hallelujah! what a Saviour!

2   Bearing shame and scoffing rude,
in my place condemned He stood;
sealed my pardon with His blood;
Hallelujah! what a Saviour!

3   Guilty, vile and helpless we;
spotless Lamb of God was He:
full atonement – can it be?
Hallelujah! what a Saviour!

4   Lifted up was He to die.,
It is finished! was His cry;
now in heaven exalted high;
Hallelujah! what a Saviour!

5   When He comes, our glorious King,
all His ransomed home to bring,
then anew this song we'll sing:
Hallelujah! what a Saviour!

459

Master, speak

MAGISTER   87 87 77

Words: Frances Ridley Havergal (1836–79)
Music: L Mason (1792–1872)

Mas-ter, speak! Thy ser-vant hear-eth, wait-ing for Thy gra - cious word,

long-ing for Thy voice that cheer-eth; Mas-ter, let it now be heard,.

I am lis-tening, Lord, for Thee; what hast Thou to say to me?

1 Master, speak! Thy servant heareth,
waiting for Thy gracious word,
longing for Thy voice that cheereth;
Master, let it now be heard,.
I am listening, Lord, for Thee;
what hast Thou to say to me?

2 Speak to me by name, O Master!
let me know it is to me;
speak, that I may follow faster,
with a step more firm and free,
where the Shepherd leads the flock
in the shadow of the rock.

3 Master, speak! though least and lowest,
let me not unheard depart;
Master, speak! for O Thou knowest
all the yearning of my heart;
knowest all its truest need;
speak, and make me blest indeed.

4 Master, speak! and make me ready,
when Thy voice is truly heard,
with obedience glad and steady
still to follow every word.
I am listening, Lord, for Thee;
Master, speak, O speak to me!

460   May God's blessing

Words and music: Cliff Barrows

461 May our worship be acceptable

Words and music: Graham Kendrick
Music arranged Christopher Norton

May our wor-ship be ac-cep-ta-ble_ in Your sight, O Lord; may our wor-ship be ac-cep-ta-ble_ in Your sight, O Lord; may the words of my mouth be pure, and the me-di-ta-tion of my heart; may our wor-ship be ac-cep-ta-ble_ in Your sight, O Lord.

462 May the fragrance

Words and music: Graham Kendrick
Music arranged David Peacock

Flowing

MEN May the fra-grance of Je - sus fill this

WOMEN May the fra-grance of Je - sus fill this place,
place,_____ may the fra-grance of

love - ly fra-grance of Je - sus,
Je - sus fill this place,_____

Chords: G Bm Asus A A#dim
ALL ris - ing   from   the   sac - ri -

Bm Bm/A E9/G# E9 Gmaj7 A9 A6
- fice_____ of lives laid down in a-do - ra -

1.2. D G G/A A | 3. D D7 *D.%* | 4. D
- tion.   - tion.   - tion.

1 MEN   May the fragrance of Jesus fill this place,
   WOMEN   may the fragrance of Jesus fill this place,
   MEN   may the fragrance of Jesus fill this place,
   WOMEN   lovely fragrance of Jesus,
   ALL   rising from the sacrifice
           of lives laid down in adoration.

2 MEN   May the glory of Jesus fill His church,
   WOMEN   may the glory of Jesus fill His church,
   MEN   may the glory of Jesus fill His church;
   WOMEN   radiant glory of Jesus,
   ALL   shining from our faces
           as we gaze in adoration.

3 MEN   May the beauty of Jesus fill my life,
   WOMEN   may the beauty of Jesus fill my life,
   MEN   may the beauty of Jesus fill my life:
   WOMEN   perfect beauty of Jesus,
   ALL   fill my thoughts, my words, my deeds,
           my all I give in adoration;
           fill my thoughts, my words, my deeds,
           my all I give in adoration.

463 May the mind of Christ my Saviour

ST LEONARDS   87 85

Words: Kate B Wilkinson (1859–1928)
Music: A C Barham Gould (1891–1953)

1 May the mind of Christ my Saviour
   live in me from day to day,
   by His love and power controlling
   all I do and say.

2 May the word of God dwell richly
   in my heart from hour to hour,
   so that all may see I triumph
   only through His power.

3 May the peace of God my Father
   rule my life in everything,
   that I may be calm to comfort
   sick and sorrowing.

4 May the love of Jesus fill me,
   as the waters fill the sea;
   Him exalting, self abasing,
   this is victory.

5 May I run the race before me,
   strong and brave to face the foe,
   looking only unto Jesus,
   as I onward go.

464 May the Lord bless you

Words and music: Susie Hare
Music arranged Christopher Norton

May the Lord bless you and keep you, make His face to shine up-on you and be gra-cious un-to you. May the Lord lift up the light of His coun-te-nance up-on you and give you peace.

465 Meekness and majesty

Words and music: Graham Kendrick
Music arranged Christopher Norton

Meek-ness and ma-jes-ty, man-hood and de-i-ty, in per-fect har-mo-ny, the man who is God: Lord of e-ter-ni-ty dwells in hu-man-i-ty, kneels in hu-mi-li-ty__ and__ wash-es our feet. *Oh, what a*

mys-te-ry,   meek-ness and   ma-jes-ty:_____bow down and

wor - ship,_____for   this is your   God,_____

__   this   is your   God!_____

God!_____   this is your   God!_____

2 Father's pure radiance,
    perfect in innocence,
    yet learns obedience
    to death on a cross:
    suffering to give us life,
    conquering through sacrifice;
    and, as they crucify,
    prays 'Father, forgive.'
      Oh what a mystery . . .

3 Wisdom unsearchable,
    God the invisible,
    Love indestructable
    in frailty appears.
    Lord of infinity,
    stooping so tenderly,
    lifts our humanity
    to the heights of His throne.
      Oh, what a mystery . . .
      this is your God!

466

Mighty in victory

Words and music: Mavis Ford

watch-ing and pray-ing, serv-ing each oth - er,___
build-ing His king - dom; then ev - ery knee shall bow,
then ev - ery tongue con-fess, Je - sus is Lord!

Mighty in victory, glorious in majesty:
every eye shall see Him when He appears,
coming in the clouds with power and glory.
    Hail to the King!
We must be ready, watching and praying,
serving each other, building His kingdom;
then every knee shall bow, then every tongue confess,
    Jesus is Lord!

467 Morning has broken

BUNESSAN 10 9 10 9

Words: Eleanor Farjeon (1881–1965)
Music: Gaelic melody
arranged Noël Tredinnick

1 Morning has broken
   like the first morning;
   blackbird has spoken
   like the first bird.
   Praise for the singing!
   Praise for the morning!
   Praise for them, springing
   fresh from the Word!

2 Sweet the rain's new fall
   sunlit from heaven,
   like the first dewfall
   on the first grass.
   Praise for the sweetness
   of the wet garden,
   sprung in completeness
   where His feet pass.

3 Mine is the sunlight!
   Mine is the morning
   born of the one light
   Eden saw play!
   Praise with elation,
   praise every morning,
   God's re-creation
   of the new day!

Music arrangement: © Noël Tredinnick/Jubilate Hymns

Words: © David Higham Associates Ltd,
5–8 Lower John Street, Golden Square, London W1R 4HA
from The Children's Bells
published by Oxford University Press

468 My God, how wonderful

WESTMINSTER CM

Words: Frederick William Faber (1814–63)
altered Horrobin/Leavers
Music: James Turle (1802–82)

1 My God, how wonderful You are,
Your majesty how bright!
How beautiful Your mercy seat,
in depths of burning light!

2 In awe I glimpse eternity,
O everlasting Lord;
by angels worshipped day and night,
incessantly adored!

3 O how I love You, Living God,
who my heart's longing hears,
and worship You with certain hope
and penitential tears!

4 Yes, I may love You, O my Lord,
almighty King of kings,
for You have stooped to live in me,
with joy my heart now sings:

5 How wonderful, how beautiful,
Your loving face must be,
Your endless wisdom, boundless power,
and awesome purity!

469 My faith looks up to Thee

OLIVET 664 6664

Words: Ray Palmer (1808–87)
Music: Lowell Mason (1792–1872)

1 My faith looks up to Thee,
Thou Lamb of Calvary,
Saviour divine:
now hear me while I pray;
take all my guilt away;
O let me from this day
be wholly Thine.

2 May Thy rich grace impart
strength to my fainting heart,
my zeal inspire.
As Thou hast died for me,
O may my love to Thee
pure, warm, and changeless be,
a living fire.

3 While life's dark maze I tread,
and griefs around me spread,
be Thou my guide;
bid darkness turn to day,
wipe sorrow's tears away,
nor let me ever stray
from Thee aside.

4 When ends life's transient dream,
when death's cold sullen stream
shall o'er me roll,
blest Saviour, then in love,
fear and distrust remove;
O bear me safe above,
a ransomed soul.

470 My goal is God Himself

Morecambe   10 10 10 10

Words: F Brook
Music: Frederic C Atkinson (1841–96)

1 My goal is God Himself, not joy nor peace,
  nor even blessing, but Himself, my God:
  'tis His to lead me there, not mine, but His
  'At any cost, dear Lord, by any road!'

2 So faith bounds forward to its goal in God,
  and love can trust her Lord to lead her there;
  upheld by Him my soul is following hard,
  till God hath full fulfilled my deepest prayer.

3 No matter if the way be sometimes dark,
  no matter though the cost be oft-times great,
  He knoweth how I best shall reach the mark,
  the way that leads to Him must needs be strait.

4 One thing I know, I cannot say Him nay;
  one thing I do, I press toward my Lord:
  My God, my glory here, from day to day,
  and in the glory there my Great Reward.

471 My God, I thank You

WENTWORTH   84 84 84

Words: Adelaide Anne Procter (1825–64)
Music: F C Maker (1844–1927)

My God, I thank You, who has made the earth so bright, so full of splen - dour and of joy, beau - ty and light; so ma - ny glo - rious things are here, no - ble and right.

1 My God, I thank You, who has made
    the earth so bright,
so full of splendour and of joy,
    beauty and light;
so many glorious things are here,
    noble and right.

2 I thank You, Lord, that You have made
    joy to abound;
so many gentle thoughts and deeds
    circling us round,
that in the darkest spot of earth
    some love is found.

3 I thank You too that all our joy
    is touched with pain;
that shadows fall on brightest hours,
    that thorns remain:
so that earth's bliss may be our guide,
    and not our chain.

4 For You, O Lord, know well how soon
    our weak heart clings,
has given us joys, tender and true,
    yet all with wings;
so that we see, gleaming on high,
    diviner things.

5 I thank You, Lord, that You have kept
    the best in store;
we have enough, yet not too much
    to long for more;
a yearning for a deeper peace
    not known before.

6 I thank You, Lord, that here our souls,
    though amply blessed,
can never find, although they seek,
    a perfect rest,
nor ever shall, until they lean
    on Jesus' breast.

My heart overflows

Words and music: Carolyn Govier

My heart o-ver-flows with a good-ly___ theme, I will add-ress my ver-ses to the King;___ my heart o-ver-flows with praise to my God, I'll give Him the love of my heart.___ ___ For He is Lord of all the earth, He's ris-en a-bove, He's

last time **to Coda**

Words and music: © 1979 Springtide/Word Music (UK), (a division of Word (UK) Ltd)
9 Holdom Avenue, Bletchley, Milton Keynes MK1 1QR, UK

My heart overflows with a goodly theme,
I will address my verses to the King;
my heart overflows with praise to my God,
I'll give Him the love of my heart.

1 For He is Lord of all the earth, He's risen above,
   He's seated at God's right hand;
   and from Him and through Him and to Him are all things,
   that His glory might fill the land.
       My heart overflows . . .

2 For He has chosen Mount Zion as His resting place,
   He says, 'Here will I dwell,
   I will abundantly bless and satisfy,
   and her saints will shout for joy.
       My heart overflows . . .

3 'Lift up your eyes round about and see,
   your heart shall thrill and rejoice,
   for the abundance of the nations is coming to you,
   I am glorifying My house.'
       My heart overflows . . .

473 My hope is built on nothing less

ST CATHERINE 88 88 88

Words: E Mote (1797–1874)
in this version Jubilate Hymns
Music: H F Hemy (1818–88)
arranged J G Walton (1821–1905)

My hope is built on no-thing less than Je-sus' blood and right-eous-ness; no me-rit of my own I claim, but whol-ly trust in Je - sus' name. *On Christ, the sol - id rock, I stand – all oth-er ground is sink-ing sand.*

1 My hope is built on nothing less
   than Jesus' blood and righteousness;
   no merit of my own I claim,
   but wholly trust in Jesus' name.
       On Christ, the solid rock, I stand –
       all other ground is sinking sand,
       all other ground is sinking sand.

2 When weary in this earthly race,
   I rest on His unchanging grace;
   in every wild and stormy gale
   my anchor holds and will not fail.
       On Christ, the solid rock . . .

3 His vow, His covenant and blood
   are my defence against the flood;
   when earthly hopes are swept away
   He will uphold me on that day.
       On Christ, the solid rock . . .

4 When the last trumpet's voice shall sound,
   O may I then in Him be found!
   clothed in His righteousness alone,
   faultless to stand before His throne.
       On Christ, the solid rock . . .

474   My life is Yours

Words and music: Ruth Hooke

Teach me the fear of the Lord, let me see Your right-eous - ness; I will kneel before You and wor - ship Christ my King.

475   My Lord, He is the fairest of the fair

Words and music: Joan Parsons
Music arranged Christopher Norton

My Lord, He is the fair-est of the fair, He is the li-ly of the val - ley, the bright and morn - ing star; His love is writ-ten deep with-in my heart,

He is the ne-ver end-ing foun - tain_____ of ev-er-last-ing

life:_____ and__ He lives,_____ He_____

lives,_____ He____ lives,_____ He____ lives in

me._____ My me._____

My Lord, what love is this

Words and music: Graham Kendrick
Music arranged Christopher Norton

1 My Lord, what love is this that pays so dearly, that I, the guilty one, may go free!

(2) so, watched Him die despised, rejected: but oh, the blood He shed flowed for me!

(3) now this love of Christ shall flow like rivers; come wash your guilt away, live again!

A - maz - ing love,

477 My peace I give unto you

Words and music: Keith Routledge

My peace I give unto you, it's a peace that the world cannot give, it's a peace that the world cannot under-stand: peace to know, peace to

Words and music: © 1975 Kenwood Music,
PO Box 356, Leighton Buzzard LU7 8WP

live,_____ My_ peace_____ I give_ un-to you._

1 My peace I give unto you,
   it's a peace that the world cannot give,
   it's a peace that the world cannot understand:
   peace to know, peace to live,
   My peace I give unto you.

2 My joy I give unto you,
   it's a joy that the world cannot give,
   it's a joy that the world cannot understand:
   joy to know, joy to live,
   My joy I give unto you.

3 My love I give unto you,
   it's a love that the world cannot give,
   it's a love that the world cannot understand:
   love to know, love to live,
   My love I give unto you.

478 My song is love unknown

LOVE UNKNOWN   66 66 44 44

Words: Samuel Crossman (1624–83)
Music: John Ireland (1879–1962)

My song is love un - known; my Sav-iour's love to
me;___ love to the love - less shown, that they might
love - ly be. O who am I, that
for my sake,___ my Lord should take frail flesh, and die?

1 My song is love unknown;
my Saviour's love to me;
love to the loveless shown,
that they might lovely be.
O who am I,
that for my sake,
my Lord should take
frail flesh, and die?

2 He came from His blest throne,
salvation to bestow;
but men made strange, and none
the longed-for Christ would know.
But O my friend,
my friend indeed,
who at my need
His life did spend.

3 Sometimes they strew His way,
and His sweet praises sing;
resounding all the day,
hosannas to their King.
Then: 'Crucify!'
is all their breath,
and for His death
they thirst and cry.

4 Why, what hath my Lord done?
What makes this rage and spite?
He made the lame to run,
He gave the blind their sight.
Sweet injuries!
yet they at these
themselves displease,
and 'gainst Him rise.

5 They rise and needs will have
my dear Lord made away:
a murderer they save,
the Prince of Life they slay.
Yet cheerful He
to suffering goes,
that He His foes
from thence might free.

6 In life, no house, no home
my Lord on earth might have;
in death, no friendly tomb,
but what a stranger gave.
What may I say?
Heaven was His home;
but mine the tomb
wherein He lay.

7 Here might I stay and sing,
no story so divine;
never was love, dear King,
never was grief like Thine.
This is my friend,
in whose sweet praise
I all my days
could gladly spend.

479 My soul doth magnify the Lord

Words: from Luke 1
Music: Unknown
arranged Betty Pulkingham

Gently

My soul doth mag-ni-fy _ the Lord, and my spi-rit hath re-joiced in God my Sav-iour. For He that is migh-ty hath done great things, and ho - ly is His name. My soul doth mag-ni-fy the Lord, my soul doth mag-ni-fy the Lord, and my spi-rit hath re-joiced in God my Sav-iour. For He that is migh-ty hath done great things, and ho - ly is His name. My soul doth name.

Music arrangement: © 1975 Celebration,
administered in Europe by Thankyou Music,
PO Box 75, Eastbourne, East Sussex BN23 6NW, UK

480   New every morning

MELCOMBE   LM

Words: J Keble (1792–1866)
Music: S Webbe (1740–1816)

New ev - ery morn - ing is the love our wak - ing and up - ris - ing prove: through sleep and dark-ness safe - ly brought, re - stored to life and power and thought.

1   New every morning is the love
    our waking and uprising prove:
    through sleep and darkness safely brought,
    restored to life and power and thought.

2   New mercies, each returning day,
    surround Your people as they pray:
    new dangers past, new sins forgiven,
    new thoughts of God, new hopes of heaven.

3   If in our daily life our mind
    be set to honour all we find,
    new treasures still, of countless price,
    God will provide for sacrifice.

4   The trivial round, the common task,
    will give us all we ought to ask:
    room to deny ourselves, a road
    to bring us daily nearer God.

5   Prepare us, Lord, in Your dear love
    for perfect rest with You above,
    and help us, this and every day,
    to grow more like You as we pray.

Name of all majesty

Majestas   66 55 66 64

Words: Timothy Dudley-Smith
Music: Michael Baughen
arranged Noël Tredinnick

Name of all ma-jes-ty, fa-thom-less mys-te-ry, King of the a-ges by an-gels a-dored; power and au-tho-ri-ty, splen-dour and dig-ni-ty, bow to His mas-tery – Je-sus is Lord!

1 Name of all majesty,
   fathomless mystery,
   King of the ages
   by angels adored;
      power and authority,
      splendour and dignity,
      bow to His mastery –
   Jesus is Lord!

2 Child of our destiny,
   God from eternity,
   love of the Father
   on sinners outpoured;
      see now what God has done
      sending His only Son,
      Christ the belovèd One –
   Jesus is Lord!

3 Saviour of Calvary,
   costliest victory,
   darkness defeated
   and Eden restored;
      born as a man to die,
      nailed to a cross on high,
      cold in the grave to lie –
   Jesus is Lord!

4 Source of all sovereignty,
   light, immortality,
   life everlasting
   and heaven assured;
      so with the ransomed, we
      praise Him eternally,
      Christ in His majesty –
   Jesus is Lord!

482   Nearer, my God, to Thee

PROPIOR DEO   64 64 664

Words: Sarah Flower Adams (1805–48)
Music: Arthur S Sullivan (1842–1900)

1 Nearer, my God, to Thee,
   nearer to Thee:
   e'en though it be a cross
   that raiseth me,
   still all my song would be
   nearer, my God, to Thee,
   nearer to Thee, nearer to Thee.

2 Though, like the wanderer,
   the sun gone down,
   darkness be over me,
   my rest a stone,
   yet in my dreams I'd be
   nearer, my God, to Thee,
   nearer to Thee, nearer to Thee.

3 There let the way appear,
   steps up to heaven;
   all that Thou sendest me,
   in mercy given;
   angels to beckon me
   nearer, my God, to Thee,
   nearer to Thee, nearer to Thee.

4 Then, with my waking thoughts
   bright with Thy praise,
   out of my stony griefs
   Bethel I'll raise;
   so by my woes to be
   nearer, my God to Thee,
   nearer to Thee, nearer to Thee.

5 Or, if on joyful wing
   cleaving the sky,
   sun, moon, and stars forgot,
   upwards I fly,
   still all my song shall be,
   nearer, my God, to Thee,
   nearer to Thee, nearer to Thee.

483   No weapon formed

Words and music: Tom Dowell

No wea-pon formed, or ar-my or king,_ shall be
a-ble to stand_ a-gainst the Lord and His a-noint-ed.
All prin-ci-pa-li-ties and pow-ers_ shall
crum-ble be-fore the Lord; and men's hearts shall

No weapon formed, or army or king,
shall be able to stand
against the Lord and His anointed.

All principalities and powers
shall crumble before the Lord;
and men's hearts shall be released,
and they shall come unto the Lord.

No weapon formed, or army or king,
shall be able to stand
against the Lord and His anointed.

484 Now dawns the Sun of righteousness

Words and music: Graham Kendrick
Music arranged Christopher Norton

1 Now dawns the Sun of_ right-eous-ness, and the dark-ness will ne - ver His
2 Laugh - ter and joy He_ will in-crease, all our bur-dens be lift - ed, op -
3 So let us go, His wit - nes - ses, spread-ing news of His king-dom of

bright-ness dim;   true light that lights the hearts of men, on - ly
- pres - sion cease;   the blood-stained bat - tle - dress be burned, and the
right - eous - ness,   till the whole world has heard the song, till the

Son of the Fa - ther,   Je - sus Christ._____
art of our war - fare   ne - ver more be learned._____
har - vest is gath-ered,   then the end shall come._____   *Tell*

out, tell out_ the_ news,   *on ev - ery street pro-claim,*   *a___*

child is born, a Son is given and Je-sus is His name! Tell

out, tell out___ the___ news, our Sav-iour Christ has come, in___

ev-ery tribe and na - tion, let songs of praise be sung, let

D.C.

songs of praise be sung!

3rd time only

or end

485   Now I have found the ground

ANCHOR   88 88 88

Words: Johann Andreas Rothe (1688–1758)
tr. John Wesley (1703–91)
altered Horrobin/Leavers
Music: Alfred Beer (1874–1963)

Now I have found the ground where-in sure my soul's an-chor may re-main — the wounds of Je - sus, for my sin be - fore the world's foun - da - tion slain;

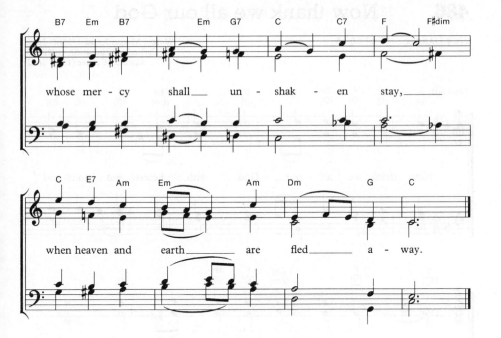

whose mer - cy shall___ un - shak - en stay,___

when heaven and earth___ are fled___ a - way.

1 Now I have found the ground wherein
sure my soul's anchor may remain –
the wounds of Jesus, for my sin
before the world's foundation slain;
whose mercy shall unshaken stay,
when heaven and earth are fled away.

2 Father, Your everlasting grace
our human thought surpassing far,
Your heart still melts with tenderness,
Your arms of love still open are
returning sinners will receive,
eternal life as they believe.

3 Your love, eternal hope, no less,
my sins consumed at Calvary!
Covered is my unrighteousness,
no spot of guilt remains on me,
while Jesu's blood through earth and skies
mercy, free, boundless mercy! cries.

4 Though waves and storms go o'er my head,
though strength, and health, and friends be gone,
though joys be withered all and dead,
though every comfort be withdrawn,
on this my steadfast soul relies –
Father, Your mercy never dies!

5 Fixed on this ground will I remain,
though my heart fail and flesh decay;
this anchor shall my soul sustain,
when earth's foundations melt away:
mercy's full power I then shall prove,
loved with an everlasting love.

486   Now thank we all our God

NUN DANKET   67 67 66 66

Words: Martin Rinkart (1586–1649)
tr. Catherine Winkworth (1829–78)
Music: J Crüger (1598–1662)

Now thank we all our God, with hearts, and hands, and voices; who won-drous things hath done, in whom His world re-joices; Who, from our mothers' arms, hath blessed us on our way with

count - less_ gifts of love, and_ still_ is_ ours to - day.

1 Now thank we all our God,
with hearts, and hands, and voices;
who wondrous things hath done,
in whom His world rejoices;
Who, from our mothers' arms,
hath blessed us on our way
with countless gifts of love,
and still is ours today.

2 O may this bounteous God
through all our life be near us,
with ever-joyful hearts
and blessèd peace to cheer us;
and keep us in His grace,
and guide us when perplexed,
and free us from all ills
in this world and the next.

3 All praise and thanks to God
the Father now be given,
the Son, and Him who reigns
with Them in highest heaven;
the one eternal God,
whom heaven and earth adore;
for thus it was, is now,
and shall be evermore.

487   Not what these hands have done

Sᴛ Bᴇᴜɴᴇs   SM

Words: Horatius Bonar (1808–89)
Music: Joseph C Bridge

Not what these hands have done can save this guil-ty soul,

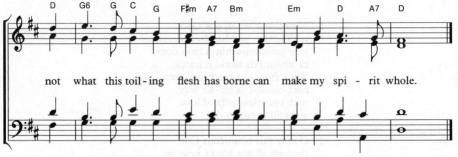

not what this toil-ing flesh has borne can make my spi - rit whole.

1   Not what these hands have done
    can save this guilty soul,
    not what this toiling flesh has borne
    can make my spirit whole.

2   Not what I feel or do
    can give me peace with God;
    not all my prayers, and sighs, and tears
    can bear my awful load.

3   Thy work alone, O Christ,
    can ease this weight of sin;
    Thy blood alone, O Lamb of God,
    can give me peace within.

4   Thy love to me, O God,
    not mine, O Lord, to Thee,
    can rid me of this dark unrest,
    and set my spirit free.

5   Thy grace alone, O God,
    to me can pardon speak;
    Thy power alone, O Son of God,
    can this sore bondage break.

6   I bless the Christ of God,
    I rest on love divine,
    and with unfaltering lip and heart,
    I call this Saviour mine.

488   O Breath of Life

SPIRITUS VITAE   98 98

Words: Elizabeth A P Head (1850–1936)
Music: Mary J Hammond (1878–1964)

1 O Breath of Life, come sweeping through us,
  revive Your Church with life and power;
  O Breath of Life, come, cleanse, renew us
  and fit Your Church to meet this hour.

2 O Breath of Love, come breathe within us,
  renewing thought and will and heart;
  come, Love of Christ, afresh to win us,
  revive Your Church in every part!

3 O Wind of God, come bend us, break us
  till humbly we confess our need;
  then, in Your tenderness remake us,
  revive, restore – for this we plead.

4 Revive us, Lord; is zeal abating
  while harvest fields are vast and white?
  Revive us, Lord, the world is waiting –
  equip Thy Church to spread the light.

489 O come and join the dance

Words and music: Graham Kendrick
Music arranged Christopher Norton

1   LEADER   O come and join the dance
                      that all began so long ago,
         ALL   when Christ the Lord was born in Bethlehem.
         LEADER   Through all the years of darkness
                      still the dance goes on and on,
         ALL   oh, take my hand and come and join the song.
         MEN   *Rejoice!*
         WOMEN   *Rejoice!*
         MEN   *Rejoice!*
         WOMEN   *Rejoice!*
         ALL   *O lift your voice and sing,*
                      and open up your heart to welcome Him.
         MEN   *Rejoice!*
         WOMEN   *Rejoice!*
         MEN   *Rejoice!*
         WOMEN   *Rejoice!*
         ALL   *and welcome now your King,*
                      for Christ the Lord was born in Bethlehem.

2   LEADER   Come shed your heavy load
                      and dance your worries all away,
         ALL   for Christ the Lord was born in Bethlehem.
         LEADER   He came to break the power of sin
                      and turn your night to day,
         ALL   oh, take my hand and come and join the song.
                      Rejoice . . .

3   *(Instrumental verse and chorus)*

4   LEADER   Let laughter ring and angels sing
                      and joy be all around,
         ALL   for Christ the Lord was born in Bethlehem.
         LEADER   And if you seek with all your heart
                      He surely can be found,
         ALL   oh, take my hand and come and join the song.
                      Rejoice . . .
                      Rejoice . . .
                      for Christ the Lord was born in Bethlehem,
                      for Christ the Lord was born in Bethlehem.

490 O come let us adore Him

ADESTE FIDELES

Music: J F Wade (1711–86)
arranged Roland Fudge

1   O come let us adore Him,
    O come let us adore Him,
    O come let us adore Him,
    Christ the Lord.

2   We'll give Him all the glory . . .

3   For He alone is worthy . . .

491   O come, all you faithful

ADESTE FIDELES   Irregular

Words: Latin, 18th century
tr. Frederick Oakley (1802–80)
altered Horrobin/Leavers
Music: J F Wade (1711–86)
arranged W H Monk (1823–89)

O come, all you faith-ful, joy-ful and tri-umph-ant, O
come now, O come_ now to Beth - le-hem;
come and be-hold Him, born the King of an - gels: O
come, let us a - dore Him, O come, let us a - dore Him, O

come, let us a - dore Him,__ Christ__ the Lord!

1 O come, all you faithful,
    joyful and triumphant,
    O come now, O come now to Bethlehem;
    come and behold Him,
    born the King of angels:
      O come, let us adore Him,
      O come, let us adore Him,
      O come, let us adore Him,
      Christ the Lord!

2 True God of true God,
    light of light eternal,
    He, who abhors not the virgin's womb;
    Son of the Father,
    begotten not created:
      O come, let us adore Him . . .

3 Sing like the angels,
    sing in exultation,
    sing with the citizens of heaven above,
    'Glory to God,
    glory in the highest':
      O come, let us adore Him . . .

4 Yes, Lord, we greet You,
    born that/*this* happy morning,
    Jesus, to You be glory given!
    Word of the Father,
    then/*now* in flesh appearing:
      O come, let us adore Him . . .

492 O come let us worship

Words and music: Iain Anderson

O come let us wor-ship and bow down,_____ let us
kneel be - fore the Lord our King;_____ let us whis - per His
name, won - der - ful name, Je - sus our Lord and
King._____ O Je - sus our Lord and King._____

last time **to Coda**

For He is Lord of all the earth,____ His

glo - ry out - shines the sun;_____ see Him clothed in His

robes of right - eous - ness, God's be - lov - èd

⊕ CODA

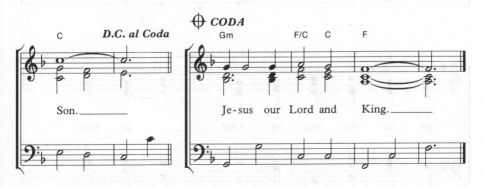

D.C. al Coda

Son.____ Je - sus our Lord and King.____

493 O come, O come, Emmanuel

VENI IMMANUEL   88 88 88

Words: from the Latin (12th century)
tr. John Mason Neale (1818–66)
Music: from a 15th century plainsong melody

In free rhythm

O come, O come, Em - man - - u - el,

and ran - som cap - tive Is - - ra - el,

that mourns in lone - ly ex - - ile here

un - til the Son of God_____ ap - pear.

Re - joice,   re - joice!   Em - man - - u - el

shall   come   to   thee,   O   Is - - ra - el.

1   O come, O come, Emmanuel,
    and ransom captive Israel,
    that mourns in lonely exile here
    until the Son of God appear.
        Rejoice, rejoice! Emmanuel
        shall come to thee, O Israel.

2   O come, O come, Thou Lord of might,
    who to Thy tribes, on Sinai's height
    in ancient times didst give the law
    in cloud and majesty and awe.
        Rejoice, rejoice . . .

3   O come, Thou rod of Jesse, free
    Thine own from Satan's tyranny;
    from depths of hell Thy people save,
    and give them victory o'er the grave.
        Rejoice, rejoice . . .

4   O come, Thou dayspring, come and cheer
    our spirits by Thine advent here;
    disperse the gloomy clouds of night,
    and death's dark shadows put to flight.
        Rejoice, rejoice . . .

5   O come, Thou key of David, come
    and open wide our heavenly home;
    make safe the way that leads on high,
    and close the path to misery.
        Rejoice, rejoice . . .

494   O for a closer walk with God

CHESHIRE   CM

Words: William Cowper (1731–1800)
Music: from Este's *Psalter*, 1592

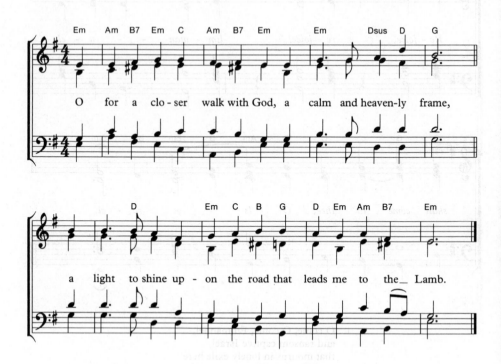

O for a clo-ser walk with God, a calm and heaven-ly frame,

a light to shine up - on the road that leads me to the_ Lamb.

1   O for a closer walk with God,
    a calm and heavenly frame,
    a light to shine upon the road
    that leads me to the Lamb.

2   Where is the blessedness I knew
    when I first saw the Lord?
    Where is that soul-refreshing view
    of Jesus and His word?

3   What peaceful hours I once enjoyed!
    how sweet their memory still!
    But they have left an aching void
    the world can never fill.

4   Return, O holy Dove! return,
    sweet messenger of rest!
    I hate the sins that made Thee mourn,
    and drove Thee from my breast.

5   The dearest idol I have known,
    whate'er that idol be,
    help me to tear it from Thy throne,
    and worship only Thee.

6   So shall my walk be close with God,
    calm and serene my frame;
    so purer light shall mark the road
    that leads me to the Lamb.

495   O for a heart to praise my God

ABRIDGE   CM

Words: Charles Wesley (1707–88)
Music: Isaac Smith (1734–1805)

O for a heart— to praise— my God,— a heart from sin— set free, a heart— that al - ways feels— Thy blood— so free - ly shed— for me.

1   O for a heart to praise my God,
a heart from sin set free,
a heart that always feels Thy blood
so freely shed for me.

2   A heart resigned, submissive, meek,
my great Redeemer's throne;
where only Christ is heard to speak,
where Jesus reigns alone:

3   A humble, lowly, contrite heart,
believing, true, and clean;
which neither life nor death can part
from Him that dwells within:

4   A heart in every thought renewed,
and full of love divine;
perfect, and right, and pure, and good,
a copy, Lord, of Thine.

5   Thy nature, gracious Lord, impart;
come quickly from above,
write Thy new name upon my heart,
Thy new, best name of love.

496   O for a thousand tongues to sing

LYNGHAM   86 86 extended

Words: Charles Wesley (1707–88) altd.
Music: T Jarman (1782–1862)

O for a thou - - sand tongues to sing my

great Re-deem-er's praise, my great Re - deem - er's

praise, the glo-ries of my God and King,

the tri-umphs of His grace! the tri-umphs of His

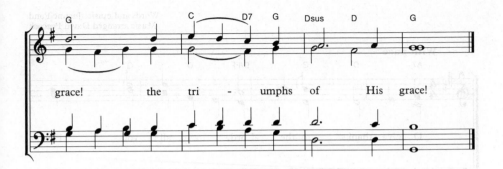

grace!   the   tri - umphs   of   His   grace!

1   O for a thousand tongues to sing
     my great Redeemer's praise,
     the glories of my God and King,
     the triumphs of His grace!

2   Jesus! the name that charms our fears,
     that bids our sorrows cease;
     'tis music in the sinner's ears,
     'tis life, and health, and peace.

3   He breaks the power of cancelled sin,
     He sets the prisoner free;
     His blood can make the foulest clean;
     His blood availed for me.

4   He speaks, and, listening to His voice,
     new life the dead receive,
     the mournful, broken hearts rejoice,
     the humble poor believe.

5   Hear Him, ye deaf; His praise, ye dumb,
     your loosened tongues employ:
     ye blind, behold your Saviour come;
     and leap, ye lame, for joy.

6   My gracious Master, and my God,
     assist me to proclaim,
     to spread through all the earth abroad,
     the honours of Thy name.

497

O give thanks to the Lord

Words and music: Joanne Pond
Music arranged David Peacock

O give thanks to the Lord, all you His peo-ple, O give thanks to the Lord, for He is good.

Let us praise, let us thank, let us ce - le-brate and dance; O give thanks to the Lord, for He is good.

498   O God, our help in ages past

St Anne   CM

Words: Isaac Watts (1674–1748) altd.
Music: William Croft (1678–1727)

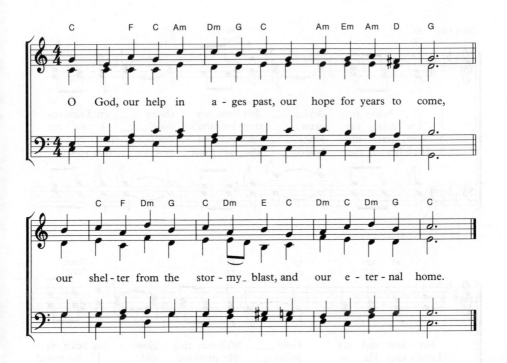

O God, our help in a-ges past, our hope for years to come,
our shel-ter from the stor-my_ blast, and our e-ter-nal home.

1 O God, our help in ages past,
   our hope for years to come,
   our shelter from the stormy blast,
   and our eternal home.

2 Under the shadow of Your throne
   Your saints have dwelt secure;
   sufficient is Your arm alone,
   and our defence is sure.

3 Before the hills in order stood,
   or earth received her frame,
   from everlasting You are God,
   to endless years the same.

4 A thousand ages in Your sight
   are like an evening gone,
   short as the watch that ends the night
   before the rising sun.

5 Time, like an ever-rolling stream,
   bears all its sons away;
   they fly forgotten, as a dream
   dies with the dawning day.

6 O God, our help in ages past,
   our hope for years to come,
   be our defence while life shall last,
   and our eternal home.

499   O happy day

Words: P Doddridge (1702–51)
Music: Ron Jones

1 O hap - py day!____ that fixed my choice____ on Thee, my
2 'Tis done, the great____ tran - sac - tion's done!____ I am my
3 Now rest, my long____ di - vid - ed heart,____ fixed on this
4 High heaven, that heard____ the so - lemn vow,____ that vow re -

Sav - iour and my God!____ Well may this glow - ing heart re -
Lord's and He is mine!____ He drew me, and____ I fol - lowed
bliss - ful cen - tre, rest;____ nor ev - er from____ the Lord de -
- newed shall dai - ly hear;____ till in life's lat - est hour I

- joice,____ and tell its rap - tures all a - broad.____
on,____ charmed to con - fess the voice di - vine.____
- part,____ with Him of ev - ery good pos - sessed.____
bow,____ and bless in death a bond so dear.____

500   O Holy Spirit breathe on me

Words and music: Norman Warren

O Ho - ly Spi - rit__ breathe on me,__

O Ho - ly Spi - rit__ breathe on me,__

and cleanse a - way my sin,_____ fill me with love with - in:__

__ O Ho - ly Spi - rit__ breathe on me!__

1   O Holy Spirit breathe on me,
     O Holy Spirit breathe on me,
     and cleanse away my sin,
     fill me with love within:
     O Holy Spirit breathe on me!

2   O Holy Spirit fill my life,
     O Holy Spirit fill my life,
     take all my pride from me,
     give me humility:
     O Holy Spirit breathe on me!

3   O Holy Spirit, make me new,
     O Holy Spirit, make me new,
     make Jesus real to me,
     give me His purity:
     O Holy Spirit breathe on me!

4   O Holy Spirit, wind of God,
     O Holy Spirit, wind of God,
     give me Your power today,
     to live for You always:
     O Holy Spirit breathe on me!

501　　O Jesus, I have promised

DAY OF REST　76 76 D

Words: J E Bode (1816–74)
Music: J W Elliott (1833–1915)

wan-der from the   path - way if Thou wilt_ be my Guide.

1 O Jesus, I have promised
   to serve Thee to the end;
   be Thou for ever near me,
   my Master and my friend.
   I shall not fear the battle
   if Thou art by my side,
   nor wander from the pathway
   if Thou wilt be my Guide.

2 O let me feel Thee near me;
   the world is ever near;
   I see the sights that dazzle,
   the tempting sounds I hear;
   my foes are ever near me,
   around me and within;
   but, Jesus, draw Thou nearer,
   and shield my soul from sin.

3 O let me hear Thee speaking
   in accents clear and still,
   above the storms of passion,
   the murmurs of self-will;
   O speak to reassure me,
   to hasten or control;
   O speak, and make me listen,
   Thou guardian of my soul.

4 O Jesus, Thou hast promised,
   to all who follow Thee,
   that where Thou art in glory
   there shall Thy servant be;
   and, Jesus, I have promised
   to serve Thee to the end;
   O give me grace to follow
   my Master and my friend.

5 O let me see Thy footmarks,
   and in them plant mine own;
   my hope to follow duly
   is in Thy strength alone;
   O guide me, call me, draw me,
   uphold me to the end;
   and then in heaven receive me,
   my Saviour and my friend!

502   O let the Son of God enfold you

Words and music: John Wimber

503(i) O little town of Bethlehem

CHRISTMAS CAROL DCM (Irregular)

Words: Phillips Brooks (1835–93)
Music: Walford Davies (1869–1941)

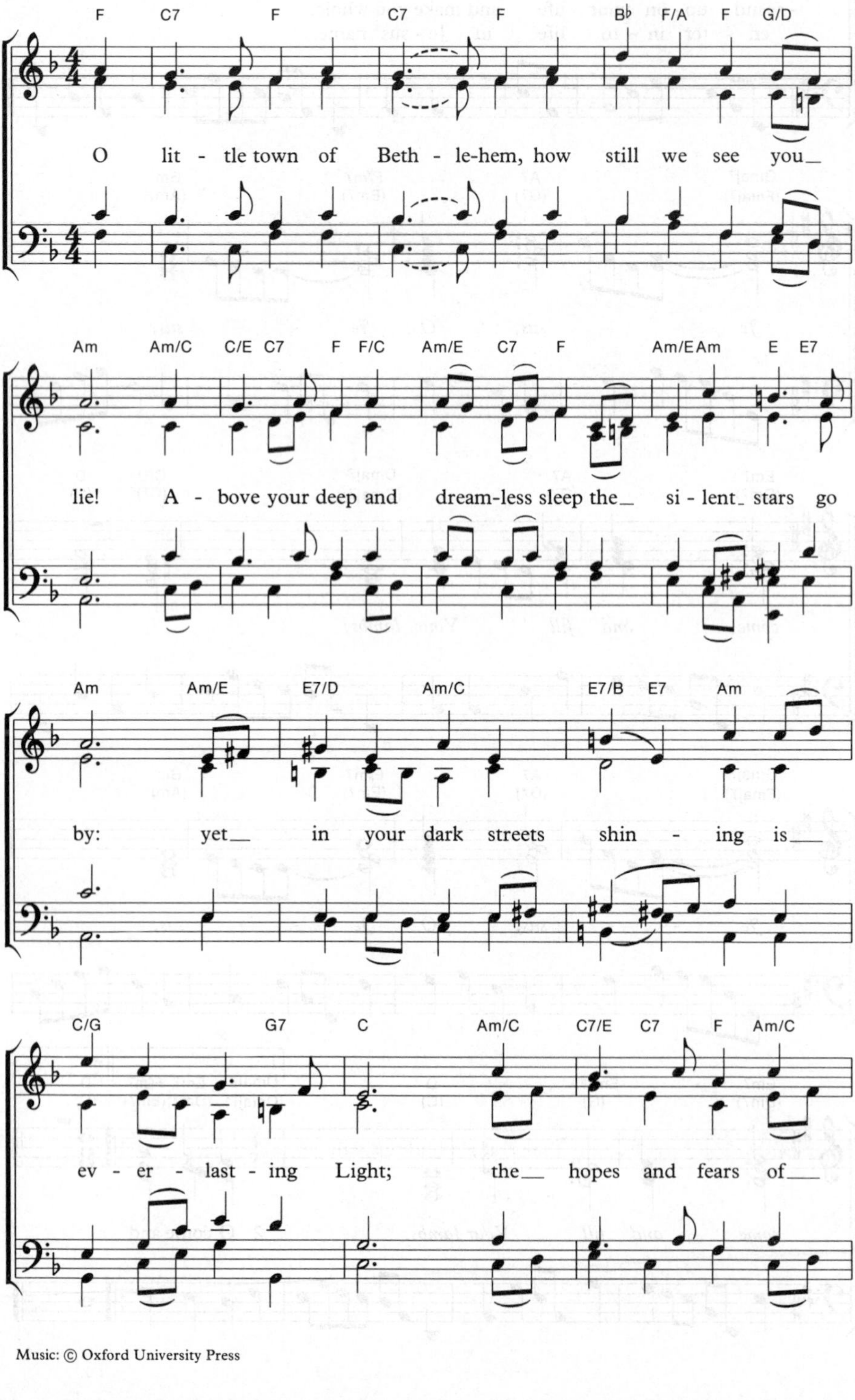

F C7 F C7 F B♭ F/A F G/D
O lit - tle town of Beth - le-hem, how still we see you_
Am Am/C C/E C7 F F/C Am/E C7 F Am/E Am E E7
lie! A - bove your deep and dream-less sleep the_ si - lent_ stars go
Am Am/E E7/D Am/C E7/B E7 Am
by: yet_ in your dark streets shin - ing is_
C/G G7 C Am/C C7/E C7 F Am/C
ev - er - last - ing Light; the_ hopes and fears of_

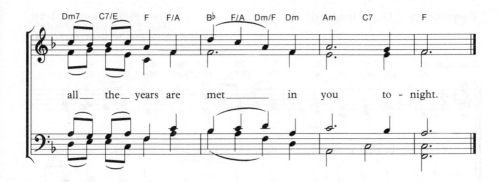

Dm7   C7/E   F   F/A   B♭   F/A   Dm/F   Dm   Am   C7   F

all — the — years are   met———   in   you   to - night.

1   O little town of Bethlehem,
    how still we see you lie!
    Above your deep and dreamless sleep
    the silent stars go by:
    yet in your dark streets shining
    is everlasting Light;
    the hopes and fears of all the years
    are met in you tonight.

2   For Christ is born of Mary;
    and, gathered all above,
    while mortals sleep, the angels keep
    their watch of wondering love.
    O morning stars, together
    proclaim the holy birth,
    and praises sing to God the King,
    and peace to men on earth.

3   How silently, how silently,
    the wondrous gift is given!
    So God imparts to human hearts
    the blessings of His heaven.
    No ear may hear His coming;
    but in this world of sin,
    where meek souls will receive Him, still
    the dear Christ enters in.

4   O holy child of Bethlehem,
    descend to us, we pray;
    cast out our sin, and enter in;
    be born in us today.
    We hear the Christmas angels
    the great glad tidings tell;
    O come to us, abide with us,
    our Lord Immanuel.

503(ii)   O little town of Bethlehem

FOREST GREEN   DCM (Irregular)

Words: Phillips Brooks (1835–93)
Music: English traditional melody
arranged R Vaughan Williams (1872–1958)

O lit-tle town of Beth-le-hem, how still we see you lie! A-bove your deep and dream-less sleep the si-lent stars go by: yet in your dark streets shin-ing is ev-er-last-ing Light; the

hopes and fears of___ all___ the_ years are met in__ you to - night.

1   O little town of Bethlehem,
    how still we see you lie!
    Above your deep and dreamless sleep
    the silent stars go by:
    yet in your dark streets shining
    is everlasting Light;
    the hopes and fears of all the years
    are met in you tonight.

2   For Christ is born of Mary;
    and, gathered all above,
    while mortals sleep, the angels keep
    their watch of wondering love.
    O morning stars, together
    proclaim the holy birth,
    and praises sing to God the King,
    and peace to men on earth.

3   How silently, how silently,
    the wondrous gift is given!
    So God imparts to human hearts
    the blessings of His heaven.
    No ear may hear His coming;
    but in this world of sin,
    where meek souls will receive Him, still
    the dear Christ enters in.

4   O holy child of Bethlehem,
    descend to us, we pray;
    cast out our sin, and enter in;
    be born in us today.
    We hear the Christmas angels
    the great glad tidings tell;
    O come to us, abide with us,
    our Lord Immanuel.

504   O Lord have mercy on me

Words and music: Carl Tuttle

Place my feet upon a_ rock, put a new song in my

heart, in my heart,_____ O Lord

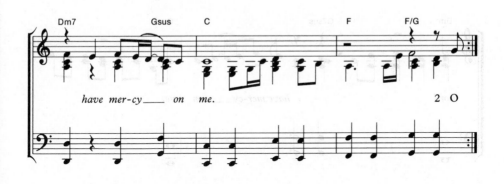

have mer-cy___ on me. 2 O

Place my feet upon a_ rock, put a new song in my_

505   O Lord most Holy God

Words and music: Wendy Churchill

Worshipfully

O Lord most Ho - ly God,   great are Your pur - po-ses,

great is Your will for us,   great is Your love.

And we re - joice in You,   and we will sing to You,

O Fa - ther have Your way,   Your will be done.

1   O Lord most Holy God,
    great are Your purposes,
    great is Your will for us,
    great is Your love.
    And we rejoice in You,
    and we will sing to You,
    O Father have Your way,
    Your will be done.

2   For You are building
    a temple without hands,
    a city without walls,
    enclosed by fire.
    A place for You to dwell,
    built out of living stones,
    shaped by a Father's hand
    and joined in love.

506 O Lord my God!

How Great Thou Art

From a Russian hymn
Words and music: Stuart K Hine

Majestically

O Lord my God! when I in awe-some won-der___ con-sid-er all the works Thy hand hath made, I see the stars, I hear the migh-ty thun-der,___ the power through-out the u-ni-verse dis-played;

Then sings my soul, my Sav-iour God, to Thee, how great Thou

art, how great Thou art! Then sings my soul, my Sav-iour God, to

Thee, how great Thou art, how great Thou art!

1 O Lord my God! when I in awesome wonder
   consider all the works Thy hand hath made,
   I see the stars, I hear the mighty thunder,
   the power throughout the universe displayed;
   Then sings my soul, my Saviour God, to Thee,
   how great Thou art, how great Thou art!
   Then sings my soul, my Saviour God, to Thee,
   how great Thou art, how great Thou art!

2 When through the woods and forest glades I wander
   and hear the birds sing sweetly in the trees;
   when I look down from lofty mountain grandeur,
   and hear the brook, and feel the gentle breeze;
   Then sings my soul . . .

3 And when I think that God His Son not sparing,
   sent Him to die – I scarce can take it in,
   that on the cross my burden gladly bearing,
   He bled and died to take away my sin:
   Then sings my soul . . .

4 When Christ shall come with shout of acclamation
   and take me home – what joy shall fill my heart!
   Then shall I bow in humble adoration
   and there proclaim, my God, how great Thou art!
   Then sings my soul . . .

507

O Lord our God

Words and music: Phil Lawson Johnston
Music arranged Christopher Norton

O Lord our God, how ma-jes-tic is Your name, the earth is filled with Your glo - ry.

O Lord our God, You are robed in ma-jes-ty, You've set Your glo-ry a-bove the hea - vens. We will mag-ni-fy, we will mag-ni-fy

the Lord en-throned in Zi - on; We will mag-ni-fy,_____ we will mag-ni-fy_____ the Lord en - throned in Zi - - - on._____

1 O Lord our God, how majestic is Your name,
  the earth is filled with Your glory.
  O Lord our God, You are robed in majesty,
  You've set Your glory above the heavens.
    We will magnify, we will magnify
    the Lord enthroned in Zion;
    We will magnify, we will magnify
    the Lord enthroned in Zion.

2 O Lord our God, You have established a throne,
  You reign in righteousness and splendour.
  O Lord our God, the skies are ringing with Your praise,
  soon those on earth will come to worship.
    We will magnify . . .

3 O Lord our God, the world was made at Your command,
  in You all things now hold together.
  Now to Him who sits on the throne and to the Lamb,
  be praise and glory and power for ever.
    We will magnify . . .

508 O Lord, our Lord

Words and music: Michael Smith

O Lord, our Lord, how ma- -jes- tic is Your name in all___ the___ earth; O Lord, our Lord, how ma- jes- tic is Your name in all___ the___

509 O Lord, the clouds are gathering

Words and music: Graham Kendrick
Music arranged Christopher Norton

Steady 4

1 O__ Lord,__ the clouds are ga-ther-ing, the fire of judge-ment
(2) Lord,__ o-ver the na-tions now, where is the dove of
(3) Lord,__ dark powers are poised to flood our streets with hate and
(4) Lord,__ Your glo-rious cross shall tower tri-um-phant in this

burns.__ How we have fall-en! O__ Lord,__ You stand ap-
peace?__ Her wings are bro-ken, O__ Lord,__ while pre-cious
fear.__ We must a-wak-en! O__ Lord,__ let love re-
land,__ e-vil con-found-ing; through the fire,__ Your suf-fering

-palled to see Your laws of love so scorned_____ and lives so
child-ren starve, the tools of war in-crease,_____ their bread is
-claim the lives that sin would sweep a-way,_____ and let Your
church dis-play the glo-ries of her Christ,_____ prais-es re-

bro - ken. MEN *Have mer-cy, Lord,* For-
sto - len. WOMEN *have mer-cy, Lord.*
king - dom come!
-sound - ing.

-give us, Lord,   ALL *Re - store us, Lord; re -vive Your church a -*
for-give us, Lord.

-gain._____ MEN *Let   just - ice flow,_   like*
WOMEN *let   just - ice flow,_*

ri - vers,   ALL *and right-eous-ness like a ne-ver-fail-ing stream.*
like ri - vers;

2 O__
3 O__   *a ne-ver-fail-ing   stream._____*
4 Yet, O

510

O Lord, You are my light

Words and music: Dave Fellingham
Music arranged Christopher Norton

O Lord, You are my light, O
Lord, You are my sal-vation; You have de-liv-ered me from
all my fear, for You are the de-fence of my life. For
my life is hid-den with Christ in God, You have con-cealed me

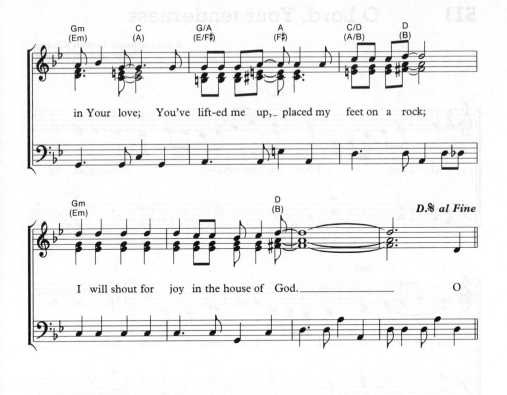

in Your love; You've lift-ed me up, placed my feet on a rock;

I will shout for joy in the house of God.

D.% al Fine

O

O Lord, You are my light,
O Lord, You are my salvation;
You have delivered me from all my fear,
for You are the defence of my life.

For my life is hidden with Christ in God,
You have concealed me in Your love;
You've lifted me up, placed my feet on a rock;
I will shout for joy in the house of God.

O Lord, You are my light . . .

511   O Lord, Your tenderness

Words and music: Graham Kendrick
Music arranged Phil Burt

O Lord, Your tenderness –
melting all my bitterness!
O Lord, I receive Your love.
O Lord, Your loveliness,
changing all my ugliness,
O Lord, I receive Your love,
O Lord, I receive Your love,
O Lord, I receive Your love.

512 O Lord, You've done great things

Words and music: Carolyn Govier

513   O Lord, You're beautiful

Words and music: Keith Green

do - ing well, ____ help me to ne - ver seek a crown,

_ for my re - ward is giv - ing glo - - ry to

You.____

D.C. al Fine

1 O Lord, You're beautiful,
   Your face is all I seek;
   for when Your eyes are on this child,
   Your grace abounds to me.

2 O Lord, please light the fire
   that once burned bright and clear;
   replace the lamp of my first love
   that burns with holy fear!

      I want to take Your word and shine it all around,
      but first help me just to live it Lord!
      And when I'm doing well,
      help me to never seek a crown,
      for my reward is giving glory to You.

3 O Lord You're beautiful,
   Your face is all I seek;
   for when Your eyes are on this child,
   Your grace abounds to me.

514 O love of God

MARTHAM   LM

Words: Horatius Bonar (1808–89)
Music: J H Maunder (1858–1920)

O love of God, how strong and true! e-ter-nal and yet ev-er new; un-com-pre-hend-ed and un-bought, be-yond all know-ledge and all thought.

1 O love of God, how strong and true!
   eternal and yet ever new;
   uncomprehended and unbought,
   beyond all knowledge and all thought.

2 O heavenly love, how precious still,
   in days of weariness and ill,
   in nights of pain and helplessness,
   to heal, to comfort, and to bless!

3 O wide-embracing, wondrous love,
   we see You in the sky above;
   we see You in the earth below,
   in seas that swell and streams that flow.

4 We see You best in Him who came
   to bear for us the cross of shame,
   sent by the Father from on high,
   our life to live, our death to die.

5 We see Your power to bless and save
   e'en in the darkness of the grave;
   still more in resurrection-light,
   we see the fulness of Your might.

6 O love of God, our shield and stay
   through all the perils of our way;
   eternal love, in You we rest,
   for ever safe, for ever blessed!

515   O Love that wilt not let me go

St Margaret   88 886

Words: George Matheson (1842–1906)
Music: A L Peace (1844–1912)

1 O Love that wilt not let me go,
   I rest my weary soul in Thee;
   I give Thee back the life I owe,
   that in Thine ocean depths its flow
   may richer, fuller be.

2 O Light that followest all my way,
   I yield my flickering torch to Thee;
   my heart restores its borrowed ray,
   that in Thy sunshine's blaze its day
   may brighter, fairer be.

3 O Joy that seekest me through pain,
   I cannot close my heart to Thee;
   I trace the rainbow through the rain,
   and feel the promise is not vain
   that morn shall tearless be.

4 O Cross that liftest up my head,
   I dare not ask to fly from Thee;
   I lay in dust life's glory dead,
   and from the ground there blossoms red
   life that shall endless be.

516   O my Saviour, lifted

DERBY   65 65

Words: William Walsham How (1823–97)
Music: Friedrich Filitz (1804–76)

1   O my Saviour, lifted
    from the earth for me,
    draw me, in Thy mercy,
    nearer unto Thee.

2   Lift my earth-bound longings,
    fix them, Lord, above;
    draw me with the magnet
    of Thy mighty love.

3   And I come, Lord Jesus;
    dare I turn away?
    No! Thy love hath conquered,
    and I come today.

4   Bringing all my burdens,
    sorrow, sin, and care;
    at Thy feet I lay them,
    and I leave them there.

517

O perfect Love

O PERFECT LOVE   11 10 11 10

Words: Dorothy Gurney (1858–1932)
Music: Joseph Barnby (1838–96)

O per-fect Love, all hu-man thought tran-scend-ing,
low-ly we kneel in prayer be-fore Your throne,
that theirs may be the__ love which knows no end-ing,
whom You for ev-er-more now join as one.

1   O perfect Love, all human thought transcending,
     lowly we kneel in prayer before Your throne,
     that theirs may be the love which knows no ending,
     whom You for evermore now join as one.

2   O perfect Life, be now their full assurance
     of tender charity, and steadfast faith,
     of patient hope, and quiet brave endurance,
     with childlike trust that fears nor pain nor death.

3   Grant them the joy which brightens earthly sorrow;
     grant them the peace which calms all earthly strife;
     and to life's day the glorious unknown morrow
     that dawns upon eternal love and life.

518   O praise ye the Lord!

HOUGHTON   55 55 65 65

Words: Henry Williams Baker (1821–77)
Music: Henry John Gauntlett (1805–76)

O praise ye the Lord! praise Him in the height; re-joice in His word, ye an-gels of light; ye hea-vens a-dore Him by whom ye were made, and wor-ship be-fore Him, in bright-ness ar-rayed.

1   O praise ye the Lord!
    praise Him in the height;
    rejoice in His word,
    ye angels of light;
    ye heavens adore Him
    by whom ye were made,
    and worship before Him,
    in brightness arrayed.

2   O praise ye the Lord!
    praise Him upon earth,
    in tuneful accord,
    ye sons of new birth;
    praise Him who has brought you
    His grace from above,
    praise Him who has taught you
    to sing of His love.

3   O praise ye the Lord!
    all things that give sound;
    each jubilant chord,
    re-echo around;
    loud organs, His glory
    forth tell in deep tone,
    and sweet harp, the story
    of what He has done.

4   O praise ye the Lord!
    thanksgiving and song
    to Him be outpoured
    all ages along:
    for love in creation,
    for heaven restored,
    for grace of salvation,
    O praise ye the Lord!

519   O Saviour Christ, I now confess

WALTON   LM

Words: Glyn L Taylor
Music: from Gardiner's *Sacred Melodies*, 1812

1   O Saviour Christ, I now confess
You are my Lord, my righteousness,
I follow Your example true,
and daily seek to be like You.

2   These waters have no power, I know,
to cleanse from sin or grace bestow.
'Tis in obedience to my Lord
that I am blessed and He's adored.

3   Buried with Christ, I die to sin,
His risen life and power within.
And victory is to me assured
as I surrender to the Lord.

4   'Tis one more step along the road
that leads me onward with my Lord.
Now fill me with the Spirit's power,
make this a pentecostal hour.

5   Baptizing nations in Your name,
Father, Son, Spirit – still the same.
In full alignment to the Lord,
their guide, their strength – the Living Word.

6   Then, only then, shall all men hear
the news, that Christ's return is near.
And men shall greet their coming Lord
by heaven and earth, for e'er adored.

Words: © 1986 Glyn L Taylor

520   O sacred head, once wounded

PASSION CHORALE   76 76 D

Words: attrib. Bernard of Clairvaux (1091–1153)
Paul Gerhardt (1607–76)
tr. James Waddell Alexander (1804–59)
Music: melody by Hans Leo Hassler (1564–1612)
arranged J B Bach (1685–1750)

does that vis-age lan-guish, which once was bright as morn!

1 O sacred head, once wounded,
   with grief and pain weighed down,
   how scornfully surrounded
   with thorns, Thine only crown!
   How pale art Thou with anguish,
   with sore abuse and scorn!
   How does that visage languish,
   which once was bright as morn!

2 O Lord of life and glory,
   what bliss till now was Thine!
   I read the wondrous story,
   I joy to call Thee mine.
   Thy grief and Thy compassion
   were all for sinners' gain;
   mine, mine was the transgression,
   but Thine the deadly pain.

3 What language shall I borrow
   to praise Thee, heavenly friend,
   for this, Thy dying sorrow,
   thy pity without end?
   Lord, make me Thine for ever,
   nor let me faithless prove;
   O let me never, never
   abuse such dying love!

4 Be near me, Lord, when dying;
   O show Thyself to me;
   and, for my succour flying,
   come, Lord, to set me free:
   these eyes, new faith receiving,
   from Jesus shall not move;
   for he who dies believing,
   dies safely through Thy love.

521   O teach me what it meaneth

RUTHERFORD   76 76 D

Words: Lucy Ann Bennett (1850–1927)
Music: Chrétian Urhan (1790–1845)

O teach me what it mean - eth, that cross up-lift - ed high,

with One, the Man of Sor - rows, con - demned to bleed and_ die!

O teach me what it cost Thee to make a sin - ner whole;

and_ teach me, Sav - iour, teach me the val - ue of a soul!

1 O teach me what it meaneth,
that cross uplifted high,
with One, the Man of Sorrows,
condemned to bleed and die!
O teach me what it cost Thee
to make a sinner whole;
and teach me, Saviour, teach me
the value of a soul!

2 O teach me what it meaneth,
that sacred crimson tide,
the blood and water flowing
from Thine own wounded side.
Teach me that if none other
had sinned, but I alone,
yet still Thy blood, Lord Jesus,
Thine only, must atone.

3 O teach me what it meaneth,
Thy love beyond compare,
the love that reacheth deeper
than depths of self-despair!
Yes, teach me, till there gloweth
in this cold heart of mine,
some feeble, pale reflection
of that pure love of thine.

4 O teach me what it meaneth,
for I am full of sin;
and grace alone can reach me,
and love alone can win.
O teach me, for I need Thee,
I have no hope beside,
the chief of all the sinners
for whom the Saviour died!

5 O infinite Redeemer!
I bring no other plea,
because Thou dost invite me
I cast myself on Thee.
Because Thou dost accept me
I love and I adore;
because Thy love constraineth,
I'll praise Thee evermore!

522 O the deep, deep love of Jesus!

EBENEZER 87 87 D

Words: Samuel Trevor Francis (1834–1925)
Music: Thomas John Williams (1869–1944)

O the deep, deep love of Je-sus!
Vast, un-mea-sured, bound-less, free; roll-ing as a
migh-ty o-cean in its ful-ness
o-ver me. Un-der-neath me, all a-round me,

is the___ cur-rent of___ Thy___ love; lead-ing___ on-ward,

lead-ing___ home-ward, to my___ glo-rious rest___ a-bove.

1 O the deep, deep love of Jesus!
  Vast, unmeasured, boundless, free;
  rolling as a mighty ocean
  in its fulness over me.
  Underneath me, all around me,
  is the current of Thy love;
  leading onward, leading homeward,
  to my glorious rest above.

2 O the deep, deep love of Jesus!
  Spread His praise from shore to shore,
  how He loveth, ever loveth,
  changeth never, nevermore;
  how He watches o'er His loved ones,
  died to call them all His own;
  how for them He intercedeth,
  watches over them from the throne.

3 O the deep, deep love of Jesus!
  Love of every love the best:
  'tis an ocean vast of blessing,
  'tis a haven sweet of rest.
  O the deep, deep love of Jesus!
  'tis a heaven of heavens to me;
  and it lifts me up to glory,
  for it lifts me up to Thee.

523　　O the valleys shall ring

Words and music: Dave Bilbrough
Music arranged Andy Silver
and Christopher Norton

May Your will___ be done,___ may Your king - dom

come!___ let it rule,___ let it reign___ in our lives.___

___ There's a shout___ in the camp___ as we ans - wer the

call,___ Hail the King!___ Hail the Lord of lords!___

524   O the bitter shame and sorrow

St Jude   87 887

Words: Theodore Monod (1836–1921)
in this version Jubilate Hymns
Music: Charles Vincent (1852–1934)

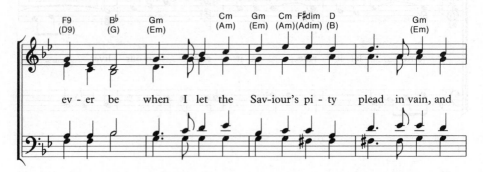

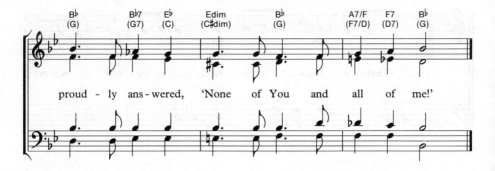

1 O the bitter shame and sorrow
that a time could ever be
when I let the Saviour's pity
plead in vain, and proudly answered,
'None of You and all of me!'

2 Yet You found me; there I saw You
dying and in agony,
heard You pray, 'Forgive them, Father',
and my wistful heart said faintly,
'Some of You and some of me.'

3 Day by day Your tender mercy,
healing, helping, full and free,
firm and strong, with endless patience
brought me lower, while I whispered,
'More of You and less of me.'

4 Higher than the highest heaven,
deeper than the deepest sea,
Lord, Your love at last has conquered:
grant me now my spirit's longing,
'All of You and none of me!'

525 O Thou who camest from above

WILTON LM

Words: Charles Wesley (1707–88)
Music: S Stanley (1767–1822)

1 O Thou who camest from above
   the pure, celestial fire to impart,
   kindle a flame of sacred love
   on the mean altar of my heart.

2 There let it for Thy glory burn,
   with inextinguishable blaze;
   and, trembling, to its source return
   in humble love and fervent praise.

3 Jesus, confirm my heart's desire
   to work and speak and think for Thee;
   still let me guard the holy fire,
   and still stir up Thy gift in me;

4 Ready for all Thy perfect will,
   my acts of faith and love repeat,
   till death Thine endless mercies seal,
   and make the sacrifice complete.

O what a gift!

Words and music: Pat Uhl Howard
Music arranged Betty Pulkingham

Joyfully, with a driving rhythm

Capo 2(Am)

O what a gift! what a won-der-ful gift!___ Who can

tell the won-ders of the Lord? Let us op - en our eyes, our

ears, and our hearts; it is Christ the Lord, it is He!

Fine

1 In the still - ness of the night___ when the
2 On the night be - fore He died___ it was
3 On the hill of Cal - va - ry___ the
4   Ear - ly on that morn - ing when the
5   Some day with the saints___ we will

From *The Johannine Hymnal*
Words and music: © 1967, 1970, 1978, 1979 American Catholic Press,
16160 South Seton Drive, South Holland, IL 60473, USA

527 O Word of God incarnate

BENTLEY   76 76 D

Words: W W How (1823–97)
Music: John Hullah (1812–84)

O Word of God in-car-nate, O wis-dom from on high, O truth un-changed, un-chang-ing, O light of our dark sky, we praise Thee for the rad-iance, that from the hal-lowed page, a

lan - tern to our foot - steps, shines on from age to age.

1   O Word of God incarnate,
    O wisdom from on high,
    O truth unchanged, unchanging,
    O light of our dark sky,
    we praise Thee for the radiance,
    that from the hallowed page,
    a lantern to our footsteps,
    shines on from age to age.

2   The Church from her dear Master
    received the gift divine,
    and still that light she lifteth
    o'er all the earth to shine:
    it is the golden casket
    where gems of truth are stored;
    it is the heaven-drawn picture
    of Christ, the living Word.

3   It floateth like a banner
    before God's host unfurled;
    it shineth like a beacon
    above the darkling world:
    it is the chart and compass
    that o'er life's surging sea,
    mid mists and rocks and quicksands
    still guide, O Christ, to Thee.

4   O make Thy Church, dear Saviour,
    a lamp of burnished gold,
    to bear before the nations
    Thy true light as of old;
    O teach Thy wandering pilgrims
    by this their path to trace,
    till, clouds and darkness ended,
    they see Thee face to face!

528   O worship the King

HANOVER   55 55 65 65

Words: Robert Grant (1779–1838)
Music: W Croft (1678–1727)

O wor - ship the King, all - glo - rious a - bove;

O grate - ful - ly sing His power and His love;

our shield and de - fen - der, the an - cient of days,

pa - vil - ioned in splen - dour, and gird - ed with praise.

1 O worship the King,
all-glorious above;
O gratefully sing
His power and His love;
our shield and defender,
the ancient of days,
pavilioned in splendour,
and girded with praise.

2 O tell of His might,
O sing of His grace,
whose robe is the light,
whose canopy, space;
His chariots of wrath
the deep thunder-clouds form,
and dark is His path
on the wings of the storm.

3 The earth, with its store
of wonders untold,
Almighty, Thy power
hath founded of old:
hath stablished it fast
by a changeless decree,
and round it hath cast,
like a mantle, the sea.

4 Thy bountiful care
what tongue can recite?
It breathes in the air,
it shines in the light,
it streams from the hills,
it descends to the plain,
and sweetly distils
in the dew and the rain.

5 Frail children of dust,
and feeble as frail,
in Thee do we trust,
nor find Thee to fail:
Thy mercies, how tender,
how firm to the end,
our Maker, defender,
Redeemer, and friend!

6 O Lord of all might,
how boundless Thy love!
while angels delight
to hymn Thee above,
the humbler creation,
though feeble their lays,
with true adoration
shall sing to Thy praise.

529   O worship the Lord

Sanctissimus   12 10 12 10 (Irregular)

Words: J S B Monsell (1811–75)
Music: W H Cook (1820–1912)

O wor-ship the Lord in the beau-ty of ho-li-ness,

bow down be - fore Him, His glo - ry pro - claim;

with gold of o - be-dience and in-cense of low-li-ness,

kneel and a - dore Him, the Lord is His name.

1 O worship the Lord in the beauty of holiness,
   bow down before Him, His glory proclaim;
   with gold of obedience and incense of lowliness,
   kneel and adore Him, the Lord is His name.

2 Low at His feet lay thy burden of carefulness,
   high on His heart He will bear it for thee,
   comfort thy sorrows, and answer thy prayerfulness,
   guiding thy steps as may best for thee be.

3 Fear not to enter His courts in the slenderness
   of the poor wealth thou wouldst reckon as thine:
   truth in its beauty and love in its tenderness:
   these are the offerings to lay on His shrine.

4 These, though we bring them in trembling and fearfulness,
   He will accept for the name that is dear;
   mornings of joy give for evenings of tearfulness,
   trust for our trembling, and hope for our fear.

5 O worship the Lord in the beauty of holiness
   bow down before Him, His glory proclaim;
   with gold of obedience and incense of lowliness,
   kneel and adore Him, the Lord is His name.

530   Oh, I will sing unto You with joy

Words and music: Shona Sauni
Music arranged Christopher Norton

Oh, I will sing un-to You with joy,__ O__ Lord, for You're the rock of my sal - va - tion; come be-fore You with thanks - giv - ing,__ and ex - tol__ You with a__ song. For You're the great - est__ King__ a - bove all__ else, You hold the depths of the earth in Your hand.

531   Oh Lord, I turn my mind to You

Words: Greg Leavers
Music: Greg Leavers and Phil Burt

1 Oh Lord,_ I turn my mind to You__ right a-
2 Oh Lord,_ I turn my eyes_ to You__ and see
3 Oh Lord,_ please speak Your word to me,__ just the
4 Oh Lord,_ please fill my heart a-new;__ I sur-

-way from the things that to-day____ I've been through. I'm so
love in Your eyes_ as You look____ to-wards me.__ I'm so un-
mes-sage I need,_ out of Your____ lov-ing heart. May I
-ren-der my pride_ which stops me____ trust-ing You._ For I

sor - ry Lord when they've cloud-ed the way____
-wor - thy Lord, yet You died_ for me;____
grasp Your truth that will set my heart free____
long that my life may____ glo-ri-fy You;____

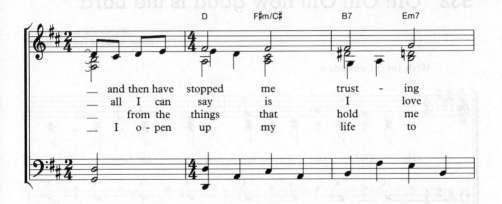

and then have stopped me trust - ing
all I can say is I love
from the things that hold me
I o - pen up my life to

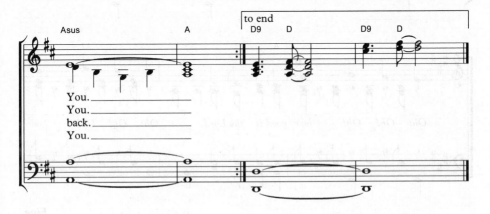

You.
You.
back.
You.

1   Oh Lord, I turn my mind to You
    right away from the things that today I've been through.
    I'm so sorry Lord when they've clouded the way
    and then have stopped me trusting You.

2   Oh Lord, I turn my eyes to You
    and see love in Your eyes as You look towards me.
    I'm so unworthy Lord, yet You died for me;
    all I can say is I love You.

3   Oh Lord, please speak Your word to me,
    just the message I need, out of Your loving heart.
    May I grasp Your truth that will set my heart free
    from the things that hold me back.

4   Oh Lord, please fill my heart anew;
    I surrender my pride which stops me trusting You.
    For I long that my life may glorify You;
    I open up my life to You.

532 Oh! Oh! Oh! how good is the Lord

Words and music: Anon
Music arranged Jeanne Harper

With joyful abandon

Oh! Oh! Oh! how good is the Lord,

Oh! Oh! Oh! how good is the Lord, Oh! Oh! Oh! how

good is the Lord, I ne-ver will for-get what He has done for me.

He gives me sal - va-tion, how good is the Lord, He

Oh! Oh! Oh! how good is the Lord,
Oh! Oh! Oh! how good is the Lord,
Oh! Oh! Oh! how good is the Lord,
I never will forget what He has done for me.

1 He gives me salvation, how good is the Lord,
  He gives me salvation, how good is the Lord,
  He gives me salvation, how good is the Lord,
  I never will forget what He has done for me.
  Oh! Oh! Oh! . . .

2 He gives me His blessings . . .
  Oh! Oh! Oh! . . .

3 He gives me His Spirit . . .
  Oh! Oh! Oh! . . .

4 He gives me His healing . . .
  Oh! Oh! Oh! . . .

5 He gives me His glory . . .
  Oh! Oh! Oh! . . .

OTHER SUITABLE VERSES MAY BE ADDED
He gives us each other . . .
He gives us His body . . .
He gives us His freedom . . . *etc.*

533   Oft in danger

UNIVERSITY COLLEGE   77 77

Words: Henry Kirke White (1785–1806) and others
Music: Henry John Gauntlett (1805–76)

1   Oft in danger, oft in woe,
    onward, Christians, onward go;
    bear the toil, maintain the strife,
    strengthened with the Bread of Life.

2   Onward, Christians, onward go!
    join the war, and face the foe;
    will ye flee in danger's hour?
    know ye not your Captain's power?

3   Let your drooping hearts be glad;
    march in heavenly armour clad;
    fight, nor think the battle long,
    victory soon shall tune your song.

4   Let not sorrow dim your eye,
    soon shall every tear be dry;
    let not fears your course impede,
    great your strength, if great your need.

5   Onward then in battle move;
    more than conquerors ye shall prove;
    though opposed by many a foe,
    Christian soldiers, onward go.

534   Oh, the joy of Your forgiveness

Words and music: Dave Bilbrough
Music arranged Christopher Norton

Oh, the joy of Your for-give-ness, slow-ly sweep-ing o-ver me; now in heart-felt a-do--ra-tion, this praise I'll__ bring to You my King; I'll wor-ship You my Lord.

535   O what a mystery I see

Words and music: Graham Kendrick
Music arranged Christopher Norton

1 O what a mystery I see, what
(2) per - fect Man, in - car - nate God, by
WOMEN (3) faith a child of His I stand, an

mar - vel - lous de - sign, that God should come as
self - less sac - ri - fice des - troyed our sin - ful
heir in Da - vid's line, roy - al de - scend-ant

one of us, a Son in Da - vid's line. Flesh
his - to - ry, all fall - en Ad - am's curse. In
by His blood des - tined by love's de - sign. MEN Fa -

of our flesh, of wo - man born, our
Him the curse to bless - ing turns, my
- thers of faith, my fa - thers now! be -

more then_ as a child of earth must I my life - time

spend – His his - to - ry, His des - ti - ny are

mine to ap - pre - hend. Oh what a_ Sav - iour,

what_ a_ Lord, O Mas - ter, Bro - ther,

friend!_____ What mi - ra - cle has

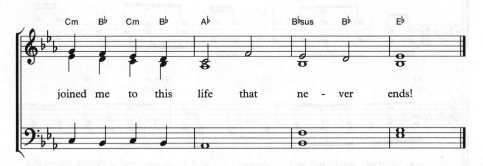

joined me to this life that ne - ver ends!

1 O what a mystery I see,
   what marvellous design,
   that God should come as one of us,
   a Son in David's line.
   Flesh of our flesh, of woman born,
   our humanness He owns;
   and for a world of wickedness
   His guiltless blood atones.

2 This perfect Man, incarnate God,
   by selfless sacrifice
   destroyed our sinful history,
   all fallen Adam's curse.
   In Him the curse to blessing turns,
   my barren spirit flowers,
   as over the shattered power of sin
   the cross of Jesus towers.

WOMEN
3 By faith a child of His I stand,
   an heir in David's line,
   royal descendant by His blood
   destined by love's design.
   MEN
   Fathers of faith, my fathers now!
   because in Christ I am,
   ALL
   and all God's promises in Him
   to me are 'Yes, amen'!

4 No more then as a child of earth
   must I my lifetime spend –
   His history, His destiny
   are mine to apprehend.
   Oh what a Saviour, what a Lord,
   O Master, Brother, friend!
   What miracle has joined me to
   this life that never ends!

536

On a hill far away

THE OLD RUGGED CROSS

Words and music: George Bennard

On a hill far a - way stood an old rug-ged cross, the

em - blem of suf-fering and shame;__ and I love that old cross where the

dear - est and best for a world of lost sin-ners was slain.__

So I'll cher - ish the *old* *rug - ged* *cross* *till my*
cross, *the* *old* *rug - ged cross,*

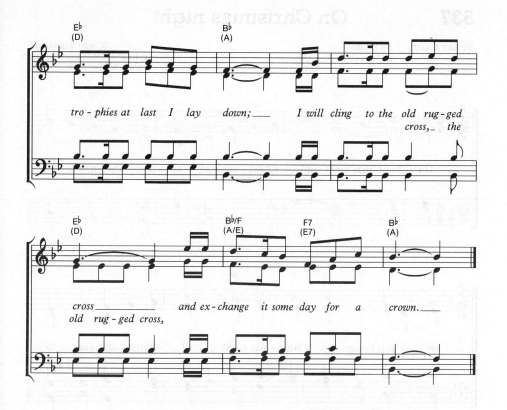

tro - phies at last I lay down; __ I will cling to the old rug-ged cross, _ the

cross _____ and ex - change it some day for a crown. __

old rug - ged cross,

1 On a hill far away stood an old rugged cross,
the emblem of suffering and shame;
and I love that old cross where the dearest and best
for a world of lost sinners was slain.
So I'll cherish the old rugged cross
till my trophies at last I lay down;
I will cling to the old rugged cross
and exchange it some day for a crown.

2 O, the old rugged cross, so despised by the world,
has a wondrous attraction for me;
for the dear Lamb of God left His glory above
to bear it to dark Calvary.
So I'll cherish . . .

3 In the old rugged cross, stained with blood so divine,
a wondrous beauty I see;
for 'twas on that old cross Jesus suffered and died
to pardon and sanctify me.
So I'll cherish . . .

4 To the old rugged cross I will ever be true,
its shame and reproach gladly bear;
then He'll call me some day to my home far away,
when His glory for ever I'll share.
So I'll cherish . . .

537 On Christmas night

SUSSEX CAROL 88 88 88

Words: Traditional
Music: English traditional melody
arranged R Vaughan Williams (1872–1958)

On Christ-mas night all Christ-ians sing to hear the news_ the

an - gels bring: on Christ-mas night all Christ - ians sing to

hear the news the an - gels bring: news of great joy,_ news of_ great

mirth, news of our mer - ci - ful_ King's birth.

Music arrangement: © Stainer & Bell Ltd,
PO Box 110, 82 High Road, London N2 9PW

1 On Christmas night all Christians sing
  to hear the news the angels bring:
  on Christmas night all Christians sing
  to hear the news the angels bring:
  news of great joy, news of great mirth,
  news of our merciful King's birth.

2 Then why should we on earth be so sad,
  since our Redeemer made us glad,
  then why should we on earth be so sad,
  since our Redeemer made us glad,
  when from our sin He set us free,
  all for to gain our liberty?

3 When sin departs before His grace,
  then life and health come in its place;
  when sin departs before His grace,
  then life and health come in its place;
  angels and men with joy may sing,
  all for to see the new-born King.

4 All out of darkness we have light,
  which made the angels sing this night:
  all out of darkness we have light,
  which made the angels sing this night:
  'Glory to God and peace to men,
  now and for evermore. Amen.'

538 On Jordan's bank, the Baptist's cry

WINCHESTER NEW   LM

Words: Charles Coffin (1676–1749)
tr. John Chandler (1806–76)
altered Horrobin/Leavers
Music: adapted from a chorale in
Musicalisches Hand-Buch, Hamburg, 1690
arranged W H Havergal (1793–1870)

On Jordan's bank the Baptist's cry announces that the Lord is nigh; come then and listen for he brings glad tidings from the King of kings.

1 On Jordan's bank the Baptist's cry
  announces that the Lord is nigh;
  come then and listen for he brings
  glad tidings from the King of kings.

2 Then cleansed be every heart from sin;
  make straight the way for God within;
  prepare we in our hearts a home,
  where such a mighty guest may come.

3 For You are our salvation, Lord,
  our refuge and our great reward;
  without Your grace we waste away,
  like flowers that wither and decay.

4 To heal the sick stretch out Your hand,
  make wholeness flow at Your command;
  sin's devastation now restore
  earth's own true loveliness once more.

5 To Him who left the throne of heaven
  to save mankind, all praise be given;
  to God the Father, voices raise,
  and Holy Spirit, let us praise.

539 Once in royal David's city

IRBY 87 87 77

Words: Cecil Frances Alexander (1823–95)
altered Horrobin/Leavers
Music: Henry John Gauntlett (1805–76)

Once in roy-al Da-vid's_ ci-ty, stood a low-ly cat-tle_ shed, where a mo-ther laid_ her ba-by, in a man-ger for_ His_ bed. Ma-ry_ was_ that mo-ther mild, Je-sus_ Christ_ her lit-tle_ child.

1 Once in royal David's city,
  stood a lowly cattle shed,
  where a mother laid her baby,
  in a manger for His bed.
  Mary was that mother mild,
  Jesus Christ her little child.

2 He came down to earth from heaven,
  who is God and Lord of all;
  and His shelter was a stable,
  and His cradle was a stall:
  with the poor and mean and lowly
  lived on earth our Saviour holy.

3 And through all His wondrous childhood
  He would honour and obey,
  love, and watch the lowly mother,
  in whose gentle arms He lay:
  Christian children all should be,
  kind, obedient, good as He.

4 For He is our childhood's pattern:
  day by day like us He grew;
  He was little, weak, and helpless,
  tears and smiles like us He knew;
  and He feels for all our sadness,
  and He shares in all our gladness.

5 And our eyes at last shall see Him,
  through His own redeeming love;
  for that child, so dear and gentle,
  is our Lord in heaven above;
  and He leads His children on
  to the place where He is gone.

6 Not in that poor lowly stable,
  with the oxen standing by,
  we shall see Him, but in heaven,
  set at God's right hand on high;
  there His children gather round,
  bright like stars, with glory crowned.

540 One day when heaven

Words: J Wilbur Chapman (1859–1918)
Music: Charles H Marsh

One day when hea - ven was filled with His prais - es, one day when sin was as black as could be,___ Je - sus came forth to be born of a vir - gin, dwelt a - mongst men, my ex - am - ple is He!___ Liv - ing, He loved me; dy - ing, He saved me; bur - ied, He

car - ried my sins far a - way,___ ris-ing, He jus - ti-fied free-ly for

ev - er: one day He's com - ing: O glo - ri - ous day.___

1 One day when heaven was filled with His praises,
   one day when sin was as black as could be,
   Jesus came forth to be born of a virgin,
   dwelt amongst men, my example is He!
       Living, He loved me; dying, He saved me;
       buried, He carried my sins far away,
       rising, He justified freely for ever:
       one day He's coming: O glorious day.

2 One day they led Him up Calvary's mountain,
   one day they nailed Him to die on the tree;
   suffering anguish, despised and rejected;
   bearing our sins, my Redeemer is He!
       Living, He loved me . . .

3 One day they left Him alone in the garden,
   one day He rested, from suffering free;
   angels came down o'er His tomb to keep vigil;
   hope of the hopeless, my Saviour is He!
       Living, He loved me . . .

4 One day the grave could conceal Him no longer,
   one day the stone rolled away from the door;
   Then He arose, over death He had conquered;
   now is ascended, my Lord evermore!
       Living, He loved me . . .

5 One day the trumpet will sound for His coming,
   one day the skies with His glory will shine;
   wonderful day, my beloved ones bringing;
   glorious Saviour, this Jesus is mine!
       Living, He loved me . . .

541   One shall tell another

Words and music: Graham Kendrick
Music arranged Christopher Norton

Lightly with increasing pace

One shall tell an-oth-er, and he shall tell his friends, hus-bands, wives and child-ren shall come fol-low-ing on. From house to house in fa-mi-lies shall more be gath-ered in; and lights will shine in ev-ery street, so warm and wel-com-ing.

Come on in and taste the new wine, the wine of the king-dom,

1 One shall tell another,
  and he shall tell his friends,
  husbands, wives and children
  shall come following on.
  From house to house in families
  shall more be gathered in;
  and lights will shine in every street,
  so warm and welcoming.
      Come on in
      and taste the new wine,
      the wine of the kingdom,
      the wine of the kingdom of God:
      here is healing and forgiveness,
      the wine of the kingdom,
      the wine of the kingdom of God.

2 Compassion of the Father
  is ready now to flow;
  through acts of love and mercy
  we must let it show.
  He turns now from His anger
  to show a smiling face,
  and longs that men should stand beneath
  the fountain of His grace.
      Come on in . . .

3 He longs to do much more than
  our faith has yet allowed,
  to thrill us and suprise us
  with His sovereign power.
  Where darkness has been darkest,
  the brightest light will shine;
  His invitation comes to us –
  it's yours and it is mine.
      Come on in . . .

542   One there is, above all others

GOUNOD   87 87 77

Words: John Newton (1725–1807)
Music: Charles Gounod (1818–93)

One there is, a - bove all oth - ers, well de - serves the name of friend; His is love be - yond a bro - ther's, cost - ly, free, and knows no end: they who once His kind - ness prove, find it ev - er - last - ing love.

1 One there is, above all others,
   well deserves the name of friend;
   His is love beyond a brother's,
   costly, free, and knows no end:
   they who once His kindness prove,
   find it everlasting love.

2 Which of all our friends, to save us,
   could, or would, have shed His blood?
   Christ, the Saviour, died to have us
   reconciled in Him to God:
   this was boundless love indeed!
   Jesus is a friend in need.

3 When He lived on earth abasèd,
   'Friend of sinners' was His name;
   now, above all glory raisèd,
   He rejoices in the same:
   still He calls them brethren, friends,
   and to all their wants attends.

4 O for grace our hearts to soften!
   teach us, Lord, at length to love.
   We, alas! forget too often
   what a friend we have above:
   but when home our souls are brought,
   we will love Thee as we ought.

543 Onward Christian soldiers

St Gertrude   65 65 with refrain

Words: S Baring-Gould (1834–1924)
Music: Arthur S Sullivan (1842–1900)

On-ward Christ-ian sol - diers, march-ing as to war,

with the cross of Je - sus go - ing on be - fore.

Christ the roy - al Mas - ter leads a - gainst the foe;

for-ward in - to bat - tle,___ see, His ban - ners go!

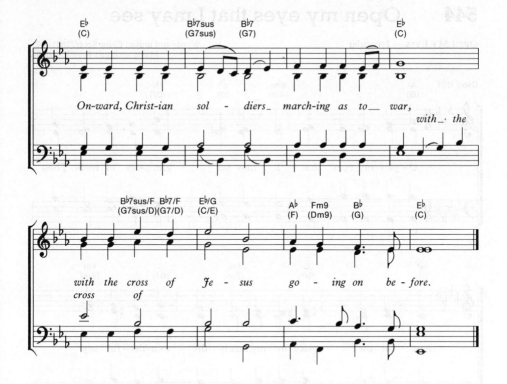

On-ward, Christ-ian sol - diers_ march-ing as to_ war,
with_ the

with the cross of Je - sus go - ing on be - fore.
cross of

1   Onward Christian soldiers, marching as to war,
with the cross of Jesus going on before.
Christ the royal Master leads against the foe;
forward into battle, see, His banners go!
Onward, Christian soldiers, marching as to war,
with the cross of Jesus going on before.

2   At the name of Jesus Satan's legions flee;
on then, Christian soldiers, on to victory.
Hell's foundations quiver at the shout of praise;
brothers, lift your voices, loud your anthems raise.
Onward, Christian soldiers . . .

3   Like a mighty army moves the Church of God;
brothers, we are treading where the saints have trod;
we are not divided, all one body we,
one in hope and calling, one in charity.
Onward, Christian soldiers . . .

4   Crowns and thrones may perish, kingdoms rise and wane,
but the Church of Jesus constant will remain;
gates of hell can never 'gainst that Church prevail;
We have Christ's own promise, and that cannot fail.
Onward, Christian soldiers . . .

5   Onward, then, ye people, join our happy throng,
blend with ours your voices in the triumph song;
glory, praise and honour unto Christ the King;
This through countless ages men and angels sing.
Onward, Christian soldiers . . .

544   Open my eyes that I may see

OPEN MY EYES   Irregular

Words and music: Clara Scott (1841–97)
Music arranged Fred P Morris

O - pen my eyes that I may see glimp-ses of truth Thou

hast for me; place in my hands the won-der - ful key

that shall un-clasp and set me free. Si - lent - ly now I

wait for Thee, rea - dy, my God, Thy will to see;

o - pen my eyes, il - lu - mine me, Spi - rit di - vine! ___

1 Open my eyes that I may see
glimpses of truth Thou hast for me;
place in my hands the wonderful key
that shall unclasp and set me free.
   Silently now I wait for Thee,
   ready, my God, Thy will to see;
   open my eyes, illumine me,
   Spirit divine!

2 Open my ears that I may hear
voices of truth Thou sendest clear;
and while the wave-notes fall on my ear,
everything false will disappear.
   Silently now I wait . . .

3 Open my mouth and let me bear
tidings of mercy everywhere;
open my heart and let me prepare
love with Thy children thus to share.
   Silently now I wait . . .

4 Open my mind, that I may read
more of Thy love in word and deed:
what shall I fear while yet Thou dost lead?
Only for light from Thee I plead.
   Silently now I wait . . .

545

Open our eyes, Lord

Words and music: Robert Cull
Music arranged David Peacock

546 Open Thou mine eyes

From Psalm 119
Words and music: C C Kerr

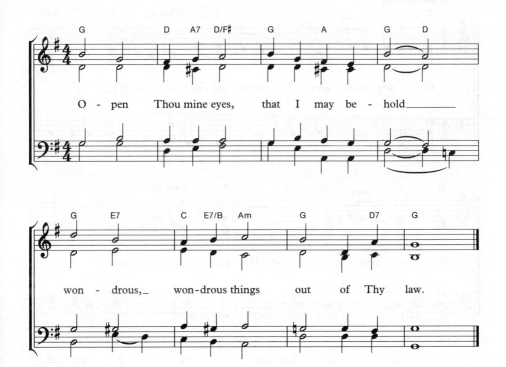

O - pen Thou mine eyes, that I may be - hold_____ won - drous,_ won-drous things out of Thy law.

Open your eyes

Words and music: Carl Tuttle
Music arranged Christopher Norton

Worshipfully

O - pen your_ eyes, see the glo - ry of the King;

lift up your_ voice, and His prais - es___ sing!

I love You, Lord, I will pro-claim:

Al - le - lu - ia! I bless Your name.

548   Our blest Redeemer

St Cuthbert   86 84

Words: Henriette Auber (1773–1862)
Music: John Bacchus Dykes (1823–76)

Our blest Re-deem-er, ere He breathed His ten-der last fare-well,

a guide, a com-fort - er be-queathed, with us to___ dwell.

1 Our blest Redeemer, ere He breathed
His tender last farewell,
a guide, a comforter bequeathed,
with us to dwell.

2 He came in semblance of a dove,
with sheltering wings outspread,
the holy balm of peace and love
on earth to shed.

3 He came in tongues of living flame,
to teach, convince, subdue;
all powerful as the wind He came,
as viewless too.

4 He comes sweet influence to impart,
a gracious, willing guest,
where He can find one humble heart
wherein to rest.

5 And His that gentle voice we hear,
soft as the breath of even,
that checks each fault, that calms each fear,
and speaks of heaven.

6 And every virtue we possess,
and every victory won,
and every thought of holiness,
are His alone.

7 Spirit of purity and grace,
our weakness, pitying, see;
O make our hearts Thy dwelling-place,
and worthier Thee.

549   Our eyes have seen the glory

Words: Roland Meredith
Music: American traditional melody
arranged Phil Burt

Our eyes have seen the glo-ry of our Sav-iour, Christ the Lord; He is seat-ed at His Fa-ther's side in love and full ac-cord; from there up-on the sons of men His Spi-rit is out-poured, all hail, as-cend-ed King!____ *Glo-ry, glo-ry hal-le-*

-lu - jah, glo - ry, glo - ry hal - le - lu - jah,

glo - ry, glo - ry hal - le - lu - jah, all hail as - cend - ed King!____

1   Our eyes have seen the glory
    of our Saviour, Christ the Lord;
    He is seated at His Father's side
    in love and full accord;
    from there upon the sons of men
    His Spirit is out-poured,
    all hail, ascended King!
        Glory, glory hallelujah,
        glory, glory hallelujah,
        glory, glory hallelujah,
        all hail ascended King!

2   He came to earth at Christmas
    and was made a man like us;
    He taught, He healed, He suffered –
    and they nailed Him to the cross;
    He rose again on Easter Day –
    our Lord victorious,
    all hail, ascended King!
        Glory, glory . . .

3   The good news of His kingdom
    must be preached to every shore,
    the news of peace and pardon,
    and the end of strife and war;
    the secret of His kingdom
    is to serve Him evermore,
    all hail, ascended King!
        Glory, glory . . .

4   His kingdom is a family
    of men of every race,
    they live their lives in harmony,
    enabled by His grace;
    they follow His example
    till they see Him face to face,
    all hail, ascended King!
        Glory, glory . . .

550 Our Father in heaven

Words: from *The Alternative Service Book 1980*
Music: John Marsh

551 Out of my bondage

JESUS, I COME   Irregular

Words: W T Sleeper (1840–1920)
Music: George C Stebbins (1846–1945)

Out of my bond-age, sor-row, and night, Je-sus, I come:

Je-sus, I come; in-to Your free-dom, glad-ness, and light,

Je-sus, I come to You.— Out of my sick-ness in-to Your health,

out of my want and in-to Your wealth, out of my sin and

in - to Your-self,   Je - sus, I come   to   You.

1   Out of my bondage, sorrow, and night,
    Jesus, I come: Jesus, I come;
    into Your freedom, gladness, and light,
    Jesus, I come to You.
    Out of my sickness into Your health,
    out of my want and into Your wealth,
    out of my sin and into Yourself,
    Jesus, I come to You.

2   Out of my shameful failure and loss,
    Jesus, I come: Jesus, I come;
    into the glorious gain of Your cross,
    Jesus, I come to You.
    Out of earth's sorrows into Your balm,
    out of life's storm and into Your calm,
    out of distress to jubilant psalm,
    Jesus, I come to You.

3   Out of unrest and arrogant pride,
    Jesus, I come: Jesus, I come;
    into Your blessèd will to abide,
    Jesus, I come to You.
    Out of myself to dwell in Your love,
    out of despair into joy from above,
    upward for ever on wings like a dove,
    Jesus, I come to You.

4   Out of the fear and dread of the tomb,
    Jesus, I come: Jesus, I come;
    into the joy and light of Your home,
    Jesus, I come to You.
    Out of the depths of ruin untold,
    into the peace of Your sheltering fold,
    ever Your glorious face to behold,
    Jesus, I come to You.

552 Our Father who is in heaven

CARIBBEAN LORD'S PRAYER

Music arrangement: Allen Percival

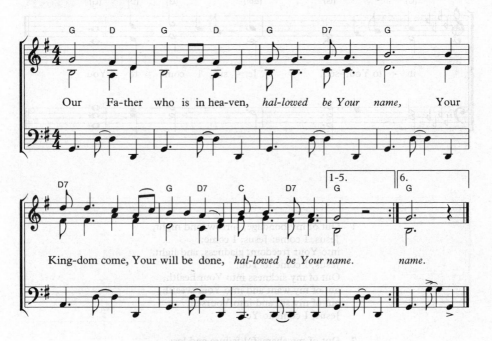

1 Our Father who is in heaven,
   hallowed be Your name,
   Your Kingdom come, Your will be done,
   hallowed be Your name.

2 On earth as it is in heaven,
   hallowed be Your name,
   give us this day our daily bread,
   hallowed be Your name.

3 Forgive us all our trespasses,
   hallowed be Your name,
   as we forgive those who trespass against us,
   hallowed be Your name.

4 And lead us not into temptation,
   hallowed be Your name,
   but deliver us from all that is evil,
   hallowed be Your name.

5 For Yours is the Kingdom, the Power and the Glory,
   hallowed be Your name,
   for ever and for ever,
   hallowed be Your name.

6 Amen, amen, it shall be so,
   hallowed be Your name,
   amen, amen, it shall be so,
   hallowed be Your name.

553   Peace I give to you

Words and music: Graham Kendrick
Music arranged Christopher Norton

1   Peace I give to you, I give to you My peace;
   peace I give to you, I give to you My peace.
   Let it flow to one another,
   let it flow, let it flow;
   let it flow to one another,
   let it flow, let it flow.

2   Love I give to you, I give to you My love;
   love I give to you, I give to you My love.
   Let it flow . . .

3   Hope I give to you, I give to you My hope;
   hope I give to you, I give to you My hope.
   Let it flow . . .

4   Joy I give to you, I give to you My joy;
   joy I give to you, I give to you My joy.
   Let it flow . . .

554 Peace is flowing like a river

Words and music: Anon
sic arranged Betty Pulkingham

Smoothly

Peace is flow-ing like a riv - er,
flow - ing out through you and me,
spread - ing out in - to the des - ert,
set - ting all the cap-tives free, set - ting all the cap-tives free.

Love is flowing . . .
Joy is flowing . . .
Faith is flowing . . .
Hope is flowing . . . *etc.*

Music arrangement: © 1974, 1975 Celebration,
administered in Europe by Thankyou Music,
PO Box 75, Eastbourne, East Sussex BN23 6NW, UK

555(i)   Peace, perfect peace

PAX TECUM   10 10

Words: E H Bickersteth (1825–1906)
Music: George Thomas Calbeck (1852–1918)
and Charles Vincent (1852–1934)

1   Peace, perfect peace, in this dark world of sin?
    The blood of Jesus whispers peace within.

2   Peace, perfect peace, by thronging duties pressed?
    To do the will of Jesus, this is rest.

3   Peace, perfect peace, with sorrows surging round?
    In Jesus' presence nought but calm is found.

4   Peace, perfect peace, with loved ones far away?
    In Jesus' keeping we are safe, and they.

5   Peace, perfect peace, our future all unknown?
    Jesus we know, and He is on the throne.

6   Peace, perfect peace, death shadowing us and ours?
    Jesus has vanquished death and all its powers.

7   It is enough: earth's struggles soon shall cease,
    and Jesus call us to heaven's perfect peace.

555(ii)   Peace, perfect peace

SONG 46   10 10

Words: E H Bickersteth (1825–1906)
Music: Orlando Gibbons (1583–1625)

Peace, per-fect peace,— in this dark world of sin?

The blood of Je-sus whis-pers peace with - in.

1   Peace, perfect peace, in this dark world of sin?
The blood of Jesus whispers peace within.

2   Peace, perfect peace, by thronging duties pressed?
To do the will of Jesus, this is rest.

3   Peace, perfect peace, with sorrows surging round?
In Jesus' presence nought but calm is found.

4   Peace, perfect peace, with loved ones far away?
In Jesus' keeping we are safe, and they.

5   Peace, perfect peace, our future all unknown?
Jesus we know, and He is on the throne.

6   Peace, perfect peace, death shadowing us and ours?
Jesus has vanquished death and all its powers.

7   It is enough: earth's struggles soon shall cease,
and Jesus call us to heaven's perfect peace.

556

Peace to you

Words and music: Graham Kendrick

Peace to you, We bless you now in the name of the Lord, Peace to you. We bless you now in the name of the Prince of Peace. Peace to you, peace to you, peace to you, peace to you.

repeat verse 3 times

rit.

Words and music: © 1988 Make Way Music,
administered in Europe by Thankyou Music,
PO Box 75, Eastbourne, East Sussex BN23 6NW, UK

557 Praise God

Words: Thomas Ken (1637–1710)
Music: Jimmy Owens

With movement

Praise God from whom all bless-ings flow; praise Him all crea-tures here be-low, praise Him a-bove ye hea-ven-ly hosts; praise Fa-ther, Son, and Ho-ly Ghost.

Optional 4-part setting

Praise God___ from whom all bless - ings flow; praise

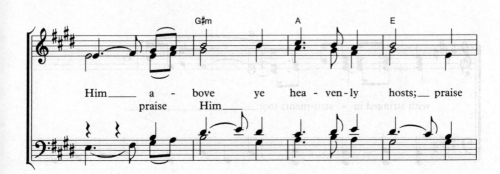

Him___ all crea - tures here___ be - low, praise

Him___ a - bove ye hea - ven - ly hosts;___ praise

praise Him___

Fa - ther, Son,___ and Ho - ly Ghost. Praise. Ghost.

558 Praise Him on the trumpet

Words and music: John Kennett
Music arranged Christopher Norton

Praise Him on the trum-pet,_ the psalt-ery and harp;

praise Him on the tim-brel and the dance;____ praise Him

with stringed in - stru-ments too;____

praise Him on the loud cym-bals, praise Him on the loud

cym - bals; let ev - ery - thing that has breath praise the

Lord!   Hal - le - lu - jah, praise the Lord;

hal - le - lu - jah, praise the Lord:___ let ev - ery - thing that has

breath praise the Lord!_____

breath praise the Lord!_____

8va bassa_____

559

Praise Him, praise Him

PRAISE HIM!   12 10 12 10 11 10 12 10

Words: Frances van Alstyne (1820–1915)
(Fanny J Crosby)
Music: C G Allen (1838–78)

1 Praise Him, praise Him! Je-sus, our bless-ed Re-deem-er!
2 Praise Him, praise Him! Je-sus, our bless-ed Re-deem-er!
3 Praise Him, praise Him! Je-sus, our bless-ed Re-deem-er!

Sing, O earth–His won-der-ful love pro-claim!
for our sins He suf-fered, and bled, and died;
heaven-ly por-tals, loud with ho-san-nas ring!

Hail Him, hail Him! high-est arch-an-gels in glo-ry;
He–our rock, our hope of e-ter-nal sal-va-tion,
Je-sus, Sav-iour, reign-eth for ev-er and ev-er:

strength and hon-our give to his ho-ly name!
hail Him, hail Him! Je-sus the cru-ci-fied!
crown Him, crown Him! Pro-phet, and Priest, and King!

Like a shep - herd, Je-sus will guard His child - ren,
Sound His prais - es— Je-sus who bore our sor - rows,
Christ is com - ing, o - ver the world vic - tor - ious,

in His arms He car-ries them all day long.___
love un - bound - ed, won-der-ful, deep and strong.__
power and glo - ry un - to the Lord be - long.__

Praise Him, praise Him! tell of His ex - cel - lent great - ness;

*Praise Him, praise Him ev - er in joy - ful song!*___

560 Praise, my soul, the King of heaven

PRAISE, MY SOUL   87 87 87

Words: H F Lyte (1793–1847)
Music: J Goss (1800–80)

Praise, my soul, the King of hea - ven;

to His feet thy tri - bute bring;__ ran - somed,

healed, re - stored, for - giv - en, who like thee His

praise should sing? Praise Him! Praise Him! Praise Him!__

Praise Him! Praise the ev - er - last - ing King.

1 Praise, my soul, the King of heaven;
   to His feet thy tribute bring;
   ransomed, healed, restored, forgiven,
   who like thee His praise should sing?
       Praise Him! Praise Him!
       Praise Him! Praise Him!
   Praise the everlasting King.

2 Praise Him for His grace and favour
   to our fathers, in distress;
   praise Him still the same for ever,
   slow to chide, and swift to bless.
       Praise Him! Praise Him!
       Praise Him! Praise Him!
   Glorious in His faithfulness.

3 Father-like He tends and spares us;
   well our feeble frame He knows;
   in His hands He gently bears us,
   rescues us from all our foes.
       Praise Him! Praise Him!
       Praise Him! Praise Him!
   Widely as His mercy flows.

4 Angels help us to adore Him;
   ye behold Him face to face;
   sun and moon, bow down before Him;
   dwellers all in time and space.
       Praise Him! Praise Him!
       Praise Him! Praise Him!
   Praise with us the God of grace.

561   Praise the Lord

From Psalm 150
Words and music:
Lee Abbey Music Workshop

Praise the Lord! Praise Him for His great-ness! Praise Him with trum-pets, harps and lyres. All liv-ing crea-tures, praise! O praise, O praise, praise the Lord! Lord!

562   Praise the Lord

Words and music: David J Hadden

Brightly with pace

Praise the Lord,__ praise God in His sanc-tu-a - ry, praise
Him in His migh-ty heavens; praise Him for His great-ness, and praise Him for_ His
power. Praise the Lord, power.
Praise Him with the sound of trum-pets,_____

praise Him with the harp and lyre,

praise Him with the tam-bour-ine_ and with danc - ing;_ let

ev-ery-thing_ that has breath praise the Lord.

Praise the Lord,
praise God in His sanctuary,
praise Him in His mighty heavens;
praise Him for His greatness,
and praise Him for His power.
Praise the Lord . . .

1 Praise Him with the sound of trumpets,
   praise Him with the harp and lyre,
   praise Him with the tambourine and with dancing;
   let everything that has breath praise the Lord.
       Praise the Lord . . .

2 Praise Him with the clash of cymbals,
   praise Him with the strings and flute,
   praise Him with the tambourine and with dancing;
   let everything that has breath praise the Lord.
       Praise the Lord . . .

563   Praise to the Holiest

GERONTIUS   CM

Words: J H Newman (1801–90)
Music J B Dykes (1823–76)

Praise to the Holiest in the height,
and in the depth be praise;
in all His words most wonderful;
most sure in all His ways.

1 Praise to the Holiest in the height,
and in the depth be praise;
in all His words most wonderful;
most sure in all His ways.

2 O loving wisdom of our God!
when all was sin and shame,
a second Adam to the fight,
and to the rescue came.

3 O wisest love! that flesh and blood
which did in Adam fail,
should strive afresh against the foe,
should strive and should prevail.

4 And that a higher gift than grace
should flesh and blood refine,
God's presence, and His very self
and essence all-divine.

5 O generous love! that He, who smote
in Man for man the foe,
the double agony in Man
for man should undergo.

6 And in the garden secretly,
and on the cross on high,
should teach His brethren, and inspire
to suffer and to die.

7 Praise to the Holiest in the height
and in the depth be praise:
in all His words most wonderful;
most sure in all His ways.

564 Praise to the Lord

LOBE DEN HERREN   14 14 47 8

Words: Joachim Neander (1650–80)
tr. Catherine Winkworth (1829–78)
Music: from *Stralsund Gesangbuch*, 1665

Praise to the Lord, the Al - migh - ty, the King of cre - a - - tion; O my soul, praise Him, for He is thy health and sal - va - tion; all ye who hear, bro - thers and sis - ters, draw near, praise Him in glad a - do - ra - tion.

1 Praise to the Lord, the Almighty, the King of creation;
O my soul, praise Him, for He is thy health and salvation;
all ye who hear,
brothers and sisters, draw near,
praise Him in glad adoration.

2 Praise to the Lord, who o'er all things so wondrously reigneth,
shelters thee under His wings, yea, so gently sustaineth:
hast thou not seen?
all that is needful hath been
granted in what He ordaineth.

3 Praise to the Lord, who doth prosper thy work, and defend thee!
surely His goodness and mercy here daily attend thee.
Ponder anew
what the Almighty can do,
who with His love doth befriend thee.

4 Praise to the Lord! O let all that is in me adore Him!
All that hath life and breath come now with praises before Him!
Let the Amen
sound from His people again:
gladly for aye we adore Him.

565   Praise You, Lord

Words and music: Nettie Rose
Music arranged Christopher Norton

praise You, Lord, for Your love for me.

1 Praise You, Lord,
for the wonder of Your healing;
praise You, Lord,
for Your love so freely given;
out-pouring, anointing,
flowing in to heal our wounds –
praise You, Lord,
for Your love for me.

2 Praise You, Lord,
for Your gift of liberation;
praise You, Lord,
You have set the captives free;
the chains that bind are broken
by the sharpness of Your sword –
praise You, Lord,
You gave Your life for me.

3 Praise You, Lord,
You have borne the depths of sorrow;
praise You, Lord,
for Your anguish on the tree;
the nails that tore Your body
and the pain that tore Your soul –
praise You, Lord,
Your tears, they fell for me.

4 Praise You, Lord,
You have turned our thorns to roses;
glory, Lord, as they bloom upon Your brow;
the path of pain is hallowed,
for Your love has made it sweet –
praise You, Lord,
and may I love You now.

566 Praise the name of Jesus

Words and music: Roy Hicks

Praise the name of Je - sus, Praise the name of Je - sus, He's my rock, He's my fort - ress, He's my de - liv - er - er, in Him will I trust; Praise the name of Je - sus.

567 Prayer is the soul's sincere desire

Nox Praecessit   CM

Words: James Montgomery (1771–1854)
Music: J Baptiste Calkin (1827–1905)

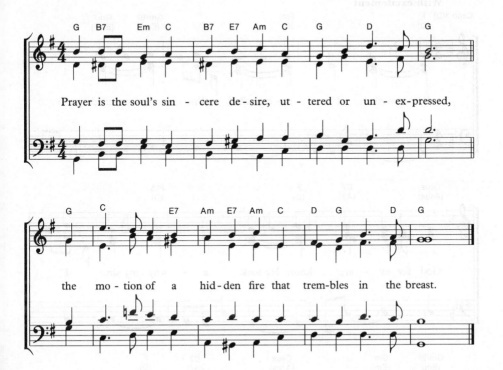

Prayer is the soul's sin - cere de - sire, ut - tered or un - ex-pressed,
the mo - tion of a hid - den fire that trem-bles in the breast.

1 Prayer is the soul's sincere desire,
   uttered or unexpressed,
   the motion of a hidden fire
   that trembles in the breast.

2 Prayer is the burden of a sigh,
   the falling of a tear,
   the upward glancing of an eye,
   when none but God is near.

3 Prayer is the simplest form of speech
   that infant lips can try;
   prayer the sublimest strains that reach
   the majesty on high.

4 Prayer is the contrite sinner's voice,
   returning from his ways;
   while angels in their songs rejoice,
   and cry, 'Behold, he prays!'

5 Prayer is the Christian's vital breath,
   the Christian's native air,
   his watchword at the gates of death;
   he enters heaven with prayer.

6 No prayer is made on earth alone;
   the Holy Spirit pleads;
   and Jesus on the eternal throne,
   for sinners intercedes.

7 O Thou by whom we come to God,
   the life, the truth, the way,
   the path of prayer Thyself hast trod;
   Lord, teach us how to pray!

Reconciled

Words and music: Mike Kerry

re-con-ciled to God,_____ hal-le-lu-jah! I'm ____

1 Reconciled, I'm reconciled,
I'm reconciled to God for ever;
know He took away my sin,
I know His love will leave me never.
Reconciled, I am His child,
I know it was on me He smiled;
I'm reconciled, I'm reconciled to God,
    hallelujah!

2 I'm justified, I'm justified,
it's just as if I'd never sinned;
and once I knew such guilty fear,
but now I know His peace with me.
Justified, I'm justified,
it's all because my Jesus died;
I'm justified, I'm justified by God,
    hallelujah!

3 I'll magnify, I'll magnify,
I'll magnify His name for ever;
wear the robe of righteousness
and bless the name of Jesus, Saviour;
magnify the One who died,
the One who reigns for me on high;
I'll magnify, I'll magnify my God.

569   Reach out and touch the Lord

Words and music: Bill Harmon

Reach out and touch the Lord as He goes by; you'll find He's not too bu-sy to hear your hearts' cry. He's pass-ing by this mo-ment your needs to sup-ply; reach out and touch the Lord as He goes by.

Words and music: © 1958 Gospel Publishing House

570   Reign in me

Words and music: Chris Bowater
Music arranged G Baker

Reign in me,_____ sove-reign Lord, reign in me,_____
reign in me,_____ sove-reign Lord,
reign in me._____ Cap - ti - vate my heart,_____
_____ let Your king-dom come,_____ es-tab-lish there Your
throne,_____ let Your will be done!_____

571 Reigning in all splendour

Words and music: Dave Bilbrough
Music arranged Christopher Norton

Reign-ing in all splen - dour - vic-to-ri-ous love;

Christ Je-sus the Sav - iour,

tran-scen-dent a - bove. _ All earth-ly do-min -

- ions and king-doms shall fall, _

572   Rejoice!

Words and music: Graham Kendrick
Music arranged Christopher Norton

Re-joice, re-joice! Christ is in___ you – the hope of glo - ry in___ our hearts. He lives, He lives! His breath is in___ you. A - rise! A migh-ty ar - my___ we a-rise!___ Now is the time for us___ to march up-on___ the land – in-to our hands He will give the ground we

claim;_____ He rides in ma-jes-ty_ to lead us in-to vic-to-ry,_ the world shall see that Christ is Lord._____

D.% al Coda

CODA

Re -

We a-rise!

We a-rise!_

We a-rise!_

8va

2 God is at work in us, His purpose to perform –
building a kingdom of power not of words;
where things impossible by faith shall be made possible:
let's give the glory to Him now.
    Rejoice, rejoice . . .

3 Though we are weak, His grace is everything we need –
we're made of clay, but this treasure is within;
He turns our weaknesses into His opportunities,
so that the glory goes to Him.
    Rejoice, rejoice . . .
    We arise! We arise! We arise!

573 Rejoice and be glad

REJOICE AND BE GLAD   Irregular

Words: Horatius Bonar (1808–89)
Music: John Jenkins Husband (1760–1825)

Re - joice and be glad! the Re - deem - er has come:

go,__ look on His cra - dle, His cross, and His tomb.

Sound His prais - es, tell the sto - ry of Him who was slain;

sound His prais - es, tell with glad - ness He now lives a - gain.

Words and music: Chris Bowater

1   Rejoice and be glad! the Redeemer has come:
  go, look on His cradle, His cross, and His tomb.
  Sound His praises, tell the story of Him who was slain;
  sound His praises, tell with gladness He now lives again.

2   Rejoice and be glad! it is sunshine at last;
  the clouds have departed, the shadows are past.
  Sound His praises . . .

3   Rejoice and be glad! for the blood has been shed;
  redemption is finished, the price has been paid.
  Sound His praises . . .

4   Rejoice and be glad! now the pardon is free;
  the just for the unjust has died on the tree.
  Sound His praises . . .

5   Rejoice and be glad! for the Lamb that was slain,
  o'er death is triumphant, and now lives again.
  Sound His praises . . .

6   Rejoice and be glad! for our King is on high;
  He pleads now for us on His throne in the sky.
  Sound His praises . . .

7   Rejoice and be glad! for He's coming again;
  He'll come in great glory, the Lamb that was slain.
  Sound His praises . . .

574 # Rejoice, rejoice, rejoice

Words and music: Chris Bowater

575   Rejoice, the Lord is King!

GOPSAL   66 66 88

Words: Charles Wesley (1707–88)
Music: G F Handel (1685–1759)

Re - joice, the Lord is King!_____ your

Lord and_ King a - dore; Mor - tals, give thanks and sing, and

tri - umph ev - er - more: *Lift up___ your heart, lift*

up your voice; re - joice, a - gain I___ say,___ re - joice.

1 Rejoice, the Lord is King!
  your Lord and King adore;
  Mortals, give thanks and sing,
  and triumph evermore:
      Lift up your heart, lift up your voice;
      rejoice, again I say, rejoice.

2 Jesus the Saviour reigns,
  the God of truth and love;
  when He had purged our stains,
  He took His seat above:
      Lift up your heart . . .

3 His kingdom cannot fail,
  He rules o'er earth and heaven;
  the keys of death and hell
  are to our Jesus given:
      Lift up your heart . . .

4 He sits at God's right hand,
  till all His foes submit,
  and bow to His command,
  and fall beneath His feet:
      Lift up your heart . . .

5 Rejoice in glorious hope;
  Jesus the Judge shall come,
  and take His servants up
  to their eternal home:
      We soon shall hear the archangel's voice;
      the trump of God shall sound, rejoice!

576   Rejoice, the Lord is risen!

Words and music: Moira Austin

Chorus overleaf

Chorus (with increased breadth and fullness)

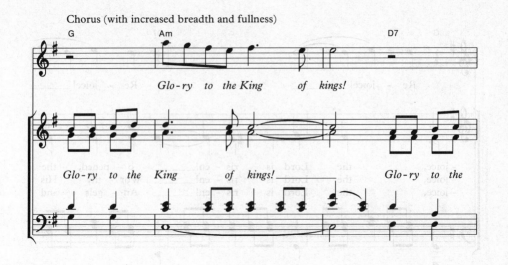

Glo-ry to the King of kings! / Glo-ry to the King of kings!_____ Glo-ry to the

Glo-ry to the Lord of lords! Je - sus, You are / Lord of lords!_____ Je-sus, we pro-claim that You are

Lord in ma - jes - ty! / Lord en-throned in ma - jes-ty!_____ Glo-ry to the

Glo-ry to the King of kings! Glo-ry to the Lord of

King of kings! Glo-ry to the Lord of lords!

lords! Je - sus, reign on high for ev-er-

Je-sus, You are reign - ing now on high for ev - er -

1.2.
- more!

3.
- more!

- more!

577   Rejoice in the Lord always

Words: from Philippians 4
Music: Traditional
arranged Evelyn Tarner

A round in 4 parts

Re - joice in the Lord al - ways, and a - gain I say re-joice! Re -

- joice in the Lord_ al - ways, and a - gain I say re - joice! Re -

- joice, re - joice, and a - gain I say re - joice! Re -

- joice, re - joice, and a - gain I say re - joice!

578 Revive Thy work, O Lord

SWABIA SM

Words: Albert Midlane (1825–1909)
Music: from a melody in J M Spiess'
Gesangbuch, 1745
arranged W H Havergal (1793–1870)

Re - vive Thy work, O Lord, Thy migh-ty __ arm make bare;

speak with the voice that wakes the dead and make Thy peo-ple hear.

1 Revive Thy work, O Lord,
Thy mighty arm make bare;
speak with the voice that wakes the dead
and make Thy people hear.

2 Revive Thy work, O Lord,
disturb this sleep of death;
quicken the smouldering embers now
by Thine almighty breath.

3 Revive Thy work, O Lord,
create soul-thirst for Thee;
and hungering for the Bread of Life
O may our spirits be!

4 Revive Thy work, O Lord,
exalt Thy precious name;
and, by the Holy Ghost, our love
for Thee and Thine inflame.

5 Revive Thy work, O Lord,
give pentecostal showers;
the glory shall be all Thine own,
the blessing, Lord, be ours.

579

Restore, O Lord

Words and music: Graham Kendrick
and Chris Rolinson

1 Re - store,   O Lord,   the hon - our of Your
2 Re - store,   O Lord,   in all the earth Your
3 Bend us,   O Lord,   where we are hard and

name!   In works of sove - reign pow - er come
fame,   and in our time re - vive the
cold,   in Your re - fin - ers fire; come

shake the earth a - gain,   that men may
Church that bears Your name,   and in Your
pu - ri - fy the gold: though suffer - ing

D   F#   Bm   Bm/A

see,   and come with rev - erent fear   to   the
anger,   Lord, re - mem - ber mer - cy,   O___
comes,   and   ev - il crou - ches near, still our

Gmaj7 F#m7   Em7   G/A   G

Liv - ing   God,___   whose King - dom
Liv - ing   God,___   whose mer - cy
Liv - ing   God___   is   reign - ing,

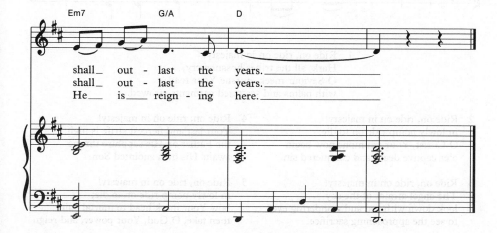

Em7   G/A   D

shall_ out - last the   years._____
shall_ out - last the   years._____
He__ is__ reign - ing here._____

580   Ride on, ride on in majesty

St Drostane   LM

Words: Henry Hart Milman (1791–1868)
Music: John Bacchus Dykes (1823–76)

1   Ride on, ride on in majesty!
Hark, all the tribes hosanna cry,
O Saviour meek, pursue Your road
with palms and scattered garments strowed.

2   Ride on, ride on in majesty!
in lowly pomp ride on to die:
O Christ, Your triumphs now begin
o'er captive death and conquered sin.

3   Ride on, ride on in majesty!
The angel armies of the sky
look down with sad and wondering eyes
to see the approaching sacrifice.

4   Ride on, ride on in majesty!
Your last and fiercest strife is nigh;
the Father on His sapphire throne
awaits His own anointed Son.

5   Ride on, ride on in majesty!
in lowly pomp ride on to die;
bow Your meek head to mortal pain,
then take, O God, Your power, and reign.

581 River wash over me

Words and music: Dougie Brown
Music arranged David Peacock

1 River, wash over me,
   cleanse me and make me new;
   bathe me, refresh me and fill me anew –
   river, wash over me.

2 Spirit, watch over me,
   lead me to Jesus' feet;
   cause me to worship and fill me anew –
   Spirit, watch over me.

3 Jesus, rule over me,
   reign over all my heart;
   teach me to praise You and fill me anew –
   Jesus, rule over me.

582(i)   Rock of ages

PETRA   77 77 77

Words: A M Toplady (1740–78)
Music: R Redhead (1820–1901)

Rock of a-ges, cleft for me, let me hide my-self in Thee;

let the wa-ter and the blood, from Thy riv-en side which flowed,

be of sin the dou-ble cure, cleanse me from its guilt and power.

1   Rock of ages, cleft for me,
     let me hide myself in Thee;
     let the water and the blood,
     from Thy riven side which flowed,
     be of sin the double cure,
     cleanse me from its guilt and power.

2   Not the labour of my hands
     can fulfil Thy law's demands;
     could my zeal no respite know,
     could my tears for ever flow,
     all for sin could not atone;
     Thou must save, and Thou alone.

3   Nothing in my hand I bring,
     simply to Thy cross I cling;
     naked, come to Thee for dress,
     helpless, look to Thee for grace;
     foul, I to the fountain fly;
     wash me, Saviour, or I die.

4   While I draw this fleeting breath,
     when mine eyes shall close in death,
     when I soar through tracts unknown,
     see Thee on Thy judgement throne;
     Rock of ages, cleft for me,
     let me hide myself in Thee.

582(ii) Rock of ages

TOPLADY   77 77 77

Words and music: A M Toplady (1740–78)

Rock of a-ges, cleft for me, let me hide my-self in Thee; let the wa-ter and the blood, from Thy riv-en side which flowed, be of sin the dou-ble cure, cleanse me from its guilt and power.

583   Safe in the shadow of the Lord

CREATOR GOD   CM

Words: Timothy Dudley-Smith
Music: Norman Warren

Safe in the sha-dow of the Lord be-neath His hand and power, I trust in Him, I trust in Him, my fort-ress and my tower.

1 Safe in the shadow of the Lord
   beneath His hand and power,
      I trust in Him,
      I trust in Him,
   my fortress and my tower.

2 My hope is set on God alone
   though Satan spreads his snare,
      I trust in Him,
      I trust in Him
   to keep me in His care.

3 From fears and phantoms of the night,
   from foes about my way,
      I trust in Him,
      I trust in Him
   by darkness as by day.

4 His holy angels keep my feet
   secure from every stone;
      I trust in Him,
      I trust in Him,
   and unafraid go on.

5 Strong in the everlasting name,
   and in my Father's care,
      I trust in Him,
      I trust in Him
   who hears and answers prayer.

6 Safe in the shadow of the Lord,
   possessed by love divine,
      I trust in Him,
      I trust in Him,
   and meet His love with mine.

584   Saviour, again to Thy dear name

ELLERS   10 10 10 10

Words: John Ellerton (1826–93)
Music: E J Hopkins (1818–1901)
arranged Arthur Sullivan (1842–1900)

1   Saviour, again to Thy dear name we raise
with one accord our parting hymn of praise;
we stand to bless Thee ere our worship cease,
then, lowly kneeling, wait Thy word of peace.

2   Grant us Thy peace upon our homeward way;
with Thee began, with Thee shall end the day;
guard Thou the lips from sin, the hearts from shame,
that in this house have called upon Thy name.

3   Grant us Thy peace, Lord, through the coming night;
turn Thou for us its darkness into light;
from harm and danger keep Thy children free,
for dark and light are both alike to Thee.

4   Grant us Thy peace throughout our earthly life,
our balm in sorrow, and our stay in strife;
then, when Thy voice shall bid our conflict cease,
call us, O Lord, to Thine eternal peace.

585 Saviour of the world

Words and music: Greg Leavers
Music arranged Phil Burt

*Begin slowly – with increasing
excitement in verses 2 and 3*

Sav-iour of the world, thank You for dy-ing on the cross. All

praise to You our ris-en Lord, Hal-le-lu-jah! Je - sus.

In the gar-den of Geth-se-ma-ne Je-sus knelt and prayed;

for He knew the time was near when He would be be - trayed.

Saviour of the world,
thank You for dying on the cross.
All praise to You our risen Lord,
Hallelujah! Jesus.

1   In the garden of Gethsemane Jesus knelt and prayed;
      for He knew the time was near when He would be betrayed.
      God gave Him the strength to cope with all that people did to hurt Him;
      soldiers laughed and forced a crown of thorns upon His head.
      Saviour of the world . . .

2   On a cross outside the city they nailed Jesus high;
      innocent, but still He suffered as they watched Him die.
      Nothing that the soldiers did could make Him lose control, for Jesus
      knew the time to die, then 'It is finished', was His cry.
      Saviour of the world . . .

3   Three days later by God's power He rose up from the dead,
      for the tomb could not hold Jesus it was as He'd said;
      victor over sin and death, He conquered Satan's power; so let us
      celebrate that Jesus is alive for evermore.
      Saviour of the world . . .

586 Saviour, Thy dying love

PHELPS   64 64 66 64

Words: Sylvanus Dryden Phelps (1816–95)
Music: Robert Lowry (1826–99)

Sav-iour, Thy dy-ing love Thou gav-est me, nor should I aught with-hold, my Lord, from Thee; in love my soul would bow, my heart ful-fil its vow, some off-ering bring Thee now, some-thing for Thee.

1 Saviour, Thy dying love
    Thou gavest me,
  nor should I aught withhold,
    my Lord, from Thee;
  in love my soul would bow,
  my heart fulfil its vow,
  some offering bring Thee now,
    something for Thee.

2 At the blest mercy-seat
    pleading for me,
  my feeble faith looks up,
    Jesus, to Thee:
  help me the cross to bear,
  Thy wondrous love declare,
  some song to raise, or prayer –
    something for Thee.

3 Give me a faithful heart,
    likeness to Thee,
  that each departing day
    henceforth may see
  some work of love begun,
  some deed of kindness done,
  some wanderer sought and won –
    something for Thee.

4 All that I am and have,
    Thy gifts so free,
  in joy, in grief, through life,
    O Lord, for Thee.
  And when Thy face I see,
  my ransomed soul shall be,
  through all eternity,
    something for Thee.

587 Search me, O God

Words: J Edwin Orr
arranged from an old Maori melody

Search me, O God, and know my heart to-day;____ try me, O Lord,____ and know my thoughts I pray: see if there be____ some wick-ed way__ in me,____

cleanse   me   from   ev - ery sin   and   set   me   free.____

1   Search me, O God, and know my heart today;
    try me, O Lord, and know my thoughts I pray:
    see if there be some wicked way in me,
    cleanse me from every sin and set me free.

2   I praise Thee, Lord, for cleansing me from sin;
    fulfil Thy word, and make me pure within;
    fill me with fire, where once I burned with shame,
    grant my desire to magnify Thy name.

3   Lord, take my life, and make it wholly Thine;
    fill my poor heart with Thy great love divine;
    take all my will, my passion, self and pride;
    I now surrender – Lord, in me abide.

4   O Holy Ghost, revival comes from Thee;
    send a revival – start the work in me:
    Thy word declares Thou wilt supply our need;
    for blessing now, O Lord, I humbly plead.

588   See, amid the winter's snow

HUMILITY   77 77 with refrain

Words: Edward Caswall (1814–78)
Music: John Goss (1800–80)

See, a-mid the win-ter's snow, born for us on earth be-low,

see, the Lamb of God ap-pears, pro-mised from e-ter-nal years.

Hail, thou ev-er-bless-èd morn! Hail, re-demp-tion's hap-py dawn!

Sing through all Je-ru-sa-lem,— Christ is born in Beth-le-hem!

1   See, amid the winter's snow,
    born for us on earth below,
    see, the Lamb of God appears,
    promised from eternal years.
        Hail, thou ever-blessèd morn!
        Hail, redemption's happy dawn!
        Sing through all Jerusalem,
        Christ is born in Bethlehem!

2   Lo, within a manger lies
    He who built the starry skies,
    He who, throned in height sublime,
    sits amid the cherubim.
        Hail, thou ever-blessèd morn . . .

3   Say, ye holy shepherds, say,
    what your joyful news today;
    wherefore have ye left your sheep
    on the lonely mountain steep?
        Hail, thou ever-blessèd morn . . .

4   As we watched at dead of night,
    Lo, we saw a wondrous light:
    angels singing, 'Peace on earth'
    told us of the Saviour's birth.
        Hail, thou ever-blessèd morn . . .

5   Sacred infant, all divine,
    what a tender love was Thine,
    thus to come from highest bliss
    down to such a world as this!
        Hail, thou ever-blessèd morn . . .

6   Teach, O teach us, holy child,
    by Thy face so meek and mild,
    teach us to resemble Thee
    in Thy sweet humility.
        Hail, thou ever-blessèd morn . . .

589 See Him lying on a bed of straw

CALYPSO CAROL   Irregular

Words and music: Michael Perry
Music arranged Stephen Coates

see the Lord_ ap-pear to men – just as poor_ as was the

sta - ble then, the Prince of glo - ry when He came.

1 See Him lying on a bed of straw:
   a draughty stable with an open door;
   Mary cradling the babe she bore –
   the Prince of glory is His name.
   O now carry me to Bethlehem
   to see the Lord appear to men –
   just as poor as was the stable then,
   the Prince of glory when He came.

2 Star of silver, sweep across the skies,
   show where Jesus in the manger lies;
   shepherds, swiftly from your stupor rise
   to see the Saviour of the world!
   O now carry . . .

3 Angels, sing the song that you began,
   bring God's glory to the heart of man;
   sing that Bethl'em's little baby can
   be salvation to the soul.
   O now carry . . .

4 Mine are riches, from Your poverty,
   from Your innocence, eternity;
   mine forgiveness by Your death for me,
   child of sorrow for my joy.
   O now carry . . .

590   Seek ye first

Words and music: Karen Lafferty
Music arranged Roland Fudge

1 Seek ye first the kingdom of God,
   and His righteousness,
   and all these things shall be added unto you.
   Allelu, alleluia.
   Seek ye first . . .

2 Man shall not live by bread alone,
   but by every word
   that proceeds from the mouth of God.
   Allelu, alleluia.
   Man shall not . . .

3 Ask and it shall be given unto you,
   seek and ye shall find;
   knock and the door shall be opened up to you.
   Allelu, alleluia.
   Ask and it shall . . .

591

Seek ye the Lord

Words and music: Joan Parsons
Music arranged Roland Fudge

ri - ver,_____ and glo - ry di - vine, if you'll
flow-ing,_____ and joy ev - er full; and there's

come to the wa-ter, if you'll taste of His
life ev - er - last-ing

wine. There is for us all._____

1 Seek ye the Lord all ye people,
turn to Him while He is near;
let the wicked forsake his own way,
and call on Him while He may hear.

2 Ho everyone who is thirsty,
come to the waters of life;
come and drink of the milk and the wine,
come without money and price.

And there is peace like a river,
and glory divine,
if you'll come to the water,
if you'll taste of His wine.
There is love ever flowing,
and joy ever full;
and there's life everlasting
for us all.

592 See Him on the cross

Words and music: Ruth Hooke

1 See Him on the cross of shame dying for
(2) laid Him in a gar-den tomb, and sealed it with a

me, bear-ing all my guilt and pain,
stone. Ma-ry wept her tears of grief – her

dy - ing for me.
pre - cious Lord had gone:

Chorus overleaf

Triumphantly

Je - sus lives, Je - sus lives, Je - sus lives in___ me:_____ I will praise Your name. 2 They

1   See Him on the cross of shame
    dying for me,
    bearing all my guilt and pain,
    dying for me.
    And how I love You,
    Jesus my Redeemer;
    You gave Your life for me, O Lord,
    now I give my life to You.
      Jesus lives, Jesus lives,
      Jesus lives in me:
      I will praise Your name.

2   They laid Him in a garden tomb,
    and sealed it with a stone.
    Mary wept her tears of grief –
    her precious Lord had gone:
    'And how I love You,
    Jesus my Redeemer';
    then she looked – the stone was rolled away –
    He had triumphed over death.
      Jesus lives . . .

593

Send forth the gospel

OMBERSLEY LM

Words: H E Fox (1841–1926)
Music: W H Gladstone (1840–91)

Lyrics under the music:

Send forth the gos - pel! Let— it run south-ward and
north - ward, east and west: tell all the earth Christ
died— and lives, He of - fers par - don, life, and rest.

1 Send forth the gospel! Let it run
 southward and northward, east and west:
 tell all the earth Christ died and lives,
 He offers pardon, life, and rest.

2 Send forth Your gospel, mighty Lord!
 Out of the chaos bring to birth
 Your own creation's promised hope;
 the better days of heaven on earth.

3 Send forth Your gospel, gracious Lord!
 Yours was the blood for sinners shed;
 Your voice still pleads in human hearts;
 to You may all Your sheep be led.

4 Send forth Your gospel, holy Lord!
 Kindle in us love's sacred flame;
 love giving all and grudging naught
 for Jesus' sake, in Jesus' name.

5 Send forth the gospel! Tell it out!
 Go, brothers, at the Master's call;
 prepare His way, who comes to reign
 the King of kings and Lord of all.

594   Send me out from here

Words and music: John Pantry
Music arranged Christopher Norton

Majestically

Send me out from here Lord, to serve a world in need; may I know no man by the coat he wears, but the heart that Je-sus sees. And may the light of Your face shine up-on me Lord— You have filled my heart with the

595
Set my spirit free

Words and music: Unknown
Music arranged Phil Burt

Set my spi-rit free that I might wor - ship You;

set my spi-rit free that I might praise Your name.

Let all bond-age go and let de - liv - erance flow;

set my spi-rit free to wor-ship You.

596 Show Your power, O Lord

Words and music: Graham Kendrick
Music arranged Christopher Norton

1 Show Your power, O Lord,_ de-mon-strate the just-ice of Your king-dom; prove Your migh-ty word,_ vin-di-cate Your name be-fore a watch-ing world.

2 Show Your power, O Lord,_ cause Your church to rise_ and take_ ac-tion; let all fear be gone;_ pow-ers of the age_ to come are break-ing through.

597

Silent night

STILLE NACHT   Irregular

Words: Joseph Mohr (1792–1848)
tr. S A Brooke (1832–1916)
Music: Franz Gruber (1787–1863)

1 Silent night, holy night!
Sleeps the world; hid from sight,
Mary and Joseph in stable bare
watched o'er the child belovèd and fair
sleeping in heavenly rest,
sleeping in heavenly rest.

2 Silent night, holy night!
Shepherds first saw the light,
heard resounding clear and long,
far and near, the angel-song:
'Christ the Redeemer is here,
Christ the Redeemer is here.'

3 Silent night, holy night!
Son of God, O how bright
love is smiling from Your face!
Strikes for us now the hour of grace,
Saviour, since You are born,
Saviour, since You are born.

598 Silver and gold

Words and music: Anon
Music arranged Betty Pulkingham

Pe-ter and John went to pray, they met a lame man on the way; he
'Sil-ver and gold have I none, but such as I have give I thee. In the

asked for alms and held out his palms, and this is what Pe-ter did
name of Je - sus Christ of Naz - a-reth, rise up and

1. say: walk!' He went walk - ing and leap - ing and
2.

prais - ing God, walk-ing and leap-ing and prais - ing God. 'In the

name of Je - sus Christ of Naz - a-reth, rise up and walk!'

599   Sing a new song to the Lord

ONSLOW SQUARE   7 7 11 8

Words: Timothy Dudley-Smith
Music: David Wilson

1 Sing a new song to the Lord, He to whom won-ders be-
2 Now to the ends of the earth, see His sal - va-tion is
3 Sing a new song and re - joice, pub - lish His prais-es a-
4 Join with the hills and the sea, thun-ders of praise to pro-

- long:_____ re - joice_____ in His tri - umph__ and
shown:_____ and still_____ He re - mem-bers____ His
- broad:_____ let voi - ces____ in cho - rus,____ with
- long:_____ in judge-ment____ and__ jus - tice____ He

tell____ of His power,_____ O sing____ to the
mer - cy____ and__ truth,_____ un - chang - ing in
trum-pet____ and__ horn,_____ re - sound____ for the
comes____ to the earth,_____ O sing____ to the

1-3.
Lord_____ a new song!
love_____ to His own.
joy_____ of the Lord!

4.
Lord_____ a new song!

600 Sing to God new songs of worship

ODE TO JOY 87 87 D

Words: from Psalm 98
Michael Baughen
Music: L van Beethoven (1770–1827)

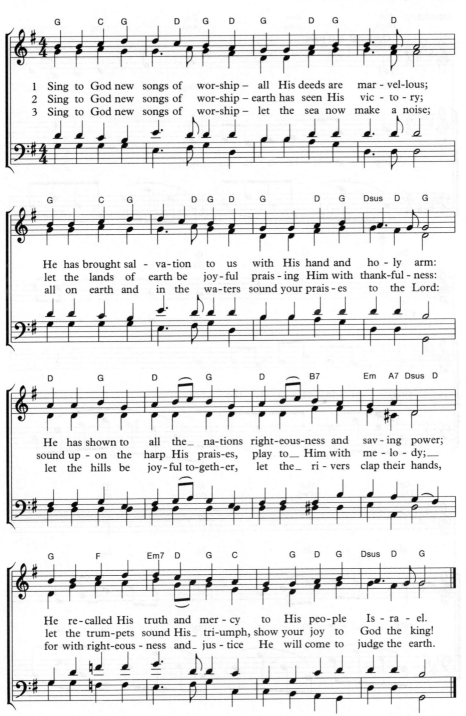

1 Sing to God new songs of wor-ship – all His deeds are mar-vel-lous;
2 Sing to God new songs of wor-ship – earth has seen His vic-to-ry;
3 Sing to God new songs of wor-ship – let the sea now make a noise;

He has brought sal-va-tion to us with His hand and ho-ly arm:
let the lands of earth be joy-ful prais-ing Him with thank-ful-ness:
all on earth and in the wa-ters sound your prais-es to the Lord:

He has shown to all the na-tions right-eous-ness and sav-ing power;
sound up-on the harp His prais-es, play to Him with me-lo-dy;
let the hills be joy-ful to-geth-er, let the ri-vers clap their hands,

He re-called His truth and mer-cy to His peo-ple Is-ra-el.
let the trum-pets sound His tri-umph, show your joy to God the king!
for with right-eous-ness and jus-tice He will come to judge the earth.

601 Sing alleluia to the Lord

Words and music: Linda Stassen
Music arranged Norman Warren

sing al - le - lu - ia to the own.

sing al - le - lu - ia to the Lord!

1 Sing alleluia to the Lord,
  sing alleluia to the Lord,
  sing alleluia, sing alleluia,
  sing alleluia to the Lord!

2 Jesus is risen from the dead,
  Jesus is risen from the dead,
  Jesus is risen, Jesus is risen,
  Jesus is risen from the dead!

3 Jesus is Lord of heaven and earth,
  Jesus is Lord of heaven and earth,
  Jesus is Lord, Jesus is Lord,
  Jesus is Lord of heaven and earth.

4 Jesus is coming for His own,
  Jesus is coming for His own,
  Jesus is coming, Jesus is coming,
  Jesus is coming for His own.

602 Sing we the King

THE GLORY SONG   10 10 10 10 with refrain

Words: C Silvester Horne (1865–1914)
Music: C H Gabriel (1856–1932)

Sing we the King who is com-ing to reign, glo-ry to Je-sus, the

Lamb that was slain; life and sal - va-tion His em-pire shall bring,

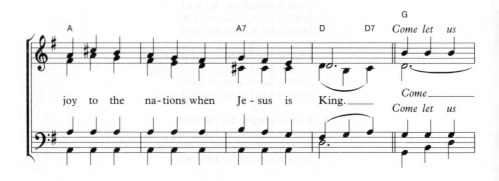

joy to the na-tions when Je - sus is King.___

Come let us
_Come___
Come let us

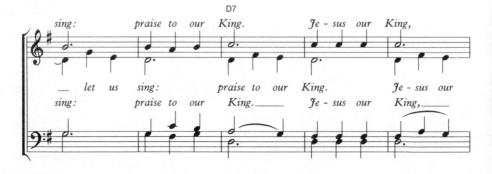

sing:___
_let us sing:___
sing:___

praise to our King.___
praise to our King.___
praise to our King.___

_Je - sus our King,___
Je - sus our King,___
_Je - sus our King,___

1 Sing we the King who is coming to reign,
glory to Jesus, the Lamb that was slain;
life and salvation His empire shall bring,
joy to the nations when Jesus is King.
Come let us sing: praise to our King.
Jesus our King, Jesus our King:
this is our song, who to Jesus belong:
glory to Jesus, to Jesus our King.

2 All men shall dwell in His marvellous light,
races long severed His love shall unite;
justice and truth from His sceptre shall spring,
wrong shall be ended when Jesus is King.
Come let us sing . . .

3 All shall be well in His kingdom of peace,
freedom shall flourish and wisdom increase;
foe shall be friend when His triumph we sing,
sword shall be sickle when Jesus is King.
Come let us sing . . .

4 Souls shall be saved from the burden of sin;
doubt shall not darken his witness within;
hell hath no terrors, and death hath no sting;
love is victorious, when Jesus is King.
Come let us sing . . .

5 Kingdom of Christ, for Thy coming we pray,
hasten, O Father, the dawn of the day;
when this new song Thy creation shall sing,
Satan is vanquished and Jesus is King.
Come let us sing . . .

603 So freely

Words and music: Dave Bilbrough
Music arranged David Peacock

Flowing, with a sense of mystery

So free - - ly___ flows the
end-less love You give___ to me;__ so free - - ly,__
__ not de - pen-dent on__ my part.__ As I am
reach-ing out,__ re-veal the love with-in Your heart;___

as I am reach-ing out,_ re-veal the love with-in Your

heart._____ 2 Com -_____

1 So freely
   flows the endless love You give to me;
   so freely,
   not dependent on my part.
   As I am reaching out,
   reveal the love within Your heart;
   as I am reaching out,
   reveal the love within Your heart.

2 Completely –
   that's the way You give Your love to me,
   completely,
   not dependent on my part.
   As I am reaching out,
   reveal the love within Your heart,
   as I am reaching out,
   reveal the love within Your heart.

3 So easy,
   I receive the love You give to me;
   so easy,
   not dependent on my part.
   Flowing out to me –
   the love within Your heart;
   flowing out to me –
   the love within Your heart.

604 Soldiers of Christ, arise

FROM STRENGTH TO STRENGTH   DSM

Words: Charles Wesley (1707–88)
Music: Edward Woodall Naylor (1867–1934)

Sol - diers of Christ, a - rise, and put your ar - mour

on, strong in the strength which God sup - plies through His e -

- ter - nal Son. Strong in the Lord of

hosts, and in His migh - ty power; who in the

strength of Je - sus trusts is more than con - que - ror.

1 Soldiers of Christ, arise,
and put your armour on,
strong in the strength which God supplies
through His eternal Son.
Strong in the Lord of hosts,
and in His mighty power;
who in the strength of Jesus trusts
is more than conqueror.

2 Stand then in His great might,
with all His strength endued;
and take, to arm you for the fight,
the panoply of God:
to keep your armour bright,
attend with constant care,
still walking in your Captain's sight
and watching unto prayer.

3 From strength to strength go on,
wrestle and fight and pray;
tread all the powers of darkness down
and win the well-fought day.
That, having all things done,
and all your conflicts past,
ye may o'ercome through Christ alone,
and stand entire at last.

605   Soon, and very soon

Words and music: Andrae Crouch

1 Soon, and very soon,
   we are going to see the King;
   soon, and very soon,
   we are going to see the King;
   soon, and very soon,
   we are going to see the King;
      alleluia, alleluia,
      we're going to see the King!

2 No more crying there . . .
      alleluia . . .

3 No more dying there . . .
      alleluia . . .
      Alleluia, alleluia, alleluia, alleluia.

4 Soon and very soon . . .
      alleluia . . .
      Alleluia, alleluia, alleluia, alleluia.

606   Soften my heart

Words and music: Graham Kendrick
Music arranged Christopher Norton

Souls of men, why will ye scatter

CROSS OF JESUS   87 87

Words: Frederick William Faber (1814–63)
Music: John Stainer (1840–1901)

1 Souls of men, why will ye scatter
   like a crowd of frightened sheep?
   Foolish hearts, why will ye wander
   from a love so true and deep?

2 Was there ever kindest shepherd
   half so gentle, half so sweet,
   as the Saviour who would have us
   come and gather round His feet?

3 There's a wideness in God's mercy,
   like the wideness of the sea;
   there's a kindness in His justice,
   which is more than liberty.

4 There is plentiful redemption
   in the blood that has been shed;
   there is joy for all the members
   in the sorrows of the Head.

5 For the love of God is broader
   than the measures of man's mind;
   and the heart of the Eternal
   is most wonderfully kind.

6 If our love were but more simple,
   we should take Him at His word,
   and our lives would be all sunshine
   in the sweetness of our Lord.

608   Speak, Lord, in the stillness

QUIETUDE   65 65

Words: Emily Mary Crawford (1864–1927)
Music: Harold Green (1871–1931)

Speak, Lord, in the still - ness, while I wait on Thee; __

hushed my heart to lis - ten in ex-pec - tan - cy.

1   Speak, Lord, in the stillness,
    while I wait on Thee;
    hushed my heart to listen
    in expectancy.

2   Speak, O blessèd Master,
    in this quiet hour;
    let me see Thy face, Lord,
    feel Thy touch of power.

3   For the words Thou speakest,
    they are life indeed;
    living Bread from heaven,
    now my spirit feed!

4   All to Thee is yielded,
    I am not my own;
    blissful, glad surrender –
    I am Thine alone.

5   Speak, Thy servant heareth!
    be not silent, Lord;
    waits my soul upon Thee
    for the quickening word!

6   Fill me with the knowledge
    of Thy glorious will;
    all Thine own good pleasure
    in Thy child fulfil.

609   Spirit of God

Words and music: Chris Bowater

Spi - rit of God, show me Je-sus;

re - move the dark - ness, let truth shine through.

Spi - rit of God, show me Je-sus;

re - veal the ful - ness of His love to me!

610   Spirit of God divine

Words and music: Colin Preston
Music arranged Chris Mitchell

fill   me   a - gain,_____   fill   me   a -

- gain,_____   O   Spi - rit   of   the   Lord._____

1 Spirit of God divine,
  fill this heart of mine
  with holy flame,
  to praise the name
  of Jesus my Lord.
      Fill me again,
      fill me again,
      fill me again,
      O Spirit of the Lord.

2 Spirit of God divine,
  fill this mouth of mine
  with holy praise,
  to set the earth ablaze
  and glorify Your name.
      Fill me again . . .

3 Spirit of God divine,
  take this heart of mine
  to Your throne this day;
  help me, I pray,
  my offering to give.
      Fill me again . . .

611   Spirit of holiness

BLOW THE WIND SOUTHERLY
12 10 12 10 12 11 12 11

Words: Christopher Idle
Music: traditional melody
arranged John Barnard

Spi - rit of ho - li - ness, wis - dom and faith - ful - ness, Wind of the

Lord, blow - ing strong - ly and free: strength of our serv - ing and

Fine

joy of our wor - ship - ping – Spi - rit of God, bring Your ful - ness to me!

You came to in - ter - pret and teach us ef - fec - tive - ly all that the

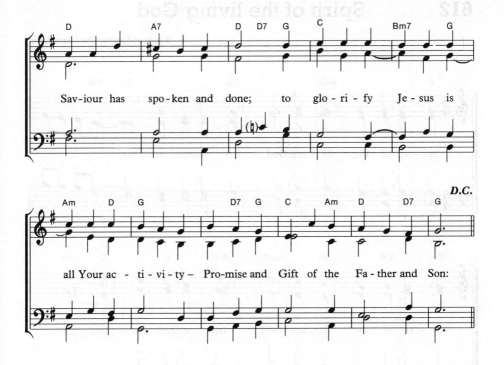

Sav-iour has spo-ken and done; to glo-ri-fy Je-sus is

all Your ac - ti - vi - ty– Pro-mise and Gift of the Fa-ther and Son:

Spirit of holiness,
wisdom and faithfulness,
Wind of the Lord,
blowing strongly and free:
strength of our serving
and joy of our worshipping –
Spirit of God,
bring Your fulness to me!

1   You came to interpret and teach us effectively
     all that the Saviour has spoken and done;
     to glorify Jesus is all Your activity –
     Promise and Gift of the Father and Son:
       Spirit of holiness . . .

2   You came with Your gifts to supply all our poverty,
     pouring Your love on the church in her need;
     You came with Your fruit for our growth to maturity,
     richly refreshing the souls that You feed:
       Spirit of holiness . . .

612   Spirit of the living God

Words and music: Paul Armstrong

613   Spirit of the living God

Words and music: Daniel Iverson
Music arranged W G Hathaway

Spi - rit of the liv - ing God, fall a-fresh on me;

Spi - rit of the liv - ing God, fall a-fresh on me;

break me, melt me, mould me, fill me;

Spi - rit of the liv - ing God, fall a-fresh on me.

614 Spirit divine

Words: Andrew Reed (1787–1862)
Music: Unknown

1 Spirit divine, attend our prayers,
   and make this house Thy home;
   descend with all Thy gracious powers,
   O come, great Spirit, come!

2 Come as the light; to us reveal
   our emptiness and woe;
   and lead us in those paths of life
   where all the righteous go.

3 Come as the fire; and purge our hearts
   like sacrificial flame;
   let our whole soul an offering be
   to our Redeemer's name.

4 Come as the Dove; and spread Thy wings,
   the wings of perfect love;
   and let Thy Church on earth become
   blest as the Church above.

5 Spirit divine, attend our prayers,
   make a lost world Thy home;
   descend with all Thy gracious powers,
   O come, great Spirit, come!

615   Stand up and bless the Lord

St Michael   SM

Words: James Montgomery (1771–1854)
Music: from the *Genevan Psalter*, 1551

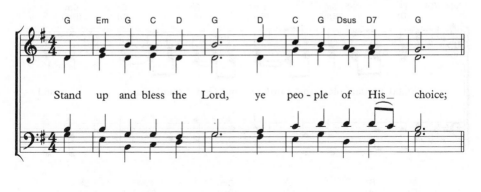

Stand up and bless the Lord, ye peo - ple of His choice;

stand up and bless the Lord your God, with heart and soul and voice.

1   Stand up and bless the Lord,
ye people of His choice;
stand up and bless the Lord your God,
with heart and soul and voice.

2   Though high above all praise,
above all blessing high;
who would not fear His holy name?
and laud and magnify?

3   O for the living flame
from His own altar brought,
O touch our lips, our minds inspire,
and wing to heaven our thought!

4   There, with benign regard,
our hymns He deigns to hear;
though unrevealed to mortal sense,
our spirits feel Him near.

5   God is our strength and song,
and His salvation ours;
then be His love in Christ proclaimed
with all our ransomed powers.

6   Stand up and bless the Lord,
the Lord your God adore;
stand up and bless His glorious name
henceforth for evermore.

616 Stand up and bless the Lord

Words and music: Andy Silver

He is gra-cious and mer - ci - ful,__ slow to an - ger and

ve - ry kind. So, stand up and bless the Lord__ your God, stand up__

__ and bless the Lord; stand up and bless the Lord

__ your God, stand up.__

617   Stand up! stand up for Jesus

MORNING LIGHT   76 76 D

Words: George Duffield (1818–88)
Music: G J Webb (1803–87)

Stand up! stand up for Je - sus! ye sol-diers of the cross,

lift high His roy - al ban - ner; it must not suf - fer loss.

From vic - tory un - to vic - tory His_ ar - my shall He lead,___

till ev - ery foe is van - quished and Christ is Lord in - deed.

1   Stand up! stand up for Jesus!
       ye soldiers of the cross,
       lift high His royal banner;
       it must not suffer loss.
       From victory unto victory
       His army shall He lead,
       till every foe is vanquished
       and Christ is Lord indeed.

2   Stand up! stand up for Jesus!
       the trumpet-call obey;
       forth to the mighty conflict
       in this His glorious day.
       Ye that are men, now serve Him
       against unnumbered foes;
       let courage rise with danger,
       and strength to strength oppose.

3   Stand up! stand up for Jesus!
       stand in His strength alone;
       the arm of flesh will fail you,
       ye dare not trust your own.
       Put on the gospel armour,
       each piece put on with prayer;
       where duty calls, or danger,
       be never wanting there.

4   Stand up! stand up for Jesus!
       the strife will not be long;
       the day the noise of battle,
       the next the victor's song.
       To him that overcometh
       a crown of life shall be;
       he with the King of glory
       shall reign eternally.

618

Sun of my soul

ABENDS   LM

Words: John Keble (1792–1866)
Music: Herbert Stanley Oakley (1830–1903)

Sun of my soul, my Sav-iour dear,
it is not night if You are near;
O may no earth-born cloud a-rise
to hide You from Your ser-vant's eyes.

1 Sun of my soul, my Saviour dear,
it is not night if You are near;
O may no earth-born cloud arise
to hide You from Your servant's eyes.

2 When the soft dews of kindly sleep
my wearied eyelids gently steep,
be my last thought, how sweet to rest
for ever on my Saviour's breast!

3 Abide with me from morn till eve,
for without You I cannot live;
abide with me when night is nigh,
for without You I dare not die.

4 If some poor wandering child of Yours
have spurned today Your holy voice,
now, Lord, the gracious work begin;
let them no more be ruled by sin.

5 Watch by the sick; enrich the poor
with blessings from Your boundless store;
be every mourner's sleep tonight,
like infant's slumbers, pure and light.

6 Come near and bless us when we wake,
ere through the world our way we take;
till in the ocean of Your love
we lose ourselves in heaven above.

619   Such love

Words and music: Graham Kendrick
Music arranged Christopher Norton

1 Such love, pure as the whitest snow;
  such love weeps for the shame I know;
  such love, paying the debt I owe;
  O Jesus, such love.

2 Such love, stilling my restlessness;
  such love, filling my emptiness;
  such love, showing me holiness;
  O Jesus, such love.

3 Such love springs from eternity;
  such love, streaming through history;
  such love, fountain of life to me;
  O Jesus, such love.

620 Sweet is the work

DEEP HARMONY   LM

Words: Isaac Watts (1674–1748)
Music: Handel Parker (1857–1928)

1 Sweet is the work, my God, my King,
to praise Thy name, give thanks and sing,
to show Thy love by morning light,
and talk of all Thy truth at night.

2 Sweet is the day of sacred rest,
no mortal cares disturb my breast;
O may my heart in tune be found,
like David's harp of solemn sound.

3 My heart shall triumph in the Lord,
and bless His works, and bless His word;
Thy works of grace, how bright they shine,
how deep Thy counsels, how divine!

4 And I shall share a glorious part,
when grace has well refined my heart,
and fresh supplies of joy are shed,
like holy oil, to cheer my head.

5 Then shall I see and hear and know
all I desired or wished below;
and every power find sweet employ
in that eternal world of joy.

621 Swing wide the gates

Words and music: Chris Bowater

622   Take, eat, this is My body

Words and music: Paul Simmons
Music arranged Christopher Norton

Words and music: © 1985 Thankyou Music,
PO Box 75, Eastbourne, East Sussex BN23 6NW, UK

623 Take heart and praise our God

CHRISTCHURCH   66 66 88

Words: David Mowbray
Music: C Steggall (1826–1905)

1 Take heart and praise our God;
  rejoice and clap your hands –
  His power our foe subdued,
  His mercy ever stands:
      Let trumpets sound and people sing,
      The Lord through all the earth is King!

2 Take heart, but sing with fear,
  exalt His worthy name;
  with mind alert and clear
  now celebrate His fame:
      Let trumpets sound . . .

3 Take heart for future days,
  for tasks as yet unknown –
  the God whose name we praise
  is seated on the throne:
      Let trumpets sound . . .

4 Take heart and trust in God
  the Father and the Son –
  God is our strength and shield,
  His Spirit guides us on:
      Let trumpets sound . . .

624

Take my life

NOTTINGHAM 77 77

Words: Frances Ridley Havergal (1836–79)
Music: Wolfgang Amadeus Mozart (1756–91)

Take my life, and let__ it be con - se - -cra - ted, Lord,_ to Thee; take__ my mo - ments and__ my days, let__ them flow__ in cease - less praise.

1 Take my life, and let it be
consecrated, Lord, to Thee;
take my moments and my days,
let them flow in ceaseless praise.

2 Take my hands, and let them move
at the impulse of Thy love;
take my feet, and let them be
swift and beautiful for Thee.

3 Take my voice, and let me sing
always, only, for my King;
take my lips, and let them be
filled with messages from Thee.

4 Take my silver and my gold,
not a mite would I withhold;
take my intellect, and use
every power as Thou shalt choose.

5 Take my will, and make it Thine;
it shall be no longer mine:
take my heart, it is Thine own;
it shall be Thy royal throne.

6 Take my love; my Lord, I pour
at Thy feet its treasure store:
take myself, and I will be
ever, only, all, for Thee.

625   Take time to be holy

TAKE TIME TO BE HOLY   11 11 11 11

Words: W D Longstaff (1822–94)
Music: G C Stebbins (1846–1945)

Take time to be ho-ly, speak oft with Thy Lord;
a-bide in Him al-ways, and feed on His Word.
Make friends of God's child-ren, help those who are weak;
for-get-ting in no-thing His bless-ing to seek.

1   Take time to be holy, speak oft with Thy Lord;
    abide in Him always, and feed on His word.
    Make friends of God's children, help those who are weak;
    forgetting in nothing His blessing to seek.

2   Take time to be holy, the world rushes on;
    spend much time in secret with Jesus alone –
    by looking to Jesus, like Him thou shalt be!
    Thy friends in thy conduct His likeness shall see.

3   Take time to be holy, let Him be thy guide;
    and run not before Him, whatever betide;
    in joy or in sorrow still follow thy Lord,
    and, looking to Jesus, still trust in His word.

4   Take time to be holy, be calm in thy soul;
    each thought and each temper beneath His control;
    thus led by His Spirit to fountains of love,
    thou soon shalt be fitted for service above.

626   Teach me Thy way

THE PATH DIVINE   64 64 66 64   Words and music: B Mansell Ramsey (1849–1923)

1 Teach me Thy way, O Lord,
   teach me Thy way!
   Thy gracious aid afford,
   teach me Thy way!
   Help me to walk aright,
   more by faith, less by sight;
   lead me with heavenly light:
   teach me Thy way!

2 When doubts and fears arise,
   teach me Thy way!
   When storms o'erspread the skies,
   teach me Thy way!
   Shine through the cloud and rain,
   through sorrow, toil, and pain;
   make Thou my pathway plain:
   teach me Thy way!

3 Long as my life shall last,
   teach me Thy way!
   Where'er my lot be cast,
   teach me Thy way!
   Until the race is run,
   until the journey's done,
   until the crown is won,
   teach me Thy way!

627 Teach me to live

Words and music: Elizabeth M Dyke

Teach me to live, day by day, in Your

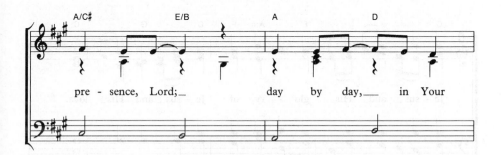

pre - sence, Lord; _ day by day, _ in Your

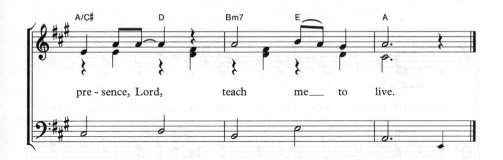

pre - sence, Lord, teach me _ to live.

1 Teach me to live, day by day,
   in Your presence, Lord;
  day by day, in Your presence, Lord,
   teach me to live.

2 Teach me to praise, day by day,
   in Your Spirit, Lord;
  day by day, in Your Spirit, Lord,
   teach me to praise.

3 Teach me to love, day by day,
   in Your power, Lord;
  day by day, in Your power, Lord,
   teach me to love.

4 Teach me to give, day by day,
   from my wealth, O Lord;
  day by day, from my wealth, O Lord,
   teach me to give.

628 Tell me the old, old story

TELL ME 76 76 D with refrain

Words: Arabella C Hankey (1834–1911) altd.
Music: W H Doane (1832–1916)

Tell me the old, old sto - ry of un - seen things a - bove,— of

Je - sus— and— His— glo - ry, of Je - sus— and His— love.

Tell me the sto - ry sim - ply, as to— a— lit - tle child, for

I am— weak and— wea - ry, and help - less— and de - filed.

Tell me the old, old sto - ry, tell me the old, old sto - ry,

tell me the old, old sto - ry of Je - sus and_ His love.

1 Tell me the old, old story
  of unseen things above,
  of Jesus and His glory,
  of Jesus and His love.
  Tell me the story simply,
  as to a little child,
  for I am weak and weary,
  and helpless and defiled.
      Tell me the old, old story,
      tell me the old, old story,
      tell me the old, old story
      of Jesus and His love.

2 Tell me the story slowly,
  that I may take it in –
  that wonderful redemption,
  God's remedy for sin.
  Tell me the story often,
  for I forget so soon:
  the early dew of morning
  has passed away at noon.
      Tell me the old . . .

3 Tell me the story softly,
  with earnest tones and grave;
  Remember! I'm the sinner
  whom Jesus came to save.
  Tell me the story always,
  if you would really be,
  in any time of trouble,
  a comforter to me.
      Tell me the old . . .

4 Tell me the same old story,
  when you have cause to fear
  that this world's empty glory
  is costing me too dear.
  Yes, and when that world's glory
  is dawning on my soul,
  tell me the old, old story;
  'Christ Jesus makes you whole.'
      Tell me the old . . .

629 Tell me the stories of Jesus

STORIES OF JESUS   84 84 54 54

Words: W H Parker (1845–1929) altd.
verse 6 by Hugh Martin (1890–1964)
altered Horrobin/Leavers
Music: F A Challinor (1866–1952)

Tell me the sto-ries of Je - sus I love to hear;___ things I would ask Him to tell me if He were here;___ scenes by the way - side, tales of the sea,___ sto - ries of Je - sus, tell them to me.___

1 Tell me the stories of Jesus
I love to hear;
things I would ask Him to tell me
if He were here;
scenes by the wayside,
tales of the sea,
stories of Jesus,
tell them to me.

2 First let me hear how the children
stood round His knee;
that I may know of His blessing
resting on me;
words full of kindness,
deeds full of grace,
signs of the love found
in Jesus' face.

3 Tell me, in words full of wonder,
how rolled the sea,
tossing the boat in a tempest
on Galilee.
Jesus then doing
His Father's will,
ended the storm saying
'Peace, peace, be still.'

4 Into the city I'd follow
the children's band,
waving a branch of the palm-tree
high in my hand;
worshipping Jesus,
yes, I would sing
loudest hosannas,
for He is King!

5 Show me that scene in the garden,
of bitter pain;
and of the cross where my Saviour
for me was slain;
and, through the sadness,
help me to see
how Jesus suffered
for love of me.

6 Gladly I'd hear of His rising
out of the grave,
living and strong and triumphant,
mighty to save:
and how He sends us
all men to bring
stories of Jesus,
Jesus, their King.

630 Tell My people

Words (chorus) and music: Leonard Bartlotti
verses and descant Jan Harrington

Verses and music arrangement: © 1975 Celebration,
administered in Europe by Thankyou Music,
PO Box 75, Eastbourne, East Sussex BN23 6NW, UK

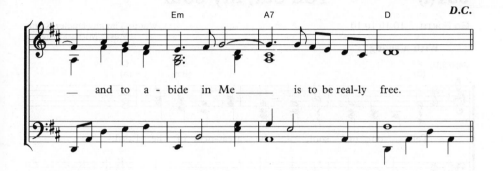

and to a - bide in Me_____ is to be real-ly free.

Optional descant for refrain

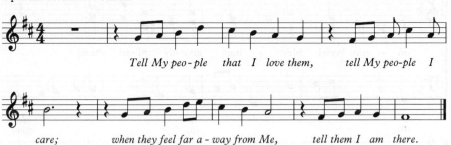

Tell My peo-ple that I love them, tell My peo-ple I

care; when they feel far a - way from Me, tell them I am there.

Tell My people I love them,
tell My people I care;
when they feel far away from Me,
tell My people I am there.

1 Tell My people I came and died
   to give them liberty;
   and to abide in Me
   is to be really free.
        Tell my people . . .

2 Tell My people where'er they go
   My comfort they can know;
   My peace and joy and love
   I freely will bestow.
        Tell my people . . .

631(i)   Tell out, my soul

Go Forth   10 10 10 10

Words: Timothy Dudley-Smith
Music: Michael Baughen

1   Tell out, my soul, the greatness of the Lord;
    unnumbered blessings give my spirit voice;
    tender to me the promise of His word;
    in God my Saviour shall my heart rejoice.

2   Tell out, my soul, the greatness of His name!
    Make known His might, the deeds His arm has done;
    His mercy sure, from age to age the same;
    His Holy name – the Lord, the Mighty One.

631(ii)   Tell out, my soul

WOODLANDS   10 10 10 10

Words: Timothy Dudley-Smith
Music: W Greatorex (1877–1949)

Tell out, my soul, the great-ness of the Lord;
un - num - bered bless-ings give my spi - rit voice;
ten - der to me the pro-mise of His word;
in God my Sav-iour shall my heart re - joice.

3 Tell out, my soul, the greatness of His might!
   powers and dominions lay their glory by;
   proud hearts and stubborn wills are put to flight,
   the hungry fed, the humble lifted high.

4 Tell out, my soul, the glories of His word!
   firm is His promise, and His mercy sure:
   tell out, my soul, the greatness of the Lord
   to children's children and for evermore!

632 Thank You for the cross

Words and music: Graham Kendrick

Thank You for the cross, the price You paid for us, how You
Now our sins are gone, all for-giv-en,
cov-ered

gave Your-self so com-plete-ly, pre-cious Lord, pre-cious Lord.
by Your blood, all for-got-ten, thank You Lord, thank You Lord.

Oh I love You Lord, real-ly love You Lord. I will

ne-ver un-der-stand why You love me.___ You're my deep-est joy,___ You're my

heart's de-light, and the great-est thing of all, O Lord, I

see: You de-light in me!

1 Thank You for the cross,
   the price You paid for us,
   how You gave Yourself
   so completely,
   precious Lord, precious Lord.
   Now our sins are gone,
   all forgiven,
   covered by Your blood,
   all forgotten,
   thank You Lord, thank You Lord.
     Oh I love You Lord,
     really love You Lord.
     I will never understand
     why You love me.
     You're my deepest joy,
     You're my heart's delight,
     and the greatest thing of all,
     O Lord, I see:
     You delight in me!

2 For our healing there
   Lord You suffered,
   and to take our fear
   You poured out Your love,
   precious Lord, precious Lord.
   Calvary's work is done,
   You have conquered,
   able now to save
   so completely,
   thank You Lord, thank You Lord.
     Oh I love You . . .

633 Thank You Jesus

Words and music: Alison Huntley
Music arranged Roland Fudge

With strength

Thank You Je - sus,_____ thank You Je - sus,_____
_____ thank You Lord_____ for lov-ing me. Thank You
Je - sus,_____ thank you Je - sus, thank You
Lord_____ for lov-ing me._____

2 You went to Calvary, there You died for me,
thank You Lord for loving me.
You went to Calvary . . .

3 You rose up from the grave, to me new life You gave,
thank You Lord for loving me.
You rose up from the grave . . .

4 You're coming back again, and we with You shall reign,
thank You Lord for loving me.
You're coming back again . . .

634 Thank You, Jesus, for Your love

Words and music: Alison Huntley
Music arranged Christopher Norton

Thank You, Je - sus, _____ for Your love to me; _____
_____ thank You, Je - sus, _____ for Your grace so free. _____
_____ I'll lift my voice to praise Your name, praise You a-gain and a-
- gain: You are ev - ery - thing, _____ You are my Lord. _____

635 Thank You Lord

Words and music: Greg Leavers
and Phil Burt

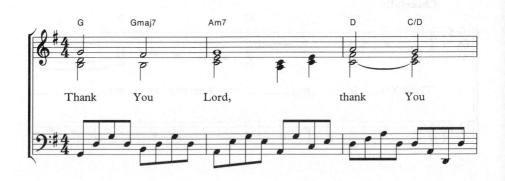

Thank You Lord, thank You

Lord that no - thing can se - pa - rate us

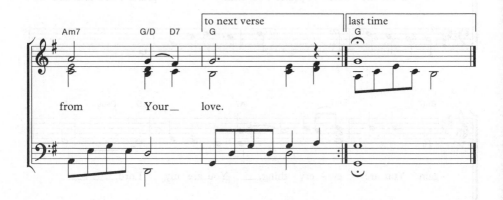

from Your_ love.

1 Thank You Lord, thank You Lord
that nothing can separate us from Your love.

2 Thank You Lord, thank You Lord
that there is no condemnation when we're in You.

CONFESSION VERSES
3 Search my heart, search my heart,
and show me the sin I need to confess to You.

4 Sorry Lord, sorry Lord,
I humbly now ask forgiveness for my sin.

5 Cleanse me Lord, cleanse me Lord,
through Your precious blood make my heart clean before You.

6 Thank You Lord, thank You Lord
that You've now removed the guilt of all my sin.

COMMUNION
7 Take this bread, take this bread,
for this is Christ's body which was broken for you.

8 Thank You Lord, thank You Lord
for dying on Calvary so that I can know You.

9 Take this cup, take this cup
and drink it remembering Jesus Christ died for you.

10 Thank You Lord, thank You Lord,
that through Your shed blood we are made one with God.

PRAISE AND WORSHIP
11 Fill me Lord, fill me Lord,
so that I might learn to live through Your power alone.

12 We love You, we love You,
we open our hearts in adoration to You.

13 Holy Lord, holy Lord,
Your name is far higher than any other name.

14 Worthy Lord, worthy Lord,
we offer our sacrifice of worship to You.

15 Reigning King, reigning King,
You're glorious in majesty, almighty in power.

636 Thank You Lord, for Your presence

Words and music: Roland Fudge

Guitar: Tune 6th string to D

thank You, we bless You, Christ Je - sus our

Lord, we thank You Lord,_____

thank You Lord._____ thank You Lord._____

Thank You Lord, for Your presence here,
thank You Lord, thank You Lord.
Thank You Lord, You remove all fear,
thank You Lord, thank You Lord.
For the love that You showed
as You poured out Your life,
we thank You, we bless You,
Christ Jesus our Lord,
we thank You Lord, thank You Lord.
Thank You Lord . . .

637 Thanks be to God

Words and music: Robert Stoodley

Thanks be to God___ who gives us the
vic - to - ry,___ gives us the vic - to - ry___ through
our Lord Je-sus Christ; our Lord Je-sus Christ.
He is a - ble to keep us from fall - ing, and to

638 Thank You God, for sending Jesus

set us free from sin:___ so let us each live

up to our call-ing, and com-mit our way_____ to Him._

Thanks be to God
    who gives us the victory,
gives us the victory
    through our Lord Jesus Christ;
thanks be to God
    who gives us the victory,
gives us the victory
    through our Lord Jesus Christ.

1 He is able to keep us from falling,
    and to set us free from sin:
    so let us each live up to our calling,
    and commit our way to Him.
       Thanks be to God . . .

2 Jesus knows all about our temptations –
    He has had to bear them too;
    He will show us how to escape them,
    if we trust Him He will lead us through.
       Thanks be to God . . .

3 He has led us from the power of darkness
    to the kingdom of His blessèd Son:
    so let us join in praise together,
    and rejoice in what the Lord has done.
       Thanks be to God . . .

4 Praise the Lord for sending Jesus
    to the cross of Calvary:
    now He's risen, reigns in power,
    and death is swallowed up in victory.
       Thanks be to God . . .

638   Thank You God, for sending Jesus

Words and music: Unknown
Music arranged Phil Burt

Thank You God, for sending Jesus;
thank You Jesus, that You came;
Holy Spirit, won't You teach us
more about His wondrous name?

639 The battle belongs to the Lord

Words and music: Jamie Owens-Collins
Music arranged Christopher Norton

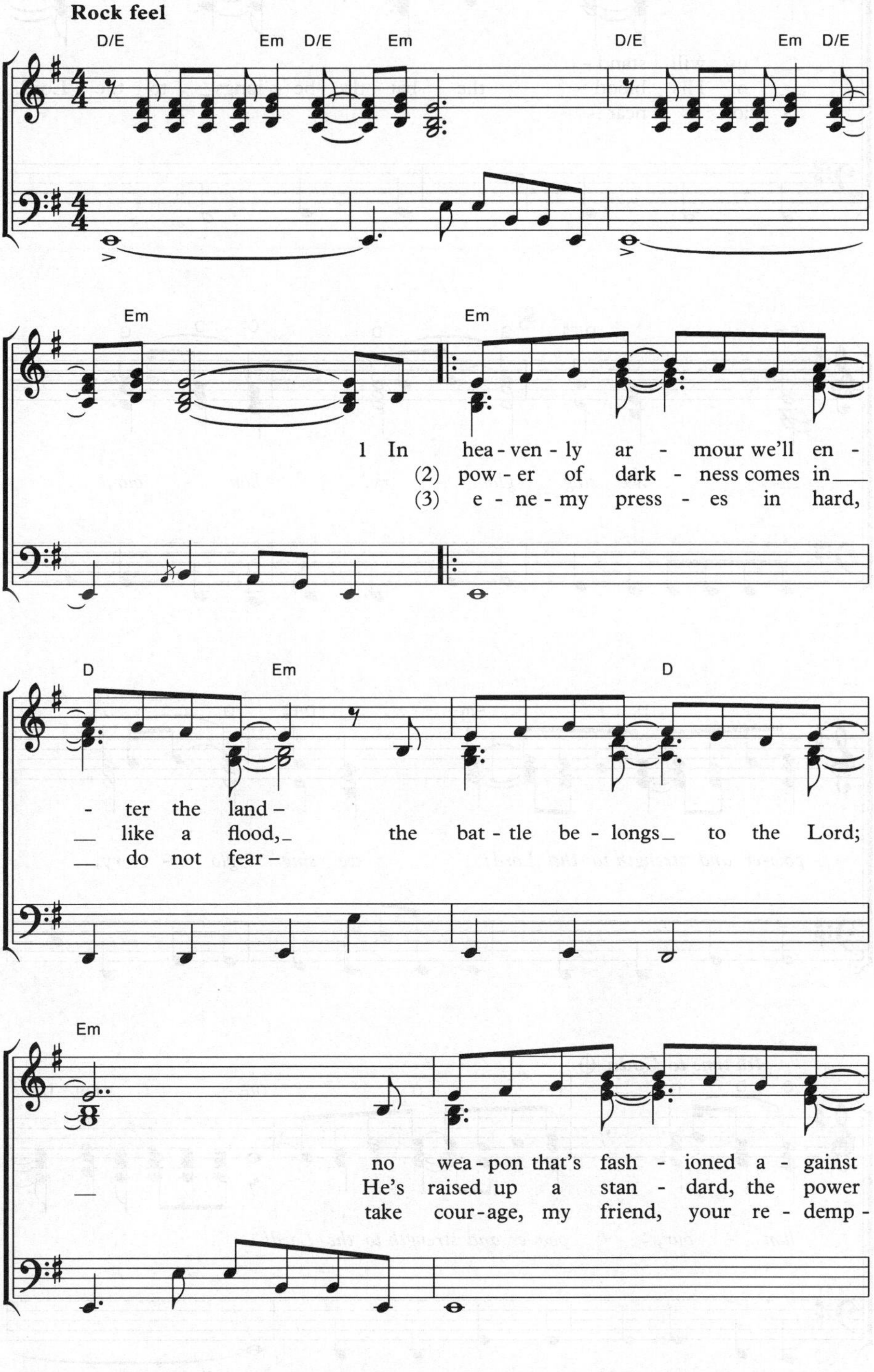

Rock feel
D/E Em D/E Em D/E Em D/E
Em Em
1 In hea-ven-ly ar - mour we'll en -
(2) pow-er of dark - ness comes in
(3) e - ne-my press - es in hard,
D Em D
- ter the land –
like a flood, the bat-tle be-longs to the Lord;
do not fear –
Em
no wea-pon that's fash - ioned a - gainst
He's raised up a stan - dard, the power
take cour-age, my friend, your re - demp -

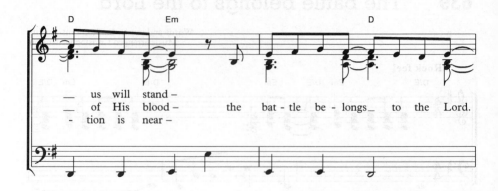

_ us will stand –
_ of His blood – the bat - tle be - longs_ to the Lord.
- tion is near –

We sing glo - ry, hon - our,

pow-er and strength to the Lord;_ we sing glo - ry,

4th time to Coda ⊕

hon - our, pow-er and strength to the Lord!_

640   The Church's one foundation

AURELIA   76 76 D

Words: Samuel John Stone (1839–1900)
Music: S S Wesley (1810–76)

The Chur-ch's one foun - da - tion is Je - sus Christ our Lord:

she is His new cre - a - tion by wa - ter and the word;

from heaven He came and sought her to be His ho - ly bride;

with His own blood He bought her, and for her life He died.

1   The Church's one foundation
     is Jesus Christ our Lord:
     she is His new creation
     by water and the word;
     from heaven He came and sought her
     to be His holy bride;
     with His own blood He bought her,
     and for her life He died.

2   Elect from every nation,
     yet one o'er all the earth,
     her charter of salvation
     one Lord, one faith, one birth,
     one holy name she blesses,
     partakes one holy food,
     and to one hope she presses,
     with every grace endued.

3   Though with a scornful wonder
     men see her sore oppressed,
     by schisms rent asunder
     by heresies distressed;
     yet saints their watch are keeping,
     their cry goes up: How long?
     and soon the night of weeping
     shall be the morn of song.

4   Mid toil and tribulation,
     and tumult of her war,
     she waits the consummation
     of peace for evermore;
     till with the vision glorious
     her longing eyes are blest,
     and the great Church victorious
     shall be the Church at rest.

5   Yet she on earth hath union
     with God the Three-in-One,
     and mystic sweet communion
     with those whose rest is won.
     O happy ones and holy!
     Lord, give us grace that we,
     like them, the meek and lowly,
     on high may dwell with Thee.

641 The day Thou gavest

St Clement   98 98

Words: John Ellerton (1826–93)
Music: C C Scholefield (1839–1904)

The day Thou gav-est, Lord, is end-ed, the dark-ness falls at Thy be-hest; to Thee our morn-ing hymns as-cend-ed, Thy praise shall sanc-ti-fy our rest.

1 The day Thou gavest, Lord, is ended,
  the darkness falls at Thy behest;
  to Thee our morning hymns ascended,
  Thy praise shall sanctify our rest.

2 We thank Thee that Thy Church unsleeping,
  while earth rolls onward into light,
  through all the world her watch is keeping,
  and rests not now by day or night.

3 As o'er each continent and island
  the dawn leads on another day,
  the voice of prayer is never silent,
  nor dies the strain of praise away.

4 The sun, that bids us rest, is waking
  our brethren 'neath the western sky,
  and hour by hour fresh lips are making
  Thy wondrous doings heard on high.

5 So be it, Lord: Thy throne shall never,
  like earth's proud empires, pass away;
  Thy kingdom stands, and grows for ever,
  till all Thy creatures own Thy sway.

642   The earth is the Lord's

Words and music: Graham Kendrick
Music arranged Christopher Norton

MEN The earth is the Lord's   MEN The
WOMEN and ev-ery-thing in it.

earth is the Lord's,   MEN The earth is the
WOMEN the work of His hands.

Lord's   ALL and all things were
WOMEN and ev-ery-thing in it,

3rd time **to Coda**

made for His glo - ry!

The moun-tains are His, the seas and the is-lands, the ci-ties and towns, the hou-ses and streets: let re-bels bow down and wor-ship be-fore Him, for all things were made for His glo-ry! The

643

The earth was dark

Words and music: John Daniels
and Phil Thompson

The earth was dark un-til You spoke – then all was light and all was peace; yet still, O God, so ma-ny___ wait to see the flame of love re-leased.___ *Lights to the world! O Light di-vine, kin-dle in us a*

*migh-ty flame,   till ev-ery heart, con-sumed by love shall rise   to*___

praise Your ho - ly name!

1 The earth was dark until You spoke –
   then all was light and all was peace;
   yet still, O God, so many wait
   to see the flame of love released.
       Lights to the world! O Light divine,
       kindle in us a mighty flame,
       till every heart, consumed by love
       shall rise to praise Your holy name!

2 In Christ You gave Your gift of life
   to save us from the depth of the night:
   O come and set our spirits free
   and draw us to Your perfect light.
       Lights to the world . . .

3 Where there is fear may we bring joy
   and healing to a world in pain:
   Lord, build Your kingdom through our lives
   till Jesus walks this earth again.
       Lights to the world . . .

4 O burn in us, that we may burn
   with love that triumphs in despair;
   and touch our lives with such a fire
   that souls may search and find You there.
       Lights to the world . . .

644

The first nowell

THE FIRST NOWELL   Irregular

Words: Author unknown (c 17th century)
in this version Jubilate Hymns
Music: English traditional carol
arranged David Willcocks

The first no - well the an - gel did

say, was to Beth - le - hem's shep - herds in fields as they

lay; in fields where they lay keep - ing their

sheep on a cold win - ter's night that was so deep:

No - well,____ no - well, no - well, no - well, born is the king___ of Is - ra - el!

1 The first nowell the angel did say,
   was to Bethlehem's shepherds in fields as they lay;
   in fields where they lay keeping their sheep
   on a cold winter's night that was so deep:
       Nowell, nowell, nowell, nowell,
       born is the king of Israel!

2 Then wise men from a country far
   looked up and saw a guiding star;
   they travelled on by night and day
   to reach the place where Jesus lay:
       Nowell, nowell . . .

3 At Bethlehem they entered in,
   on bended knee they worshipped Him;
   they offered there in His presence
   their gold and myrrh and frankincense:
       Nowell, nowell . . .

4 Then let us all with one accord
   sing praises to our heavenly Lord;
   for Christ has our salvation wrought
   and with His blood mankind has bought:
       Nowell, nowell . . .

645   The God of Abraham praise

LEONI   66 84 D

Words: Thomas Olivers (1725–99) altd.
Music: from a Hebrew melody
Thomas Olivers (1725–99)

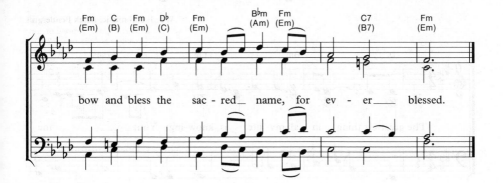

bow and bless the sac - red_ name, for ev - er_ blessed.

1 The God of Abraham praise,
   who reigns enthroned above,
   Ancient of everlasting days,
   and God of love.
   Jehovah, great I AM!
   by earth and heaven confessed;
   we bow and bless the sacred name,
   for ever blessed.

2 The God of Abraham praise,
   at whose supreme command
   from earth we rise, and seek the joys
   at His right hand;
   we all on earth forsake,
   its wisdom, fame, and power;
   and Him our only portion make,
   our shield and tower.

3 The God of Abraham praise,
   whose all-sufficient grace
   shall guide us all our happy days,
   in all our ways:
   He is our faithful friend;
   He is our gracious God;
   and He will save us to the end,
   through Jesus' blood.

4 He by Himself has sworn –
   we on His oath depend –
   we shall, on eagles' wings upborne,
   to heaven ascend:
   we shall behold His face,
   we shall His power adore,
   and sing the wonders of His grace
   for evermore.

5 The whole triumphant host
   give thanks to God on high:
   'Hail, Father, Son, and Holy Ghost!'
   they ever cry.
   Hail, Abraham's God and ours!
   We join the heavenly lays;
   and celebrate with all our powers
   His endless praise.

646 The greatest thing

Words and music: Mark Pendergras

2 The greatest thing in all my life
   is loving You;
the greatest thing in all my life
   is loving You;
I want to love You more;
   I want to love You more.
The greatest thing in all my life
   is loving You.

3 The greatest thing in all my life
   is serving You;
the greatest thing in all my life
   is serving You;
I want to serve You more;
   I want to serve You more.
The greatest thing in all my life
   is serving You.

647   The head that once was crowned

St Magnus   CM

Words: Thomas Kelly (1769–1855)
Music: J Clark (c1670–1707)

1   The head that once was crowned with thorns
    is crowned with glory now;
    a royal diadem adorns
    the mighty victor's brow.

2   The highest place that heaven affords
    is His by sovereign right;
    the King of kings and Lord of lords,
    He reigns in perfect light.

3   The joy of all who dwell above,
    the joy of all below,
    to whom He manifests His love,
    and grants His name to know.

4   To them the cross, with all its shame,
    with all its grace is given;
    their name an everlasting name,
    their joy the joy of heaven.

5   They suffer with their Lord below;
    they reign with Him above;
    their profit and their joy, to know
    The mystery of His love.

6   The cross He bore is life and health,
    though shame and death to Him:
    His people's hope, His people's wealth,
    their everlasting theme.

648 The heavens declare

Words and music: Andy Silver

The hea-vens de-clare the glo-ry of God, and the hea-vens pro-claim the work of His hands; and day af-ter day they pour forth speech, and night af-ter night they dis-play what He knows.

649

The King of love

DOMINUS REGIT ME · 87 87

Words: Henry Williams Baker (1821–77)
Music: John Bacchus Dykes (1823–76)

1 The King of love my Shepherd is,
   whose goodness faileth never;
   I nothing lack if I am His
   and He is mine for ever.

2 Where streams of living water flow
   my ransomed soul He leadeth,
   and where the verdant pastures grow
   with food celestial feedeth.

3 Perverse and foolish oft I strayed;
   but yet in love He sought me,
   and on His shoulder gently laid,
   and home rejoicing brought me.

4 In death's dark vale I fear no ill
   with Thee, dear Lord, beside me;
   Thy rod and staff my comfort still,
   Thy cross before to guide me.

5 Thou spread'st a table in my sight;
   Thy unction grace bestoweth;
   and O what transport of delight
   from Thy pure chalice floweth!

6 And so through all the length of days
   Thy goodness faileth never;
   Good Shepherd, may I sing Thy praise
   within Thy house for ever!

650   The King is among us

Words and music: Graham Kendrick
Music arranged Chris Rolinson

The King is a-mong us, His Spi-rit is here: let's draw near and wor-

- ship, let songs fill the air!

2 He

1 The King is among us,
   His Spirit is here:
   let's draw near and worship,
   let songs fill the air!

2 He looks down upon us,
   delight in His face,
   enjoying His children's love,
   enthralled by our praise.

3 For each child is special,
   accepted and loved –
   a love gift from Jesus
   to His Father above.

4 And now He is giving
   His gifts to us all;
   for no one is worthless
   and each one is called.

5 The Spirit's anointing
   on all flesh comes down,
   and we shall be channels
   for works like His own:

6 We come now believing
   Your promise of power,
   for we are Your people
   and this is Your hour.

651 The kingdom of God

HANOVER 10 10 11 11

Words: Bryn Rees (1911–83)
Music: *A New Supplement to the New Version*, 1708

The king-dom of God is jus-tice and joy,
for Je-sus re-stores what sin would de-stroy;
God's pow-er and glo-ry in Je-sus we know,
and here and here-af-ter the king-dom shall grow.

1   The kingdom of God
        is justice and joy,
    for Jesus restores
        what sin would destroy;
    God's power and glory
        in Jesus we know,
    and here and hereafter
        the kingdom shall grow.

2   The kingdom of God
        is mercy and grace,
    the captives are freed,
        the sinners find place,
    the outcast are welcomed
        God's banquet to share,
    and hope is awakened
        in place of despair.

3   The kingdom of God
        is challenge and choice,
    believe the good news,
        repent and rejoice!
    His love for us sinners
        brought Christ to His cross,
    our crisis of judgement
        for gain or for loss.

4   God's kingdom is come,
        the gift and the goal,
    in Jesus begun,
        in heaven made whole;
    the heirs of the kingdom
        shall answer His call,
    and all things cry glory
        to God all in all!

652 The light of Christ

Words and music: Donald Fishel
Music arranged Betty Pulkingham

Flowing

Part 1 The light of Christ has come in-to the world; the light of Christ

Part 2 The light of Christ has come in-to the world; the

last time **to Coda**

Christ has come in-to the world.

light of Christ has come.

1 All men must be__ born a-gain to__ see the King-dom of
2 God gave up His__ on-ly Son out of love__ for the
3 The light of God has__ come to us so that we might have sal -

God;   the__ wa-ter and the__ Spi - rit bring new__
world, so that all____ men who be-lieve in Him will__
- va-tion; from the dark-ness of our__ sins we walk in-to

life__ in God's love.__
live__ for____ ev - er.
glo - ry with Christ Je - sus.

CODA
world.

653 The Lord has given

Words and music: Unknown
Music arranged Phil Burt

hand, we'll march right on to the vic-to-ry side,___ right in-to Ca-naan's land.___

1 The Lord has given a land of good things,
  I will press on and make them mine;
  I'll know His power, I'll know His glory,
  and in His kingdom I will shine.
      With the high praises of God in our mouth,
      and a two-edged sword in our hand,
      we'll march right on to the victory side,
      right into Canaan's land.

2 Gird up your armour, ye sons of Zion,
  gird up your armour, let's go to war;
  we'll win the battle with great rejoicing
  and so we'll praise Him more and more.
      With the high praises . . .

3 We'll bind their kings in chains and fetters,
  we'll bind their nobles tight in iron,
  to execute God's written judgement –
  march on to glory, sons of Zion!
      With the high praises . . .

654   The Lord has led forth

Words and music: Chris Bowater
Music arranged Phil Burt

The Lord has led forth His peo-ple with joy,_____ and His cho-sen ones with sing - ing, sing - ing; the Lord has led forth His peo-ple with joy,_____ and His cho-sen ones with sing - ing.

Fine

He has given to them___ the lands of the na-
- tions, to pos - sess the fruit and keep His laws, and praise,___
___ praise His name.___ The

D.%. al Fine

Chords: Bm, F#m / Bm, F#m, G, D/F# / Em7, G/A, A7

The Lord has led forth His people with joy,
and His chosen ones with singing, singing;
the Lord has led forth His people with joy,
and His chosen ones with singing.
He has given to them the lands of the nations,
to possess the fruit and keep His laws,
and praise, praise His name.
The Lord has led forth His people with joy,
and His chosen ones with singing, singing;
the Lord has led forth His people with joy,
and His chosen ones with singing.

655 The Lord is a great and mighty King

-200Words and music: Diane Davis

-200The Lord is a great and migh-ty King,

just and gen-tle with ev-e-ry-thing;

so with hap-pi-ness___ we sing,

and let His prais-es ring. ring.___

-200Words and music: © 1973 GIA Publications Inc,
7404 S Mason Avenue, Chicago, IL 60638, USA

The Lord is a great and mighty King,
just and gentle with everything;
so with happiness we sing,
and let His praises ring.

1 We are His voice, we His song;
   let us praise Him all day long. Alleluia.
   The Lord is a great ...

2 We are His body here on earth;
   from above He gave us birth. Alleluia.
   The Lord is a great ...

3 For our Lord we will stand,
   sent by Him to every land. Alleluia.
   The Lord is a great ...

4 The Lord our God is one,
   Father, Spirit, and the Son. Alleluia.
   The Lord is a great ...

656(i)   The Lord is King!

CHURCH TRIUMPHANT   LM

Words: Josiah Conder (1789–1855)
Music: J W Elliott (1833–1915)

The Lord is King! lift up thy voice, O earth, and all ye heavens re-joice; from world to world the joy shall ring, 'The Lord om-ni-po-tent is King!'

1 The Lord is King! lift up thy voice,
   O earth, and all ye heavens rejoice;
   from world to world the joy shall ring,
   'The Lord omnipotent is King!'

2 The Lord is King! who then shall dare
   resist His will, distrust His care,
   or murmur at His wise decrees,
   or doubt His royal promises?

3 The Lord is King! Child of the dust,
   the Judge of all the earth is just;
   holy and true are all His ways:
   let every creature speak His praise.

4 He reigns! ye saints, exalt your strains;
   your God is King, your Father reigns;
   and He is at the Father's side,
   the man of love, the crucified.

5 One Lord, one empire, all secures;
   He reigns, and life and death are yours,
   through earth and heaven one song shall ring,
   'The Lord omnipotent is King!'

656(ii)   The Lord is King!

NIAGARA   LM

Words: Josiah Conder (1789–1855)
Music: R Jackson (1840–1914)

The Lord is King! lift up thy voice, O earth, and all ye heavens re - joice; from world to world the joy shall ring, 'The Lord om - ni - po - tent is King!'

1 The Lord is King! lift up thy voice,
O earth, and all ye heavens rejoice;
from world to world the joy shall ring,
'The Lord omnipotent is King!'

2 The Lord is King! who then shall dare
resist His will, distrust His care,
or murmur at His wise decrees,
or doubt His royal promises?

3 The Lord is King! Child of the dust,
the Judge of all the earth is just;
holy and true are all His ways:
let every creature speak His praise.

4 He reigns! ye saints, exalt your strains;
your God is King, your Father reigns;
and He is at the Father's side,
the man of love, the crucified.

5 One Lord, one empire, all secures;
He reigns, and life and death are yours,
through earth and heaven one song shall ring,
'The Lord omnipotent is King!'

657 The Lord is King

Words and music: Graham Kendrick

Triumphantly

The Lord is King, He is migh-ty in bat-tle, work-ing won-ders, glor-ious in ma - jes - ty. The Lord is King – so ma-jes-tic in pow-er! His right hand has shat-tered the e - ne - my.

658 The Lord is my strength

Words and music: Roland Fudge

With breadth

The Lord_____ is my strength and my song,_____ the Lord_____ is my strength and my song,_____ and He has be-come_____ my sal - va - tion.

659 The Lord reigns

Words and music: Angela Pack

Steadily

The Lord reigns,_____ the Lord reigns,_____ He is robed_____ in ma-jes-ty,_____ the Lord is robed_____ in ma-jes-ty,_____

and He is gird - ed with

strength._____ The Lord has es-

-tab - lished the world,_____

it shall ne - ver be moved;_____

Thy throne is es - tab - lished of old,_____ Thou art from ev - er - last - ing. strength._____

D.C. ⊕ CODA

The Lord reigns, the Lord reigns,
He is robed in majesty,
the Lord is robed in majesty,
and He is girded with strength.

1   The Lord has established the world,
    it shall never be moved;
    Thy throne is established of old,
    Thou art from everlasting.
      The Lord reigns . . .

2   The floods have lifted up, O Lord,
    lifted up their voice;
    mightier than the thunder of the waves,
    the Lord on high is mighty.
      The Lord reigns . . .

660 The Lord's my Shepherd

CRIMOND CM

Words: Francis Rous (1579–1659)
revised for *Scottish Psalter*, 1650
Music: melody by Jessie S Irvine (1836–87)

The Lord's my Shepherd, I'll not want;
He makes me down to lie
in pastures green; He leadeth me
the quiet waters by.

1 The Lord's my Shepherd, I'll not want;
He makes me down to lie
in pastures green; He leadeth me
the quiet waters by.

2 My soul He doth restore again,
and me to walk doth make
within the paths of righteousness,
e'en for His own name's sake.

3 Yea, though I walk through death's dark vale,
yet will I fear none ill;
for Thou art with me, and Thy rod
and staff me comfort still.

4 My table Thou hast furnished
in presence of my foes;
my head Thou dost with oil anoint,
and my cup overflows.

5 Goodness and mercy all my life
shall surely follow me;
and in God's house for evermore
my dwelling-place shall be.

661 The Lord's Prayer

Music: Joseph Lees

662 The love of Christ who died for me

Words: Timothy Dudley-Smith
Music: Phil Burt

The love of Christ who died for me
is more than mind can know,
His mer-cy mea - sure-less and free to
meet the debt I owe.

1 The love of Christ who died for me
   is more than mind can know,
   His mercy measureless and free
   to meet the debt I owe.

2 He came my sinful cause to plead,
   He laid His glories by,
   for me a homeless life to lead,
   a shameful death to die.

3 My sins I only see in part,
   my self-regarding ways;
   the secret places of my heart
   lie bare before His gaze.

4 For me the price of sin He paid;
   my sins beyond recall
   are all alike on Jesus laid,
   He died to bear them all.

5 O living Lord of life, for whom
   the heavens held their breath,
   to see, triumphant from the tomb,
   a love that conquers death.

6 Possess my heart that it may be
   Your kingdom without end,
   O Christ who died for love of me
   and lives to be my friend.

663

The price is paid

Words and music: Graham Kendrick
Music arranged David Peacock

Unhurried

The price is paid: come, let us en-ter in to all that Je-sus died to make our own. For ev-ery sin more than e-nough He gave, and bought our free-dom from each guil-ty stain. *The price is* paid, *Al-le-lu - ia— a-maz-ing grace, so strong and sure! And so with*

all my heart, my life in ev-ery part,_ I live to thank You for_ the price You paid.

The price is

1 The price is paid:
        come, let us enter in
    to all that Jesus died
        to make our own.
    For every sin
        more than enough He gave,
    and bought our freedom
        from each guilty stain.
    The price is paid, Alleluia –
    amazing grace,
    so strong and sure!
    And so with all my heart,
    my life in every part,
    I live to thank You
    for the price You paid.

2 The price is paid:
        see Satan flee away –
    for Jesus, crucified,
        destroys his power.
    No more to pay!
        Let accusation cease:
    in Christ there is
        no condemnation now!
    The price is paid, . . .

3 The price is paid:
        and by that scourging cruel,
    He took our sicknesses
        as if His own.
    And by His wounds,
        His body broken there,
    His healing touch may now
        by faith be known.
    The price is paid, . . .

4 The price is paid:
        'Worthy the Lamb!' we cry –
    eternity shall never
        cease His praise.
    The Church of Christ
        shall rule upon the earth:
    in Jesus' name
        we have authority!
    The price is paid, . . .

664   The Spirit lives

WALK IN THE LIGHT

Words and music: Damien Lundy

The Spi-rit lives to set us free, walk, walk in the light; He

binds us all in u-ni-ty, walk, walk in the light.

Walk in the light,_ walk in the light,_

walk in the light,_ walk in the light of the Lord.

1 The Spirit lives to set us free,
   walk, walk in the light;
   He binds us all in unity,
   walk, walk in the light.
       Walk in the light,
       walk in the light,
       walk in the light,
       walk in the light of the Lord.

2 Jesus promised life to all,
   walk, walk in the light;
   the dead were wakened by His call,
   walk, walk in the light.
       Walk in the light . . .

3 He died in pain on Calvary,
   walk, walk in the light;
   to save the lost like you and me,
   walk, walk in the light.
       Walk in the light . . .

4 We know His death was not the end,
   walk, walk in the light;
   He gave His Spirit to be our friend,
   walk, walk in the light.
       Walk in the light . . .

5 By Jesus' love our wounds are healed,
   walk, walk in the light;
   the Father's kindness is revealed,
   walk, walk in the light.
       Walk in the light . . .

6 The Spirit lives in you and me,
   walk, walk in the light;
   His light will shine for all to see,
   walk, walk in the light.
       Walk in the light . . .

665 The Spirit of the Lord

Words and music: Chris Bowater

The steadfast love

... sus, on-ly *Je* - - - *sus* — it is *Je-sus, Sav-iour,*

heal-er and bap-tiz-er, and the migh - ty King, the *vic-tor and de-liv-erer — He is*

Lord, He is *Lord,* He is *Lord.*

1 The Spirit of the Lord,
    the sovereign Lord, is on me,
    because He has anointed me
    to preach good news to the poor:
        Proclaiming Jesus, only Jesus –
        it is Jesus, Saviour, healer and baptizer,
        and the mighty King, the victor and deliverer –
        He is Lord, He is Lord, He is Lord.

2 And He has called on me
    to bind up all the broken hearts,
    to minister release to every
    captivated soul:
        Proclaiming Jesus . . .

3 Let righteousness arise
    and blossom as a garden;
    let praise begin to spring in every
    tongue and nation:
        Proclaiming Jesus . . .

666   The steadfast love

Words and music: Edith McNeill

The guitar chords and piano arrangement are not designed to be used together.

soul, there-fore I will hope in Him. *The stead-fast*

Verses 2-4

2 The Lord— is good to those who wait for Him, to the soul that
3 The Lord— will not cast off for ev - er, but will have com -
4 So let us ex-am-ine all our ways,_____ and re - turn_

seeks_ Him: it is good_ that we should wait_ qui - et - ly_____
-pas - sion: for_ He does not will - ing_ ly af-flict or
to the Lord: let us lift up our hearts_ and_ hands_____

for the sal - va-tion of the Lord.
grieve the_ sons_ of_ men. *The stead - fast*
to_____ God_ in_ heaven.

Words and music © 1989 Make Way Music,
administrated in Europe by Thankyou Music,
P.O. Box 75, Eastbourne, East Sussex BN23 6NW, UK.

667 The trumpets sound

Words and music: Graham Kendrick
Music arranged Christopher Norton

The trum-pets sound, the an - gels sing, the feast is rea-dy to_ be-gin; the gates of heaven are o - pen wide, and Je - sus wel-comes you_ in-side.

repeat 1st time only

Sing with thank-ful-ness songs of pure_ de-light, come and re - vel in hea-ven's love_ and light;

1   The trumpets sound, the angels sing,
    the feast is ready to begin;
    the gates of heaven are open wide,
    and Jesus welcomes you inside.
    The trumpets sound . . .
       Sing with thankfulness songs of pure delight,
       come and revel in heaven's love and light;
       take your place at the table of the King,
       the feast is ready to begin,
       the feast is ready to begin.

2   Tables are laden with good things,
    O taste the peace and joy He brings;
    He'll fill you up with love divine,
    He'll turn your water into wine.
       Sing with thankfulness . . .

3   The hungry heart He satisfies,
    offers the poor His paradise;
    now hear all heaven and earth applaud
    the amazing goodness of the Lord.
       Sing with thankfulness . . .

668 The world was in darkness

RICH AND FREE   10 9 10 10 with refrain

Words: verses 1 and 2 Seth Sykes
verse 3 Glyn L Taylor
Music: Richard Maxwell, William Wirges
and Seth Sykes

The world was in dark-ness in sin and shame; man-kind was lost, and then Je-sus came. He car-ried our sins to Cal-va-ry's tree, He hung there, and bled there, for you and me.

Thank You Lord, for sav-ing my soul. Thank You Lord, for

mak-ing me whole. Thank You Lord, for giv-ing to me,____

Thy great sal - va - tion so rich____ and free.

1   The world was in darkness in sin and shame;
mankind was lost, and then Jesus came.
He carried our sins to Calvary's tree,
He hung there, and bled there, for you and me.
Thank You Lord, for saving my soul.
Thank You Lord, for making me whole.
Thank You Lord, for giving to me
Thy great salvation so rich and free.

2   Lord Jesus came down from His throne on high;
ready to live and willing to die.
For all of the pain and the suffering He bore,
I'll love Him and thank Him for evermore.
Thank You Lord . . .

3   To You I surrender my all today,
the debt I owe, I ne'er could repay,
I'll serve You with joy wherever You lead,
with this great assurance, You'll meet my need.
Thank You Lord . . .

669 Then I saw a new heaven and earth

Words: Christopher Idle
Music: Norman Warren

Then I saw a new heaven and earth, for the first had passed a -

-way; and the ho - ly ci - ty, come down from God, like a

bride on her wed - ding day: and I know how He loves His

own, for I heard His great voice tell, they would be His peo - ple, and

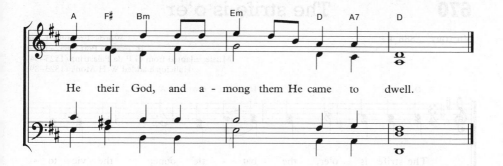

He their God, and a-mong them He came to dwell.

1 Then I saw a new heaven and earth,
for the first had passed away;
and the holy city, come down from God,
like a bride on her wedding day:
and I know how He loves His own,
for I heard His great voice tell,
they would be His people, and He their God,
and among them He came to dwell.

2 He will wipe away every tear,
even death shall die at last;
there'll be no more crying, or grief, or pain,
they belong to the world that's past:
and the One on the throne said 'Look!
I am making all things new';
He is A and Z, He is first and last,
and His words are exact and true.

3 So the thirsty can drink their fill
at the fountain giving life;
but the gates are shut on all evil things,
on deceit and decay and strife:
with foundations and walls and towers,
like a jewel the city shines;
with its streets of gold and its gates of pearl,
in a glory where each combines.

4 As they measured its length and breadth
I could see no temple there,
for its only temple is God the Lord
and the Lamb in that city fair:
and it needs neither sun nor moon
in a place which knows no night,
for the city's lamp is the Lamb Himself
and the glory of God its light.

5 And I saw by the sacred throne
flowing water, crystal clear;
and the tree of life with its healing leaves
and its fruit growing all the year:
so the worshippers of the Lamb
bear His name, and see His face;
and they reign and serve and for ever live
to the praise of His glorious grace.

670

The strife is o'er

VICTORY   888 4

Words: From the Latin
tr. Francis Pott (1832–1909)
Music: adapted from G P da Palastrina (1525–94)
Hallelujah added W H Monk (1823–89)

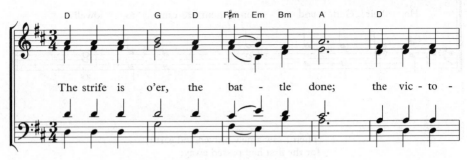

1 The strife is o'er, the battle done;
   the victory of life is won;
   the song of triumph has begun:
    Hallelujah!

2 The powers of death have done their worst,
   but Christ their legions has dispersed;
   let shouts of holy joy outburst:
    Hallelujah!

3 The three sad days have quickly sped:
   He rises glorious from the dead;
   all glory to our risen Head:
    Hallelujah!

4 He broke the bonds of death and hell;
   the bars from heaven's high portals fell;
   let hymns of praise His triumph tell:
    Hallelujah!

5 Lord, by the stripes which wounded Thee,
   from death's dread sting Thy servants free,
   that we may live, and sing to Thee;
    Hallelujah!

671 There is a fountain

St Mary   CM

Words: William Cowper (1731–1800)
Music: from Pry's *Psalter*, 1621

There is a foun-tain filled with blood drawn
from Em-man-uel's veins; and sin-ners, plunged be-
-neath that flood, lose all their guil-ty stains.

1 There is a fountain filled with blood
drawn from Emmanuel's veins;
and sinners, plunged beneath that flood,
lose all their guilty stains.

2 The dying thief rejoiced to see
that fountain in his day;
and there may I, as vile as he,
wash all my sins away.

3 Dear dying Lamb! Your precious blood
shall never lose its power,
till all the ransomed Church of God
be saved, to sin no more.

4 E'er since, by faith, I saw the stream
Your flowing wounds supply,
redeeming love has been my theme,
and shall be till I die.

5 Then in a nobler, sweeter song,
I'll sing Your power to save,
when this poor lisping, stammering tongue
lies silent in the grave.

672   There is a name I love to hear

Words: F Whitfield
Music: W H Rudd

There is a name I love to hear, I love to speak_ its worth;_____ it sounds like mu - sic in my ear, the sweet - est name on earth._____

O how I love the Sav - iour's name, O how I
How I love_ the Sav - iour's name,_____ how I

love   the   Sav - iour's   name,   O   how   I   love   the
love___ the   Sav - iour's   name, how   I   love,   I   love___ the

Sav - iour's   name,   the   sweet - est   name   on   earth.   (on   earth.)
Sav - iour's   name,

1   There is a name I love to hear,
     I love to speak its worth;
     it sounds like music in my ear,
     the sweetest name on earth.
          O how I love the Saviour's name,
          O how I love the Saviour's name,
          O how I love the Saviour's name,
          the sweetest name on earth.

2   It tells me of a Saviour's love,
     who died to set me free;
     it tells me of His precious blood,
     the sinner's perfect plea.
          O how I love . . .

3   It tells of one whose loving heart
     can feel my deepest woe,
     who in my sorrow bears a part
     that none can bear below.
          O how I love . . .

4   It bids my trembling heart rejoice,
     it dries each rising tear;
     it tells me in a 'still, small voice'
     to trust and never fear.
          O how I love . . .

5   Jesus, the name I love so well,
     the name I love to hear!
     No saints on earth its worth can tell,
     no heart conceive how dear!
          O how I love . . .

673   There is a Redeemer

Words and music: Melody Green

There is a Re-deem - - er,
Je - sus, God's own Son,_____ pre-cious Lamb of
God, Mes-si - ah, ho - - ly One.
Thank You, O my Fa - ther, for giv-ing us Your

Son,_____ and leav - ing Your Spi - rit till the

work__ on__ earth is done. done.

1 There is a Redeemer,
   Jesus, God's own Son,
   precious Lamb of God, Messiah,
   holy One.
       Thank You, O my Father,
       for giving us Your Son,
       and leaving Your Spirit
       till the work on earth is done.

2 Jesus my Redeemer,
   name above all names,
   precious Lamb of God, Messiah,
   O for sinners slain:
       Thank You . . .

3 When I stand in glory
   I will see His face,
   and there I'll serve my King for ever
   in that holy place.
       Thank You . . .

674 There is a green hill

HORSLEY   CM

Words: Cecil Frances Alexander (1818–95)
Music: W Horsley (1774–1858)

1 There is a green hill far away
   without a city wall,
   where the dear Lord was crucified,
   who died to save us all.

2 We may not know, we cannot tell
   what pains He had to bear;
   but we believe it was for us
   He hung and suffered there.

3 He died that we might be forgiven,
   He died to make us good,
   that we might go at last to heaven,
   saved by His precious blood.

4 There was no other good enough
   to pay the price of sin;
   He only could unlock the gate
   of heaven, and let us in.

5 O dearly, dearly has He loved,
   and we must love Him too,
   and trust in His redeeming blood,
   and try His works to do.

675   There is no condemnation

Words and Music: Joan Parsons
Music arranged Andy Silver
and Christopher Norton

There is no con-dem-na - tion for those who are in Christ,

for the Spi-rit of life in Christ has set me free.

O He's a-live, He's a-live, He's a - live, O He's a-

-live, He's a - live, He's a - live, praise the Lord.

2   If the Spirit of Him who raised Christ from the dead
be born in you, then He will give you life.
O He's alive, . . .

3   If God be for us, who can be against us?
For He who sent His Son will freely give us all things.
O He's alive, . . .

676 There is no love like the love of Jesus

THE LOVE OF JESUS   10 6 10 6 with refrain

Words: W E Littlewood (1831–86)
Music: T E Perkins (1831–1912)

There is no love like the love of Je - sus,
ne - ver to fade or fall, till in - to the fold of the
peace of God__ He has ga - thered us all.
Je - sus' love, pre - cious love, bound-less and pure and free! O

turn to that love, wea-ry wand-ering soul, Je-sus plead - eth with   thee.

1 There is no love like the love of Jesus,
   never to fade or fall,
   till into the fold of the peace of God
   He has gathered us all.
     Jesus' love, precious love,
     boundless and pure and free!
     O turn to that love, weary wandering soul,
     Jesus pleadeth with thee.

2 There is no heart like the heart of Jesus,
   filled with a tender love,
   no throb nor throe that our hearts can know
   but He feels it above.
     Jesus' love . . .

3 O let us hark to the voice of Jesus!
   O may we never roam,
   till safe we rest on His loving breast
   in the dear heavenly home.
     Jesus' love . . .

677   *There is none holy as the Lord*

Words and music: Gary Garrett

Not too slowly

There is none ho-ly as the Lord, there is none be - side Thee; nei-ther is there a - ny rock like our God, there is none ho-ly as the Lord.

678 There's a quiet understanding

Words and music: Tedd Smith

Words and music: © 1973 Hope Publishing Co, Carol Stream, IL 60188, USA

679   There's a light upon the mountains

THERE'S A LIGHT UPON THE MOUNTAINS
15 15 15 15

Words: Henry Burton (1840–1930)
Music: M L Wostenholm (1887–1959)

There's a light up-on the moun-tains, and the day is at the spring, when our eyes shall see the beau-ty and the glo-ry of the King; wea-ry was our heart with wait-ing, and the night-watch seemed so long; but His tri-umph-day is

break-ing, and we hail__ it__ with__ a song.__

1 There's a light upon the mountains, and the day is at the spring,
  when our eyes shall see the beauty and the glory of the King;
  weary was our heart with waiting, and the night-watch seemed so long;
  but His triumph-day is breaking, and we hail it with a song.

2 In the fading of the starlight we can see the coming morn;
  and the lights of men are paling in the splendours of the dawn:
  for the eastern skies are glowing as with light of hidden fire,
  and the hearts of men are stirring with the throbs of deep desire.

3 There's a hush of expectation, and a quiet in the air;
  and the breath of God is moving in the fervent breath of prayer:
  for the suffering, dying Jesus is the Christ upon the throne,
  and the travail of our spirit is the travail of His own.

4 He is breaking down the barriers, He is casting up the way;
  He is calling for His angels to build up the gates of day:
  but His angels here are human, not the shining hosts above;
  for the drum-beats of His army are the heart-beats of our love.

5 Hark! we hear a distant music, and it comes with fuller swell;
  'tis the triumph-song of Jesus, of our King, Immanuel:
  Zion, go ye forth to meet Him; and, my soul, be swift to bring
  all thy sweetness and thy dearest for the triumph of our King!

680 There's a song for all the children

IN MEMORIAM   86 76 76 76

Words: Albert Midlane (1825–1909)
in this version Jubilate Hymns
Music: John Stainer (1840–1901)

There's a song for all the child-ren that makes the hea-vens ring,—— a song that ev-en an-gels can ne-ver ne-ver sing;—— they praise Him as their Mak-er and see Him glo-ri--fied,—— but we can call Him Sav-iour be-cause for us He died.

1   There's a song for all the children
    that makes the heavens ring,
    a song that even angels
    can never never sing;
    they praise Him as their Maker
    and see Him glorified,
    but we can call Him Saviour
    because for us He died.

2   There's a place for all the children
    where Jesus reigns in love,
    a place of joy and freedom
    that nothing can remove;
    a home that is more friendly
    than any home we know,
    where Jesus makes us welcome
    because He loves us so.

3   There's a friend for all the children
    to guide us every day,
    whose care is always faithful
    and never fades away;
    there's no-one else so loyal –
    His friendship stays the same;
    He knows us and He loves us,
    and Jesus is His name.

681

There's a sound

BATTLE HYMN

Words and music: Graham Kendrick

There's a sound on the wind like a vic-to-ry song; lis-ten now, let it rest on your soul.

It's a song that I learned from a hea-ven-ly King, it's a song of a bat-tle

royal._____ 2 There's a _____ Come on hea-ven's

child-ren,_____ the ci-ty_____ is in sight.

There will be____ no sad-ness on the oth - er side.

1   There's a sound on the wind like a victory song;
listen now, let it rest on your soul.
It's a song that I learned from a heavenly King,
it's a song of a battle royal.

2   There's a loud shout of victory that leaps from our hearts,
as we wait for our conquering King.
There's a triumph resounding from dark ages past,
to the victory song we now sing.
    Come on heaven's children,
    the city is in sight.
    There will be no sadness
    on the other side.

3   There'll be crowns for the conquerors and white robes to wear,
there will be no more sorrow or pain;
and the battles of earth shall be lost in the sight,
of the glorious Lamb that was slain.

4   Now the King of the ages approaches the earth,
He will burst through the gates of the sky;
and all men shall bow down to His beautiful name;
we shall rise with a shout, we shall fly!
    Come on . . .

(repeat verse 4)

682

There's a way back

Words and music: E H Swinstead

There's a way back to God from the dark paths of sin; there's a
door that is o-pen and you may go in: at Cal-va-ry's cross is
where you be-gin, when you come as a sin-ner to Je - sus.

683 There's a wideness in God's mercy

CROSS OF JESUS   87 87

Words: Frederick William Faber (1814–63) altd.
Music: John Stainer (1840–1901)

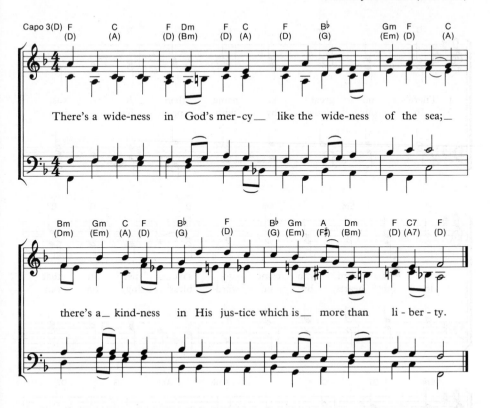

1   There's a wideness in God's mercy
    like the wideness of the sea;
    there's a kindness in His justice
    which is more than liberty.

2   There is plentiful redemption
    in the blood that has been shed;
    there is joy for all the members
    in the sorrows of the Head.

3   There is grace enough for thousands
    of new worlds as great as this;
    there is room for fresh creations
    in that upper home of bliss.

4   For the love of God is broader
    than the measures of man's mind;
    and the heart of the Eternal
    is most wonderfully kind.

5   But we make His love too narrow
    by false limits of our own;
    and we magnify His strictness
    with a zeal He will not own.

6   If our love were but more simple
    we should take Him at His word;
    and our lives would be illumined
    by the presence of our Lord.

684 There's no greater name

Words and music: Michael Baughen

Words and music: © Michael Baughen/Jubilate Hymns

2 Let ev-ery-thing that's be-neath the ground, let ev-ery-thing in the world a-round, let ev-ery-thing ex-alt-ed on high____ bow at Je-sus' name.____

D.C. al Fine

1   There's no greater name than Jesus,
    name of Him who came to save us;
    in that saving name so gracious
    every knee shall bow.

2   Let everything that's beneath the ground,
    let everything in the world around,
    let everything exalted on high
    bow at Jesus' name.

3   In our minds, by faith professing,
    in our hearts, by inward blessing,
    on our tongues, by words confessing,
    Jesus Christ is Lord.

685 Therefore the redeemed

Words and music: Ruth Lake
Music arranged Christopher Norton

Therefore the redeemed of the Lord shall return, and come with singing unto Zion, and everlasting joy shall be upon their head. Therefore the redeemed head. They shall obtain gladness and

joy,_____ and sor-row and mourn-ing__ shall flee a-

-way. There-fore the re-deemed of the Lord shall re-

-turn,_____ and come with sing-ing_ un-to Zi-on,_ and ev-er-

-last-ing_ joy shall be up-on their head._____

686 Therefore we lift our hearts

Words and music: Colin Green
Music arranged Norman Warren

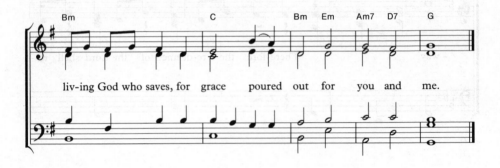

1 Therefore we lift our hearts in praise,
   sing to the living God who saves,
   for grace poured out for you and me.

2 There for everyone to see,
   there on the hill at Calvary,
   Jesus died for you and me.

3 There for sad and broken men
   He rose up from the grave again,
   and reigns on high for you and me.

4 There for such great pain and cost
   the Spirit came at Pentecost,
   and comes in power for you and me.

5 Therefore we lift our hearts in praise,
   sing to the living God who saves,
   for grace poured out for you and me.

687   These are the facts

YVONNE   10 10 11 10

Words: Michael Saward
Music: Norman Warren

2 These are the facts as we have received them:
Christ has fulfilled what the Scriptures foretold,
Adam's whole family in death had been sleeping,
Christ through His rising restores us to life.

3 These are the facts as we have received them:
we, with our Saviour, have died on the cross;
now, having risen, our Jesus lives in us,
gives us His Spirit and makes us His home.

4 These are the facts as we have received them:
we shall be changed in the blink of an eye,
trumpets shall sound as we face life immortal,
this is the victory through Jesus our Lord.

5 These are the facts as we have received them,
these are the truths that the Christian believes,
this is the basis of all of our preaching:
Christ died for sinners and rose from the tomb.

688   They that wait upon the Lord

Words and music: Andy Silver

They that wait up-on the Lord shall re-new their strength, and mount on ea - gles wings. They that wait up-on the Lord shall re-new their strength, and mount on ea - gles wings.

They will run and not grow wea-ry,_____

they will walk and not be faint._____ Those whose

hope_____ is in the Lord_____ shall re-

D.C. al Fine

-new_____ their strength._____

689 Thine be the glory

MACCABAEUS   10 11 11 11 with refrain

Words: Edmond Budry (1854–1932)
tr. R Birch Hoyle (1875–1939)
Music: G F Handel (1685–1759)

Thine be the glo - ry, ri - sen,_ con-quering Son,
end - less_ is the vic - tory Thou o'er death hast won;
an - gels_ in bright rai - ment rolled the stone a - way,
kept the_ fold - ed grave-clothes where Thy bo - dy lay.

1 Thine be the glory, risen, conquering Son,
   endless is the victory Thou o'er death hast won;
   angels in bright raiment rolled the stone away,
   kept the folded grave-clothes where Thy body lay.
       Thine be the glory, risen, conquering Son,
       endless is the victory Thou o'er death hast won.

2 Lo! Jesus meets us, risen from the tomb;
   lovingly He greets us, scatters fear and gloom;
   let the Church with gladness hymns of triumph sing,
   for her Lord now liveth; death hath lost its sting.
       Thine be the glory . . .

3 No more we doubt Thee, glorious Prince of life;
   life is nought without Thee: aid us in our strife;
   make us more than conquerors, through Thy deathless love:
   bring us safe through Jordan to Thy home above.
       Thine be the glory . . .

690   This Child

Words and music: Graham Kendrick
Music arranged Christopher Norton

Calypso

This Child, se - cret - ly comes in the night, oh, this Child, hid - ing a hea - ven - ly light, oh, this Child, com - ing to us like a stran - ger, this hea - ven - ly Child. *This* Child, hea - ven come down now to be with us here, hea - ven - ly love

_ and mer - cy ap - pear, soft-ly in awe___ and won - der come

near   to this hea - ven-ly Child.   This

Child.   This   Child.

1 This Child, secretly comes in the night,
   oh, this Child, hiding a heavenly light,
   oh, this Child, coming to us like a stranger,
   this heavenly Child.
       This Child, heaven come down now to be with us here,
       heavenly love and mercy appear,
       softly in awe and wonder come near
       to this heavenly Child.

2 This Child, rising on us like the sun,
   oh this Child, given to light everyone,
   oh this Child, guiding our feet on the pathway
   to peace on earth.
       This Child, heaven come down . . .

3 This Child, raising the humble and poor,
   oh this Child, making the proud ones to fall;
   this Child, filling the hungry with good things,
   this heavenly Child.
       This Child, heaven come down . . .
       This Child, heaven come down . . .

691 This is the day

Words: Les Garrett
Music: Fiji Island folk melody
Music arranged Roland Fudge

Joyfully

1 This is the day, this is the day that the
2 This is the day, this is the day when He
3 This is the day, this is the day when the

Lord has made, that the Lord has made.
rose a - gain, when He rose a - gain.
Spi - rit came, when the Spi - rit came.

We will re - joice, we will re - joice and be

glad in it, and be glad in it.

This is the day that the Lord has＿ made,
This is the day when He rose a - gain,
This is the day when the Spi - rit＿ came,

we will re - joice and be glad in＿ it.

This is the day,   this is the day   that the
This is the day,   this is the day   when He
This is the day,   this is the day   when the

Lord   hath   made.
rose   a   -   gain.
Spi   -   rit   came.

Words and music © Greg Leavers and Phil Burt

692   This is what our Saviour said

Words and music: Greg Leavers
and Phil Burt

This is what our Sav-iour said, He will re-turn to the

earth in pow - er, com - ing on the clouds from heaven,

all earth shall see Him and bow be-fore Him. He is the Al-pha and O-me-ga,

Who is, and who was, and who is to come;_ once He was dead and be -

- hold He now is liv-ing for ev - er - more.   - men!

1   This is what our Saviour said,
    He will return to the earth in power,
    coming on the clouds from heaven,
    all earth shall see Him and bow before Him.
    He is the Alpha and Omega,
    Who is, and who was, and who is to come;
    once He was dead and behold He now is
    living for evermore.

2   With a shout and trumpet sound
    He'll fetch His bride for the marriage feast,
    and then we'll see Him face to face,
    joining all heaven in praise and worship.
    Blessing and glory and thanksgiving
    be to the Lamb reigning now and forever;
    honour and power belong to Jesus,
    come quickly Lord, amen!

693   Thou art the everlasting word

PALMYRA   86 86 88

Words: Josiah Conder (1789–1855)
Music: Joseph Summers (1843–1916)

Thou art the ev - er - last - ing Word, the
Fa - ther's on - ly Son; God man - i - fest - ly
seen and heard, and Heaven's be - lov - èd One: *Wor-thy, O Lamb of*
God, art Thou that ev - ery knee to Thee should bow.

1   Thou art the everlasting Word,
      the Father's only Son;
      God manifestly seen and heard,
      and Heaven's belovèd One:
          Worthy, O Lamb of God, art Thou
          that every knee to Thee should bow.

2   In Thee most perfectly expressed
      the Father's glories shine;
      of the full Deity possessed,
      eternally divine:
          Worthy, O Lamb of God . . .

3   True image of the infinite,
      whose essence is concealed;
      brightness of uncreated light;
      the heart of God revealed:
          Worthy, O Lamb of God . . .

4   But the high mysteries of Thy name
      an angel's grasp transcend;
      the Father only – glorious claim!
      the Son can comprehend:
          Worthy, O Lamb of God . . .

5   Throughout the universe of bliss,
      the centre Thou, and sun;
      the eternal theme of praise is this,
      to heaven's belovèd One:
          Worthy, O Lamb of God . . .

694   Thou art my God

Words and music: Tony Hopkins
Music arranged Roland Fudge

Rich and broad

Thou art my God and I will praise Thee; Thou art my God, I will ex - alt Thee. O give thanks un - to the Lord, for He is good; for His mer - cy en - dur - eth for ev - er.

695 Thou art the Way

St James   CM

Words: George Washington Doane (1799–1859)
Music: Raphael Courteville (1675–1735)

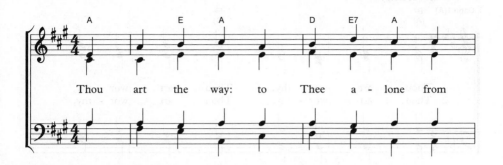

Thou art the way: to Thee a - lone from

sin and death we___ flee: and he who would the

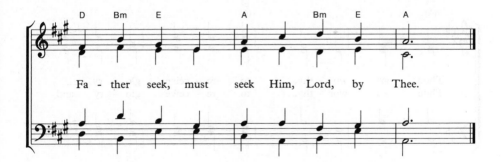

Fa - ther seek, must seek Him, Lord, by Thee.

1 Thou art the way: to Thee alone
   from sin and death we flee:
   and he who would the Father seek,
   must seek Him, Lord, by Thee.

2 Thou art the truth: Thy word alone
   true wisdom can impart;
   Thou only canst inform the mind
   and purify the heart.

3 Thou art the life: the rending tomb
   proclaims Thy conquering arm;
   and those who put their trust in Thee
   nor death nor hell shall harm.

4 Thou art the way, the truth, the life;
   grant us that way to know,
   that truth to keep, that life to win,
   whose joys eternal flow.

696   Thou art worthy

Words and music: Pauline Michael Mills
verse 2 by Tom Smail

Thou hast cre - a - ted, hast all things cre - a - ted, for
Thou hast re - deemed us; hast ran - somed and cleaned us,

Thou hast cre - a - ted all things;____
by Thy blood set - ting us free.____ In

and for Thy plea - sure they are cre - a - ted:____
white robes ar - rayed us, kings and priests made us, and

Thou art wor - thy, O Lord.____
we are reign - ing in Thee.____

697 Thou didst leave Thy throne

MARGARET Irregular

Words: Emily Elizabeth Steele Elliott (1836–97)
Music: T R Matthews (1826–1910)

Thou didst leave Thy throne and Thy king-ly crown, when Thou
cam-est to earth for me; but in Beth-le-hem's home was there
found no room for Thy ho-ly na-ti-vi-ty: O
come to my heart, Lord Je-sus, there is room in my heart for Thee.

1   Thou didst leave Thy throne
    and Thy kingly crown,
    when Thou camest to earth for me;
    but in Bethlehem's home
    was there found no room
    for Thy holy nativity:
    O come to my heart, Lord Jesus,
    there is room in my heart for Thee.

2   Heaven's arches rang
    when the angels sang,
    proclaiming Thy royal degree;
    but of lowly birth
    cam'st Thou, Lord, on earth,
    and in great humility:
    O come to my heart, Lord Jesus,
    there is room in my heart for Thee.

3   The foxes found rest,
    and the birds their nest,
    in the shade of the cedar-tree;
    but Thy couch was the sod,
    O Thou Son of God,
    in the deserts of Galilee;
    O come to my heart, Lord Jesus,
    there is room in my heart for Thee.

4   Thou camest, O Lord,
    with the living word
    that should set Thy people free;
    but, with mocking scorn,
    and with crown of thorn,
    they bore Thee to Calvary:
    O come to my heart, Lord Jesus,
    Thy cross is my only plea.

5   When heaven's arches ring,
    and her choirs shall sing,
    at Thy coming to victory,
    let Thy voice call me home,
    saying, 'Yet there is room,
    there is room at my side for thee!'
    And my heart shall rejoice, Lord Jesus,
    when Thou comest and callest for me.

698   Thou, Lord, hast given Thyself

SPRINGFIELD   11 10 11 10

Words: R D Browne
Music: H J Gauntlett (1805–76)

1 Thou, Lord, hast giv-en Thy-self for our heal-ing;
poured out Thy life that our souls might be freed. Love, from the heart of the
Fa-ther, re-veal-ing light for our dark-ness and grace for our need.

2 Sav-iour of men, our hu-ma-ni-ty shar-ing,
give us a_ pas-sion for souls that are lost. Help us to fol-low, Thy
gos-pel de-clar-ing; dai-ly to serve Thee and count not the cost.

3 Pray we for men who to-day in their blind-ness
wan-der from Thee and Thy king-dom of truth: grant them a sight of Thy
great lov-ing-kind-ness, Lord of their man-hood and guide of their youth.

4 Come, Holy Spirit, to cleanse and renew us:
   purge us from evil and fill us with power:
   thus shall the waters of healing flow through us;
   so shall revival be born in this hour.

5 Give to Thy Church, as she tells forth the story,
   strength for her weakness and trust for her fears;
   make her a channel of grace for Thy glory,
   answer her prayers in the midst of the years.

Words: © R D Browne

699 Thou, whose almighty word

MOSCOW

Words: John Marriott (1780–1825)
Music: Felice de Giardini (1716–96)

1 Thou, whose almighty word
chaos and darkness heard,
and took their flight;
hear us, we humbly pray,
and where the Gospel day
sheds not its glorious ray,
let there be light!

2 Thou, who didst come to bring,
on Thy redeeming wing,
healing and sight;
health to the sick in mind,
sight to the inly blind,
O now to all mankind
let there be light!

3 Spirit of truth and love,
Life-giving, holy Dove,
speed forth Thy flight;
move on the water's face,
bearing the lamp of grace,
and in earth's darkest place
let there be light!

4 Blessèd and holy Three,
glorious Trinity,
wisdom, love, might;
boundless as ocean's tide,
rolling in fullest pride,
through the earth, far and wide
let there be light!

700   Thou who wast rich

FRAGRANCE   98 98 98

Words: Frank Houghton
Music: French Carol melody
arranged C H Kitson

Thou who wast rich beyond all splendour, all for love's sake becamest poor, thrones for a manger didst surrender sapphire-paved courts for stable floor. Thou who wast rich beyond all

splen - dour,   all   for love's   sake___   be - cam - est   poor.

1   Thou who wast rich beyond all splendour,
    all for love's sake becamest poor,
    thrones for a manger didst surrender
    sapphire-paved courts for stable floor.
    Thou who wast rich beyond all splendour,
    all for love's sake becamest poor.

2   Thou who art God beyond all praising,
    all for love's sake becamest man;
    stooping so low, but sinners raising
    heavenwards by Thine eternal plan.
    Thou who art God beyond all praising,
    all for love's sake becamest man.

3   Thou who art love beyond all telling,
    Saviour and King, we worship Thee.
    Immanuel, within us dwelling,
    make us what Thou wouldst have us be.
    Thou who art love beyond all telling,
    Saviour and King, we worship Thee.

701 Thou wilt keep him in perfect peace

Words: Anon
Music: Robert Witty
arranged Paul Beckwith

1 Thou wilt keep him in perfect peace, (*3 times*)
   whose mind is stayed on Thee.

2 Marvel not that I say unto you, (*3 times*)
   ye must be born again.

3 Though your sins as scarlet be, (*3 times*)
   they shall be white as snow.

4 If the Son shall make you free, (*3 times*)
   ye shall be free indeed.

5 They that wait upon the Lord, (*3 times*)
   they shall renew their strength.

6 Whom shall I send and who will go? (*3 times*)
   Here I am Lord, send me.

702 Through all the changing scenes

WILTSHIRE CM

Words: Nahum Tate (1652–1715)
and Nicholas Brady (1639–1726)
Music: G T Smart (1776–1867)

1 Through all the changing scenes of life,
   in trouble and in joy,
   the praises of my God shall still
   my heart and tongue employ.

2 Of His deliverance I will boast,
   till all that are distressed
   from my example comfort take,
   and charm their griefs to rest.

3 O magnify the Lord with me,
   with me exalt His name;
   when in distress to Him I called,
   He to my rescue came.

4 The hosts of God encamp around
   the dwellings of the just;
   deliverance He affords to all
   who on His succour trust.

5 O make but trial of His love;
   experience will decide
   how blest they are, and only they,
   who in His truth confide.

6 Fear Him, ye saints, and you will then
   have nothing else to fear;
   make you His service your delight,
   He'll make your wants His care.

Through our God

Words and music: Dale Garratt
Music arranged Christopher Norton

Through our God____ we shall do val - iant-ly, it is

He____ who will tread down our e - ne-mies; we'll

sing____ and shout His vic - to-ry:___ Christ is

King! For God____ has won the vic - to-ry____ and

Words and music: © 1979 Scripture in Song,
administered in Europe by Thankyou Music,
PO Box 75, Eastbourne, East Sussex BN23 6NW, UK

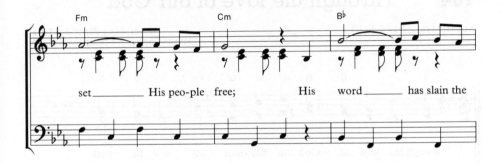

set_____ His peo-ple free; His word_____ has slain the

e - ne - my,___ the earth shall stand and see that – through our

⊕ *CODA*

Christ   is   King,

Christ   is   King,   Christ   is   King!

704   Through the love of our God

SOUTHGATE   84 84 88 84

Words: Mary Peters (1813–56)
Music: Thomas B Southgate (1814–68)

Through the love of God our Sav-iour all will be well;

free and change-less is His fa-vour, all,___ all is well.

Pre-cious is the blood that heals us, per-fect_ is the grace that seals us,

strong the hand stretched out to shield us; all_____ must be well.

1   Through the love of God our Saviour
        all will be well;
    free and changeless is His favour,
        all, all is well.
    Precious is the blood that heals us,
    perfect is the grace that seals us,
    strong the hand stretched out to shield us;
        all must be well.

2   Though we pass through tribulation,
        all will be well;
    ours is such a full salvation,
        all, all is well.
    Happy, still in God confiding;
    fruitful, if in Christ abiding;
    holy, through the Spirit's guiding;
        all must be well.

3   We expect a bright tomorrow;
        all will be well;
    faith can sing, through days of sorrow
        'All, all is well.'
    On our Father's love relying,
    Jesus every need supplying,
    or in living or in dying,
        all must be well.

705 Thy hand, O God, has guided

THORNBURY   76 76 D

Words: E H Plumptre (1821–91)
Music: Basil Harwood (1859–1949)

- cord;_____ and both of____ this bear wit - ness: One
Church, one Faith, one Lord._____

1 Thy hand, O God, has guided
Thy flock, from age to age;
the wondrous tale is written,
full clear on every page;
our fathers owned Thy goodness,
and we their deeds record;
and both of this bear witness:
One Church, one Faith, one Lord.

2 Thy heralds brought glad tidings
to greatest as to least;
they bade men rise and hasten
to share the great King's feast;
and this was all their teaching
in every deed and word;
to all alike proclaiming:
One Church, one Faith, one Lord.

3 Through many a day of darkness,
through many a scene of strife,
the faithful few fought bravely
to guard the nation's life.
Their gospel of redemption,
sin pardoned, man restored,
was all in this enfolded:
One Church, one Faith, one Lord.

4 Thy mercy will not fail us,
nor leave Thy work undone;
with Thy right hand to help us,
the victory shall be won;
and then, by men and angels,
Thy name shall be adored,
and this shall be their anthem:
One Church, one Faith, one Lord.

706 Thy loving-kindness

Words and music: Hugh Mitchell
Music arranged Roger Mayor

Thy lov-ing-kind - ness is bet-ter than life,
Thy lov-ing-kind - ness is bet-ter than life;
my lips shall praise Thee, thus will I bless Thee;
Thy lov-ing-kind-ness is bet - ter than life.

2 I lift my hands up unto Thy name,
I lift my hands up unto Thy name;
my lips shall praise Thee, thus will I bless Thee;
Thy loving-kindness is better than life.

707   Timeless love!

Words: Timothy Dudley-Smith
Music: Norman Warren

Time-less love! We sing the sto - ry, praise His won - ders, tell His
By His faith - ful - ness sur - round - ed, north and south His_ hand pro -
Truth and right - eous-ness en - throne Him, just and e - qual_ are His

worth; love more fair than hea - ven's glo - ry, love more
- claim; earth and hea - ven formed and found - ed, skies and
ways; more than hap - py, those who own Him, more than

firm than an - cient earth! Tell His faith - ful - ness a -
seas de - clare His name! Wind and storm o - bey His
joy, their songs of praise! Sun and shield and great re -

- broad, who is like_ Him? Praise the Lord!
word, who is like_ Him? Praise the Lord!
- ward, who is like_ Him? Praise the Lord!

708 To God be the glory!

Words: Frances van Alstyne (1820–1915)
(Fanny J Crosby)
Music: W H Doane (1832–1916)

To God be the glo - ry! great things He hath done; so
loved He the world that He gave us His Son; who yield - ed His
life an a - tone - ment for sin, and op - ened the
life gate that all may go in. *Praise the Lord, praise the Lord! let the*

1 To God be the glory! great things He hath done;
   so loved He the world that He gave us His Son;
   who yielded His life an atonement for sin,
   and opened the life gate that all may go in.
      Praise the Lord, praise the Lord!
      let the earth hear His voice;
      praise the Lord, praise the Lord!
      let the people rejoice:
      O come to the Father,
      through Jesus the Son
      and give Him the glory;
      great things He hath done!

2 O perfect redemption, the purchase of blood!
   to every believer the promise of God;
   the vilest offender who truly believes,
   that moment from Jesus a pardon receives.
      Praise the Lord . . .

3 Great things He hath taught us, great things He hath done,
   and great our rejoicing through Jesus the Son;
   but purer, and higher, and greater will be
   our wonder, our rapture, when Jesus we see.
      Praise the Lord . . .

709   To Him we come

LIVING LORD   98 88 83

Words: James E Seddon (1915–83)
Music: Patrick Appleford

To Him we come — Je - sus Christ our Lord, God's — own liv - ing Word, His dear Son: in Him there is — no east and west, in Him all na - tions shall be blessed; to all He of - fers peace and rest — lov - ing — Lord!

Music: © 1960 Josef Weinberger Ltd,
12–14 Mortimer Street, London W1N 7RD

1   To Him we come –
    Jesus Christ our Lord,
    God's own living Word,
    His dear Son:
    in Him there is no east and west,
    in Him all nations shall be blessed;
    to all He offers peace and rest –
        loving Lord!

2   In Him we live –
    Christ our strength and stay,
    life and truth and way,
    friend divine:
    His power can break the chains of sin,
    still all life's storms without, within,
    help us the daily fight to win –
        living Lord!

3   For Him we go –
    soldiers of the cross,
    counting all things loss
    Him to know;
    going to every land and race,
    preaching to all redeeming grace,
    building His church in every place –
        conquering Lord!

4   With Him we serve –
    His the work we share
    with saints everywhere,
    near and far;
    one in the task which faith requires,
    one in the zeal which never tires,
    one in the hope His love inspires –
        coming Lord!

5   Onward we go –
    faithful, bold, and true,
    called His will to do
    day by day
    till, at the last, with joy we'll see
    Jesus, in glorious majesty;
    live with Him through eternity –
        reigning Lord!

710   To Him who is able to keep us

Words and music: Andy Silver

To Him who is able to keep us,
to keep us from falling away,
who'll bring us, spotless and joyful,
into God's presence one day.
To the only God our Saviour,
through Jesus Christ our Lord
be glory, majesty, might and power,
now, always – amen.

711 True-hearted, whole-hearted

TRUE-HEARTED   11 10 11 10

Words: Frances Ridley Havergal (1836–79)
altered Horrobin/Leavers
Music: Josiah Booth (1852–1930)

True - heart-ed, whole - heart-ed, faith - ful and loy - al,

King of our lives, by Your grace we'll stay true! Un-der Your stand-ard, ex-

-alt - ed and roy - al, strong in Your strength, we will bat - tle for You!

Peal out the watch - word, and si - lence it ne - ver,

song of our spi-rits, re-joic-ing and free: 'True-heart-ed, whole-heart-ed,

now and for ev-er, King of our lives, by Your grace we will be!'

1 True-hearted, whole-hearted, faithful and loyal,
King of our lives, by Your grace we'll stay true!
Under Your standard, exalted and royal,
strong in Your strength, we will battle for You!
Peal out the watchword, and silence it never,
song of our spirits, rejoicing and free:
'True-hearted, whole-hearted, now and for ever,
King of our lives, by Your grace we will be!'

2 True-hearted, whole-hearted! fullest allegiance
yielding each day to our glorious King!
Valiant endeavour and loving obedience
freely and joyously now would we bring.
Peal out the watchword . . .

3 True-hearted! Saviour, You know all our story,
weak are the hearts that we lay at Your feet;
sinful and treacherous, yet, for Your glory,
heal them and cleanse them from sin and deceit.
Peal out the watchword . . .

4 True-hearted, whole-hearted! Saviour, all-glorious,
take Your great power and You reign alone,
over our wills and affections victorious –
freely surrendered and wholly Your own.
Peal out the watchword . . .

712 Turn your eyes upon Jesus

Words and music: Helen H Lemmel

O soul, are you wea-ry and trou-bled? No light in the dark-ness you see?_____ There's light for a look at the Sav-iour, and life more a-bun-dant and free!

Turn your eyes up-on Je-sus, look full in His

Words and music: 1922, 1950 Singspiration/MPI Ltd/United
Nations Music Publishers Ltd/Boosey & Hawkes Music
Publishers Ltd

won - der - ful face;＿＿＿＿ and the things of earth will grow

strange - ly dim in the light of His glo - ry and grace.＿＿

1 O soul, are you weary and troubled?
   No light in the darkness you see?
   There's light for a look at the Saviour,
   and life more abundant and free!
        Turn your eyes upon Jesus,
        look full in His wonderful face;
        and the things of earth will grow strangely dim
        in the light of His glory and grace.

2 Through death into life everlasting
   He passed and we follow Him there;
   over us sin no more hath dominion,
   for more than conquerors we are!
        Turn your eyes . . .

3 His word shall not fail you He promised;
   believe Him, and all will be well:
   then go to a world that is dying,
   His perfect salvation to tell.
        Turn your eyes . . .

713 Tonight

Words and music: Graham Kendrick
Music arranged Christopher Norton

to find___ it was___ all

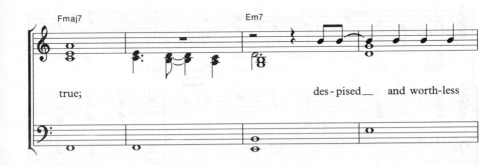

true;   des-pised___ and worth-less

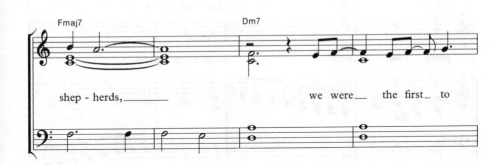

shep-herds,_____   we were___ the first___ to

know!_____

714   Unto us a Boy is born!

PUER NOBIS   76 77

Words: German (15th century)
tr. Percy Dearmer (1867–1936)
Music: German carol melody
arranged Geoffrey Shaw (1879–1943)

Un - to us a boy is born! King of all cre - a - tion, came He to a world for-lorn, the Lord of ev - ery na - tion, the Lord of ev - ery na - tion.

1   Unto us a boy is born!
King of all creation,
came He to a world forlorn,
the Lord of every nation,
the Lord of every nation.

2   Cradled in a stall was He
with sleepy cows and asses;
but the very beasts could see
that He all men surpasses,
that He all men surpasses.

3   Herod then with fear was filled:
'A Prince,' he said, 'in Jewry!'
All the little boys he killed
at Bethlehem in his fury,
at Bethlehem in his fury.

4   Now may Mary's Son, who came
so long ago to love us,
lead us all with hearts aflame
unto the joys above us,
unto the joys above us.

5   Alpha and Omega He!
Let the organ thunder,
while the choir with peals of glee
doth rend the air asunder,
doth rend the air asunder!

715   Victory is on our lips

Words and music: Diane Fung
Music arranged Roland Fudge

716 We are a chosen people

Words and music: David J Hadden

Triumphantly

We are a cho - - sen peo - ple, a roy - al priest - hood, a ho - ly na - tion be - long - ing to God. We are a God. You have called us out of dark - ness

to de-clare_____ Your praise;_

we ex-alt_____ You__   and en-throne__ You,_

D.C. al Fine

glo-ri-fy_____ Your   name.__

We are a chosen people,
a royal priesthood,
a holy nation belonging to God.

1 You have called us out of darkness
   to declare Your praise;
   we exalt You and enthrone You,
   glorify Your name.
      We are a chosen people . . .

2 You have placed us into Zion,
   in the new Jerusalem;
   thousand thousand are their voices,
   singing to the Lamb.
      We are a chosen people . . .

717   We are here to praise You

Words and music: Graham Kendrick
Music arranged David Peacock

We are here to praise You, lift our hearts and sing; we are here to give You the best that we can bring. And it is our

love rising from our hearts —
give You pleasure and de - light —

We are here to praise You,
lift our hearts and sing;
we are here to give You
the best that we can bring.
And it is our love
rising from our hearts –
everything within us cries:
'Abba Father!'
Help us now to give You
pleasure and delight –
heart and mind and will that say:
'I love You, Lord.'

718   We are marching

Words and music: Graham Kendrick
Music arranged Christopher Norton

We are march-ing in the great pro-ces-sion, sing-ers and dan-cers, and mu-si-cians; with the great con-gre-ga-tion we are mov-ing on-ward, ev-er fur-ther and deep-er in-to the heart of God.

O give thanks to the Lord, for His

D.S al Fine

love will ne - ver end.   2 It's a march of___

1 We are marching
   in the great procession,
   singers and dancers,
   and musicians;
   with the great congregation
   we are moving onward,
   ever further and deeper
   into the heart of God.
       O give thanks to the Lord,
       for His love will never end.

2 It's a march of victory,
   it's a march of triumph,
   lifting Jesus higher
   on a throne of praise.
   With the banner of love
   flying over us,
   ever further and deeper
   into the heart of God.
       O give thanks . . .

3 We will go to the nations,
   spreading wide the fragrance
   of the knowledge of Jesus
   into every place.
   Hear the great cloud of witnesses
   cheer us onward,
   ever further and deeper
   into the heart of God.
       O give thanks . . .

4 And the whole creation
   waits in expectation
   of the full revelation
   of the sons of God;
   as we march through history
   to our blood-bought destiny,
   ever further and deeper
   into the heart of God.

   Ever further and deeper
   into the heart of God.

719 We are moving on

Words and music: Ian Traynar
Music arranged Christopher Norton

We are mov-ing on in-to a deep ap-pre-ci - a-tion_ of the

love which flows from Fa-ther out to ev-ery child of God;_ of the

grace with which He han-dles ev-ery min-ute si - tu - a-tion, how He

wants the best for ev-ery-one who gives to Him his all.___

1   We are moving on into
    a deep appreciation
    of the love which flows from Father out
    to every child of God;
    of the grace with which He handles
    every minute situation,
    how He wants the best for everyone
    who gives to Him his all.
        Grace it seems is all He has,
        and one big open heart;
        and it's so good
        being loved by You, my Lord.

2   We will know and understand
    His purposes more clearly,
    O the mystery of the things He does
    in making us more whole.
    With His love He woos us,
    by His grace He sets us free;
    we can only trust Him
    and just hold on to His hand.
        Grace it seems . . .

720   We believe

Words and music: Graham Kendrick
Music arranged Roger Mayor

1 We be-lieve in God the Fa - ther, ma - ker of the u - ni - verse, and in Christ His Son our sav-iour, come to us by vir - gin birth. We be-lieve He died to save us, bore our sins, was cru - ci - fied; then from death He rose vic - to-rious, a - scen - ded to the Fa - ther's side.

2 We be-lieve He sends His Spi - rit on His church with gifts of power; God, His word of truth af - firm-ing, sends us to the na - tions now. He will come a - gain in glo-ry, judge the liv - ing and the dead: ev - ery knee shall bow be - fore Him, then must ev - ery tongue con - fess.

8va

721   We break this bread

Words: from *The Alternative Service Book 1980*
Music: Chris Rolinson
Music arranged Christopher Norton

we are one bo - dy, _____ be-cause we all_ share, we

1.
all share in one bread. _____ Though we are

2.
all share in one bread. _____

1 MEN   We break this bread
             to share in the body of Christ:
   WOMEN   we break this bread
             to share in the body of Christ:
   ALL   though we are many,
             we are one body,
             because we all share,
             we all share in one bread.

2 MEN   We drink this cup
             to share in the body of Christ:
   WOMEN   we drink this cup
             to share in the body of Christ:
   ALL   though we are many,
             we are one body,
             because we all share,
             we all share in one cup.

722 We bring the sacrifice of praise

Words and music: Kirk Dearman

We bring the sac-ri-fice of praise in-to the house of the Lord; we bring the sac-ri-fice of praise in-to the house of the Lord; Lord; and we of-fer up to You the sac-ri-

-fi - ces of thanks-giv - ing; and we of - fer up to

You_____ the sac-ri - fi - ces of joy.

We bring the sacrifice of praise
into the house of the Lord;
we bring the sacrifice of praise
into the house of the Lord;
we bring the sacrifice of praise
into the house of the Lord;
we bring the sacrifice of praise
into the house of the Lord;
and we offer up to You
the sacrifices of thanksgiving;
and we offer up to You
the sacrifices of joy.

723 We come as guests invited

PASSION CHORALE   76 76 D

Words: Timothy Dudley-Smith
Music: Hans Hassler (1564–1612)
arranged J S Bach (1685–1750)

We come as guests in - vi - ted when Je - sus bids us dine, His friends on earth u - ni - ted to share the bread and wine; the bread of life is bro - ken, the wine is free - ly poured for

us,_ in_ so - lemn to - ken of_ Christ our dy - ing_ Lord.

1 We come as guests invited
when Jesus bids us dine,
His friends on earth united
to share the bread and wine;
the bread of life is broken,
the wine is freely poured
for us, in solemn token
of Christ our dying Lord.

2 We eat and drink, receiving
from Christ the grace we need,
and in our hearts believing
on Him by faith we feed;
with wonder and thanksgiving
for love that knows no end,
we find in Jesus living
our ever-present friend.

3 One bread is ours for sharing,
one single fruitful vine,
our fellowship declaring
renewed in bread and wine –
renewed, sustained and given
by token, sign and word,
the pledge and seal of heaven,
the love of Christ our Lord.

724 We come unto our father's God

THE GOLDEN CHAIN 87 87 887

Words: Thomas Hornblower Gill (1819–1906)
Music: Joseph Barnby (1838–96)

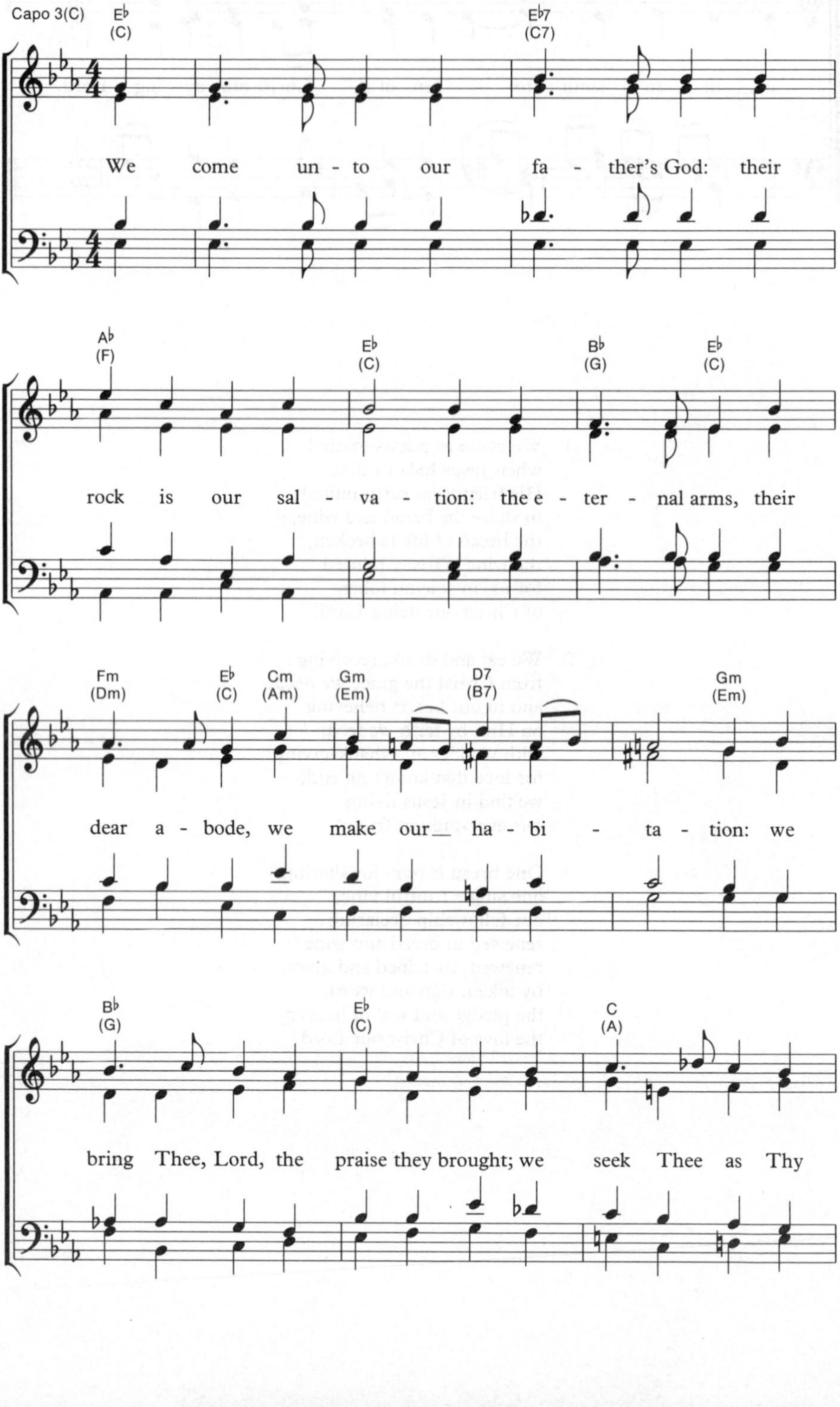

Capo 3(C)
E♭ (C) E♭7 (C7)
We come un - to our fa - ther's God: their
A♭ (F) E♭ (C) B♭ (G) E♭ (C)
rock is our sal - va - tion: the e - ter - nal arms, their
Fm (Dm) E♭ (C) Cm (Am) Gm (Em) D7 (B7) Gm (Em)
dear a - bode, we make our ha - bi - ta - tion: we
B♭ (G) E♭ (C) C (A)
bring Thee, Lord, the praise they brought; we seek Thee as Thy

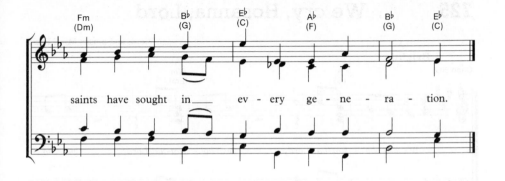

saints have sought in___ ev - ery ge - ne - ra - tion.

1 We come unto our father's God:
    their rock is our salvation:
    the eternal arms, their dear abode,
    we make our habitation:
    we bring Thee, Lord, the praise they brought;
    we seek Thee as Thy saints have sought
    in every generation.

2 The fire divine, their steps that led,
    still goeth bright before us;
    the heavenly shield, around them spread,
    is still high holden o'er us;
    the grace those sinners that subdued,
    the strength those weaklings that renewed,
    doth vanquish, doth restore us.

3 The cleaving sins that brought them low
    are still our souls oppressing;
    the tears that from their eyes did flow
    fall fast, our shame confessing;
    as with Thee, Lord, prevailed their cry,
    so now our prayer ascends on high,
    and bringeth down Thy blessing.

4 Their joy unto their Lord we bring;
    their song to us descendeth:
    the Spirit who in them did sing
    to us His music lendeth.
    His song in them, in us, is one;
    we raise it high, we send it on –
    the song that never endeth!

5 Ye saints to come, take up the strain,
    the same sweet theme endeavour!
    Unbroken be the golden chain,
    keep on the song for ever!
    Safe in the same dear dwelling-place,
    rich with the same eternal grace,
    bless the same boundless giver!

725

We cry, Hosanna, Lord

Words and music: Mimi Farra

1 Be-hold, our Sav-iour comes! be-hold the Son of our
2 Child-ren wave their palms as the King of all kings rides
3 He comes to set us free, He gives us lib - er -

We cry hosanna, Lord;
yes, hosanna, Lord;
yes, hosanna, Lord, to You:
we cry hosanna, Lord;
yes, hosanna, Lord;
yes, hosanna, Lord, to You!

1   Behold, our Saviour comes!
    behold the Son of our God!
    He offers Himself, and He comes among us,
    a lowly servant to all.
        We cry hosanna . . .

2   Children wave their palms
    as the King of all kings rides by;
    should we forget to praise our God,
    the very stones would sing.
        We cry hosanna . . .

3   He comes to set us free,
    He gives us liberty;
    His victory over death is the eternal sign
    of God's love for us.
        We cry hosanna . . .

726   We declare Your majesty

Words and music: Malcolm du Plessis
Music arranged Roger Mayor

We de - clare Your ma - jes - ty,___ we pro - claim that Your name_ is ex - alt - ed;___ for You reign mag - ni - fi - cent - ly, rule vic - to - ri - ous - ly, and Your power is shown through - out the earth. And we ex -

- claim_____ and we ex - claim   our God is migh - ty,_____ lift up Your

name,_____ lift up Your name   for You are ho - ly._____ Sing it a -

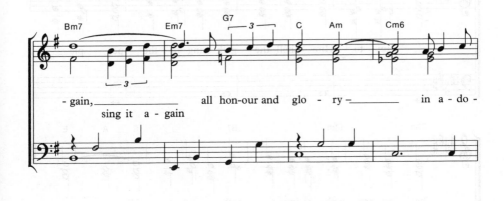

- gain,_____ sing it a - gain   all hon-our and glo - ry -_____ in a - do -

- ra - tion we bow be-fore Your throne!_____

We are gathering

727

Words and music: Anon

1 We are gathering together unto Him . . .

2 We are offering together unto Him . . .

3 We are singing together unto Him . . .

4 We are praying together unto Him . . .

728   We have a gospel to proclaim

FULDA   LM

Words: Edward J Burns
Music: W Gardiner's *Sacred Melodies*, 1815

1 We have a gospel to proclaim,
   good news for men in all the earth;
   the gospel of a saviour's name:
   we sing His glory, tell His worth.

2 Tell of His birth at Bethlehem,
   not in a royal house or hall
   but in a stable dark and dim:
   the Word made flesh, a light for all.

3 Tell of His death at Calvary,
   hated by those He came to save;
   in lonely suffering on the cross
   for all He loved, His life He gave.

4 Tell of that glorious Easter morn:
   empty the tomb, for He was free;
   He broke the power of death and hell
   that we might share His victory.

5 Tell of His reign at God's right hand,
   by all creation glorified;
   He sends His Spirit on His church
   to live for Him, the Lamb who died.

6 Now we rejoice to name Him king:
   Jesus is Lord of all the earth;
   this gospel-message we proclaim:
   we sing His glory, tell His worth.

729   We have come into His house

Words and music: © 1976 Canticle Publications Inc,
1900 West 47th Place, Mission, Kansas 66205, USA

Lord, wor - ship Him, Christ___ the Lord.___

1 We have come into His house,
   and gathered in His name to worship Him.
   We have come into His house,
   and gathered in His name to worship Him.
   We have come into His house,
   and gathered in His name to worship Christ the Lord,
   worship Him, Christ the Lord.

2 So forget about yourself
   and concentrate on Him and worship Him.
   So forget about yourself
   and concentrate on Him and worship Him.
   So forget about yourself
   and concentrate on Him and worship Christ the Lord,
   worship Him, Christ the Lord.

3 Let us lift up holy hands
   and magnify His name and worship Him.
   Let us lift up holy hands
   and magnify His name and worship Him.
   Let us lift up holy hands
   and magnify His name and worship Christ the Lord,
   worship Him, Christ the Lord.

730   We have heard a joyful sound

LIMPSFIELD   73 73 77 73

Words: Priscilla Owens (1829–1907)
Music: Josiah Booth (1852–1929)

1 We have heard a joy - ful sound: Je - sus saves!___
2 Sing a - bove the bat - tle's strife: Je - sus saves!___
3 Give the winds a migh - ty voice: Je - sus saves!___

Spread the glad - ness all___ a-round: Je - sus saves!___
By His death and end - less life, Je - sus saves!___
Let the na - tions now___ re-joice: Je - sus saves!___

Bear the news to ev - ery land, climb the steeps and cross the waves;
Sing it soft - ly through the gloom, when the heart for mer - cy craves;
Shout sal - va - tion full___ and free to ev - ery strand that o - cean laves –

On - ward! 'tis our Lord's com-mand: Je - sus saves!___
sing in tri - umph o'er___ the tomb: Je - sus saves!___
this our song of vic - to - ry: Je - sus saves!___

731   We love the place, O God

QUAM DILECTA   66 66

Words: William Bullock (1798–1874)
and H W Baker (1821–77)
Music: Henry Lascelles Jenner (1820–98)

We love the place, O God, where - in Thine hon-our dwells;
the joy of Thine a - bode all earth - ly joy ex - cels.

1   We love the place, O God,
wherein Thine honour dwells;
the joy of Thine abode
all earthly joy excels.

2   It is the house of prayer,
wherein Thy servants meet;
and Thou, O Lord, art there,
Thy chosen flock to greet.

3   We love the word of life,
the word that tells of peace,
of comfort in the strife,
and joys that never cease.

4   We love to sing below
of mercies freely given;
but O we long to know
the triumph-song of heaven.

5   Lord Jesus, give us grace,
on earth to love Thee more,
in heaven to see Thy face,
and with Thy saints adore.

732

We plough the fields

WIR PFLÜGEN   76 76 D with refrain

Words: Matthias Claudius (1740–1815)
tr. Jane Montgomery Campbell (1817–78)
altered Horrobin/Leavers
Music: J A P Schulz (1747–1800)

We plough the fields and scat - ter the good seed on the land,

but it is fed and wa - tered by God's al - migh - ty hand;

He sends the snow in win - ter, the warmth to swell the grain,

the breez - es and the sun - shine and soft re - fresh - ing rain.

All good gifts a - round_ us are sent from heaven a - bove,

then thank the Lord, O thank the Lord, for all___ His love.

1 We plough the fields and scatter
   the good seed on the land,
   but it is fed and watered
   by God's almighty hand;
   He sends the snow in winter,
   the warmth to swell the grain,
   the breezes and the sunshine
   and soft refreshing rain.
   All good gifts around us
   are sent from heaven above,
   then thank the Lord, O thank the Lord,
   for all His love.

2 He only is the Maker
   of all things near and far;
   He paints the wayside flower,
   He lights the evening star;
   the wind and waves obey Him,
   by Him the birds are fed;
   much more to us, His children,
   He gives our daily bread.
   All good gifts . . .

3 We thank You then, O Father,
   for all things bright and good,
   the seed-time and the harvest,
   our life, our health, our food.
   Accept the gifts we offer
   for all Your love imparts;
   we come now, Lord, to give You
   our humble, thankful hearts.
   All good gifts . . .

733   We praise You, we bless You

St Luke   11 11 11 11

Words: Frances van Alstyne (1820–1915)
(Fanny J Crosby)
altered Horrobin/Leavers
Music: Anon

We praise You, we bless You, our Sav - iour di - vine,
all power and do - min - ion are Yours for all time!
We sing of___ Your mer - cy with joy - ful ac - claim,
for You have re - deemed us: all praise to Your name!

1 We praise You, we bless You, our Saviour divine,
all power and dominion are Yours for all time!
We sing of Your mercy with joyful acclaim,
for You have redeemed us: all praise to Your name!

2 All honour and praise to Your excellent name,
Your love is unchanging – for ever the same!
We bless and adore You, O Saviour and King;
with joy and thanksgiving Your praises we sing!

3 The strength of the hills and the depths of the sea,
the earth and its fulness, Yours always shall be;
and yet to the lowly You listen with care,
so ready their humble petitions to hear.

4 Your infinite goodness our tongues shall employ;
You give to us richly all things to enjoy;
we'll follow Your footsteps, we'll rest in Your love,
and soon we shall praise You in mansions above!

734 We really want to thank You, Lord

Words: Ed Baggett
verse 3 after T Ken (1637–1710)
Music: Ed Baggett
arranged Betty Pulkingham

We real - ly want to thank You, Lord, we real - ly want to

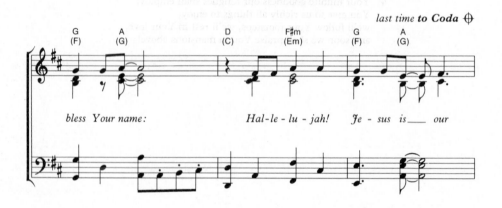

bless Your name: Hal-le-lu-jah! Je - sus is___ our

last time **to Coda** ⊕

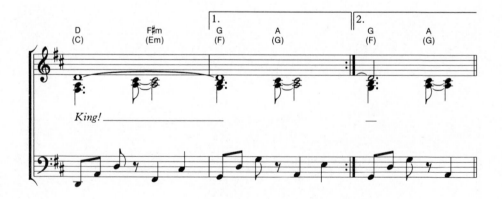

King!___

235   We Feast on Thee

D (C)   F#m (Em)   G (F)   A (G)

1 We thank You, Lord,   for Your gift   to   us,_____   Your
2 We thank You Lord,   for our   life   to - geth - er,   to
3 Praise God from whom   all____   bless - ings flow,_____   praise

D (C)   F#m (Em)   G (F)   A (G)   D (C)   F#m (Em)

life   so   rich   be - yond com-pare,   the   gift of Your bo - dy
live and move in the love   of Christ,   Your   ten - der-ness_ which
Him all crea - tures   here be - low,_   praise Him_ a - bove   you

G (F)   A (G)   D (C)   G (F)   A (G)

here   on_ earth   of   which   we_ sing and   share._
sets   us_ free   to   serve_   You_ with our   lives._
heaven-ly_ host,   praise Fa-ther, Son and Ho - ly   Ghost.

⊕ CODA

D.C. al Coda

D (C)   G (F)   D (C)

King!_____

735

We rest on Thee

FINLANDIA   11 10 11 10 11 10

Words: Edith Gilling Cherry (1872–97)
Music: Jean Sibelius (1865–1957)

We rest on Thee, our shield and our de-fend-er!

we go not forth a - lone a - gainst the foe;

strong in Thy strength, safe in Thy keep - ing ten - der,

we rest on Thee, and in Thy name we go.

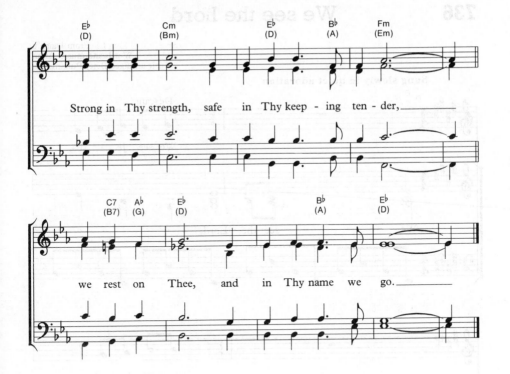

Strong in Thy strength, safe in Thy keep - ing ten - der,_____
we rest on Thee, and in Thy name we go._____

1 We rest on Thee, our shield and our defender!
we go not forth alone against the foe;
strong in Thy strength, safe in Thy keeping tender,
we rest on Thee, and in Thy name we go.
Strong in Thy strength, safe in Thy keeping tender,
we rest on Thee, and in Thy name we go.

2 Yes, in Thy name, O Captain of salvation!
in Thy dear name, all other names above;
Jesus our righteousness, our sure foundation,
our Prince of glory and our King of love.
Jesus our righteousness, our sure foundation,
our Prince of glory and our King of love.

3 We go in faith, our own great weakness feeling,
and needing more each day Thy grace to know:
yet from our hearts a song of triumph pealing,
'We rest on Thee, and in Thy name we go.'
Yet from our hearts a song of triumph pealing,
'We rest on Thee, and in Thy name we go.'

4 We rest on Thee, our shield and our defender!
Thine is the battle, Thine shall be the praise;
when passing through the gates of pearly splendour,
victors, we rest with Thee, through endless days.
When passing through the gates of pearly splendour,
victors, we rest with Thee, through endless days.

736

We see the Lord

From Isaiah 6
Words and music: Anon
Music arranged Betty Pulkingham

Sung slowly in quiet adoration

We see Je - sus,

We see the Lord,

we see Je - sus.

we see the Lord, and He is

High,_____ He is high,_____

high and lift - ed up, and His train fills the tem - ple; He is

He is high.

high and lift-ed up, and His train fills the tem-ple. The

An-gels cry, 'Ho-ly', the an-gels cry, 'Ho-ly', the

an-gels cry, 'Ho-ly', the an-gels cry, 'Ho-ly', the

an - gels cry, 'Ho - ly is the Lord.'_____

an - gels cry, 'Ho - ly is the Lord.'

737   We shall stand

Words and music: Graham Kendrick
Music arranged Christopher Norton

We shall stand, ___ with our feet on the Rock; ___ what-ev-er men ___ may say, ___ we'll lift Your name up high ___ and we shall walk ___ through the dark - est ___ night; ___ set-ting our fa - ces like flint, we'll walk in-to ___ the ___ light!

738

We sing the praise

WARRINGTON   LM

Words: Thomas Kelly (1769–1855)
Music: R Harrison (1748–1810)

1 We sing the praise of Him who died,
   of Him who died upon the cross;
   the sinner's hope let men deride,
   for this we count the world but lost.

2 Inscribed upon the cross we see,
   in shining letters, 'God is love';
   He bears our sins upon the tree,
   He brings us mercy from above.

3 The cross! it takes our guilt away,
   it holds the fainting spirit up;
   it cheers with hope the gloomy day
   and sweetens every bitter cup.

4 It makes the coward spirit brave,
   and nerves the feeble arm for fight;
   it takes the terror from the grave,
   and gilds the bed of death with light.

5 The balm of life, the cure of woe,
   the measure and the pledge of love;
   the sinner's refuge here below,
   the angels theme in heaven above.

739   We will sing of our Redeemer

Words and music: Gordon Brattle

740   We three kings of Orient are

Words and music: J H Hopkins (1820–91)
Words altered Horrobin/Leavers

We three kings of Or - i - ent are, bear - ing
gifts we tra - vel a - far, field and foun - tain,
moor and moun - tain, fol - low - ing yon - der star:
O___ star of won - der, star of night, star with

roy - al beau - ty bright, west - ward lead - ing, still pro -
ceed - ing, guide us to the per - fect light.

1 We three kings of Orient are,
   bearing gifts we travel afar,
   field and fountain, moor and mountain,
   following yonder star:
       O star of wonder, star of night,
       star with royal beauty bright,
       westward leading, still proceeding,
       guide us to the perfect light.

2 Born a King on Bethlehem plain,
   gold I bring to crown Him again:
   King for ever, ceasing never,
   over us all to reign.
       O star of wonder . . .

3 Frankincense for Jesus have I,
   God on earth yet Priest on high;
   prayer and praising all men raising:
   worship is earth's reply.
       O star of wonder . . .

4 Myrrh is mine: its bitter perfume
   tells of His death and Calvary's gloom;
   sorrowing, sighing, bleeding, dying,
   sealed in a stone-cold tomb.
       O star of wonder . . .

5 Glorious now, behold Him arise,
   King, and God, and sacrifice!
   Heaven sings out 'Alleluia',
   'Amen' the earth replies.
       O star of wonder . . .

741   We Your people

Words and music: Adrian Snell

Moderato

1 We Your peo - ple bow be - fore_ You bro - ken and a -
3 Fa - ther, in this hour of dan - ger we will turn to

- shamed; we have turned on Your cre - a - tion,
You: O for - give us, Lord, for - give us

crushed the life You free - ly_ gave.
and our lives and faith re - new.

2 Lord, have mer - cy on Your child - ren
4 Pour Your Ho - ly Spi - rit on_ us,

1 We Your people bow before You
broken and ashamed;
we have turned on Your creation,
crushed the life You freely gave.

2 Lord, have mercy on Your children
weeping and in fear:
for You are our God and Saviour,
Father in Your love draw near.

3 Father, in this hour of danger
we will turn to You:
O forgive us, Lord, forgive us
and our lives and faith renew.

4 Pour Your Holy Spirit on us,
set our hearts aflame:
all shall see Your power in the nations,
may we bring glory to Your name.

We'll sing a new song

Words and music: Diane Fung

Lively

We'll sing a new song___ of glo-rious tri-umph,___ for we see the gov-ern-ment of God in our lives; lives. He is

Words and music: © 1978 Springtide/
Word Music (UK), (a division of Word (UK) Ltd)
9 Holdom Avenue, Bletchley, Milton Keynes MK1 1QR, UK

crowned   God of the whole world, crowned,

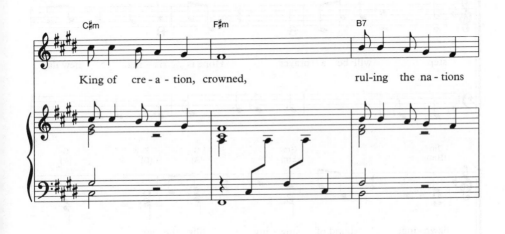

King of cre - a - tion, crowned,   rul-ing the na - tions

now.   now.

743 We'll walk the land

Words and music: Graham Kendrick
Music arranged Christopher Norton

Rhythmically

Capo 3(D)

1 We'll walk the land with hearts on fire; and ev-ery

step will be a prayer. Hope is ris-ing, new day

dawn-ing; sound of sing-ing fills the air.

1.

2 Two thou-sand

2.3.

Let the flame burn

Words and music: © 1989 Make Way Music,
administered in Europe by Thankyou Music,
PO Box 75, Eastbourne, East Sussex BN23 6NW, UK

bright - er in the heart of the dark - ness, turn - ing

night to glo-rious day. Let the song grow loud-er, as our love grows

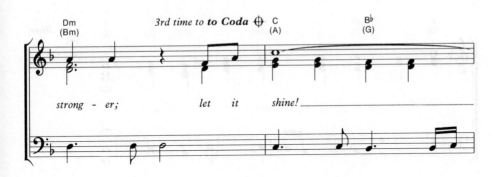

strong - er; let it shine!

let it shine!

3 We'll walk for ___   Let the flame burn

___   let it shine!_____   let it

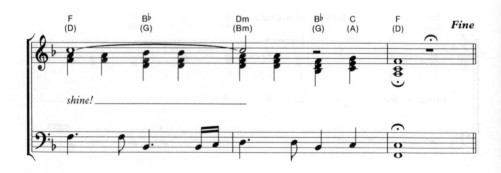

shine!_____

shine!_____   Let the flame burn

1 We'll walk the land with hearts on fire;
   and every step will be a prayer.
   Hope is rising, new day dawning;
   sound of singing fills the air.

2 Two thousand years, and still the flame
   is burning bright across the land.
   Hearts are waiting, longing, aching,
   for awakening once again.
     Let the flame burn brighter
     in the heart of the darkness,
     turning night to glorious day.
     Let the song grow louder,
     as our love grows stronger;
     let it shine! let it shine!

3 We'll walk for truth, speak out for love;
   in Jesus' name we shall be strong,
   to lift the fallen, to save the children,
   to fill the nation with Your song.
     Let the flame . . .

744
We've a story to tell

MESSAGE   10 8 87 with refrain

Words: Colin Sterne (1862–1926)
Music: H E Nichol (1862–1926)

We've a sto - ry to tell to the na - tions, that shall
turn their hearts to the right; a sto - ry of truth and sweet - ness, a
sto - ry of peace and light,___ a sto - ry of peace and light:
For the dark - ness shall turn to dawn - ing, and the

dawn - ing to noon - day bright,＿ and Christ's great king - dom shall

come on earth, the king - dom of love and light.

1 We've a story to tell to the nations,
   that shall turn their hearts to the right;
   a story of truth and sweetness,
   a story of peace and light,
   a story of peace and light:
       For the darkness shall turn to dawning,
       and the dawning to noon-day bright,
       and Christ's great kingdom shall come on earth,
       the kingdom of love and light.

2 We've a song to be sung to the nations,
   that shall lift their hearts to the Lord;
   a song that shall conquer evil,
   and shatter the spear and sword,
   and shatter the spear and sword:
       For the darkness . . .

3 We've a message to give to the nations,
   that the Lord who reigneth above
   hath sent us His Son to save us,
   and show us that God is love,
   and show us that God is love:
       For the darkness . . .

4 We've a Saviour to show to the nations,
   who the path of sorrow has trod,
   that all of the world's great peoples,
   might come to the truth of God,
   might come to the truth of God:
       For the darkness . . .

745

Were you there?

American Folk Hymn
Music arranged Francis Westbrook (1903–1975)

Were you there when they cru-ci-fied my Lord?—

— Were you there when they cru - ci - fied my

Lord?— Oh!—

Some-times it caus - es me to trem-ble, trem-ble,

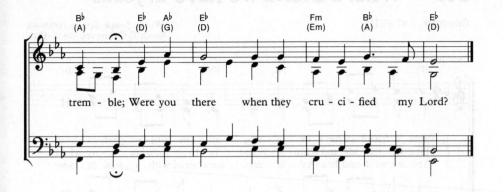

trem - ble; Were you there when they cru - ci - fied my Lord?

1 Were you there when they crucified my Lord?
   Were you there when they crucified my Lord?
   Oh! Sometimes it causes me to tremble, tremble, tremble;
   Were you there when they crucified my Lord?

2 Were you there when they nailed Him to the tree?
   Were you there when they nailed Him to the tree?
   Oh! Sometimes it causes me to tremble, tremble, tremble;
   Were you there when they nailed Him to the tree?

3 Were you there when they laid Him in the tomb?
   Were you there when they laid Him in the tomb?
   Oh! Sometimes it causes me to tremble, tremble, tremble;
   Were you there when they laid Him in the tomb?

4 Were you there when God raised Him from the dead?
   Were you there when God raised Him from the dead?
   Oh! Sometimes it causes me to tremble, tremble, tremble;
   Were you there when God raised Him from the dead?

746   What a friend we have in Jesus

CONVERSE   87 87 D

Words: Joseph Scriven (1819–86)
Music: C C Converse (1832–1918)

1 What a friend we have in Je - sus, all our sins and griefs to bear!
2 Have we tri - als and temp - ta - tions? Is there trou - ble a - ny-where?
3 Are we weak and hea - vy - la - den, cum-bered with a load of care?

What a pri - vi - lege to car - ry ev - ery-thing to God in prayer!
We should ne - ver be dis - cour - aged: take it to the Lord in prayer!
Pre - cious Sav - iour still our re - fuge, take it to the Lord in prayer!

O what peace we of - ten for - feit, O what need-less pain we bear –
Can we find a friend so faith - ful, who will all our sor-rows share?
Do thy friends des - pise, for - sake thee? Take it to the Lord in prayer!

all be - cause we do not car - ry ev - ery-thing to God in prayer!
Je - sus knows our ev - ery weak - ness – take it to the Lord in prayer!
In His arms He'll take and shield thee, thou wilt find a so - lace there.

747   # What a mighty God we serve

Words: Unknown
Music: Zulu working song
arranged Phil Burt

1   What a mighty God we serve . . .
     (*4 times*)

2   He created you and me . . .

3   He has all the power to save . . .

4   Let us praise the living God . . .

5   What a mighty God we serve . . .

748 What a wonderful change

Words: Rufus H McDaniel (1850–1940)
Music: Charles H Gabriel (1856–1932)

What a won-der-ful change in my life has been wrought since Je-sus came in-to my heart! I have light in my soul for which long I had sought, since Je-sus came in-to my heart!

Since Je-sus came in-to my heart, since
Since Je-sus came in, came in-to my heart, since

Je-sus came in-to my heart, floods of joy o'er my soul like the
Je-sus came in, came in-to my heart,

sea bil-lows roll, since Je - sus came in - to my heart!

1 What a wonderful change in my life has been wrought
   since Jesus came into my heart!
   I have light in my soul for which long I had sought,
   since Jesus came into my heart!
      Since Jesus came into my heart,
      since Jesus came into my heart,
      floods of joy o'er my soul
      like the sea billows roll,
      since Jesus came into my heart!

2 I have ceased from my wandering and going astray
   since Jesus came into my heart!
   And my sins which were many are all washed away
   since Jesus came into my heart!
      Since Jesus came . . .

3 I'm possessed of a hope that is steadfast and sure,
   since Jesus came into my heart!
   And no dark clouds of doubt now my pathway obscure,
   since Jesus came into my heart!
      Since Jesus came . . .

4 There's a light in the valley of death now for me,
   since Jesus came into my heart!
   And the gates of the city beyond I can see,
   since Jesus came into my heart!
      Since Jesus came . . .

5 I shall go there to dwell in that city, I know,
   since Jesus came into my heart!
   and I'm happy, so happy, as onward I go,
   since Jesus came into my heart!
      Since Jesus came . . .

749   What child is this

GREENSLEEVES   87 87 with refrain

Words: William Chatterton Dix (1837–98)
Music: English traditional melody

What child is this, who, laid to rest on Ma-ry's lap is
sleep - ing? Whom an - gels greet with an - thems sweet, while
shep - herds watch are keep - ing? *This, this is*
Christ the King, whom shep - herds guard and an - gels sing:

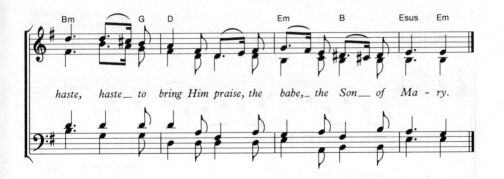

haste,   haste___ to   bring Him praise, the   babe,___ the   Son___ of   Ma - ry.

1   What child is this, who, laid to rest
      on Mary's lap is sleeping?
      Whom angels greet with anthems sweet,
      while shepherds watch are keeping?
        This, this is Christ the King,
        whom shepherds guard and angels sing:
        haste, haste to bring Him praise,
        the babe, the Son of Mary.

2   Why lies He in such mean estate,
      where ox and ass are feeding?
      Good Christian fear: for sinners here
      the silent Word is pleading.
        This, this is Christ . . .

3   So bring Him incense, gold, and myrrh,
      come, peasant, king, to own Him.
      The King of kings salvation brings,
      let loving hearts enthrone Him.
        This, this is Christ . . .

750

What kind of love is this

Words and music:
Bryn and Sally Haworth

Moderato

What kind of love__ is this,__
kind of love__ is this?__

that__ gave it-self__ for me?
A__ love I've ne - ver known.

I did - n't e - ven__
I am the__

1.
guil - ty one, yet I

v.2

Words and music: © 1983 Signalgrade Ltd,
48 Chatsworth Avenue, Raynes Park, London SW20 8J2

1 What kind of love is this,
   that gave itself for me?
   I am the guilty one,
   yet I go free.
   What kind of love is this?
   A love I've never known.
   I didn't even know His name,
   what kind of love is this?

2 What kind of man is this,
   that died in agony?
   He who had done no wrong
   was crucified for me.
   What kind of man is this,
   who laid aside His throne
   that I may know the love of God?
   What kind of man is this?

3 By grace I have been saved,
   it is the gift of God.
   He destined me to be His son,
   such is His love.
   No eye has ever seen,
   no ear has ever heard,
   nor has the heart of man conceived,
   what kind of love is this?

751

When all Your mercies

CONTEMPLATION   CM

Words: Joseph Addison (1672–1719)
Music: F A Gore Ouseley (1825–89)

1   When all Your mercies, O my God,
        my rising soul surveys,
    transported with the view, I'm lost
        in wonder, love, and praise.

2   Unnumbered comforts on my soul
        Your tender care bestowed,
    before my infant heart conceived
        from whom those comforts flowed.

3   Ten thousand thousand precious gifts
        my daily thanks employ,
    nor is the least a cheerful heart
        that tastes those gifts with joy.

4   Through every period of my life
        Your goodness I'll pursue,
    and after death, in distant worlds,
        the glorious theme renew.

5   Through all eternity to You
        a joyful song I'll raise;
    for O eternity's too short
        to utter all Your praise!

752

When He comes

Words and music: Sue Read
Music arranged Andy Silver
and Christopher Norton

1 When He comes we'll see just a child; no war-rior Lord but a ba-by so mild. The Lord says: 'Beth - le - hem, though you are but small, in___ you shall be born the King.' When He comes, when He comes.___

Words and music: © 1985 Thankyou Music,
PO Box 75, Eastbourne, East Sussex BN23 6NW, UK

tears: for the Lord will wipe them all a-way.___ And on that

day, men shall be bro-thers, re-con-ciled to God and each o-ther; the world shall

see the King in His glo-ry, when_ He comes._____

Verse 3 – use verse 2 accompaniment

3 When He comes He'll be of Da-vid's line,

the migh-ty God and ru-ler di-vine. They'll call Him

Won-der-ful___ and Coun-sel-lor, and His king-dom shall ne-ver cease.

Back to the chorus

___ When He comes, when_ He comes._____

753

When I feel the touch

Words and music:
Keri Jones and Dave Matthews

When I feel the touch_____ of Your hand up-on my life,_____ it caus-es me to sing a song, that I love You, Lord. So from deep with- -in_____ my spi-rit sing - eth un - to Thee,_____ You are my King, You are my God, and I love You, Lord.

Words and music: © 1978 Springtide/Word Music (UK), (a division of Word (UK) Ltd)
9 Holdom Avenue, Bletchley, Milton Keynes MK1 1QR, UK

754   When I look into Your holiness

Words and music: Anon
Music arranged Phil Burt

When I look in-to Your ho - li - ness,____ when I gaze in - to Your love - li - ness, when all things that sur-round be-come sha-dows in the light of You.____ When I've found the joy__ of reach-ing Your

heart,____ when my will be-comes en-throned in Your

love,____ when all things that sur - round be - come

sha - dows in the light of You.____ I wor-ship

You,____ I wor-ship You;____ the

rea-son I live_____ is to wor-ship You._____ I wor-ship

You,_____ I wor-ship You;_____ the

rea-son I live_____ is to wor-ship You._____

When I look into Your holiness,
when I gaze into Your loveliness,
when all things that surround
become shadows in the light of You.

When I've found the joy of reaching Your heart,
when my will becomes enthroned in Your love,
when all things that surround
become shadows in the light of You.

I worship You, I worship You;
the reason I live is to worship You.
I worship You, I worship You;
the reason I live is to worship You.

When I survey

ROCKINGHAM LM

Words: Isaac Watts (1674–1748)
Music: E Miller (1731–1807)

Capo 1(D)

1 When I survey the wondrous cross
   on which the Prince of glory died,
   my richest gain I count but loss,
   and pour contempt on all my pride.

2 Forbid it, Lord, that I should boast,
   save in the death of Christ my God:
   all the vain things that charm me most,
   I sacrifice them to His blood.

3 See from His head, His hands, His feet,
   sorrow and love flow mingled down:
   did e'er such love and sorrow meet,
   or thorns compose so rich a crown?

4 Were the whole realm of nature mine,
   that were an offering far too small,
   love so amazing, so divine,
   demands my soul, my life, my all.

756 When morning gilds the skies

LAUDES DOMINI   666 D

Words: tr. from the German by
Edward Caswall (1814–78)
Music: J Barnby (1838–96)

When morn-ing gilds the skies,__ my heart a-wak-ing cries:__ May Je-sus Christ be praised! A-like at work and prayer__ to Je-sus I re-pair;__ may Je-sus Christ be praised!

1 When morning gilds the skies,
   my heart awaking cries:
      May Jesus Christ be praised!
   Alike at work and prayer
   to Jesus I repair;
      may Jesus Christ be praised!

2 Does sadness fill my mind?
   a solace here I find –
      may Jesus Christ be praised!
   When evil thoughts molest,
   with this I shield my breast –
      may Jesus Christ be praised!

3 Be this, when day is past,
   of all my thoughts the last:
      May Jesus Christ be praised!
   The night becomes as day,
   when from the heart we say:
      May Jesus Christ be praised!

4 To God, the Word, on high
   the hosts of angels cry:
      May Jesus Christ be praised!
   Let mortals, too, upraise
   their voice in hymns of praise:
      May Jesus Christ be praised!

5 Let earth's wide circle round
   in joyful notes resound:
      May Jesus Christ be praised!
   Let air, and sea, and sky,
   from depth to height, reply:
      May Jesus Christ be praised!

6 Be this while life is mine,
   my canticle divine:
      May Jesus Christ be praised!
   Be this the eternal song
   through all the ages long:
      May Jesus Christ be praised!

757

When peace like a river

Words: Horatio G Spafford (1828–88)
Music: Philip P Bliss
arranged Phil Burt

When peace like a___ ri - ver at - tend - eth my
way, when sor - rows like sea - bil - lows roll;_____ what-
-ev - er my lot You have taught me to say, 'It is___
well, it is well with my soul.'_____ _It is_
(well with my soul)

well,_____ with my soul;_____ it is
(it   is   well)   (with my   soul)

well,   it   is   well   with   my   soul._____

1   When peace like a river attendeth my way,
    when sorrows like sea-billows roll;
    whatever my lot You have taught me to say,
    'It is well, it is well with my soul.'
        It is well with my soul;
        it is well, it is well with my soul.

2   Though Satan should buffet, if trials should come,
    let this blessed assurance control,
    that Christ has regarded my helpless estate,
    and has shed His own blood for my soul.
        It is well . . .

3   My sin – O the bliss of this glorious thought –
    my sin – not in part – but the whole
    is nailed to His cross; and I bear it no more;
    praise the Lord, praise the Lord, O my soul.
        It is well . . .

4   For me, be it Christ, be it Christ hence to live!
    if Jordan above me shall roll.
    No pang shall be mine, for in death as in life
    You will whisper Your peace to my soul.
        It is well . . .

5   But Lord, it's for You – for Your coming we wait,
    the sky, not the grave, is our goal:
    O trump of the angel! O voice of the Lord!
    Blessed hope! blessed rest of my soul.
        It is well . . .

758 When the Lord in glory comes

GLORIOUS COMING 77 77 77 D

Words: Timothy Dudley-Smith
Music: Michael Baughen
and D G Wilson

1 When the Lord in glo-ry comes, not the trum-pets, not the drums, not the an-them, not the psalm, not the thun-der, not the calm, not the shout the hea-vens raise, not the cho-rus, not the praise,

2 When the Lord is seen a-gain, not the glo-ries of His reign, not the light-nings through the storm, not the ra-diance of His form, not His pomp and power a-lone, not the splen-dours of His throne,

3 When the Lord to hu-man eyes shall be-stride our nar-row skies, not the child of hum-ble birth, not the car-pen-ter of earth, not the man by all de-nied, not the vic-tim cru-ci-fied,

not   the si - len - ces sub - lime,   not   the sounds of space and
not   His robe and   di - a - dems,   not   the gold and not the
but   the God who   died to save,   but   the vic - tor of the

time,   but His voice   when He ap - pears   shall be
gems,   but His face   up - on my sight   shall be
grave,   He it is   to whom I fall,   Je - sus

mu - sic to my ears;   but His voice   when He ap - pears   shall be
dark - ness in - to light;   but His face   up - on my sight   shall be
Christ, my all in all;   He it is   to whom I fall,   Je - sus

mu - sic to   my   ears._____
dark - ness in - to   light._____
Christ, my   all in   all._____

759   When the trumpet of the Lord

ROLL CALL

Words and music: James M Black (1856–1938)

1 When the trum - pet of the Lord shall sound, and
2 On that bright and cloud - less morn - ing when the
3 Let us la - bour for the Mas - ter from the

time shall be no more, and the morn-ing breaks, e - ter - nal, bright, and
dead in Christ shall rise, and the glo - ry of His re - sur - rec - tion
dawn till set - ting sun, let us talk of all His won-derous love and

fair; when the saved of earth shall gath - er o - ver
share; when His cho - sen ones shall gath - er to their
care; then when all of life is o - ver, and our

on the oth - er shore, and the roll is called up yon-der, I'll be there.
home be-yond the skies, and the roll is called up yon-der, I'll be there.
work on earth is done, and the roll is called up yon-der, I'll be there.

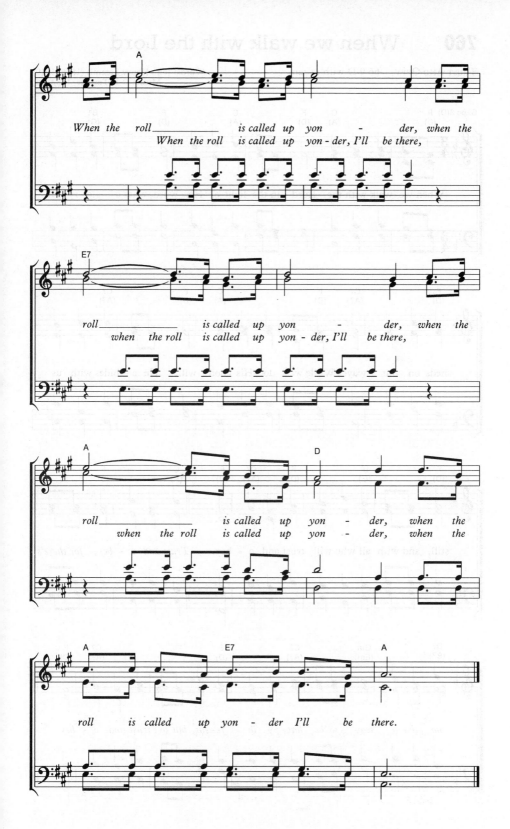

When the roll_____ is called up yon - der, when the
When the roll   is called up yon - der, I'll be there,

roll_____ is called up yon - der, when the
when the roll   is called up yon - der, I'll be there,

roll_____ is called up yon - der, when the
when the roll   is called up yon - der, when the

roll   is called up yon - der I'll be there.

760 When we walk with the Lord

TRUST AND OBEY   66 9 D with refrain

Words: John Henry Sammis (1846–1919)
Music: D B Towner (1833–96)

When we walk with the Lord in the light of His word, what a glo-ry He

sheds on our way! While we do His good will, He a-bides with us

still, and with all who will trust and o-bey. *Trust and o-bey, for there's*

no oth-er way to be hap-py in Je-sus, but to trust and o-bey.

1 When we walk with the Lord
  in the light of His word,
  what a glory He sheds on our way!
  While we do His good will,
  He abides with us still,
  and with all who will trust and obey.
    Trust and obey,
    for there's no other way
    to be happy in Jesus,
    but to trust and obey.

2 Not a shadow can rise,
  not a cloud in the skies,
  but His smile quickly drives it away;
  not a doubt nor a fear,
  not a sigh nor a tear,
  can abide while we trust and obey.
    Trust and obey . . .

3 Not a burden we bear,
  not a sorrow we share,
  but our toil He doth richly repay;
  not a grief nor a loss,
  not a frown nor a cross,
  but is blest if we trust and obey.
    Trust and obey . . .

4 But we never can prove
  the delights of His love,
  until all on the altar we lay;
  for the favour He shows,
  and the joy He bestows
  are for them who will trust and obey.
    Trust and obey . . .

5 Then in fellowship sweet,
  we will sit at His feet,
  or we'll walk by His side in the way.
  What He says we will do,
  where He sends we will go,
  never fear, only trust and obey.
    Trust and obey . . .

761 When to our world the Saviour came

CHURCH TRIUMPHANT   LM

Words: Timothy Dudley-Smith
Music: James W Elliott (1833–1915)

1 When to our world the Saviour came,
   the sick and helpless heard His name;
   and in their weakness longed to see
   the healing Christ of Galilee.

2 That good physician! night and day
   the people thronged about His way;
   and wonder ran from soul to soul –
   'The touch of Christ has made us whole!'

3 His praises then were heard and sung
   by opened ears and loosened tongue,
   while lightened eyes could see and know
   the healing Christ of long ago.

4 Of long ago – yet living still,
   who died for us on Calvary's hill;
   who triumphed over cross and grave,
   His healing hands stretched forth to save.

5 Those wounded hands are still the same,
   and all who serve that saving Name
   may share today in Jesus' plan –
   the healing Christ of every man.

6 Then grant us, Lord, in this our day,
   to hear the prayers the helpless pray;
   give to us hearts their pain to share,
   make of us hands to tend and care.

7 Make us Your hands! for Christ to live,
   in prayer and service, swift to give;
   till all the world rejoice to find
   the healing Christ of all mankind.

762 Wherever I am

Words and music: Anon
Music arranged David Peacock

Quite fast

Wher-ev-er I am I'll praise Him, when-ev-er I can I'll praise Him; for His love sur- -rounds me like a sea; I'll praise the name of Je-sus, lift up the name of Je-sus, for the name of Je-sus lift-ed me.

Words: Copyright control

763 Where the Lord walks

NAHUM

Based on the book of Nahum
Words and music: Anne Horrobin
and Sue Cartwright
Music arranged Phil Burt

Where the Lord walks, storms a-rise,— the clouds are the dust raised by His feet;— the earth shakes when the Lord ap-pears, the world and its peo-ple trem-ble.

You, Ni-ne-veh, are a wick-ed ci-ty, your

peo - ple__ plot a-gainst Me;   you've made My peo - ple

D.C. al Fine

Is - ra - el suf - fer, but now I'm going to set them   free.

Where the Lord walks, storms arise,
the clouds are the dust raised by His feet;
the earth shakes when the Lord appears,
the world and its people tremble.

1 You, Nineveh, are a wicked city,
   your people plot against Me;
   you've made My people Israel suffer,
   but now I'm going to set them free.
   Where the Lord walks . . .

2 The Lord will always protect His people,
   He'll care for those who trust Him;
   but turn against Him, oppose the Lord,
   and His judgement then is death.
   Where the Lord walks . . .

3 I say to my people Israel,
   a messenger is bringing good news;
   stand in the victory I've given you,
   for your enemy has been destroyed.
   Where the Lord walks . . .

764   # While shepherds watched

WINCHESTER OLD   CM

Words: Nahum Tate (1652–1715)
Music: Tate's *Psalms*, 1592

1 While shepherds watched their flocks by night,
 all seated on the ground,
 the angel of the Lord came down
 and glory shone around.

2 'Fear not,' said he – for mighty dread
 had seized their troubled mind –
 'Glad tidings of great joy I bring
 to you and all mankind:

3 'To you in David's town this day
 is born of David's line,
 a Saviour, who is Christ the Lord.
 And this shall be the sign:

4 'The heavenly babe you there shall find
 to human view displayed,
 all meanly wrapped in swaddling bands,
 and in a manger laid.'

5 Thus spake the angel; and forthwith
 appeared a shining throng
 of angels praising God, who thus
 addressed their joyful song:

6 'All glory be to God on high,
 and to the earth be peace;
 goodwill henceforth from heaven to men
 begin and never cease!'

765   Who can cheer the heart

ALL THAT THRILLS MY SOUL

Words and music: Thoro Harris

1 Who can cheer the heart like Je - sus, _ by His pres-ence all di - vine?
2 Love of Christ so free - ly giv - en, _ grace of God be-yond de-gree,
3 What a won-der-ful re-demp-tion! Nev-er can a mor-tal know
4 Ev - ery need His hand sup-ply - ing, _ ev-ery good in Him I see;
5 By the cry-stal flow-ing ri - ver, _ with the ran-somed I will sing,

True and ten - der, pure and pre-cious, O how blest to call Him mine!
mer - cy high - er than the hea - ven, _ deep - er than the deep-est sea.
how my sin, though red like crim-son, _ can be whit-er than the snow.
on His strength di - vine re - ly-ing, _ He is all in all to me.
and for ev - er and for ev - er, _ praise and glo - ri - fy the King.

All that thrills my soul is Je - sus; He is more than life to me; (to me;)

and the fair-est of ten thou - sand, _ in my bless-ed Lord I see.

766 Who can sound

Words and music: Graham Kendrick
Music arranged Christopher Norton

na - tion,   up - on the   na - tion have   mer - cy
na - tion,   up - on the   na - tion have   mer - cy
na - tion,   up - on the   na - tion have   mer - cy

Lord!
Lord!   2   We have   Lord!_____
Lord!   3   Who can

1   Who can sound the depths of sorrow
    in the Father heart of God,
    for the children we've rejected,
    for the lives so deeply scarred?
    And each light that we've extinguished
    has brought darkness to our land:
    upon the nation, upon the nation
    have mercy Lord!

2   We have scorned the truth You gave us,
    we have bowed to other lords,
    we have sacrificed the children
    on the altars of our gods.
    O let truth again shine on us,
    let Your holy fear descend:
    upon the nation, upon the nation
    have mercy Lord!

MEN

3   Who can stand before Your anger;
    who can face Your piercing eyes?
    For You love the weak and helpless,
    and You hear the victims' cries.

ALL

    Yes, You are a God of justice,
    and Your judgement surely comes:
    upon the nation, upon the nation
    have mercy Lord!

WOMEN

4   Who will stand against the violence?
    Who will comfort those who mourn?
    In an age of cruel rejection,
    who will build for love a home?

ALL

    Come and shake us into action,
    come and melt our hearts of stone:
    upon Your people, upon Your people,
    have mercy Lord!

5   Who can sound the depths of mercy
    in the Father heart of God?
    For there is a Man of sorrows
    who for sinners shed His blood.
    He can heal the wounds of nations,
    He can wash the guilty clean:
    because of Jesus, because of Jesus,
    have mercy Lord!

767   Who is He, in yonder stall

WHO IS HE   77 with refrain   Words and music: Benjamin Russell Hanby (1833–67)

1   Who is He, in yonder stall,
at whose feet the shepherds fall?
'Tis the Lord! O wondrous story!
'Tis the Lord! the King of Glory!
At His feet we humbly fall;
crown Him, crown Him Lord of all.

2   Who is He, in yonder cot,
bending to His toilsome lot?
'Tis the Lord . . .

3   Who is He, in deep distress,
fasting in the wilderness?
'Tis the Lord . . .

4   Who is He, that stands and weeps
at the grave where Lazarus sleeps?
'Tis the Lord . . .

5   Lo, at midnight, who is He
prays in dark Gethsemane?
'Tis the Lord . . .

6   Who is He, in Calvary's throes,
asks for blessings on His foes?
'Tis the Lord . . .

7   Who is He that from the grave
comes to heal and help and save?
'Tis the Lord . . .

8   Who is He that from His throne
rules through all the worlds alone?
'Tis the Lord . . .

768   Who is like unto Thee

Words and music: popular version of original by
Judy Horner Montemayor
Music arranged Roland Fudge

Alternative guitar chords for use
without piano part, in brackets

Who is like un-to Thee,_____ O____ Lord a-mong gods?_____

_ Who is like un-to Thee?_____ Glo-rious in

ho - li-ness, fear-ful in prais - es, do-ing

won - ders;_____ who_ is like un-to Thee?_____

769 Who is on the Lord's side?

ARMAGEDDON   65 65 D with refrain

Words: Frances Ridley Havergal (1836–79)
Music: J Goss (1800–80)

Who is on the Lord's side? Who will serve the King? Who will be His help-ers oth-er lives to bring? Who will leave the world's side? Who will face the foe? Who is on the Lord's side? Who for Him will go? By Thy call of mer-cy, by Thy grace di-vine, we are on the Lord's side; Sav-iour, we are Thine.

1   Who is on the Lord's side?
    Who will serve the King?
    Who will be His helpers
    other lives to bring?
    Who will leave the world's side?
    Who will face the foe?
    Who is on the Lord's side?
    Who for Him will go?
    By Thy call of mercy,
    by Thy grace divine,
    we are on the Lord's side;
    Saviour, we are Thine.

2   Not for weight of glory,
    not for crown or palm,
    enter we the army,
    raise the warrior-psalm;
    but for love that claimeth
    lives for whom He died:
    he whom Jesus nameth
    must be on His side.
    By Thy love constraining,
    by Thy grace divine,
    we are on the Lord's side;
    Saviour, we are Thine.

3   Fierce may be the conflict,
    strong may be the foe,
    but the King's own army
    none can overthrow.
    Round His standard ranging,
    victory is secure,
    for His truth unchanging
    makes the triumph sure.
    Joyfully enlisting,
    by Thy grace divine,
    we are on the Lord's side;
    Saviour, we are Thine.

4   Chosen to be soldiers
    in an alien land,
    chosen, called, and faithful,
    for our captain's band;
    in the service royal
    let us not grow cold;
    let us be right loyal,
    noble, true and bold.
    Master, Thou wilt keep us,
    by Thy grace divine,
    always on the Lord's side,
    Saviour, always Thine.

770 Will your anchor hold

Words: Priscilla Jane Owens (1829–99)
Music: W J Kirkpatrick (1838–1921)

Will your an-chor hold in the storms of life, when the clouds un-fold their

wings of strife? When the strong tides lift, and the ca-bles strain, will your

an-chor drift, or__ firm re-main? *We have an-chor that keeps the soul*

stead-fast and sure while the bil-lows roll; fast-ened to the rock which

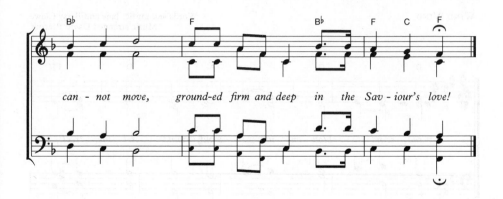

can - not   move,   ground-ed firm and deep   in   the   Sav - iour's   love!

1 Will your anchor hold in the storms of life,
   when the clouds unfold their wings of strife?
   When the strong tides lift, and the cables strain,
   will your anchor drift, or firm remain?
   We have an anchor that keeps the soul
   steadfast and sure while the billows roll;
   fastened to the rock which cannot move,
   grounded firm and deep in the Saviour's love!

2 Will your anchor hold in the straits of fear,
   when the breakers roar and the reef is near?
   While the surges rage, and the wild winds blow,
   shall the angry waves then your bark o'erflow?
   We have an anchor . . .

3 Will your anchor hold in the floods of death,
   when the waters cold chill your latest breath?
   On the rising tide you can never fail,
   while your anchor holds within the veil.
   We have an anchor . . .

4 Will your eyes behold through the morning light,
   the city of gold and the harbour bright?
   Will you anchor safe by the heavenly shore,
   when life's storms are past for evermore?
   We have an anchor . . .

771

Wind, wind blow on me

WIND WIND

Words and music: Jane and Betsy Clowe
Music arranged David Peacock

Wind, wind blow on me;__ wind, wind set me free!__

Wind, wind my Fa-ther sent the bless-èd Ho-ly Spi - rit.____

Je-sus told us all a-bout You, how we could not live with-out_ You;

with His blood the pow-er bought to help us live the life He taught.

Wind, wind blow on me;
wind, wind set me free!
Wind, wind my Father sent
the blessèd Holy Spirit.

1   Jesus told us all about You,
how we could not live without You;
with His blood the power bought
to help us live the life He taught.
    Wind, wind . . .

2   When we're weary You console us,
when we're lonely You enfold us,
when in danger You uphold us,
blessèd Holy Spirit.
    Wind, wind . . .

3   When into the church You came,
it was not in Your own but Jesus' name:
Jesus Christ is still the same –
He sends the Holy Spirit.
    Wind, wind . . .

4   Set us free to love our brothers,
set us free to live for others,
that the world the Son might see,
and Jesus' name exalted be.
    Wind, wind . . .

772

With all my heart

Words and music: Paul Field
Music arranged Christopher Norton

1   With all my heart I thank You Lord.
      With all my heart I thank You Lord.
      For this bread and wine we break,
      for this sacrament we take,
      for the forgiveness that You make,
      I thank You Lord.

2   With all my soul I thank You Lord.
      With all my soul I thank You Lord.
      For this victory that You've won,
      for this taste of things to come,
      for this love that makes us one,
      I thank You Lord.

3   With all my voice I thank You Lord.
      With all my voice I thank You Lord.
      For the sacrifice of pain,
      for the Spirit and the flame,
      for the power of Your name,
      I thank You Lord.

773   With harps and viols

THE NEW SONG   11 12 with refrain

Words: Arthur Tappan Pierson (1837–1911)
Music: Philip Bliss (1838–76)

With harps and with viols there stand a great throng

in the presence of Jesus, and sing this new song:

Unto Him who has loved us and washed us from sin,

unto Him be the glory for ever! Amen.

1   With harps and with viols
        there stand a great throng
    in the presence of Jesus,
        and sing this new song:
        Unto Him who has loved us
        and washed us from sin,
        unto Him be the glory
        for ever! Amen.

2   All these once were sinners,
        defiled in His sight,
    now arrayed in pure garments
        in praise they unite:
        Unto Him who has . . .

3   He's made of the rebel
        a priest and a king,
    He has bought us, and taught us
        this new song to sing:
        Unto Him who has . . .

4   How helpless and hopeless
        we sinners had been,
    if He never had loved us
        till cleansed from our sin!
        Unto Him who has . . .

5   Aloud in His praises
        our voices shall ring,
    so that others, believing,
        this new song shall sing:
        Unto Him who has . . .

774   With joy we meditate the grace

St Stephen   CM

Words: Isaac Watts (1614–1748) altd.
Music: William Jones (1726–1800)

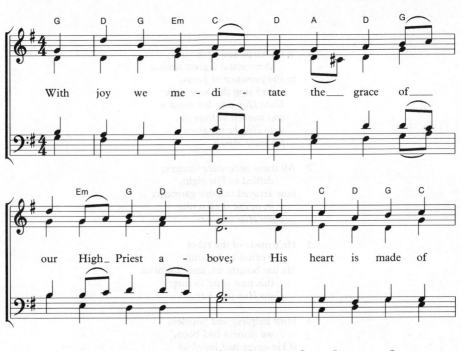

1   With joy we meditate the grace
    of our High Priest above;
    His heart is made of tenderness,
    it overflows with love.

2   Touched with a sympathy within,
    He knows our feeble frame;
    He knows what sore temptations mean,
    for He has felt the same.

3   He, in the days of feeble flesh,
    poured out His cries and tears;
    and now exalted feels afresh
    what every member bears.

4   He'll never quench the smoking flax,
    but raise it to a flame;
    the bruisèd reed He never breaks,
    nor scorns the meanest name.

5   Then let our humble faith address
    His mercy and His power;
    we shall obtain delivering grace
    in the distressing hour.

775   With my heart I worship You

Words and music: Norman Warren

ALTERNATIVE VERSES:

With my lips I praise You . . .

With my life I serve You . . .

776 Wonderful Counsellor

Words and music: Paul Armstrong

Won-der-ful_ Coun-sel-lor,_ the Migh-ty God,_____ the
Ev-er-last-ing Fa-ther, the Prince_ of Peace, the Prince of
Peace, the Ev-er-last-ing Fa-ther, the Migh - ty
God._____ Won-der-ful_ Coun-sel-lor,_

Words and music: © 1980 Springtide/Word Music (UK), (a division of Word (UK) Ltd)
9 Holdom Avenue, Bletchley, Milton Keynes MK1 1QR, UK

777 Wonderful Counsellor, Jesus

Words and music: Bill Yarger

1 Won - der - ful
2 Migh - ty God,
3 Ev - er - last - ing
4 Prince of Peace,
5 Won - der - ful

Coun - sel - lor	Je - sus:	
Son of God,	Je - sus;	
Fa - ther,	Je - sus;	
rule my heart,	Je - sus;	
Coun - sel - lor	Je - sus;	

search me,	know me,	Je - sus;
Name a - bove all	o - ther names,	Je - sus;
Ho - ly and un -	change - a - ble,	Je - sus;
know my ev - ery	an - xious thought,	Je - sus;
Migh - ty God,	Son of God,	Je - sus;

Words and music: © Maranatha! Music (USA)/Word Music (UK), (a division of Word (UK) Ltd)
9 Holdom Avenue, Bletchley, Milton Keynes MK1 1QR, UK
For British Isles, Republic of Ireland, Continent of Europe (Exc Benelux)

1 Wonderful Counsellor Jesus:
   search me, know me, Jesus;
   lead me, guide me, Jesus –
   Wonderful Counsellor Jesus.

2 Mighty God, Son of God, Jesus;
   Name above all other names, Jesus:
   glorify, magnify, Jesus –
   Mighty God, Son of God, Jesus.

3 Everlasting Father, Jesus;
   Holy and unchangeable, Jesus:
   fill me with Your presence, Jesus –
   Everlasting Father, Jesus.

4 Prince of Peace, rule my heart, Jesus;
   know my every anxious thought, Jesus;
   calm my fears, dry my tears, Jesus –
   Prince of Peace, rule my heart, Jesus.

5 Wonderful Counsellor Jesus;
   Mighty God, Son of God, Jesus;
   Everlasting Father, Jesus –
   Prince of Peace, rule my heart, Jesus.

778 Within the veil

Words and music: Ruth Dryden

Quiet and gentle

With - in the veil_____ I now would come,_____ in - to the ho - ly place_____ to look up - on Thy face._____ I see such beau - ty there,_____ no oth - er can com - pare,_____ I wor - ship Thee, my Lord,_____ with - in the veil.

779 Worthy art thou, O Lord

Words and music: Dave Richards
Music arranged Roger Mayor

780

Worthy is the Lamb

Music arranged Roland Fudge

1 Worthy is the Lamb;
   Worthy is the Lamb;
   Worthy is the Lamb;
   Worthy is the Lamb.

2 Holy is the Lamb . . .   4 Praises to the Lamb . . .

3 Precious is the Lamb . . .   5 Glory to the Lamb . . .

6 Jesus is our Lamb . . .

781 Worthy is the Lamb seated

Words and music: David J Hadden

Triumphantly

Wor-thy is the Lamb seat-ed on the throne, wor-thy is the Lamb who was slain, to re-ceive po-wer and rich-es, and wis-dom and strength, hon-our and glo-ry, glo-ry and praise, for ev-er and ev-er-more.

Words and music: © 1983 Restoration Music Ltd/Lifestyle Music Ltd,
PO Box 356, Leighton Buzzard LU7 8WP

782 Worthy, O worthy are You Lord

Words and music: Mark S Kinzer

Wor-thy, O wor-thy are You Lord, wor-thy to be thanked and praised and wor-shipped and a-dored; wor-thy, O wor-thy are You Lord, wor-thy to be thanked and praised and wor-shipped and a-dored.

783 Ye holy angels bright

DARWELL'S 148TH   66 66 44 44

Words: Richard Baxter (1615–91) and others
Music: John Darwell (1731–89)

Ye ho-ly an-gels bright, who wait at God's right hand, or through the realms of___ light fly___ at your Lord's com - mand, as - sist our song, or else the theme too high doth seem for mor - tal tongue.

1 Ye holy angels bright,
  who wait at God's right hand,
  or through the realms of light
  fly at your Lord's command,
    assist our song,
    or else the theme
    too high doth seem
    for mortal tongue.

2 Ye blessèd souls at rest,
  who see your Saviour's face,
  whose glory, e'en the least
  is far above our grace,
    God's praises sound,
    as in His sight
    with sweet delight
    ye do abound.

3 Ye saints, who toil below,
  adore your heavenly King,
  and onward as ye go
  some joyful anthem sing;
    take what He gives
    and praise Him still,
    through good and ill,
    who ever lives!

4 My soul, bear thou thy part,
  triumph in God above:
  and with a well-tuned heart
  sing thou the songs of love!
    Let all thy days
    till life shall end,
    whate'er He send,
    be filled with praise.

784
Ye servants of God

LAUDATE DOMINUM   55 55 65 65

Words: Charles Wesley (1707–88)
Music: C H H Parry (1848–1918)

Ye ser-vants of__ God, your Mas-ter pro-claim, and pub-lish a - broad__ His won-der-ful name; the name all - vic-tor-ious__ of__ Je-sus ex - tol; His king-dom is glo-rious, and rules o - ver all.

1 Ye servants of God,
  your Master proclaim,
  and publish abroad
  His wonderful name;
  the name all-victorious
  of Jesus extol;
  His kingdom is glorious,
  and rules over all.

2 God ruleth on high,
  almighty to save;
  and still He is nigh,
  His presence we have;
  the great congregation
  His triumph shall sing,
  ascribing salvation
  to Jesus our King.

3 'Salvation to God
  who sits on the throne',
  let all cry aloud,
  and honour the Son:
  the praises of Jesus
  the angels proclaim,
  fall down on their faces,
  and worship the Lamb.

4 Then let us adore,
  and give Him His right –
  all glory and power,
  all wisdom and might:
  all honour and blessing,
  with angels above;
  and thanks never-ceasing,
  and infinite love.

785   Yes, power belongs to You, O Lord

Words and music: Colin Preston
Music arranged Chris Mitchell

Yes, power be-longs to You, O Lord, in You we put our trust; You are sove-reign o - ver all,_ great are You. Great in Your mer - cy, Lord, great in Your love, a migh-ty war-rior in whom we trust.

Glo-ri-fy Your name, glo-ri-fy Your name,

glo-ri-fy Your name.

1 Don't wor-ry a-bout the
2 Do not fear_ nor
3 Be still and know that

op - po - si - tion, for I stand with the few;
be dis - mayed, the bat - tle is not yours;
I am God,_ and wait up - on My word,

the proud, the vio-lent
you shall not need to
res - pond-ing to My

god-less man___ will know I stand with you.
fight, but stand and see sal - va - tion of the Lord.
Spi-rit's voice,_ with your breath and praise do war.

Yes,

786

Yes, God is good

Williams   LM

Words: John Hampden Gurney (1802–62)
Music: from *Templi Carmina*, 1829

1 Yes, God is good – in earth and sky,
   from ocean depths and spreading wood,
   ten thousand voices seem to cry:
   God made us all, and God is good.

2 The sun that keeps his trackless way,
   and downward pours his golden flood,
   night's sparkling hosts, all seem to say
   in accents clear that God is good.

3 The joyful birds prolong the strain,
   their song with every spring renewed;
   the air we breathe, and falling rain,
   each softly whispers: God is good.

4 I hear it in the rushing breeze;
   the hills that have for ages stood,
   the echoing sky and roaring seas,
   all swell the chorus: God is good.

5 Yes, God is good, all nature says,
   by God's own hand with speech endued;
   and man, in louder notes of praise,
   should sing for joy that God is good.

6 For all Your gifts we bless You, Lord,
   but chiefly for our heavenly food,
   Your pardoning grace, Your quickening word,
   these prompt our song, that God is good.

787 Yesterday, today, for ever

788 You are beautiful

Words and music: Mark Altrogge
Music arranged Christopher Norton

Majestically

You are beau-ti-ful be-yond des-crip - tion,___ too mar-vel-lous for words,

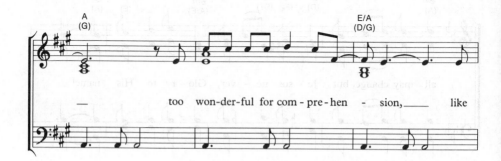

___ too won-der-ful for com-pre-hen - sion,___ like

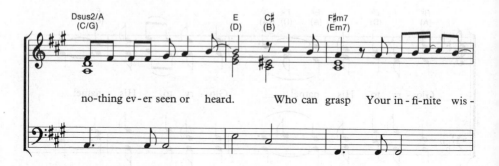

no-thing ev - er seen or heard. Who can grasp Your in - fi-nite wis-

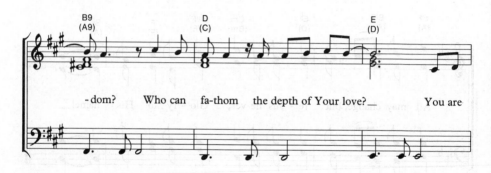

-dom? Who can fa-thom the depth of Your love?__ You are

789 You are coming

Beverley 87 887 77 77

Words: Frances Ridley Havergal (1836–79)
altered Horrobin/Leavers
Music: William Henry Monk (1823–89)

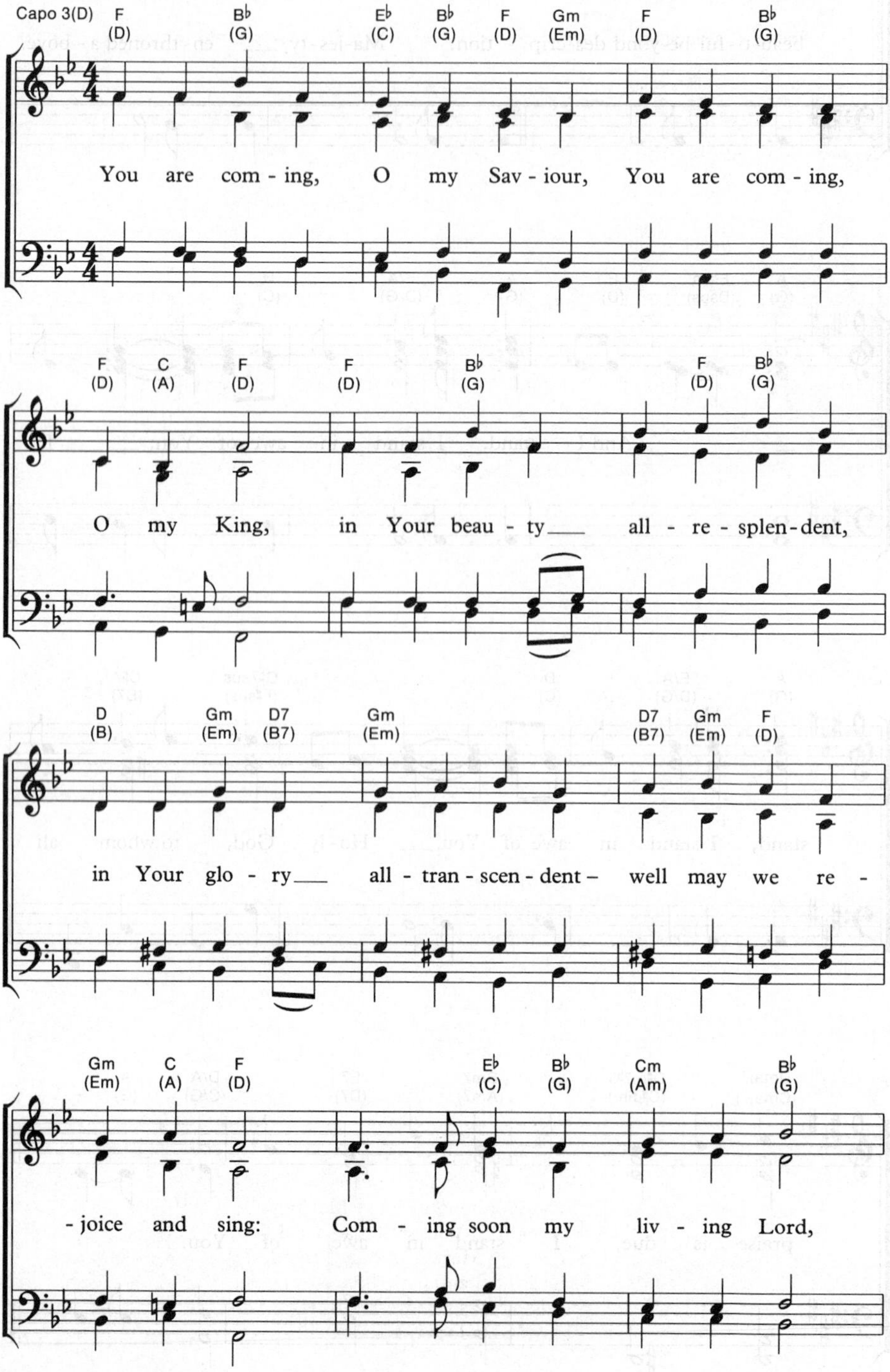

Capo 3(D)
F (D) B♭ (G) E♭ (C) B♭ (G) F (D) Gm (Em) F (D) B♭ (G)
You are com - ing, O my Sav - iour, You are com - ing,
F (D) C (A) F (D) F (D) B♭ (G) F (D) B♭ (G)
O my King, in Your beau - ty all - re - splen - dent,
D (B) Gm (Em) D7 (B7) Gm (Em) D7 (B7) Gm (Em) F (D)
in Your glo - ry all - tran - scen - dent – well may we re -
Gm (Em) C (A) F (D) E♭ (C) B♭ (G) Cm (Am) B♭ (G)
- joice and sing: Com - ing soon my liv - ing Lord,

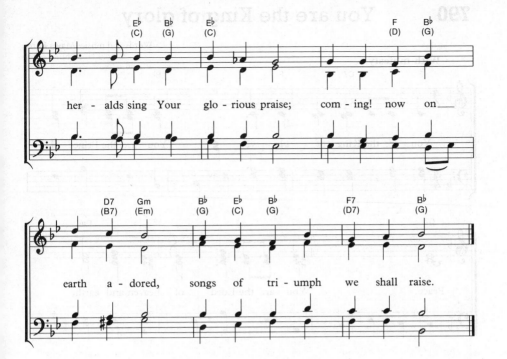

her - alds sing Your glo - rious praise; com - ing! now on___ earth a - dored, songs of tri - umph we shall raise.

1 You are coming, O my Saviour,
   You are coming, O my King,
   in Your beauty all-resplendent,
   in Your glory all-transcendent –
   well may we rejoice and sing:
   Coming soon my living Lord,
   heralds sing Your glorious praise;
   coming! now on earth adored,
   songs of triumph we shall raise.

2 You are coming, You are coming,
   we shall meet You on Your way,
   we shall see You, we shall see You,
   we shall bless You, we shall show You
   all our hearts could never say.
   What an anthem that will be,
   ringing out eternally,
   earth's and heaven's praises meet,
   at Your own all glorious feet!

3 O the joy to see You reigning,
   You, my own belovèd Lord!
   Every tongue Your name confessing,
   worship, honour, glory blessing
   brought to You with glad accord –
   You, my Master and my Friend,
   vindicated and enthroned,
   unto earth's remotest end
   glorified, adored, and owned!

790   You are the King of glory

Words and music: Mavis Ford

With majesty

You are the King of glo-ry, You are the Prince of Peace, You are the Lord of heaven and earth, You're the Son of right-eous-ness. An-gels bow down be-fore You, wor-ship and a-dore, for You have the words of e-ter-nal life,___ You are Je-sus Christ the

Lord._____ Ho - san-na to the Son of Da - vid!_____ Ho -

- san-na to the King of___ kings!   Glo-ry in the high - est

hea - ven, for Je - sus the Mes-si - ah reigns!

You are the King of glory,
You are the Prince of Peace,
You are the Lord of heaven and earth,
You're the Son of righteousness.
Angels bow down before You,
worship and adore,
for You have the words of eternal life,
You are Jesus Christ the Lord.
Hosanna to the Son of David!
Hosanna to the King of kings!
Glory in the highest heaven,
for Jesus the Messiah reigns!

791

You are the mighty King

Words and music: Eddie Espinosa
Music arranged Roger Mayor

And I praise Your name,

and I praise Your name.

D.C. al Fine

1 You are the mighty King,
  the living Word;
  master of everything –
  You are the Lord.
     And I praise Your name,
     and I praise Your name.

2 You are almighty God,
  Saviour and Lord;
  Wonderful Counsellor,
  You are the Lord.
     And I praise Your name,
     and I praise Your name.

3 You are the Prince of Peace,
  Emmanuel;
  Everlasting Father,
  You are the Lord.
     And I love Your name,
     and I love Your name.

4 You are the mighty King,
  the living Word;
  master of everything,
  You are the Lord.

792

You are the Vine

Words and music: Danny Daniels
Music arranged Christopher Norton

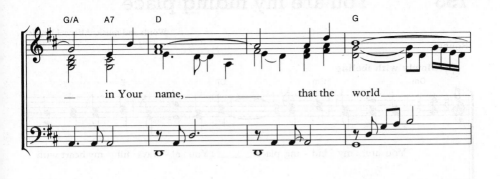

in Your name,_____ that the world_____

___ will sure - ly know_____ that You have

D.C. al Coda

pow - er to heal and to save._____

✠ *CODA*

- bid - ing in You._____

793   You are my hiding place

Words and music: Michael Ledner

Round

794

You are worthy

Words and music: John Daniel Lawtum

795 You laid aside Your majesty

Words and music: Noel Richards
Music arranged Roger Mayor

You laid a-side Your ma-jes-ty, gave up ev-ery-thing for me, suf-fered at the hands of those You had cre-a-ted; You took all my guilt and shame, when You died and rose a-gain; now to-day You reign in

Words and music: © 1985 Thankyou Music,
PO Box 75, Eastbourne, East Sussex BN23 6NW, UK

heaven and earth ex - alt - ed. I real-ly want to wor-ship You, my

Lord, You have won my heart and I am Yours for ev-er and ev - er:

I will love You. You are the on-ly one who died for

me, gave Your life___ to set me free, so I lift my voice to You

___ in a - do - ra - tion._____

796 You shall go out with joy

Words and music: Stuart Dauermann
Music arranged Roland Fudge

With joy

You shall go out with joy__ and be led forth with peace, and the

moun-tains and the hills shall break forth be-fore you. There'll be

shouts of joy__ and the trees of the field shall__ clap, shall clap their

hands, and the trees of the field shall clap their hands, and the

trees of the field shall clap their hands, and the trees of the field shall

clap their hands, and you'll go out with joy._____

You shall go out with joy
    and be led forth with peace,
and the mountains and the hills
    shall break forth before you.
There'll be shouts of joy
    and the trees of the field
shall clap, shall clap their hands,
and the trees of the field
    shall clap their hands,
and the trees of the field
    shall clap their hands,
and the trees of the field
    shall clap their hands,
and you'll go out with joy.

797   Your love is to me

Words and music: Richard Taylor
Music arranged Phil Burt

Your love is to me like an ev-er-flow-ing stream, Your love is to me like an ev-er-flow-ing stream, reach-ing out Lord. Lord we need Your love, yes, we need Your

love,   we   need   Your   love   to make it   through;___

_   Lord we   need   Your   love,   yes,   we   need   Your

love,   we   need   Your   love   to make it   through.___

Your love is to me like an ever-flowing stream,
Your love is to me like an ever-flowing stream,
Your love is to me like an ever-flowing stream
reaching out Lord.

Lord we need Your love,
yes, we need Your love,
we need Your love to make it through;
Lord we need Your love,
yes, we need Your love,
we need Your love to make it through.

798   Yours, Lord, is the greatness

Words and music: Helen Thomas
Music arranged Andy Silver
and Christopher Norton

Yours, Lord, is the great-ness, the pow-er, the glo-ry; Yours, Lord, is the great-ness, the vic-to-ry, the ma-jes-ty. For ev-ery-thing in hea-ven and earth is Yours, You are the King, su-preme o-ver all.

CODA: ma-jes-ty.

2   All riches and honour come from You;
    You are our God, You make us strong.
    Yours, Lord . . .

3   And now, our God, we give You thanks,
    we praise Your glorious name.
    Yours, Lord . . .

Copyright Addresses

Alexanders Copyright Trust, c/o S W Grant, 12 Lawrie Park Crescent, Sydenham, London SE26 6HD

American Catholic Press, 16160 South Seton Drive, South Holland, IL 60473 USA

M C & M M Austin, 4 Burkes Close, Beaconsfield, Bucks. HP9 1ES

J M Barnes, 15 South Canterbury Road, Canterbury, Kent CT1 3LH

Cliff Barrows, Melody Lane, Rt 9 No Parker Road, Greenville, SC 2960 USA

Bible Society, Stonehill Green, Westlea Down, Swindon SN5 7DG

A & C Black (Publishers) Ltd, Howard Road, Eaton Socon, Huntington, Cambs. PE19 3EZ

Fred Bock Music, PO Box 333 Tarzana, CA 91356 USA

Boosey & Hawkes Music Publishers, 295 Regent Street, London W1R 8JH

Gordon Brattle, c/o N A M Cooke, 52 Birch Grove, Ealing Common, London W3 9SR

Breitkopf & Hartel, Buch-und Musikverlag, Walkmühl Strasse 52, D-6200 Weisbaden 1, W Germany

R Browne, 5 Avondale Road, Trowbridge, Wiltshire

E J Burns, Christ Church Vicarage, 6 Watling Street Road, Fulwood, Preston, Lancs. PR2 4DY

Catacombs Productions, J S Craggs Management Services, PO Box 4124 Station A, Victoria, BC V8X 3X4 Canada

Canticle Publications, c/o House Group Music, 2712 West 104th Terrace, Leaworth, IL 66236 USA

Central Board of Finance of the Church of England, Church House, Great Smith Street, London SW1

K Chance, Glaubensentrum, Gruner Plaz 12, 3340 Wolfenbuttel, W Germany

Chappell Music, 129 Park Street, London W1Y 3EA

Cherry Lane Music Ltd, 75 High Street, Needham Market, Ipswich, Suffolk 1P6 8AN

Christian Fellowship of Columbia, 4600 Christian Fellowship Road, Columbia, MS 65203 USA

Paul S Deeming, 8987 St Louis Avenue, St Louis, MS 63114 USA

Colin C Duckworth, 44 Margerson Road, Ben Rhydding, Ilkley, West Yorks. LS29 8QD

Timothy Dudley-Smith, Rectory Meadow, Bramerton, Norwich NR14 7DW

E M Dyke, 32 Woodlands Close, Harrogate, N. Yorks. HG2 7AZ

William Elkin Music Services, Station Road Industrial Estate, Salhouse, Norwich, Norfolk NR13 6NY

Paul Field, 26 Demesne Road, Wallington, Surrey SM6 8PP

Franciscan Communications, 1229 South Santee Street, Los Angeles, CA 90015 USA

Gaither Music Company, Copyright Management, PO Box 737, Alexandria, IN 46001, USA

GIA Publications Inc, 7404 S. Mason Avenue, Chicago, IL 60638 USA

J S Graggs Management Services, PO Box 4124, Station A, Victoria BC V8X 3X4, Canada

Gospel Publishing House, 1445 Boonville Avenue, Springfield, MS 65802 USA

D R Gould, 34 Pollards Drive, Horsham, West Sussex RH16 4AL

Jeanne Harper, Stanfords, 27 Munster Green, Haywards Heath, West Sussex RH16 4AL

David Higham Associates, 5–8 Lower John Street, Golden Square, London W1R 4HA

High-Fye Music, Campbell Connelly Co Ltd, 8–9 Frith Street, London W1V 5TZ

Hope Publishing, 380 South Main Place, Carol Stream, IL 60188 USA

Hymns Ancient & Modern, St Mary's Works, St Mary's Plain, Norwich, Norfolk NR3 3BH

Integrity's Hosanna! Music, Glyndley Manor, Stone Cross, Pevensey, East Sussex BN24 5BS

International Music Publications, Woodford Trading Estate, Southend Road, Woodford Green, Essex IG8 8HN

InterVarsity Press, 5206 Main Street, PO Box 1400, Downers End, IL 60515 USA

John Ireland Trust, 35 St Mary's Mansions, St Mary's Terrace. London W2 1SQ

W F Jabusch, University of St Mary of the Lake, Mundelein Seminary, Mundelein, IL 60060 USA

Francis Jackson, Nether Garth, Acklam, Moulton, Yorks. YR7 9RG

A M Jones, 22 Wentworth Road, Chilwell, Nottingham NG9 4FP

Roger Jones (Christian Music Ministries), 325 Bromford Road, Hodge Hill, Birmingham B36 8ET

Jubilate Hymns, c/o 61 Chessel Avenue, Southampton S02 4DY

Kenwood Music, Lifestyle Music Ltd, PO Box 356, Leighton Buzzard, Beds. LU7 8WP

B K M Kerr, Wayside Cottage, Friston Hill, East Dene, Eastbourne, East Sussex BN20 0BP

Bob Kilpatrick Music, PO Box 493194, Redding, CA 96049 USA

Lindsey Music, 23 Hitchin Street, Biggleswade, Beds. SG18 8AX

Manna Music Inc, 25510 Avenue Stanford, Suite 101, Valencia, CA 91355 USA

Andrew Maries, St Cuthbert's Centre, Peasholme Green, York YO1 2PW

Dr John Marsh, The Vicarage, 36 Manor Road, Ossett, West Yorkshire WF5 0AU

Marshall Morgan & Scott, Middlesex House, 34–42 Cleveland Street, London W1P 5FB

Kevin Mayhew Ltd, The Paddock, Rattlesbury, Bury St Edmunds, Suffolk

Meadowgreen MusicIMP, Woodford Trading Estate, Southend Road, Woodford Green, Essex IG8 8HN

Methodist Church Division of Education & Youth, 2 Chester House, Pages Lane, Muswell Hill, London N10 1PR

Methodist Publishing House, 20 Ivatt Way, Peterborough, Cambs. PE3 7PG

Rev Roland Meredith, The Rectory, 13 Station Road, Witney, Oxfordshire OX8 6BH

Moody Bible Insititute, 820 N. La Salle Street, Chicago, IL 60610 USA

A R Mowbray Ltd, Artillery House, Artillery Row, London SW1P 1RT

Music Publishing International, 75 High Street, Needham Market, Suffolk IP6 8AN

Mustard Seed Music, Lifestyle Music Ltd, PO Box 356, Leighton Buzzard, Beds. LU7 8WP

National Young Life Campaign, Spring Cottage, Spring Road, Leeds, West Yorks. LF6 1AD

Nazarene Publishing House, Box 419527, Kansas City, MO 64141 USA

New Song Ministries, PO Box 11662, Costa Mesa, CA 92627 USA

Novello & Co Ltd, 8–10 Lower James Street, London W1R 3PL

Overseas Missionary Fellowship, 2 Cluny Road, Singapore 1025, Republic of Singapore

Oxford University Press, Music Department, Walton Street, Oxford OX2 6DP

Patch Music/Peer Music, Peer-Southern Organisation, 8 Denmark Street, London WC1 8LT

Colin Preston, 81 Howth Drive, Woodley, Reading, Berks.

The Public Trustee Office, Stewart House, Kingsway, London WC2B 6JX

M E Rees, 5a Thornwood Road, Epping, Essex CM16 6SX

Restoration Music Ltd, Lifestyle Music Ltd, PO Box 356, Leighton Buzzard, Beds. LU7 8WP

John Richards, Renewal Servicing, PO Box 17, Shepperton, Middlesex TW17 8NU

Joan Robinson, 47 Woodlands Road, Beaumont, Lancaster

Rocksmith Music/Leosong Copyright Service, 7–8 Greenland Place, London NW1 0AT

R Rusbridge, 9 Springfield House, Cotham Road, Bristol BS6 6DQ

Salvationist Publishing & Supplies Ltd, 117–121 Judd Street, London WC1H 9NN

Pete Sanchez Jnr, 4723 Hickory Downs, Houston, TX 77084 USA

Scripture Gift Mission, Radstock House, 3 Ecclestone Street, London SW1W 9LZ

Scripture Union, 130 City Road, London EC1V 2NJ

Signalgrade Music Ltd, 48 Chatsworth Avenue, Raynes Park, London SW20 8JZ

C Simmonds, School House, 81 Clapham Road, Bedford MK41 7RB

Stainer & Bell Ltd, PO Box 110, 82 High Road, London N2 9PW

Straightway Music, Gaither Copyright Management, PO Box 737, Alexandria, IN 46001 USA

C L Taylor, 59 Baldwin Avenue, Eastbourne, East Sussex

Thankyou Music Ltd, 1 St Annes Road, Eastbourne, East Sussex BN21 3UN

Gordon Thompson Music, a division of Warner/Chappell Music Canada Ltd, 85 Scarsdale Road, Unit 101, Don Mills, Ontario, M3B 2R2 Canada

J Tyrrell, 41 Minster Road, Godalming, Surrey

Josef Weinberger Ltd, 12–14 Mortimer Street, London W1N 7RD

Whole Armor Publishing, 2828 Azalea Place, Nashville, TN 37204 USA

Word Music (UK) Ltd, 9 Holdom Avenue, Bletchley, Milton Keynes MK1 1QU

Word of God Music, PO Box 8617, Ann Arbor, MI 48107 USA

Youth with a Mission, Schloss Hurlach, 8931 Hurlach I, W. Germany

Phil Burt, Roland Fudge, Ruth Hooke, Peter Horrobin, Horrobin/Leavers, Anne Horrobin, Greg Leavers, Andy Silver, c/o Marshall Pickering, Middlesex House, 34–42 Cleveland Street, London W1P 5FB

USA and Canada

Benson Company Inc, 365 Great Circle Road, Nashville, TN 37228 USA

C A Music Services, 2021 N Brower, Simi Valley, CA 93065 USA

Celebration Music, Maranatha! Music, PO Box 1396, Costa Mesa, CA 92628 USA

Fairhill Music, PO Box 933, Newbury Park, CA 91320 USA

Friends First Music, Dawn Treader Music, Straightway Music, Gaither Copyright Management, PO Box 737, Alexandria, IN 46001 USA

Latter Rain Music, Sparrow Corporation, PO Box 2120, 9255 Deering Avenue, Chatsworth, CA 91311 USA

LexiconSpectra Music Copyright Management Inc., 1102 17th Avenue South, Suite 400, Nashville, TN 57212 USA

Lillenas Publishing Company, Box 419527, Kansas City, MO 64141 USA

Meadowgreen Music Inc, 8 Music Square West, Nashville, TN 37202 USA

Mercy Publishing, PO Box 65004, Ahaheim, CA 92815 USA

People of Destiny, 7881-8 Beechcroft Avenue, Gaithersbury, MO 20879 USA

Rocksmith Music, c/o Trust Music Management, 6255 Sunset Blvd, Suite 723, Hollywood, CA 90028 USA

RodeheaverNorman Claydon Publishing, Word Inc, 5221 N O'Connor Blvd, Suite 1000, Irving, TX 75039 USA

Star Song Music, 2325 Crestmoor, Nashville, TN 37215 USA

Timothy Dudley-Smith, Jubilate Hymns, Hope Publishing Company, 380 South Main Place, Carol Stream, IL 60188 USA

Warner Chappell Music Corp, 9000 Sunset Boulvard, Los Angeles, CA 90069, USA

Word Music, c/o Word Inc, 5221 N O'Connor Boulvard, Suite 1000, Irving, TX 75039 USA

Rest of world

Acts Music, c/o New Spilkins Pharmacy, 187 Main Street, Kenilworth, Johannesburg 2190, Republic of South Africa

Australia and New Zealand

Genesis Music, PO Box 26, Auburn 2144, Australia

Maranatha! Music, Thankyou Music, Integrity's Hosanna! Music, Mercy Publishing, Restoration Music, Canticle Publications, Celebration, Scripture in Song, Scripture in Song, PO Box 17161, Greenlane, Auckland, New Zealand

Straightway Music, Word Australia Ltd, 140 Canterbury Road, Kilsyth, Vic 3137, Australia

Word Australia Ltd, 140 Canterbury Road, Kilsyth, Vic 3137, Australia

Subject Index

Contents

Titles which differ from first lines are shown in italics
Numbers in brackets refer to the number of the item in Mission Praise 1 (1–282),
Mission Praise 2 (283–647), and Mission Praise Supplement (648–758).

Section A: The Godhead

A5. The Holy Spirit

A6. The Trinity

Section B: The Church of Jesus Christ

Section C: Seasons of the Christian Year

Section D: Living the Christian Life

Section E: Other Subjects

Index of Tunes

Metrical Index

888 4
VICTORY, 670

88 86
HE LIFTED ME
(with refrain), 333

888 6
MISERICORDIA, 396(ii)
WOODWORTH, 396(i)

88 87
EWHURST, 257
OLD YEAVERING, 419

88 88 D
JANE, 286

88 886
ST MARGARET, 515

88 88 88
ANCHOR, 485
CAREY (SURREY), 197
GIESSEN, 168
MELITA, 122
SAGINA, 33
ST CATHERINE, 473
SUSSEX CAROL, 537
VENI IMMANUEL, 493

888 D
MONMOUTH, 320

98 88 83
LIVING LORD, 435, 709

98 98
SPIRITUS VITAE, 488
ST CLEMENT, 641

98 98 98
FRAGRANCE, 700

10 4 66 66 10 4
LUCKINGTON, 404

10 4 10 4 10 10
SANDON, 399

10 4 10 7 4 10
WONDERFUL LOVE, 94

10 6 10 6
THE LOVE OF JESUS
(with refrain), 676

10 8 87
MESSAGE (with refrain), 744

10 8 10 8
BUNESSAN, 71

10 8 11 8
I'LL SEE JESUS
(with refrain), 277

10 9 10 9
BUNESSAN, 467

10 9 10 10
RICH AND FREE
(with refrain), 668

10 10
CRUCIFER (with refrain), 417
I NEED THEE (with refrain),
288
PAX TECUM, 555(i)
SONG 46, 555(ii)

10 10 10 4
SINE NOMINE, 148

10 10 10 10
ELLERS, 584
EVENTIDE, 4
GO FORTH, 631(i)
MORECAMBE, 470
SLANE, 51
THE GLORY SONG
(with refrain), 602
TOULON, 230
WOODLANDS, 631(ii)
YANWORTH, 178

10 10 10 10 4
IT PASSETH KNOWLEDGE,
349

10 10 10 10 10 10
YORKSHIRE, 80

10 10 11 10
YVONNE, 687

10 10 11 11
HANOVER, 651

10 11 11 11
CHEDWORTH, 440
MACCABAEUS (with refrain),
689

11 10 11 10
EPIPHANY HYMN, 65
GREAT IS THY
FAITHFULNESS
(with refrain), 200
LORD OF THE YEARS, 428
O PERFECT LOVE, 517
SPRINGFIELD, 698
TRUE-HEARTED, 711

11 10 11 10 11 10
FINLANDIA, 98, 735

11 11 11 5
CLOISTERS, 441

11 11 11 11
CRADLE SONG, 47
MONTGOMERY, 243
ST DENIO, 327
ST LUKE, 733
TAKE TIME TO BE HOLY,
625

11 11 11 11 11
LAND OF HOPE AND
GLORY, 75

11 12
THE NEW SONG
(with refrain), 773

11 12 11 10
O SOLE MIO (with refrain),
116

11 12 12 10
NICAEA, 237

11 14
CELEBRATIONS
(with refrain), 83

12 10 12 10
SANCTISSIMUS, 529

12 10 12 10 11 10 12 10
PRAISE HIM!, 559

12 10 12 10 12 11 12 11
BLOW THE WIND
SOUTHERLY, 611

12 12 12 7
O LORD JESUS HOW LONG
(with refrain), 347

13 13 13 8 10 10 13 8
MARCHING THROUGH
GEORGIA, 86

14 14 47 8
LOBE DEN HERREN, 564

15 15 15 15
THERE'S A LIGHT UPON
THE MOUNTAINS, 679

Irregular
ADESTE FIDELES, 491
BENSON, 189
BLESSED ASSURANCE, 59
CALYPSO CAROL, 589
CHRIST'S OWN PEACE, 434
IN DULCI JUBILO, 196
JESUS, I COME, 551
LONDONDERRY AIR, 266,
442
MARGARET, 697
MOUNTAIN CHRISTIANS,
154
OPEN MY EYES, 544
REJOICE AND BE GLAD,
573
STILLE NACHT, 597
THE FIRST NOWELL, 644

Index of First Lines